Recently, everyone's been using the term "power spot," and from what I hear, if you use this term, you can make visiting shrines and temples somewhat fashionable (well, that's what I've been told, anyway). I'd like to use this term and travel around to various places, but recently it's gotten tough to get very far from home.

—HIROSHI SHIIBASHI, 2009

HIROSHI SHIIBASHI debuted in BUSINESS JUMP magazine with *Aratama*. **NURA: RISE OF THE YOKAI CLAN** is his breakout hit. He was an assistant to manga artist Hirohiko Araki, the creator of *Jojo's Bizarre Adventure*. *Steel Ball Run* by Araki is one of his favorite manga.

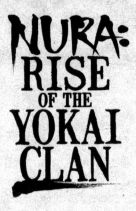

NURA: RISE OF THE YOKAI CLAN
VOLUME 4
SHONEN JUMP Manga Edition

Story and Art by HIROSHI SHIIBASHI

Translation — Yoshihiro Watanabe, Cindy Yamaguchi
Adaptation — Mark Giambruno
Touch-up Art and Lettering — Gia Cam Luc
Graphics and Cover Design — Fawn Lau
Editors — Joel Enos, Rebecca Downer, Daniel Gillespie

NURARIHYON NO MAGO © 2008 by Hiroshi
Shiibashi. All rights reserved. First published in
Japan in 2008 by SHUEISHA Inc., Tokyo. English
translation rights arranged by SHUEISHA Inc.

Printed in the U.S.A.

Published by VIZ Media, LLC
P.O. Box 77010
San Francisco, CA 94107

10 9 8 7 6 5 4 3 2 1
First printing, August 2011

www.viz.com   www.shonenjump.com

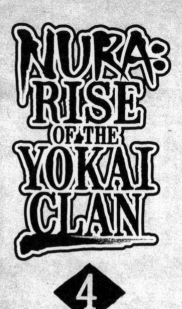

NURA: RISE OF THE YOKAI CLAN

4

THE 88 DEMONS OF SHIKOKU

STORY AND ART BY
HIROSHI SHIIBASHI

CHARACTERS

NURARIHYON

Rikuo's grandfather and the Lord of Pandemonium. He intends to pass leadership of the Nura clan—leaders of the yokai world—to Rikuo.

RIKUO NURA

Though he appears to be a human boy, he's actually the grandson of Nurarihyon, a yokai. His grandfather's blood makes him one-quarter yokai, and he transforms into a yokai at times.

KIYOTSUGU

Rikuo's classmate. He has adored yokai ever since he was saved by Rikuo in his yokai form, leading him to form the "Kiyojuji Paranormal Patrol."

KANA IENAGA

Rikuo's classmate and a childhood friend. Even though she hates scary things, she's a member of the Kiyojuji Paranormal Patrol for some reason.

YUKI-ONNA

A yokai of the Nura clan who is in charge of looking after Rikuo. She disguises herself as a human and attends the same school as Rikuo to protect him from danger. When in human form, she goes by the name Tsurara Oikawa.

YURA KEIKAIN

Rikuo's classmate and a descendant of the Keikain family of onmyoji. She transferred into Ukiyoe Middle School to do field training in yokai exorcism. She has the power to control her shikigami and uses them to destroy yokai.

NATSUMI TORII

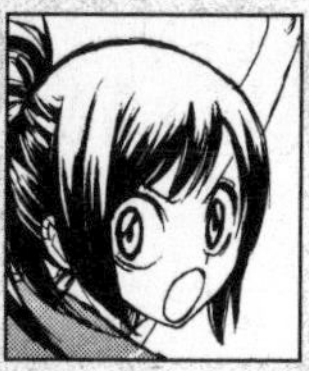

A member of the Kiyojuji Paranormal Patrol, she was forced by Yura to train in the art of self-protection against yokai, but she's really gotten into it lately.

SAORI MAKI

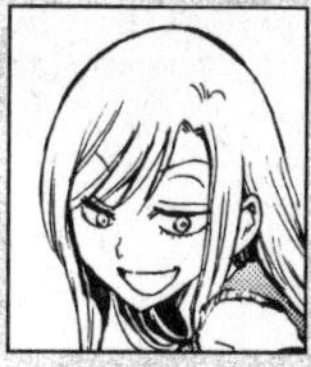

Although she participates in the Kiyojuji Paranormal Patrol, she has no particular interest in yokai. She's an early bloomer.

KUBINASHI

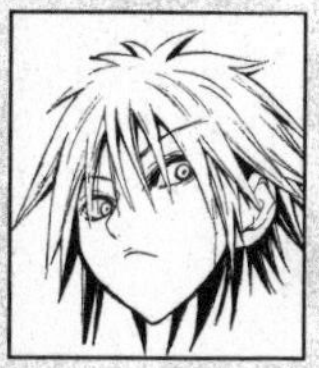

A Nura clan yokai. He joined the ranks of Rikuo's guards ever since the boy became the official successor to the Supreme Commander. Handsome, but has low tolerance for alcohol.

AOTABO

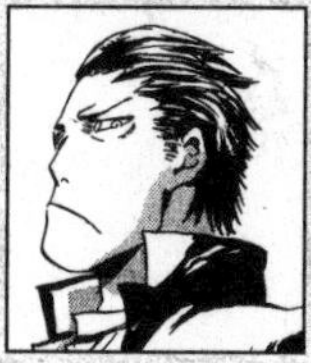

Another Nura clan yokai who, along with Yuki-Onna, looks after and protects Rikuo when he attends school. He uses the name Kurata when disguised as a human.

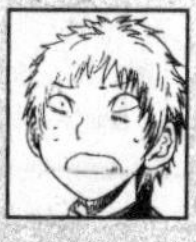

SHIMA

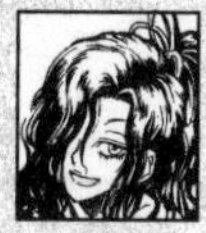

KEJORO

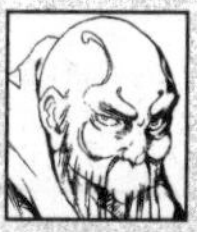

MOKUGYO-DARUMA

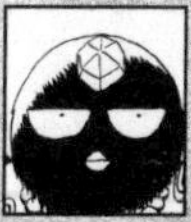

KARASU-TENGU

STORY SO FAR

Rikuo Nura is a seventh-grader at Ukiyoe Middle School. At first glance, he appears to be just another normal boy. But he's actually the grandson of the yokai Supreme Commander Nurarihyon, and is now the Underboss of the Nura clan, the leading organization for the yokai in the region. He is expected to become the third Supreme Commander like his grandfather, but in the meantime lives his days as a human being.

Rikuo wins his final battle against Gyuki at Mt. Nejireme, but stops Gyuki from taking his own life when he discovers that Gyuki's rebellion sprang from his concern and loyalty for the Nura clan. The incident leads Rikuo to ardently commit to becoming the Third and that role's responsibility for looking after the yokai in the clan. At the Nura clan assembly, he is officially named Underboss, and it is decided that he will succeed the Supreme Commander if no other candidate appears before he turns thirteen. Gyuki was found not guilty after that.

Meanwhile, Nura clan boss Hihi and his group are annihilated by a mysterious force, but Nurarihyon shows little concern about his own safety to the panicked yokai of his clan as he sneaks off, unguarded. When Muchi, a yokai from Shikoku, confronts and attacks him, the Supreme Commander's true Meikyo Shisui is revealed! He spectacularly crushes Muchi, but...

TABLE OF CONTENTS

NURA:RISE OF THE YOKAI CLAN

Act 25: The Seven Phantom Travelers

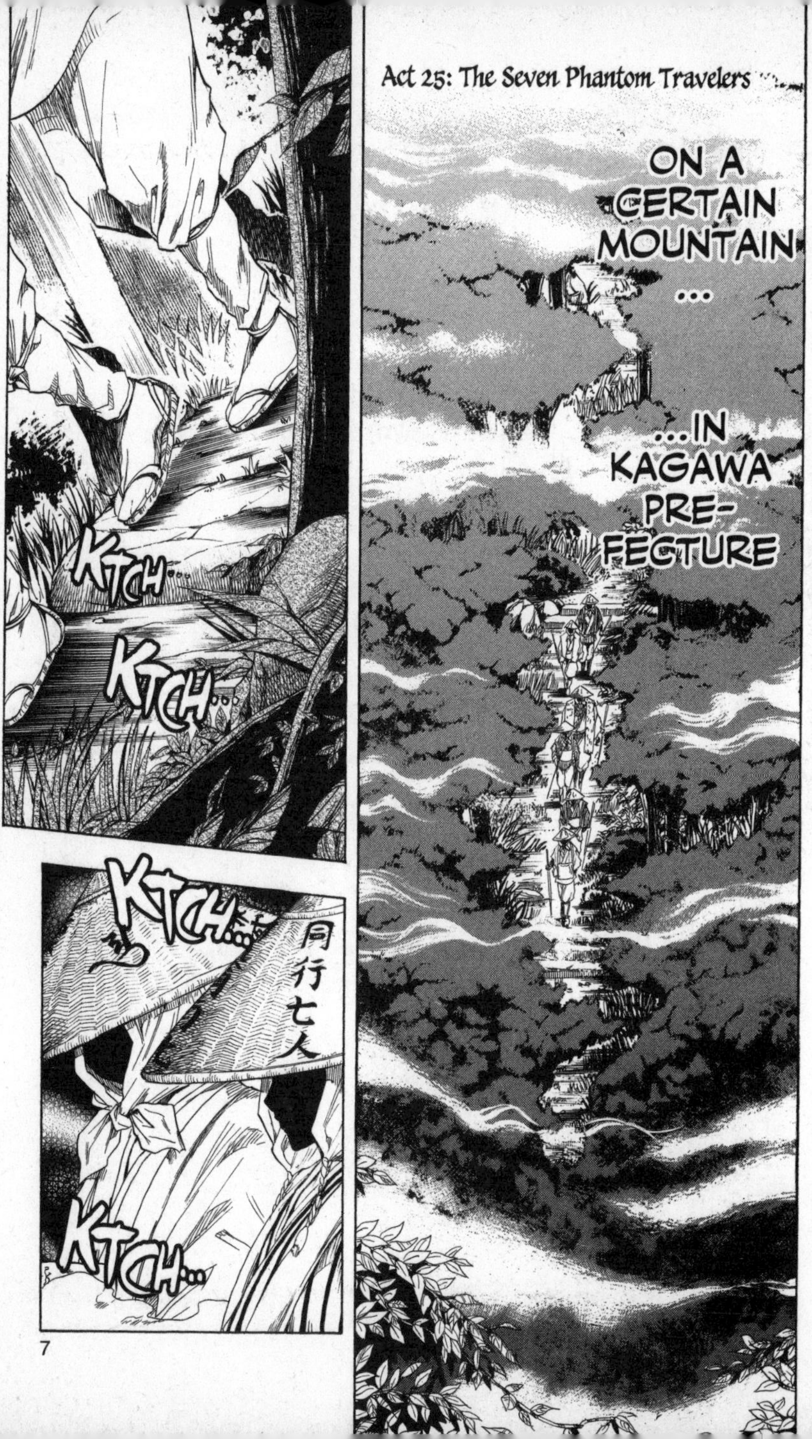
ON A CERTAIN MOUNTAIN ...
...IN KAGAWA PRE-FECTURE
KTCH...
KTCH...
KTCH...
同行七人
KTCH...

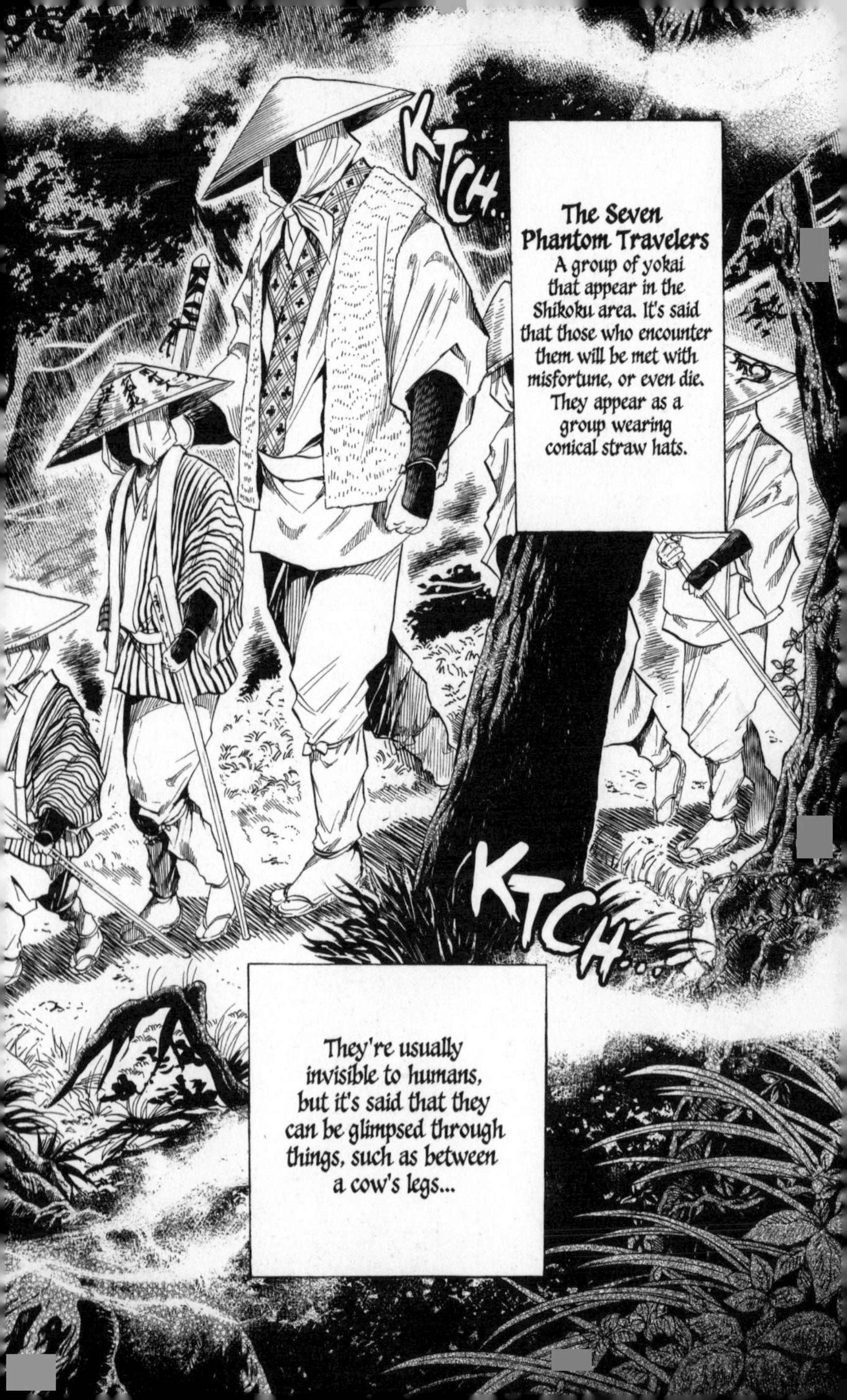
KTCH...
The Seven Phantom Travelers
A group of yokai that appear in the Shikoku area. It's said that those who encounter them will be met with misfortune, or even die. They appear as a group wearing conical straw hats.
KTCH...
They're usually invisible to humans, but it's said that they can be glimpsed through things, such as between a cow's legs...

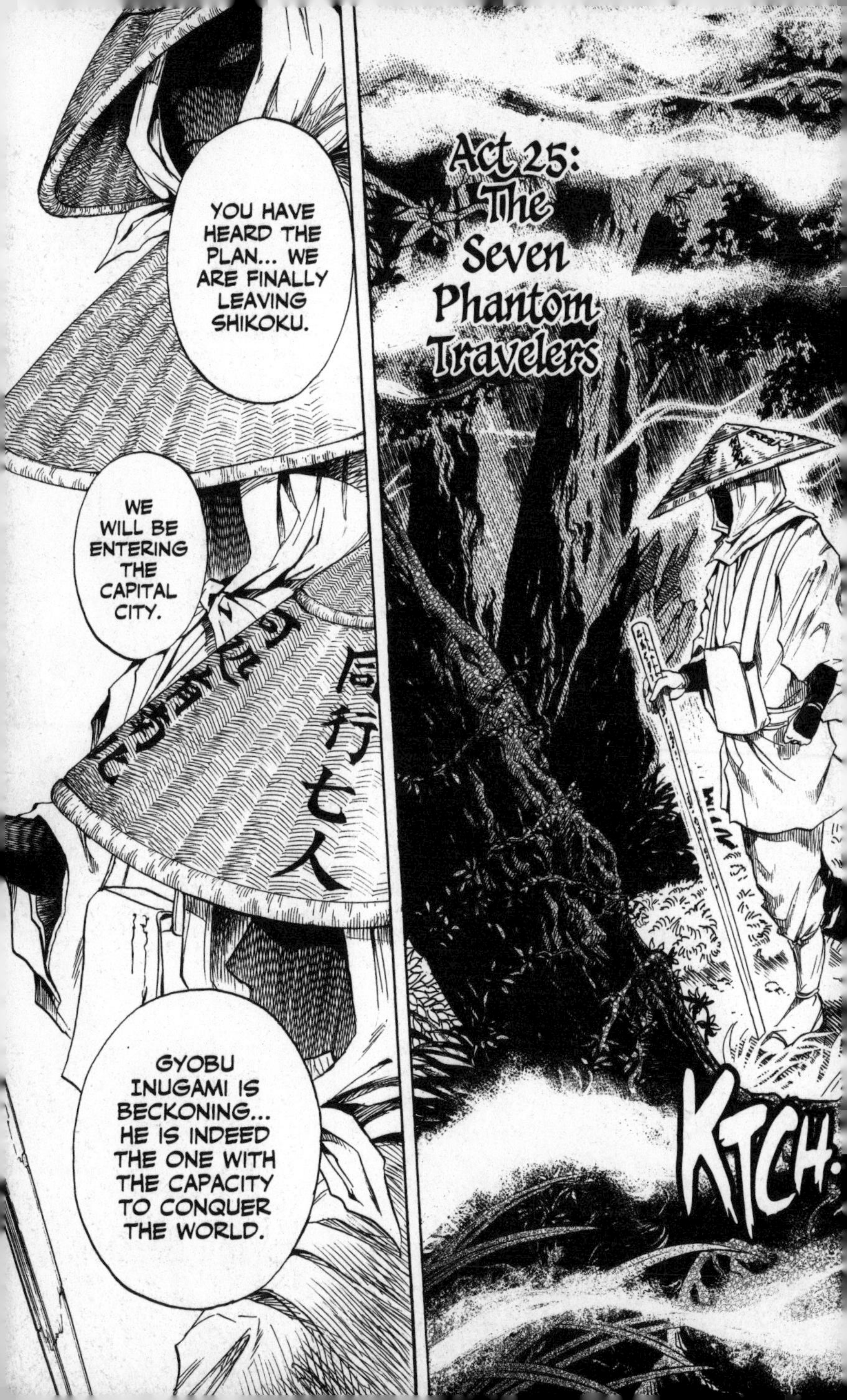
Act 25: The Seven Phantom Travelers
KTCH...
YOU HAVE HEARD THE PLAN... WE ARE FINALLY LEAVING SHIKOKU.
WE WILL BE ENTERING THE CAPITAL CITY.
GYOBU INUGAMI IS BECKONING... HE IS INDEED THE ONE WITH THE CAPACITY TO CONQUER THE WORLD.

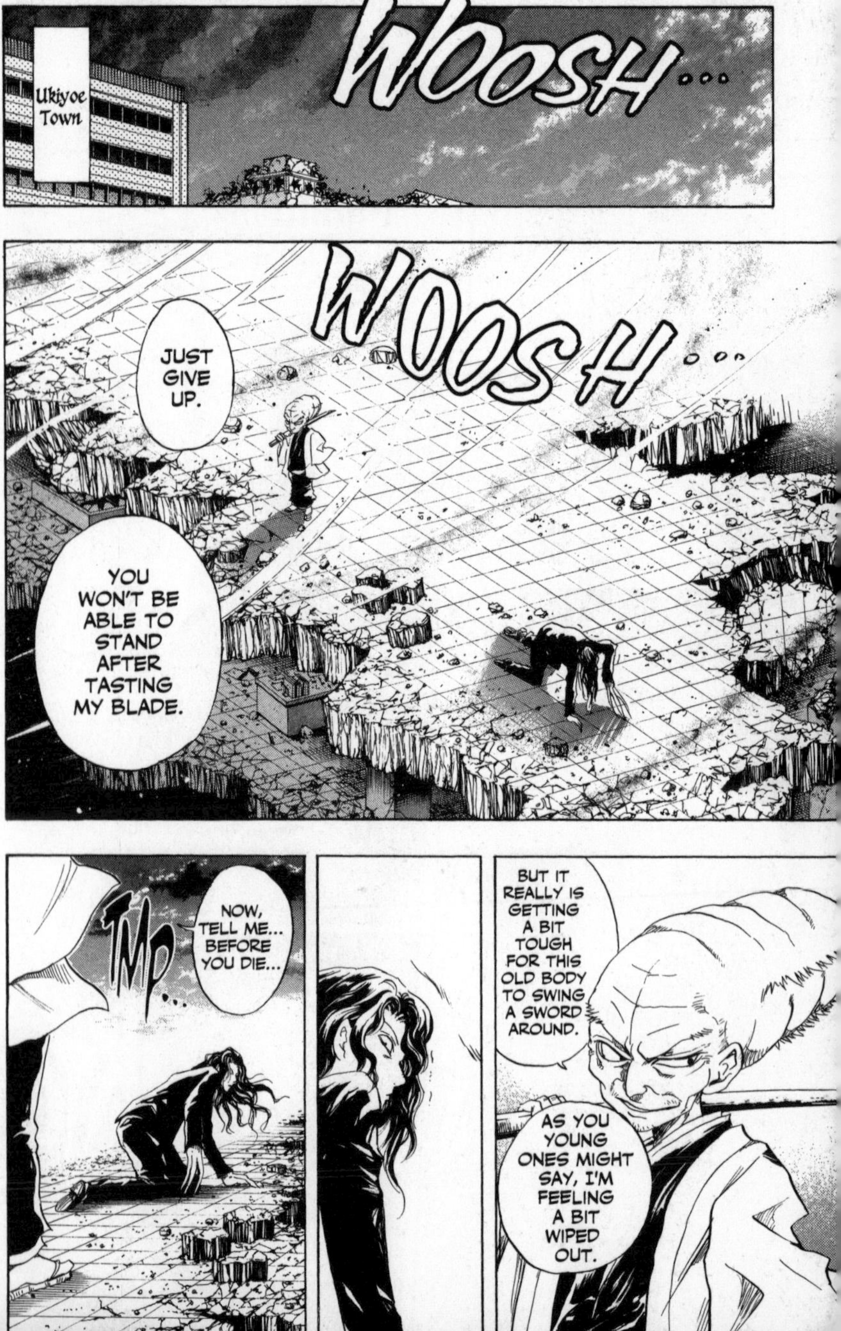
Ukiyoe Town
WOOSH...
WOOSH...
JUST GIVE UP.
YOU WON'T BE ABLE TO STAND AFTER TASTING MY BLADE.
BUT IT REALLY IS GETTING A BIT TOUGH FOR THIS OLD BODY TO SWING A SWORD AROUND.
AS YOU YOUNG ONES MIGHT SAY, I'M FEELING A BIT WIPED OUT.
TMP...
NOW, TELL ME... BEFORE YOU DIE...

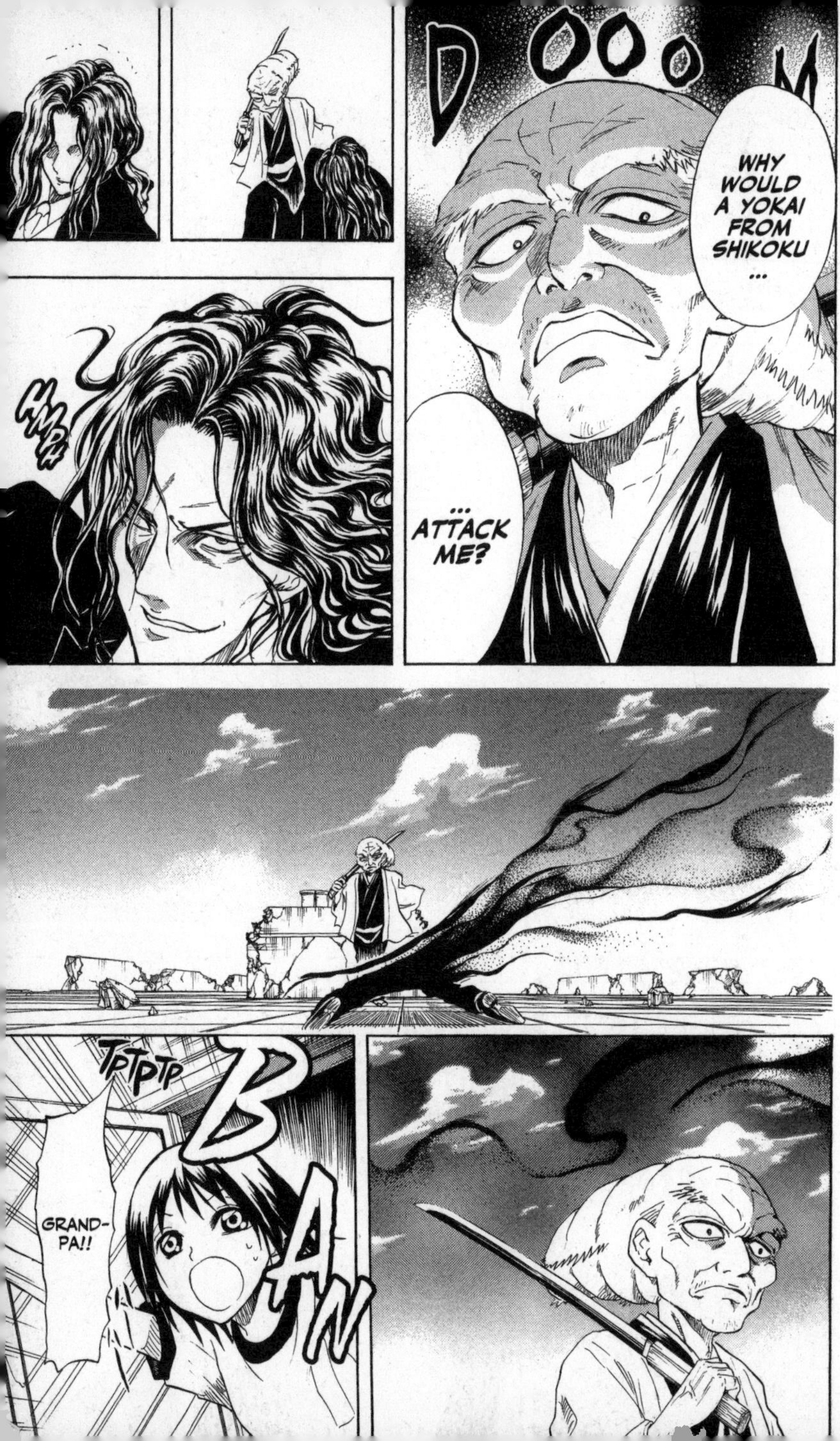
DOOOM
WHY WOULD A YOKAI FROM SHIKOKU ...
... ATTACK ME?
HMPH
TPTPTP
BAN
GRAND-PA!!

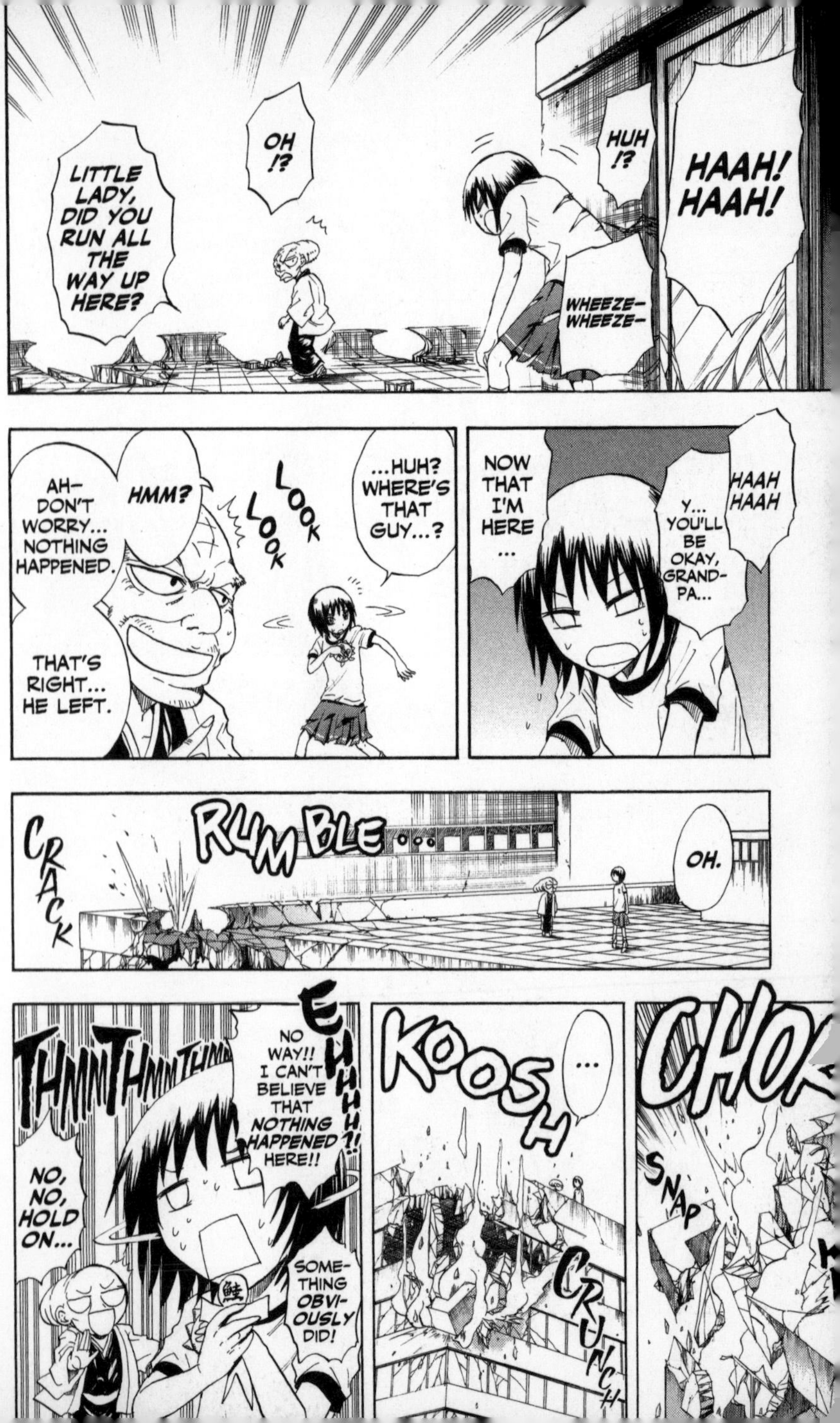
HAAH! HAAH!
WHEEZE- WHEEZE-
HUH !?
OH !?
LITTLE LADY, DID YOU RUN ALL THE WAY UP HERE?
HAAH HAAH
NOW THAT I'M HERE...
Y... YOU'LL BE OKAY, GRAND-PA...
...HUH? WHERE'S THAT GUY...?
LOOK LOOK
HMM?
AH- DON'T WORRY... NOTHING HAPPENED.
THAT'S RIGHT... HE LEFT.
OH.
RUMBLE
CRACK
CHOK
SNAP
...
KOOSH
CRUNCH
EHHHHH?!
NO WAY!! I CAN'T BELIEVE THAT NOTHING HAPPENED HERE!!
SOME-THING OBVI-OUSLY DID!
THMMTHMMTHMM
NO, NO, HOLD ON...

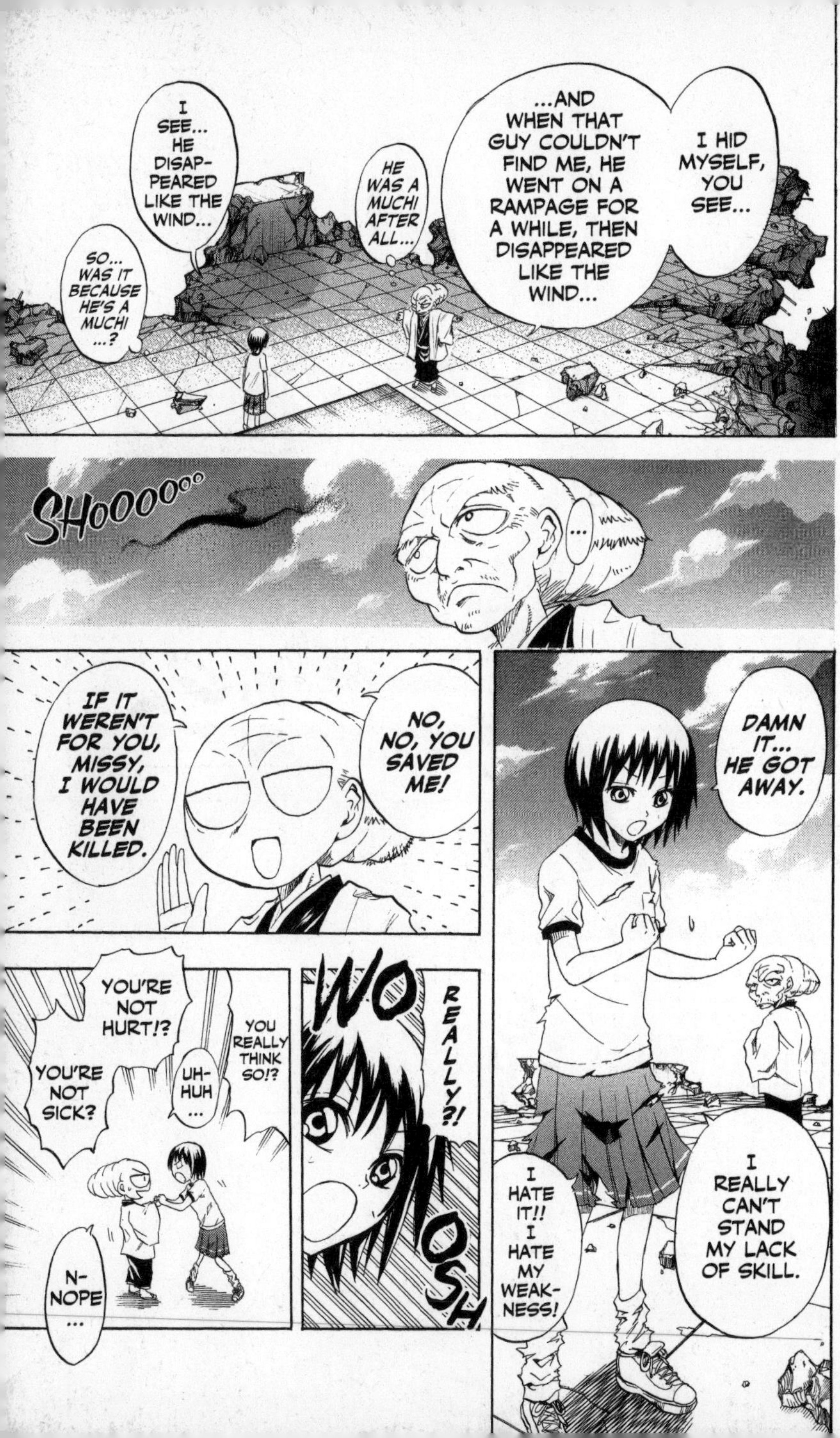
I HID MYSELF, YOU SEE...
...AND WHEN THAT GUY COULDN'T FIND ME, HE WENT ON A RAMPAGE FOR A WHILE, THEN DISAPPEARED LIKE THE WIND...
HE WAS A MUCHI AFTER ALL...
I SEE... HE DISAPPEARED LIKE THE WIND...
SO... WAS IT BECAUSE HE'S A MUCHI ...?
...
SHOOOOOO
DAMN IT... HE GOT AWAY.
I REALLY CAN'T STAND MY LACK OF SKILL.
I HATE IT!! I HATE MY WEAKNESS!
NO, NO, YOU SAVED ME!
IF IT WEREN'T FOR YOU, MISSY, I WOULD HAVE BEEN KILLED.
REALLY?!
WOOSH
YOU REALLY THINK SO!?
UH-HUH...
YOU'RE NOT HURT!?
YOU'RE NOT SICK?
N-NOPE...

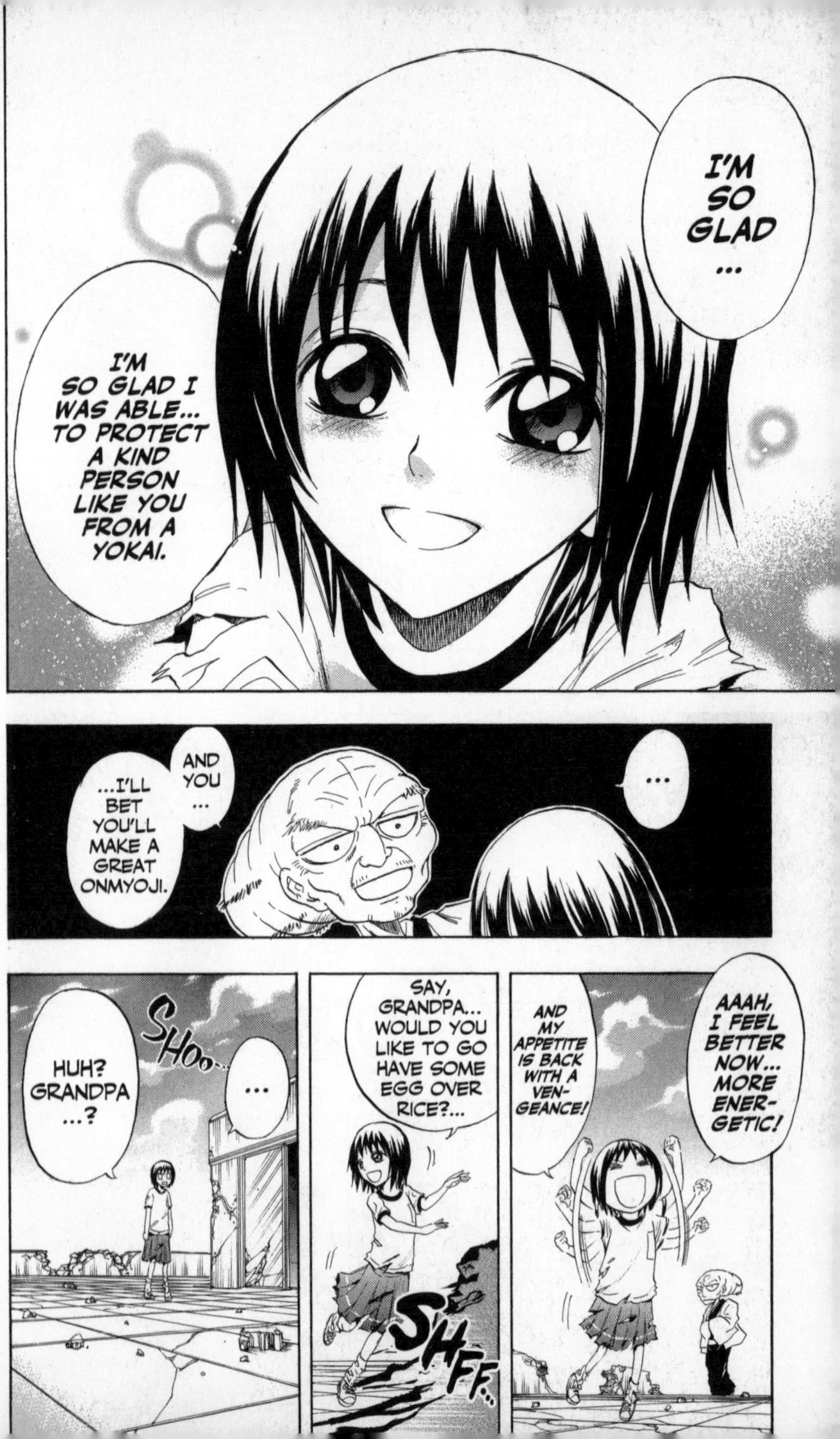
I'M SO GLAD ...
I'M SO GLAD I WAS ABLE... TO PROTECT A KIND PERSON LIKE YOU FROM A YOKAI.
...
AND YOU ...
...I'LL BET YOU'LL MAKE A GREAT ONMYOJI.
AAAH, I FEEL BETTER NOW... MORE ENER-GETIC!
AND MY APPETITE IS BACK WITH A VEN-GEANCE!
SAY, GRANDPA... WOULD YOU LIKE TO GO HAVE SOME EGG OVER RICE?...
SHFF...
SHOO...
...
HUH? GRANDPA ...?

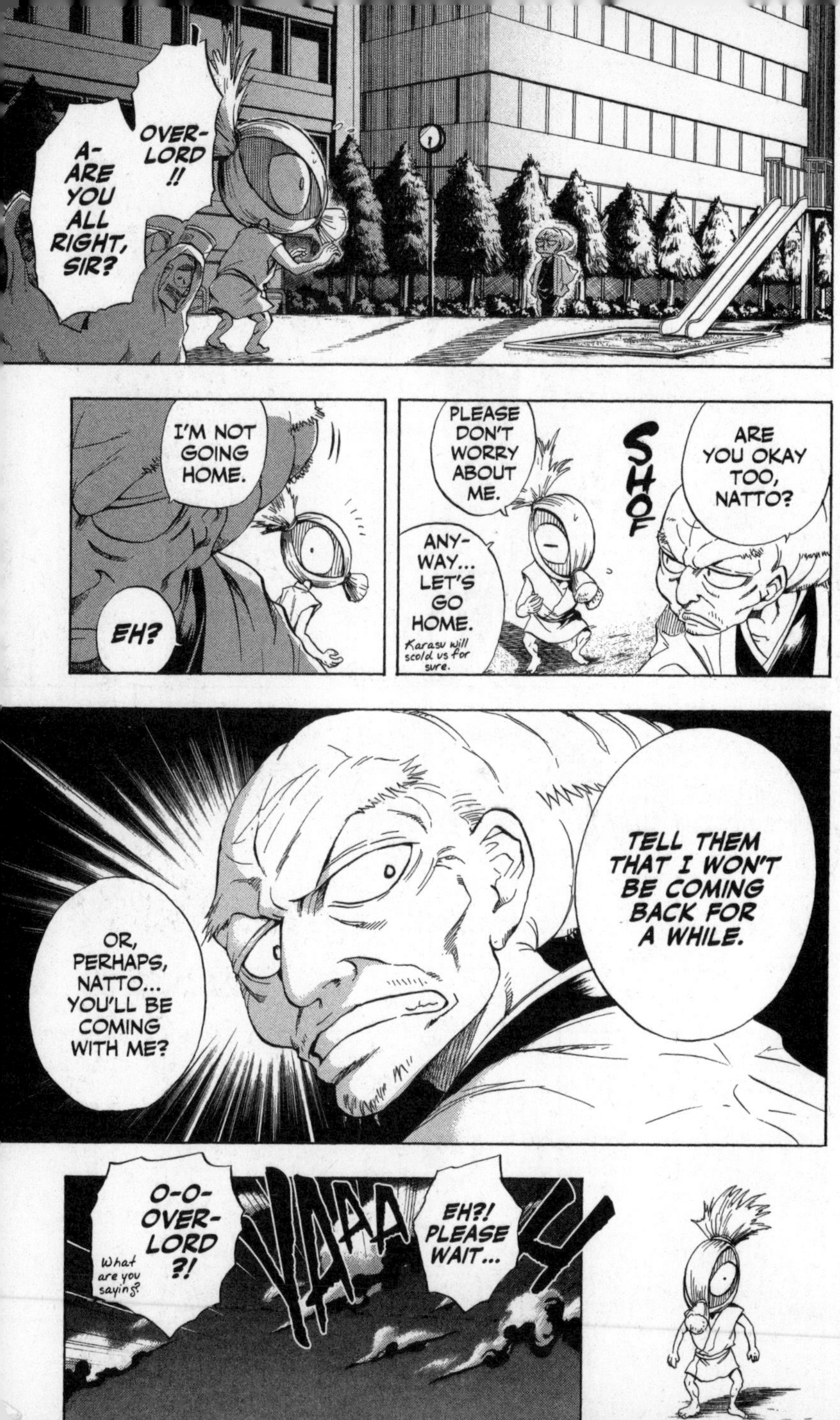
OVER-LORD!!
A-ARE YOU ALL RIGHT, SIR?
ARE YOU OKAY TOO, NATTO?
SHOF
PLEASE DON'T WORRY ABOUT ME.
ANY-WAY... LET'S GO HOME.
Karasu will scold us for sure.
I'M NOT GOING HOME.
EH?
TELL THEM THAT I WON'T BE COMING BACK FOR A WHILE.
OR, PERHAPS, NATTO... YOU'LL BE COMING WITH ME?
EH?! PLEASE WAIT...
O-O-OVER-LORD?!
What are you saying?

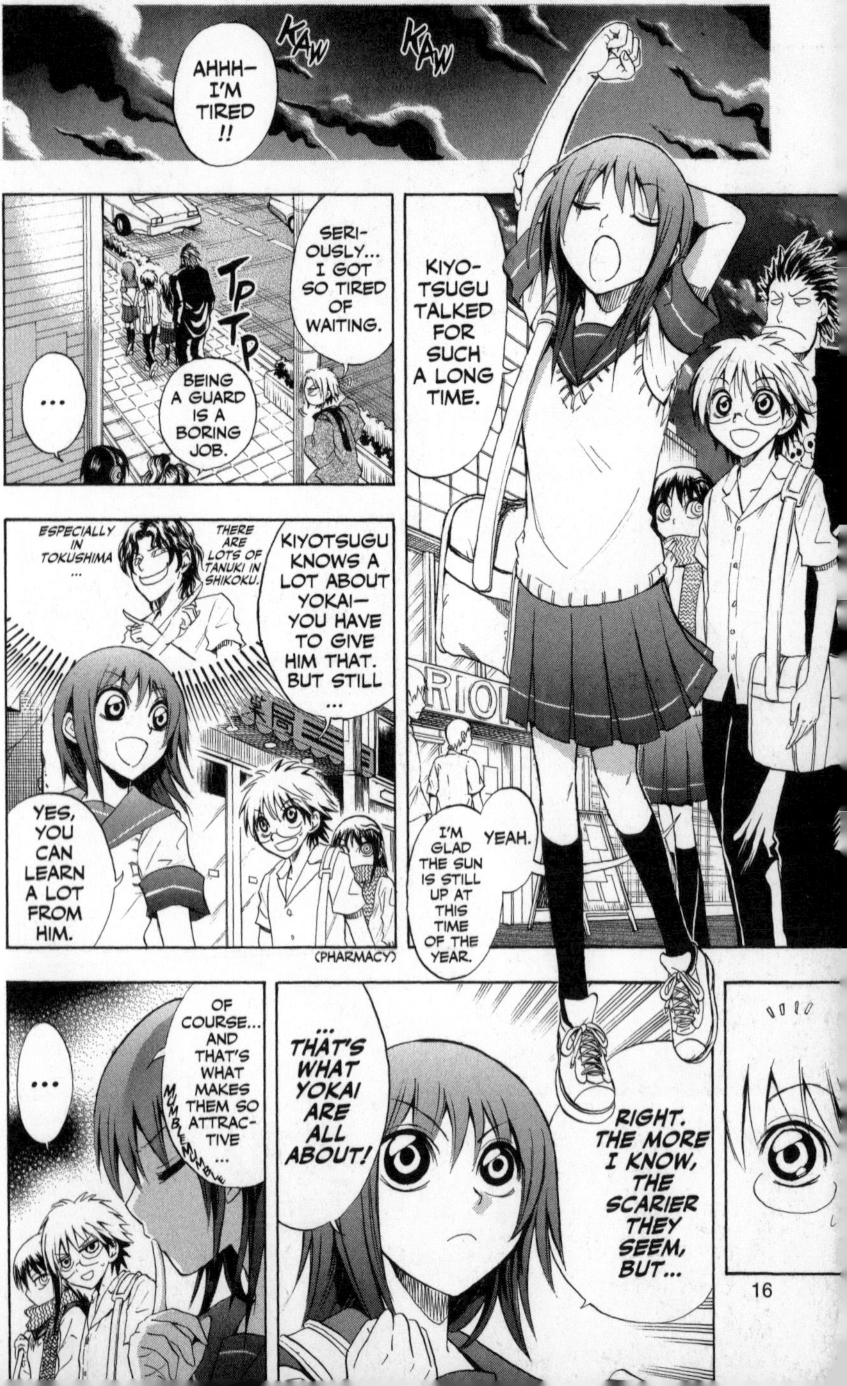
KAW
KAW
AHHH— I'M TIRED !!
KIYOTSUGU TALKED FOR SUCH A LONG TIME.
SERIOUSLY... I GOT SO TIRED OF WAITING.
TP TP
BEING A GUARD IS A BORING JOB.
...
I'M GLAD THE SUN IS STILL UP AT THIS TIME OF THE YEAR.
YEAH.
KIYOTSUGU KNOWS A LOT ABOUT YOKAI— YOU HAVE TO GIVE HIM THAT. BUT STILL ...
THERE ARE LOTS OF TANUKI IN SHIKOKU.
ESPECIALLY IN TOKUSHIMA ...
YES, YOU CAN LEARN A LOT FROM HIM.
(PHARMACY)
RIGHT. THE MORE I KNOW, THE SCARIER THEY SEEM, BUT...
... THAT'S WHAT YOKAI ARE ALL ABOUT!
OF COURSE... AND THAT'S WHAT MAKES THEM SO ATTRACTIVE ...
MUMBLE MUMBLE
...

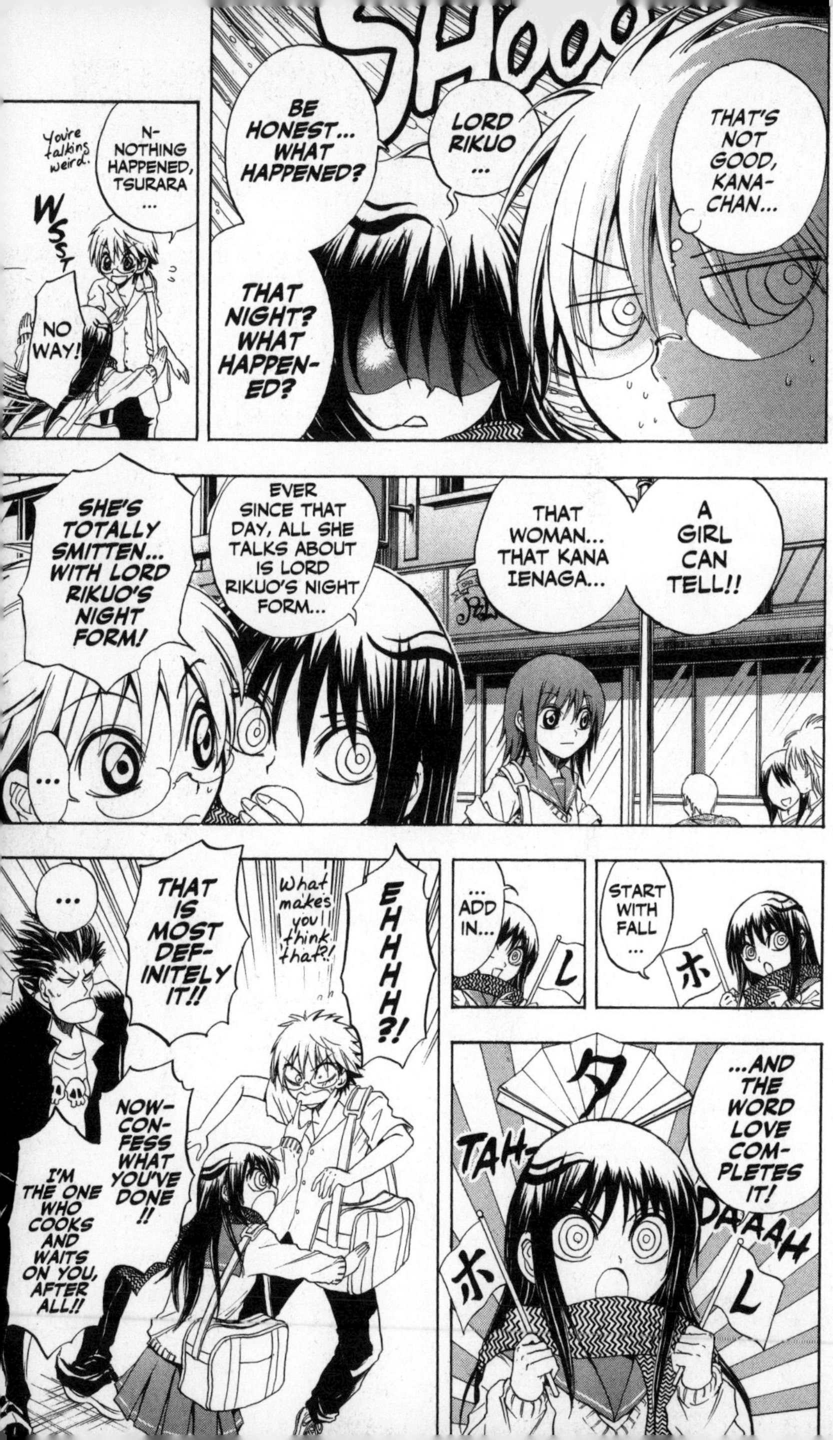

SHOOO
THAT'S NOT GOOD, KANA-CHAN...
LORD RIKUO...
BE HONEST... WHAT HAPPENED?
THAT NIGHT? WHAT HAPPENED?
N-NOTHING HAPPENED, TSURARA...
You're talking weird.
WSST
NO WAY!
A GIRL CAN TELL!!
THAT WOMAN... THAT KANA IENAGA...
EVER SINCE THAT DAY, ALL SHE TALKS ABOUT IS LORD RIKUO'S NIGHT FORM...
SHE'S TOTALLY SMITTEN... WITH LORD RIKUO'S NIGHT FORM!
...
START WITH FALL...
ホ
... ADD IN...
レ
...AND THE WORD LOVE COMPLETES IT!
タ
TAH-DAAAH
EHHHHH?!
What makes you think that?!
THAT IS MOST DEFINITELY IT!!
...
NOW—CONFESS WHAT YOU'VE DONE!!
I'M THE ONE WHO COOKS AND WAITS ON YOU, AFTER ALL!!

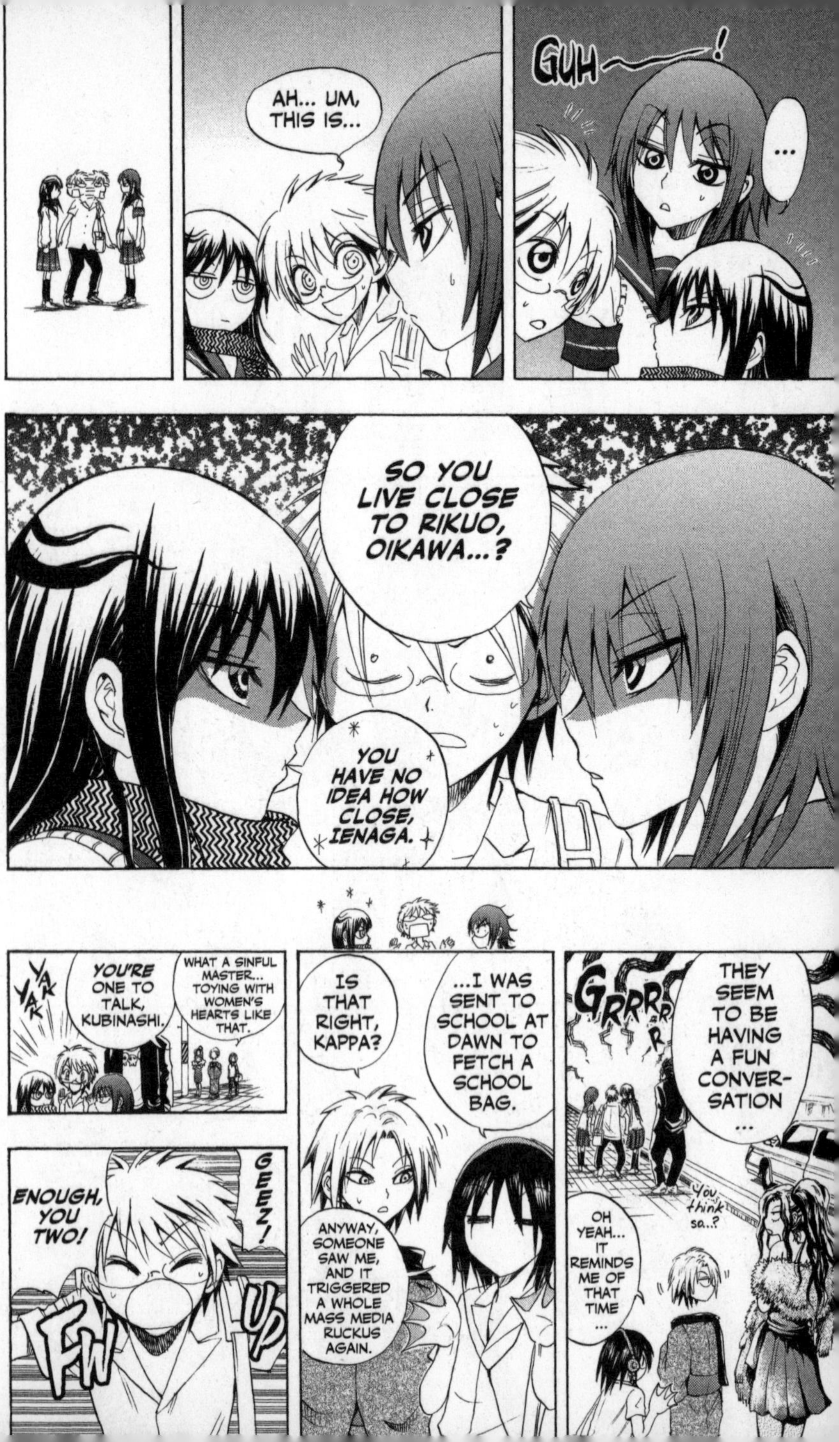
GUH—!
...
AH... UM, THIS IS...
SO YOU LIVE CLOSE TO RIKUO, OIKAWA...?
YOU HAVE NO IDEA HOW CLOSE, IENAGA.
GRRRRR
THEY SEEM TO BE HAVING A FUN CONVERSATION...
You think so..?
OH YEAH... IT REMINDS ME OF THAT TIME...
...I WAS SENT TO SCHOOL AT DAWN TO FETCH A SCHOOL BAG.
IS THAT RIGHT, KAPPA?
ANYWAY, SOMEONE SAW ME, AND IT TRIGGERED A WHOLE MASS MEDIA RUCKUS AGAIN.
WHAT A SINFUL MASTER... TOYING WITH WOMEN'S HEARTS LIKE THAT.
YOU'RE ONE TO TALK, KUBINASHI.
YAK YAK
GEEZ!
ENOUGH, YOU TWO!
FWUP

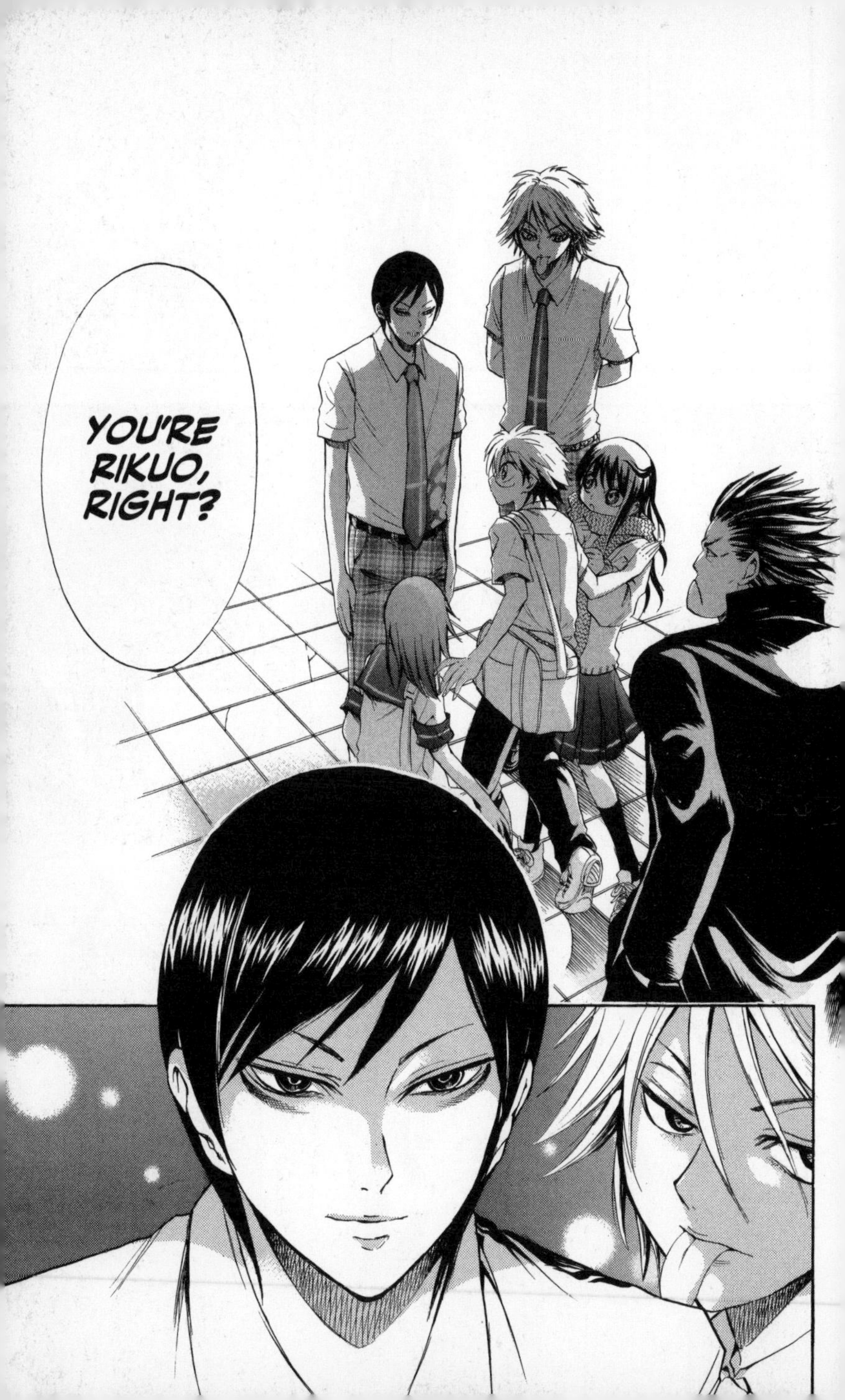
YOU'RE RIKUO, RIGHT?

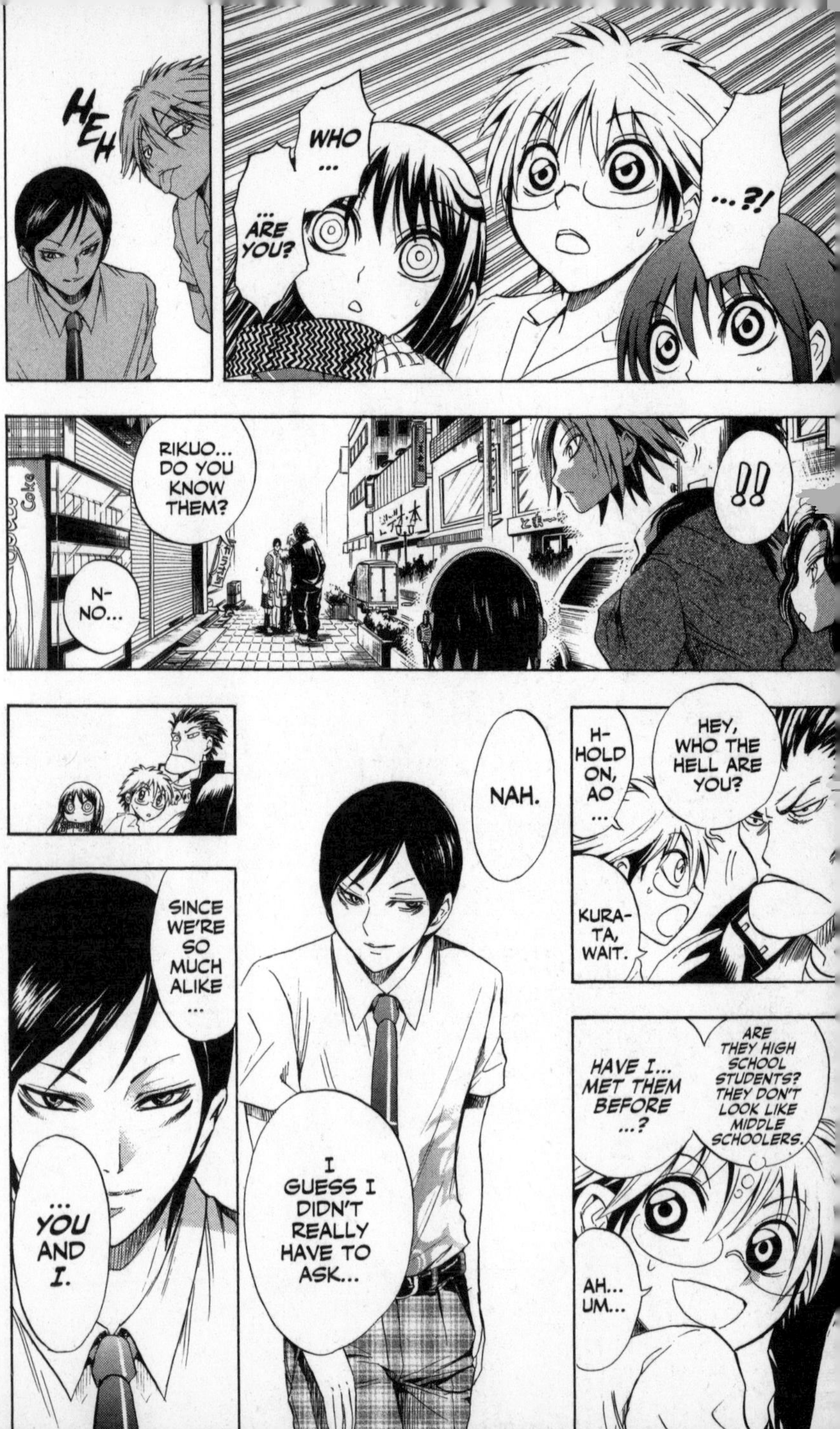
...?!
WHO ...
... ARE YOU?
HEH
!!
RIKUO... DO YOU KNOW THEM?
N-NO...
HEY, WHO THE HELL ARE YOU?
H-HOLD ON, AO ...
KURATA, WAIT.
ARE THEY HIGH SCHOOL STUDENTS? THEY DON'T LOOK LIKE MIDDLE SCHOOLERS.
HAVE I... MET THEM BEFORE ...?
AH... UM...
NAH.
I GUESS I DIDN'T REALLY HAVE TO ASK...
SINCE WE'RE SO MUCH ALIKE ...
... YOU AND I.

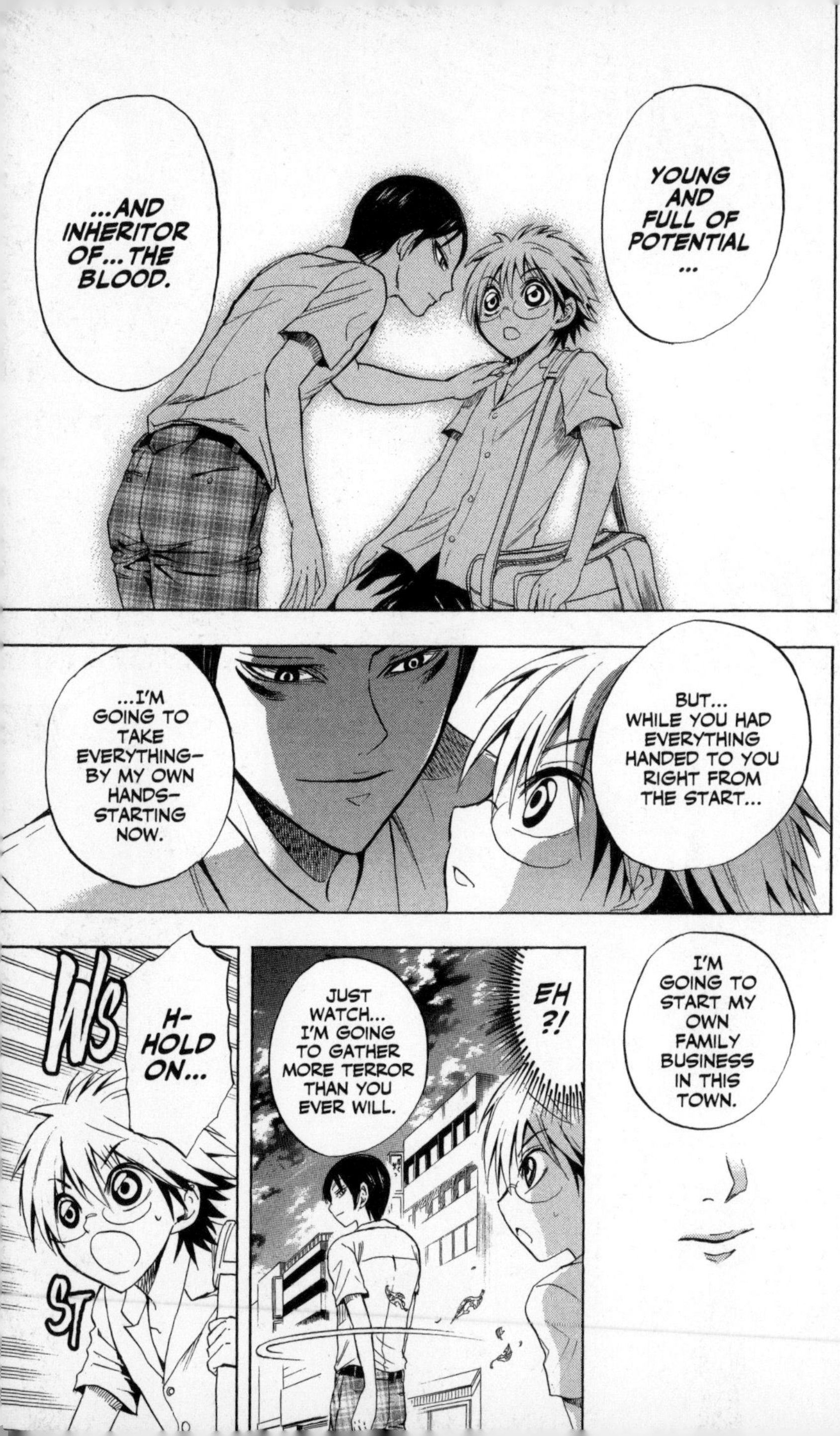
YOUNG AND FULL OF POTENTIAL ...
...AND INHERITOR OF...THE BLOOD.
BUT... WHILE YOU HAD EVERYTHING HANDED TO YOU RIGHT FROM THE START...
...I'M GOING TO TAKE EVERYTHING- BY MY OWN HANDS- STARTING NOW.
I'M GOING TO START MY OWN FAMILY BUSINESS IN THIS TOWN.
EH ?!
JUST WATCH... I'M GOING TO GATHER MORE TERROR THAN YOU EVER WILL.
WS
H- HOLD ON...
ST

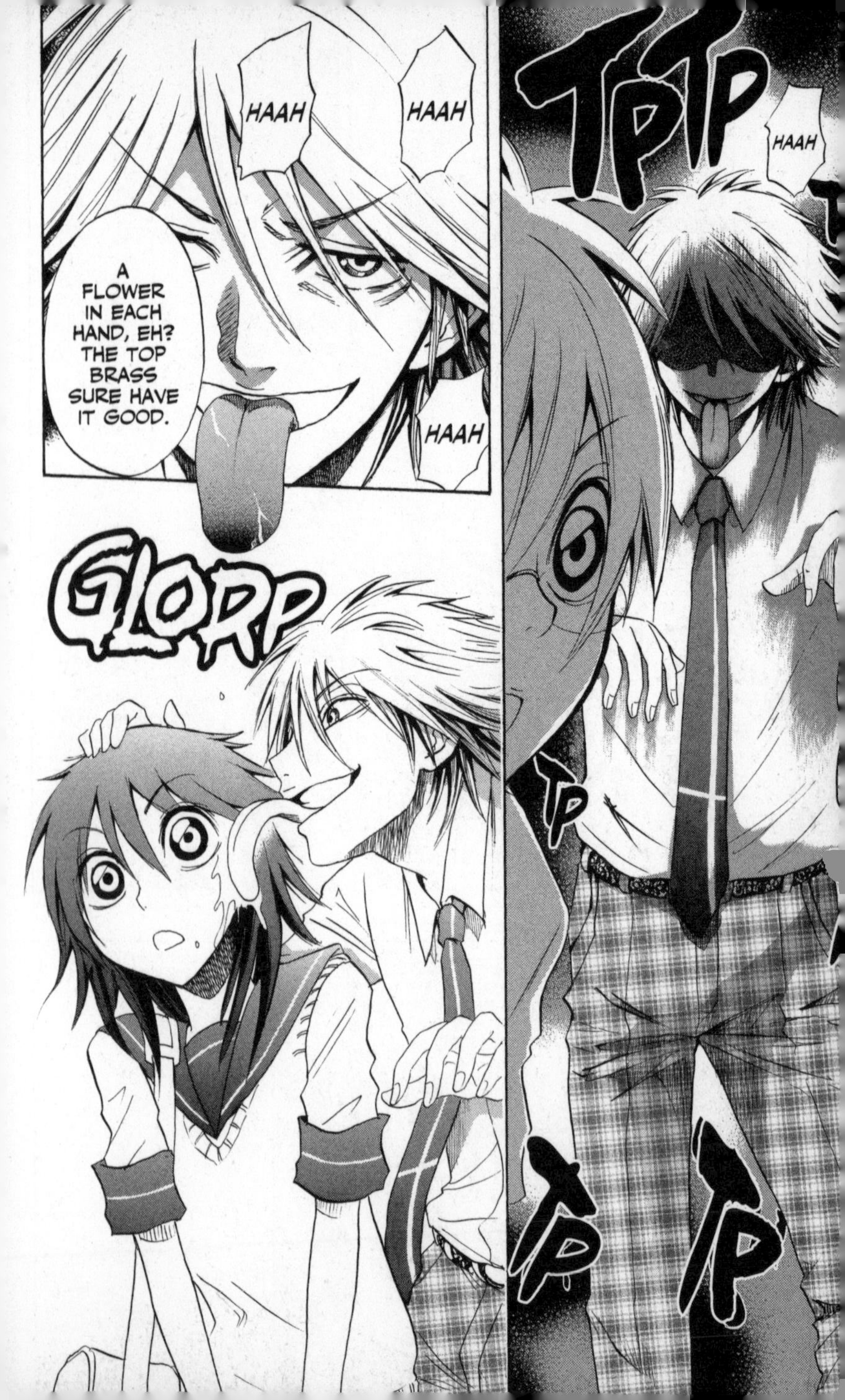
TPTP
HAAH
TP
TP TP
HAAH HAAH
A FLOWER IN EACH HAND, EH? THE TOP BRASS SURE HAVE IT GOOD.
HAAH
GLORP

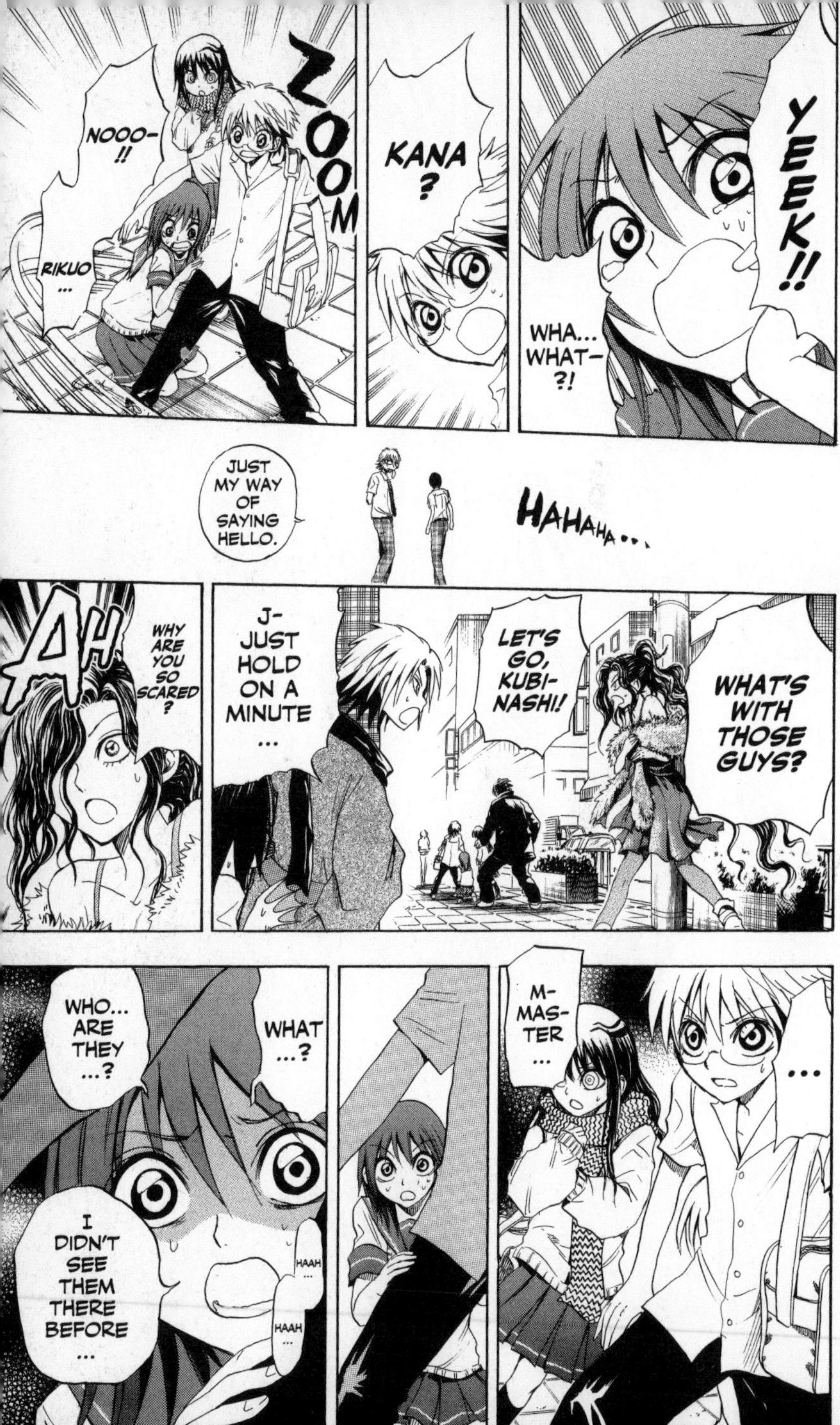
YEEK!!
WHA... WHAT-?!
KANA?
ZOOM
NOOO-!!
RIKUO...
HAHAHA...
JUST MY WAY OF SAYING HELLO.
WHAT'S WITH THOSE GUYS?
LET'S GO, KUBI-NASHI!
J-JUST HOLD ON A MINUTE...
WHY ARE YOU SO SCARED?
AH
M-MASTER...
...
WHAT...?
HAAH...
HAAH...
WHO... ARE THEY...?
I DIDN'T SEE THEM THERE BEFORE...

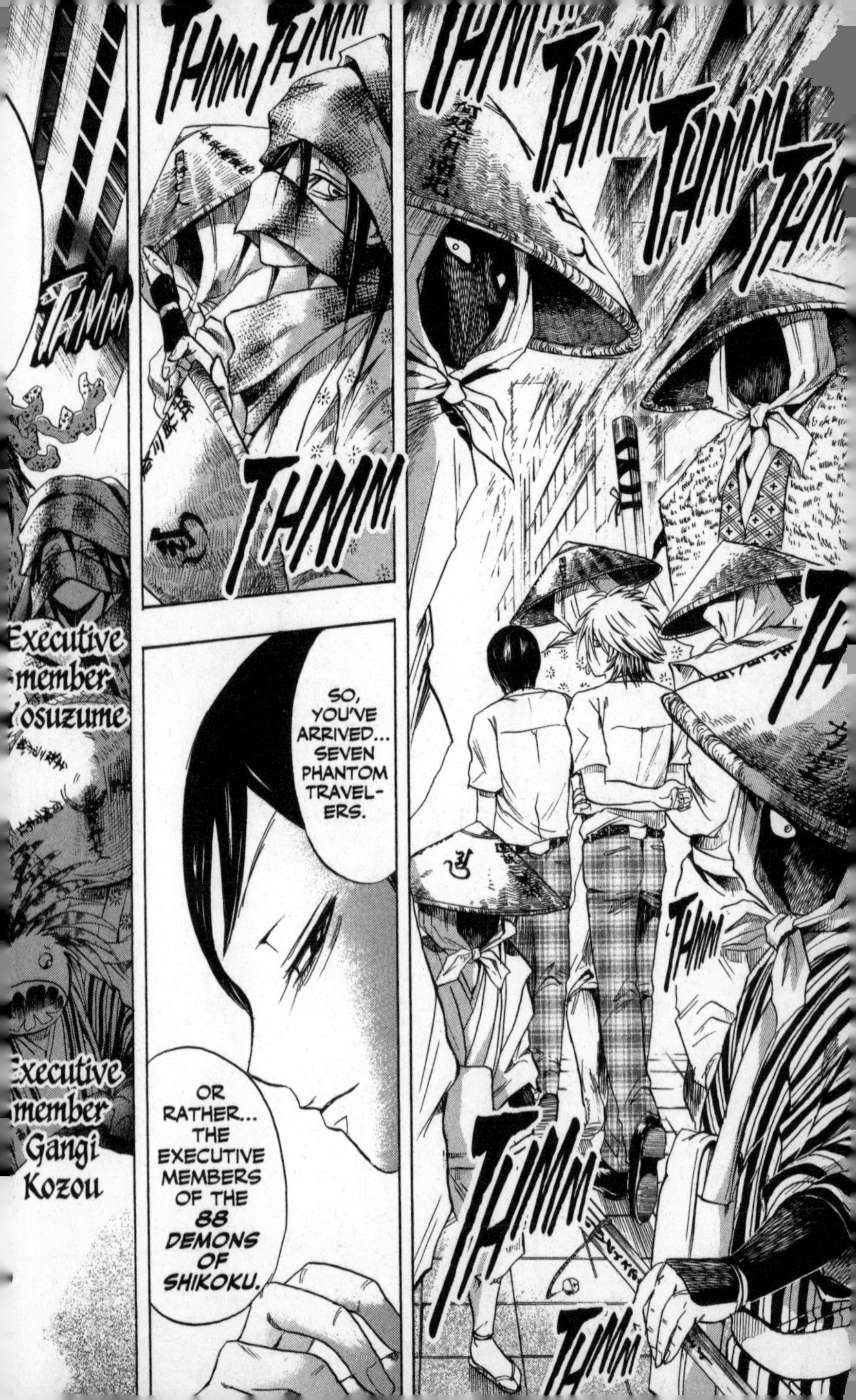
THMM
THMM
THMM
THMM
THMM
THMM
THMM
THMM THMM
THMM
SO, YOU'VE ARRIVED... SEVEN PHANTOM TRAVEL-ERS.
OR RATHER... THE EXECUTIVE MEMBERS OF THE 88 DEMONS OF SHIKOKU.
THMM
Executive member Yosuzume
Executive member Gangi Kozou

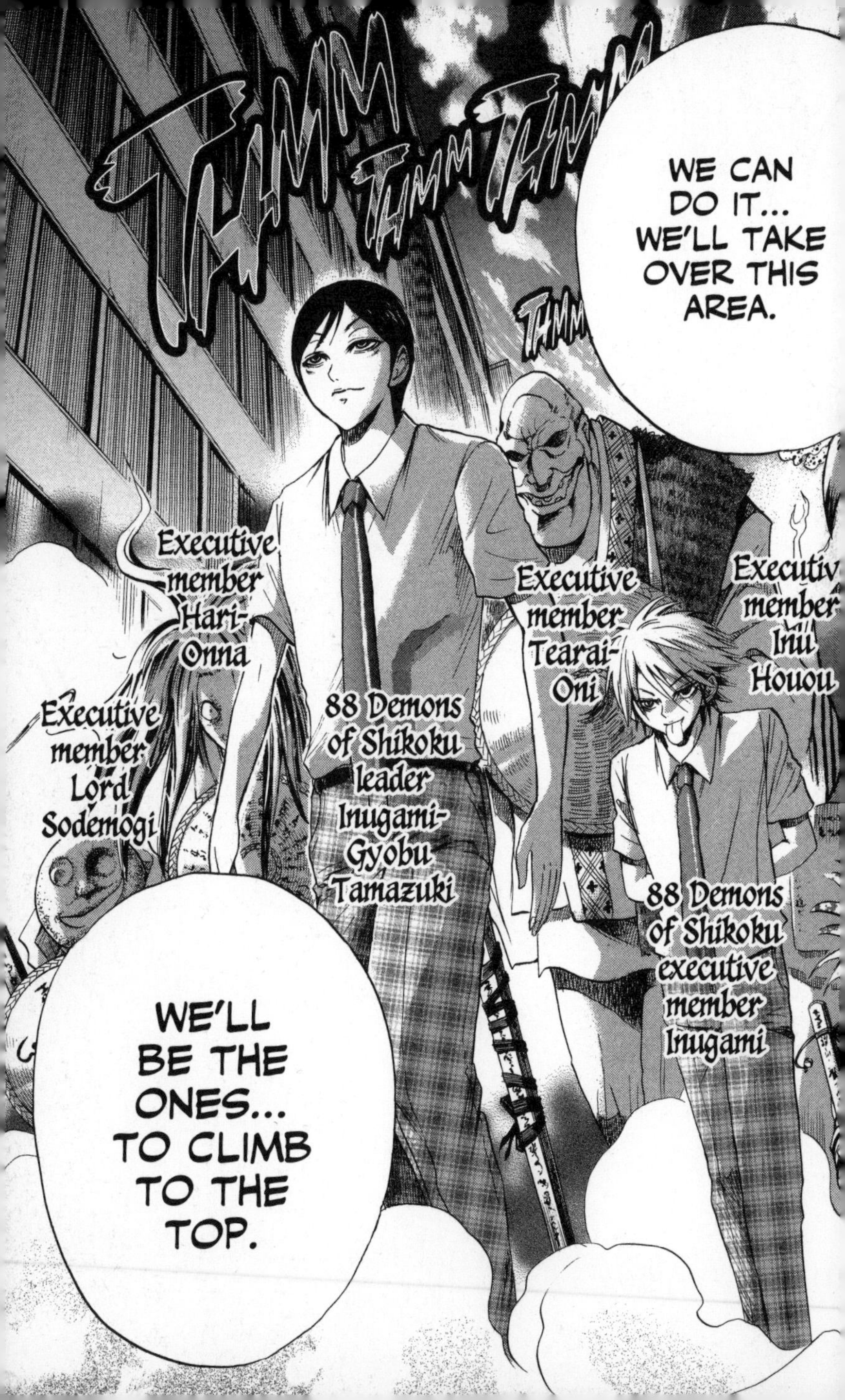
WE CAN DO IT... WE'LL TAKE OVER THIS AREA.
TAMM TAMM TAMM
Executiv member Inu Houou
88 Demons of Shikoku executive member Inugami
Executive member Tearai-Oni
88 Demons of Shikoku leader Inugami-Gyobu Tamazuki
Executive member Hari-Onna
Executive member Lord Sodemogi
WE'LL BE THE ONES... TO CLIMB TO THE TOP.

My personal favorites are these two.

Sodemogi-sama:
Professional
Tochi-gami Assassin

Muchi:
Professional
Yokai Assassin

They probably got along well.

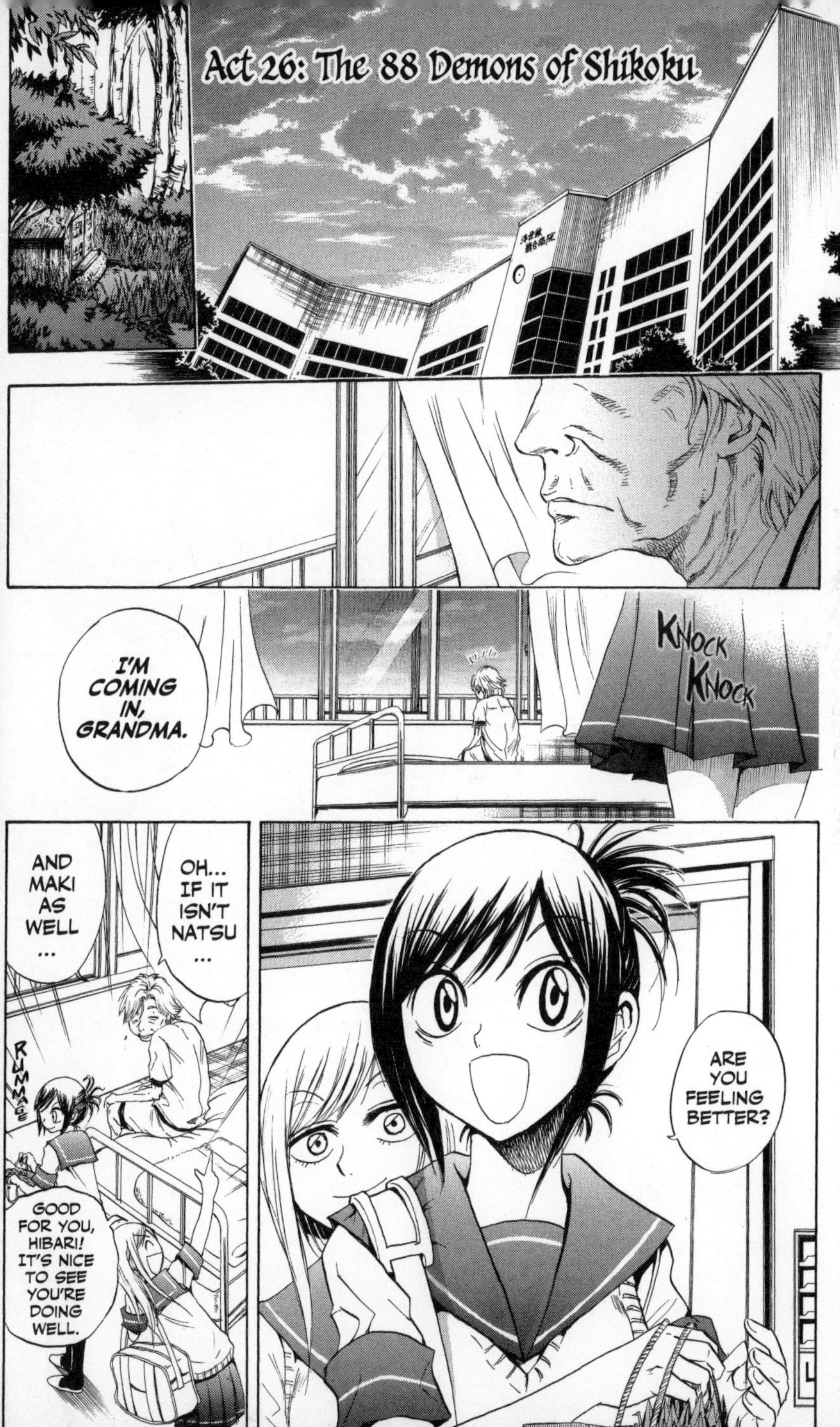
Act 26: The 88 Demons of Shikoku
KNOCK KNOCK
I'M COMING IN, GRANDMA.
ARE YOU FEELING BETTER?
OH... IF IT ISN'T NATSU...
AND MAKI AS WELL...
RUMMAGE
GOOD FOR YOU, HIBARI! IT'S NICE TO SEE YOU'RE DOING WELL.

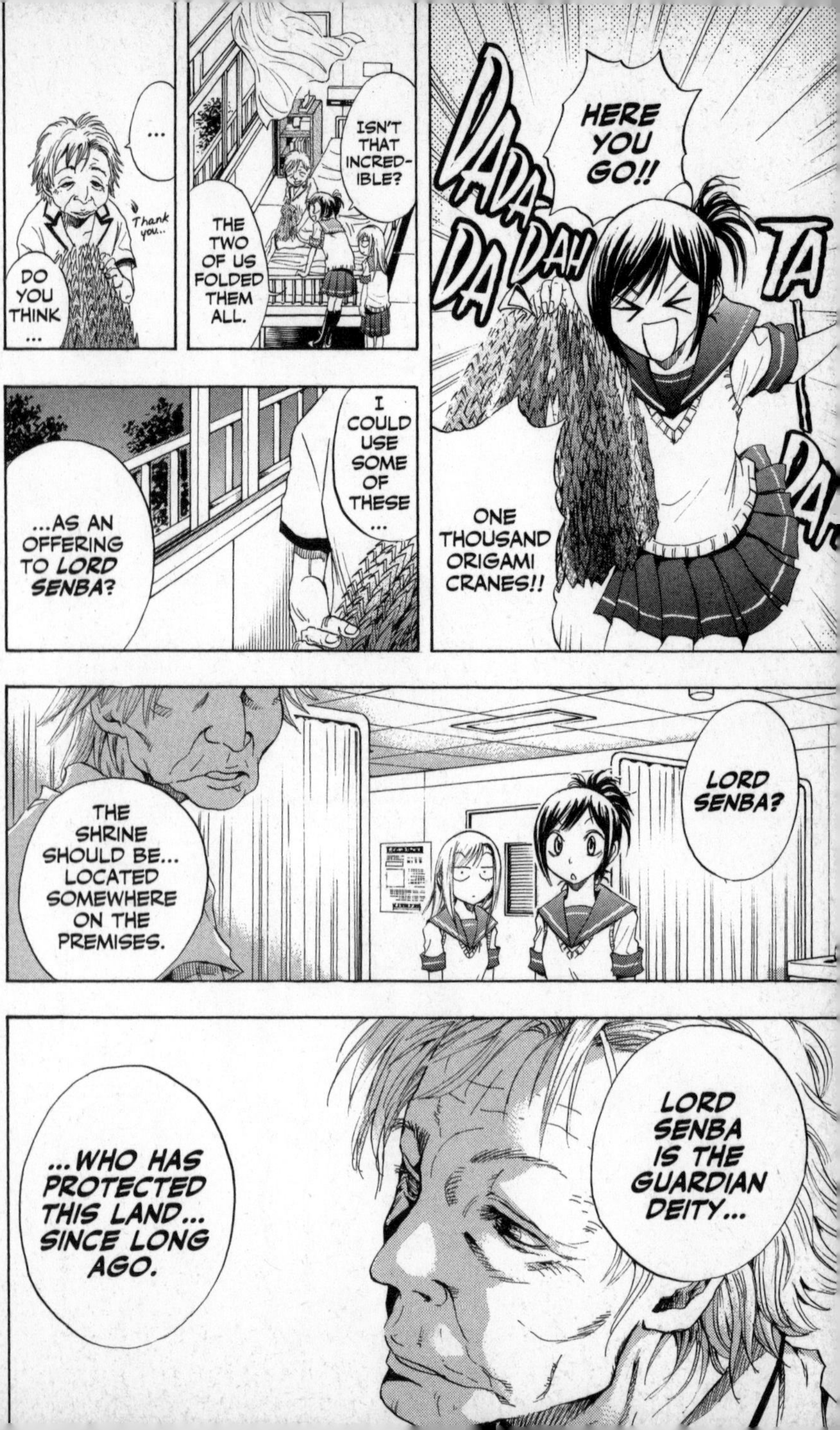
HERE YOU GO!!
DADA-DA DAH
TA-DA
ONE THOUSAND ORIGAMI CRANES!!
ISN'T THAT INCREDIBLE?
THE TWO OF US FOLDED THEM ALL.
...
Thank you...
DO YOU THINK ...
I COULD USE SOME OF THESE ...
...AS AN OFFERING TO LORD SENBA?
LORD SENBA?
THE SHRINE SHOULD BE... LOCATED SOMEWHERE ON THE PREMISES.
LORD SENBA IS THE GUARDIAN DEITY...
...WHO HAS PROTECTED THIS LAND... SINCE LONG AGO.

Act 26: The 88 Demons of Shikoku

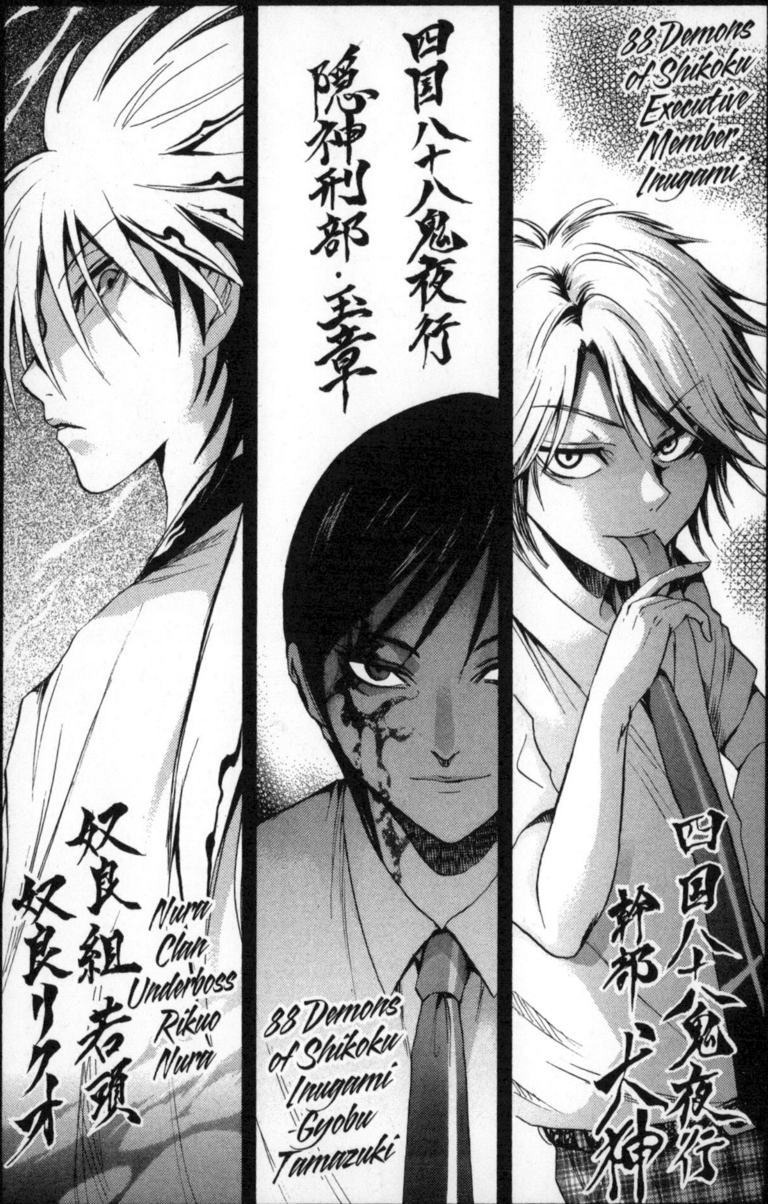
88 Demons of Shikoku Executive Member Inugami
四国八十八鬼夜行
幹部 犬神
四国八十八鬼夜行
隠神刑部・玉章
88 Demons of Shikoku Inugami-Gyobu Tamazuki
奴良組若頭
奴良リクオ
Nura Clan Underboss Rikuo Nura

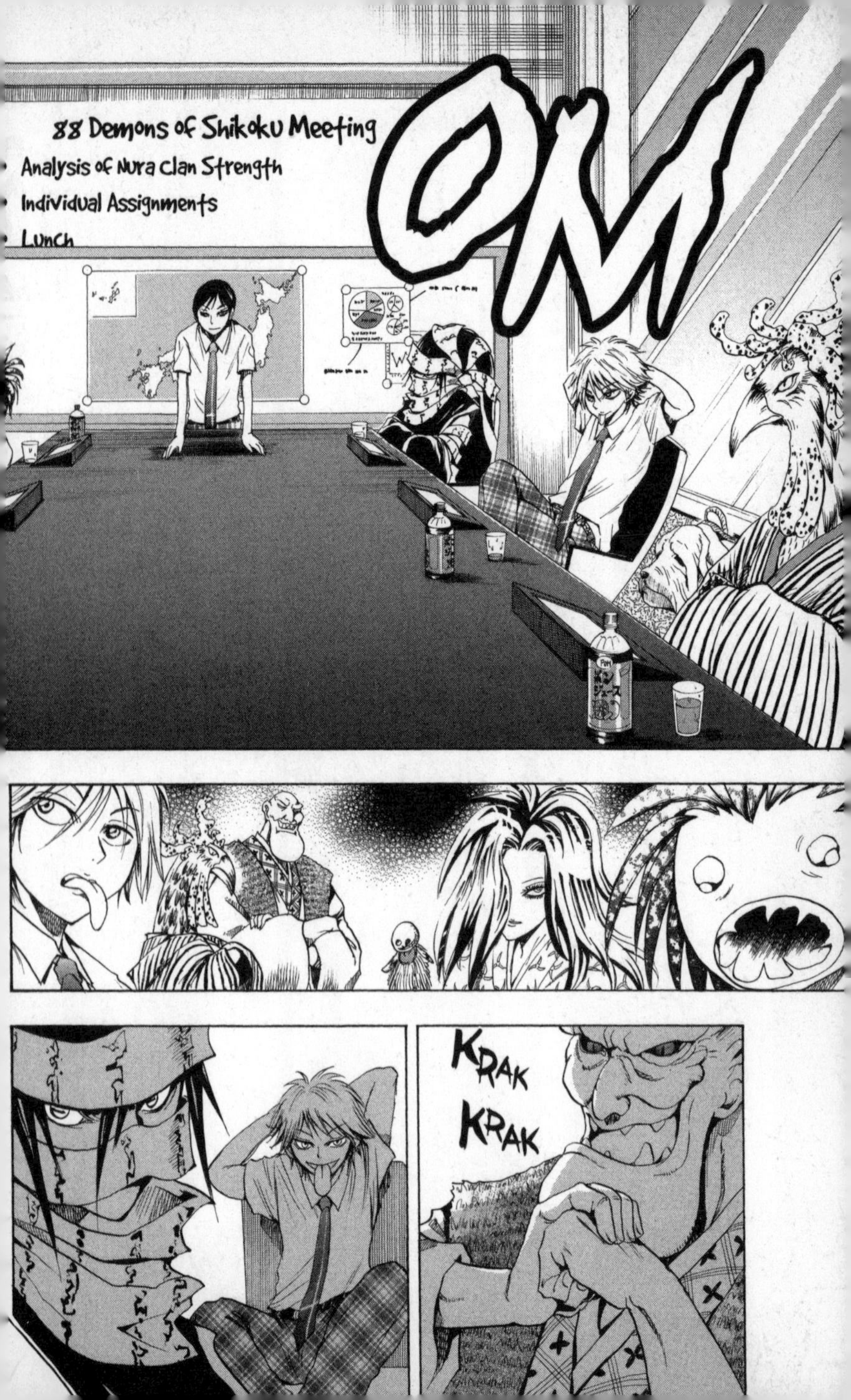
88 Demons of Shikoku Meeting
Analysis of Nura Clan Strength
Individual Assignments
Lunch
OM
KRAK
KRAK

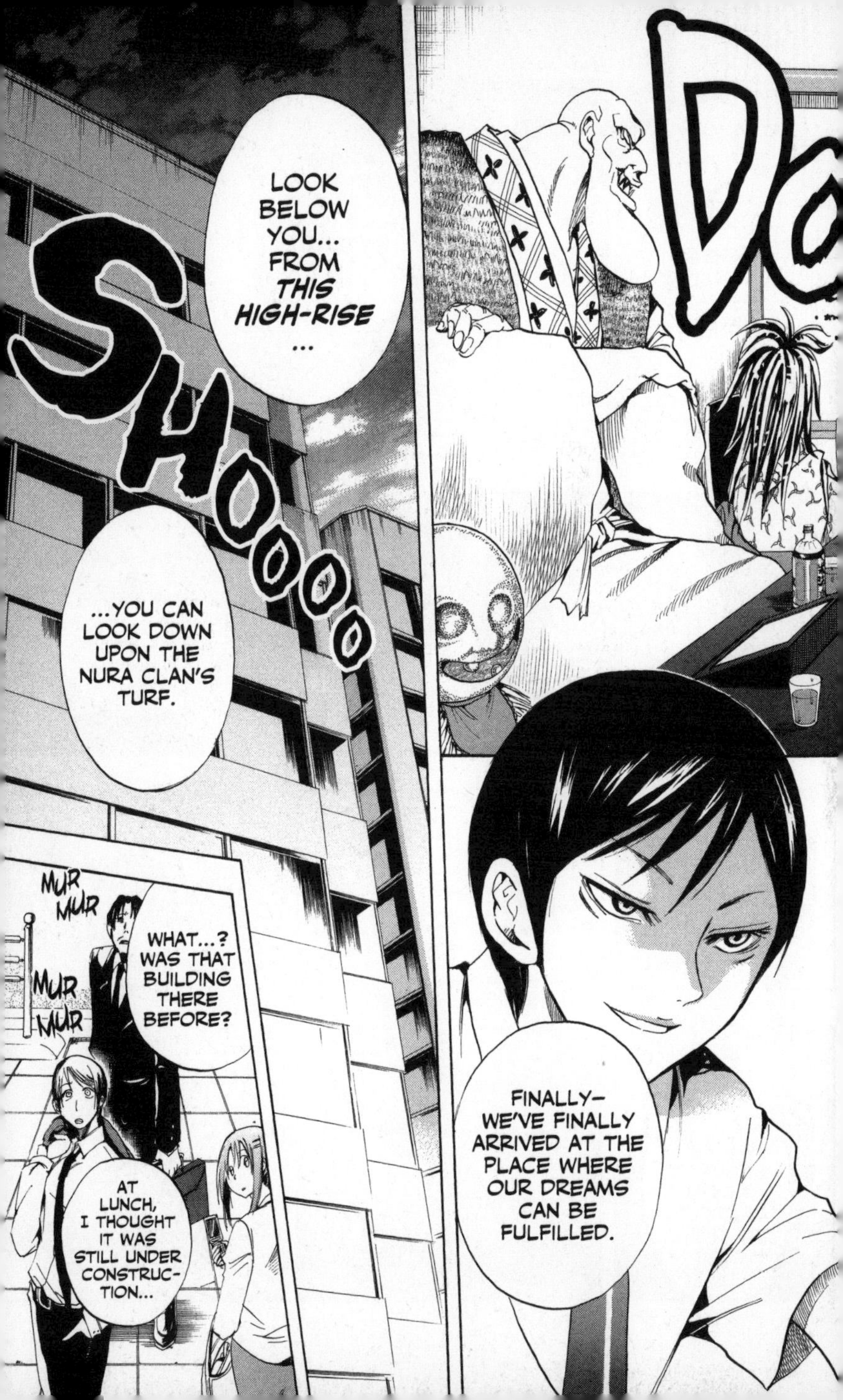
DO
LOOK BELOW YOU... FROM THIS HIGH-RISE...
SHOOOOO
...YOU CAN LOOK DOWN UPON THE NURA CLAN'S TURF.
FINALLY— WE'VE FINALLY ARRIVED AT THE PLACE WHERE OUR DREAMS CAN BE FULFILLED.
MUR MUR
MUR MUR
WHAT...? WAS THAT BUILDING THERE BEFORE?
AT LUNCH, I THOUGHT IT WAS STILL UNDER CONSTRUCTION...

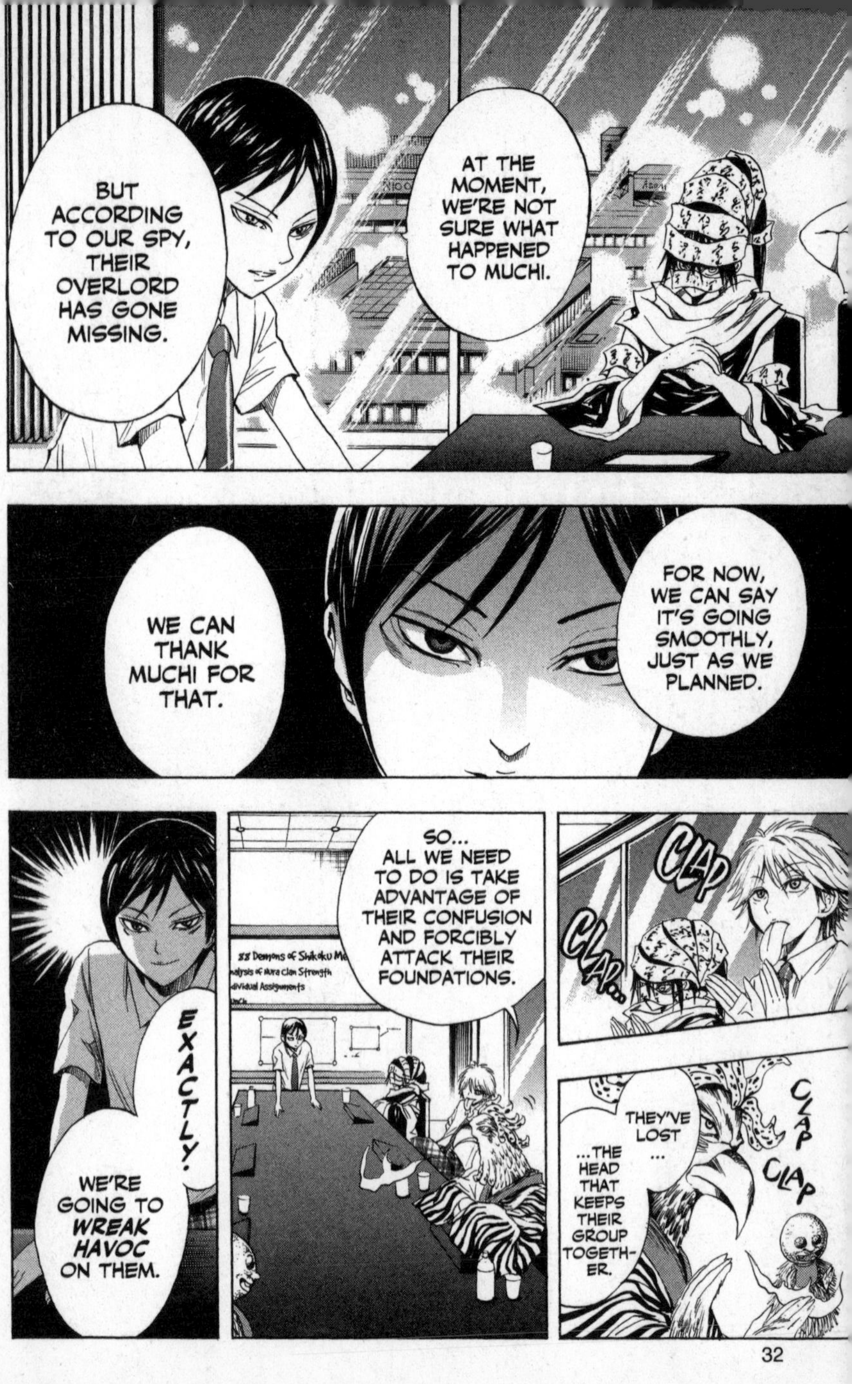
AT THE MOMENT, WE'RE NOT SURE WHAT HAPPENED TO MUCHI.
BUT ACCORDING TO OUR SPY, THEIR OVERLORD HAS GONE MISSING.
FOR NOW, WE CAN SAY IT'S GOING SMOOTHLY, JUST AS WE PLANNED.
WE CAN THANK MUCHI FOR THAT.
CLAP
CLAP...
THEY'VE LOST ...
...THE HEAD THAT KEEPS THEIR GROUP TOGETH-ER.
CLAP
CLAP
SO... ALL WE NEED TO DO IS TAKE ADVANTAGE OF THEIR CONFUSION AND FORCIBLY ATTACK THEIR FOUNDATIONS.
EXACTLY.
WE'RE GOING TO *WREAK HAVOC* ON THEM.

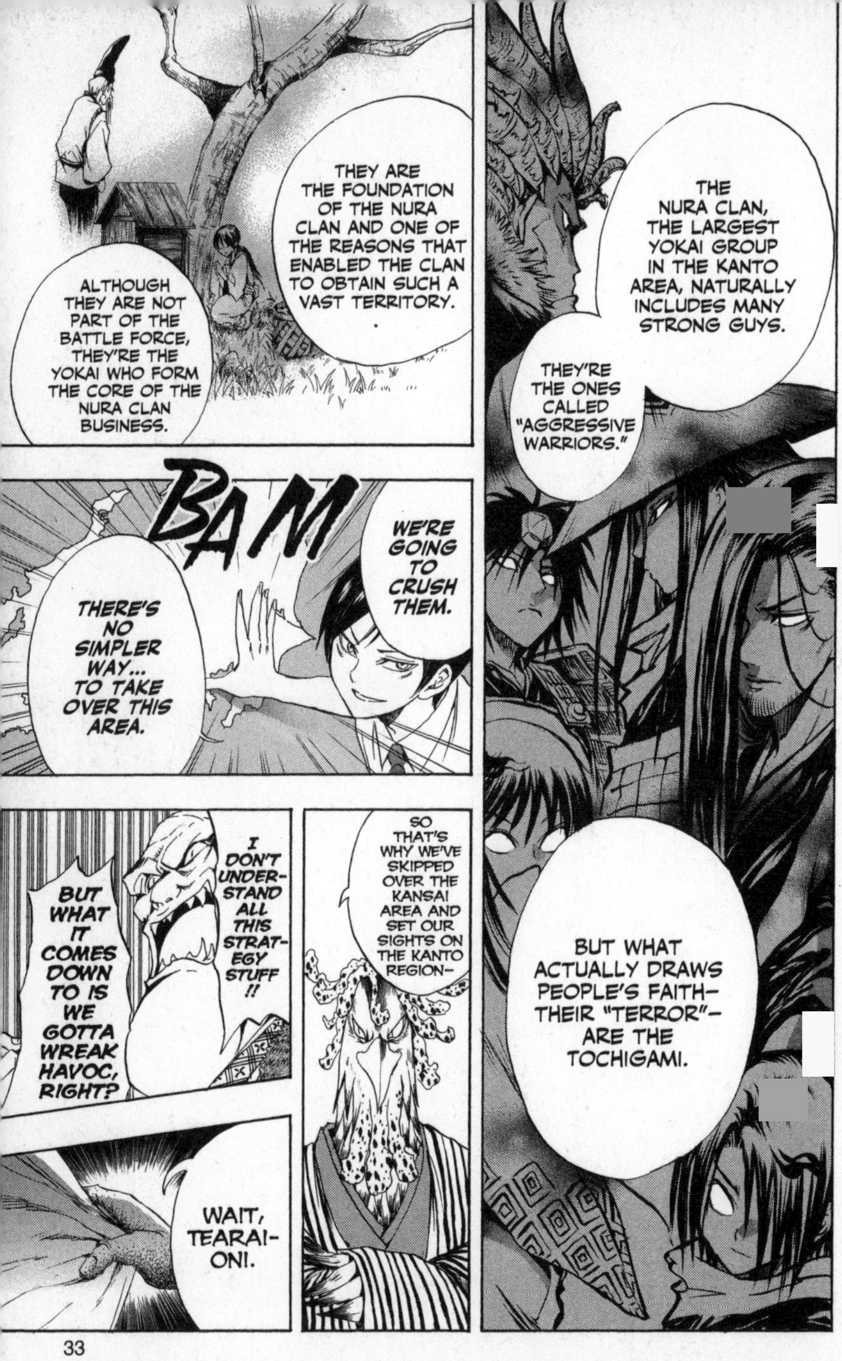
THE NURA CLAN, THE LARGEST YOKAI GROUP IN THE KANTO AREA, NATURALLY INCLUDES MANY STRONG GUYS.
THEY'RE THE ONES CALLED "AGGRESSIVE WARRIORS."
BUT WHAT ACTUALLY DRAWS PEOPLE'S FAITH—THEIR "TERROR"—ARE THE TOCHIGAMI.
THEY ARE THE FOUNDATION OF THE NURA CLAN AND ONE OF THE REASONS THAT ENABLED THE CLAN TO OBTAIN SUCH A VAST TERRITORY.
ALTHOUGH THEY ARE NOT PART OF THE BATTLE FORCE, THEY'RE THE YOKAI WHO FORM THE CORE OF THE NURA CLAN BUSINESS.
BAM
WE'RE GOING TO CRUSH THEM.
THERE'S NO SIMPLER WAY... TO TAKE OVER THIS AREA.
SO THAT'S WHY WE'VE SKIPPED OVER THE KANSAI AREA AND SET OUR SIGHTS ON THE KANTO REGION—
I DON'T UNDER-STAND ALL THIS STRAT-EGY STUFF!!
BUT WHAT IT COMES DOWN TO IS WE GOTTA WREAK HAVOC, RIGHT?
WAIT, TEARAI-ONI.

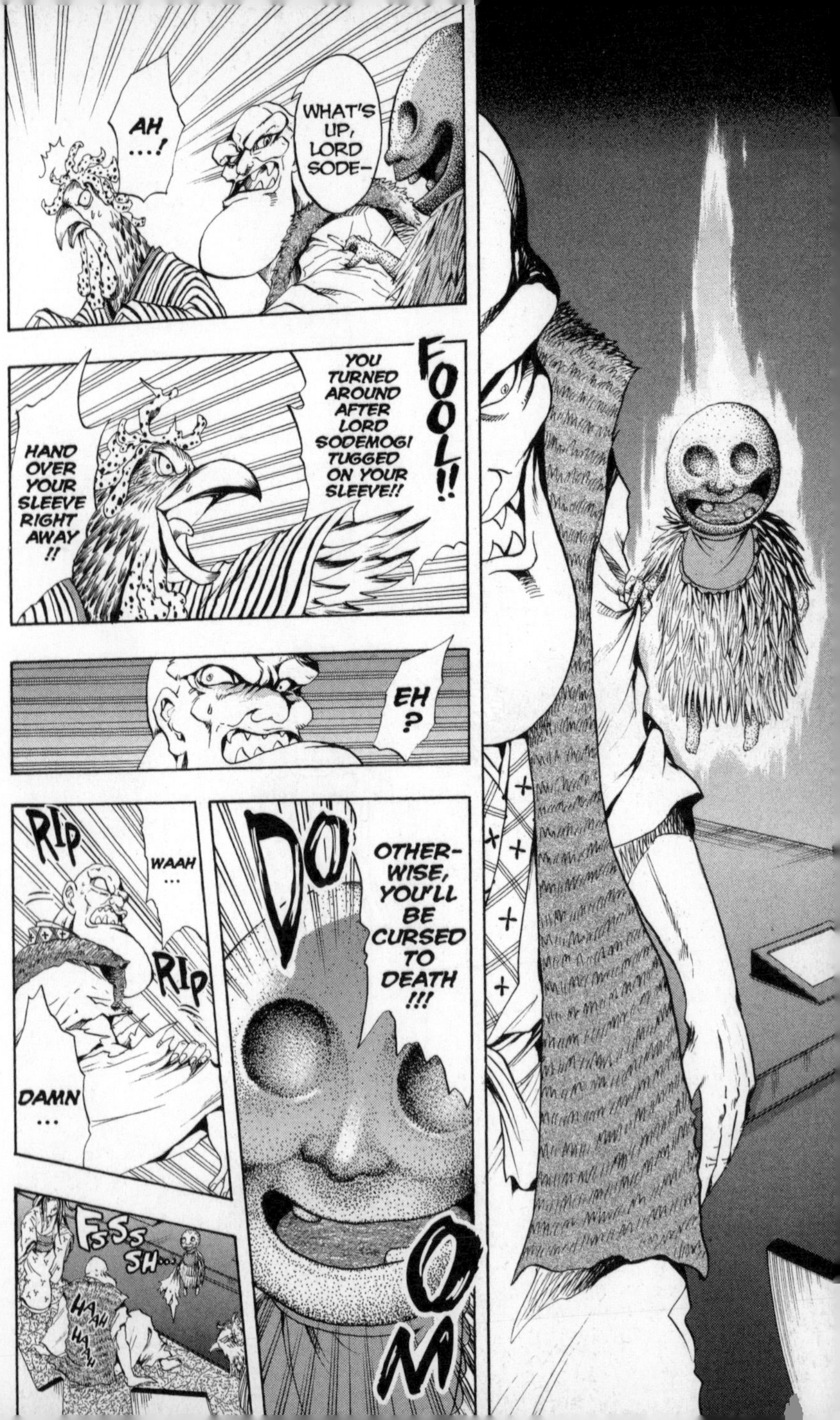
WHAT'S UP, LORD SODE-
AH ...!
FOOL!!
YOU TURNED AROUND AFTER LORD SODEMOGI TUGGED ON YOUR SLEEVE!!
HAND OVER YOUR SLEEVE RIGHT AWAY !!
EH ?
DOOM
OTHER-WISE, YOU'LL BE CURSED TO DEATH !!!
RIP
WAAH ...
RIP
DAMN ...
FSSSSH...
HAAH HAAH

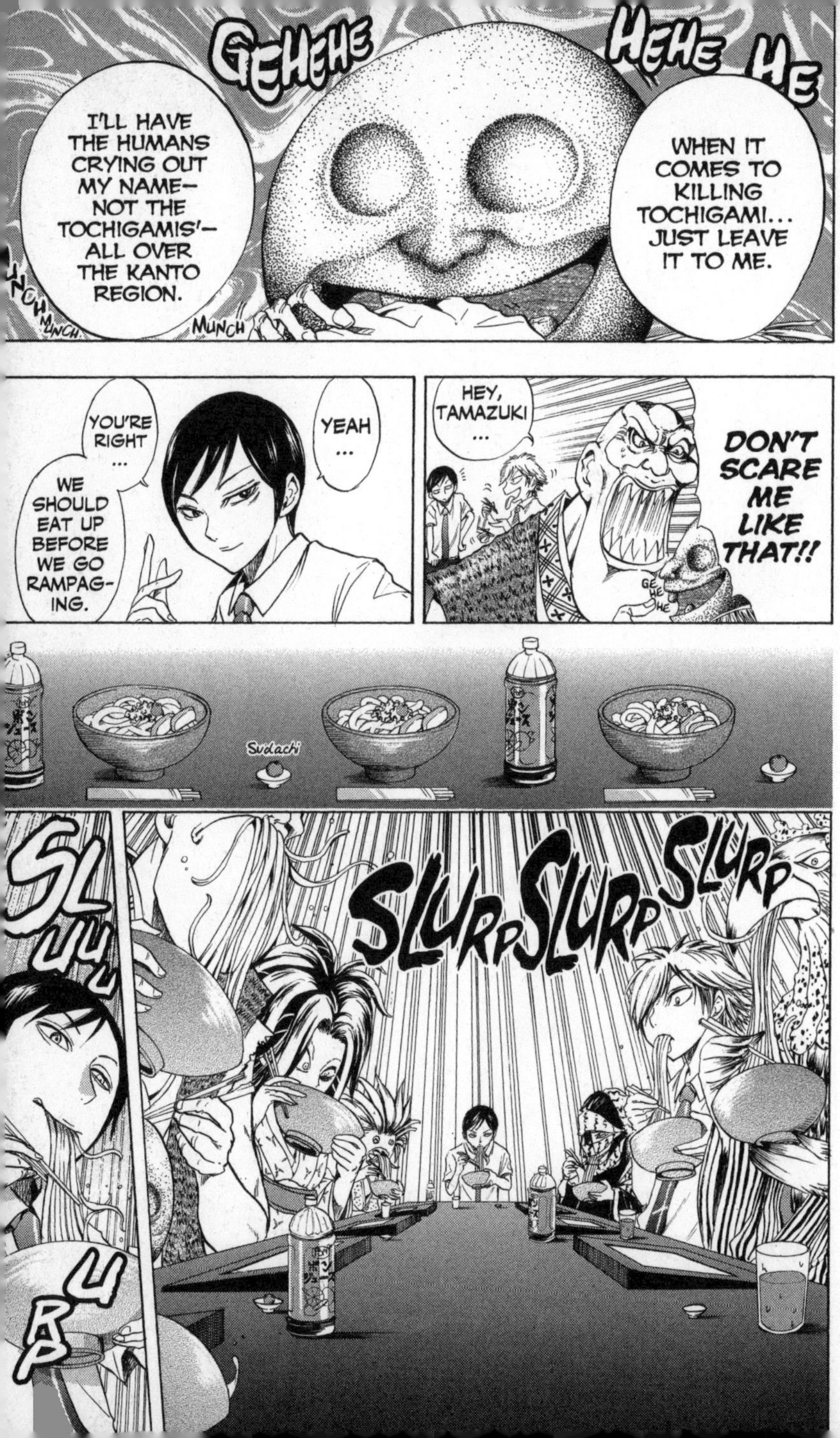
HEHE HE
WHEN IT COMES TO KILLING TOCHIGAMI... JUST LEAVE IT TO ME.
GEHEHE
I'LL HAVE THE HUMANS CRYING OUT MY NAME—NOT THE TOCHIGAMIS'—ALL OVER THE KANTO REGION.
MUNCH
HEY, TAMAZUKI...
DON'T SCARE ME LIKE THAT!!
GE HE HE
YEAH...
YOU'RE RIGHT... WE SHOULD EAT UP BEFORE WE GO RAMPAGING.
Sudachi
SLURP SLURP SLURP
SLUUUURP

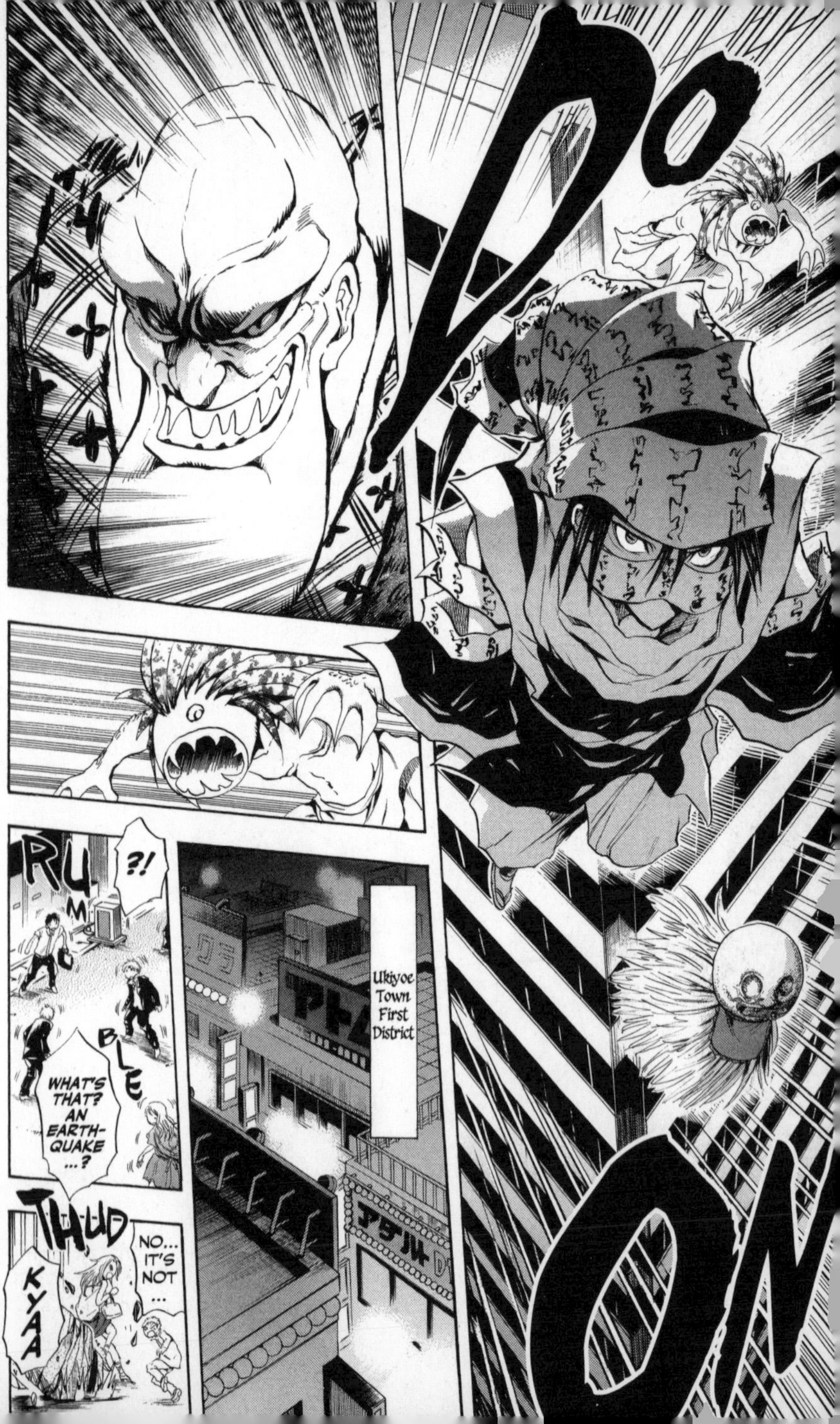
DO
ON
Ukiyoe Town First District
RUMBLE
?!
WHAT'S THAT? AN EARTH-QUAKE ...?
THUD
NO... IT'S NOT ...
KYAA

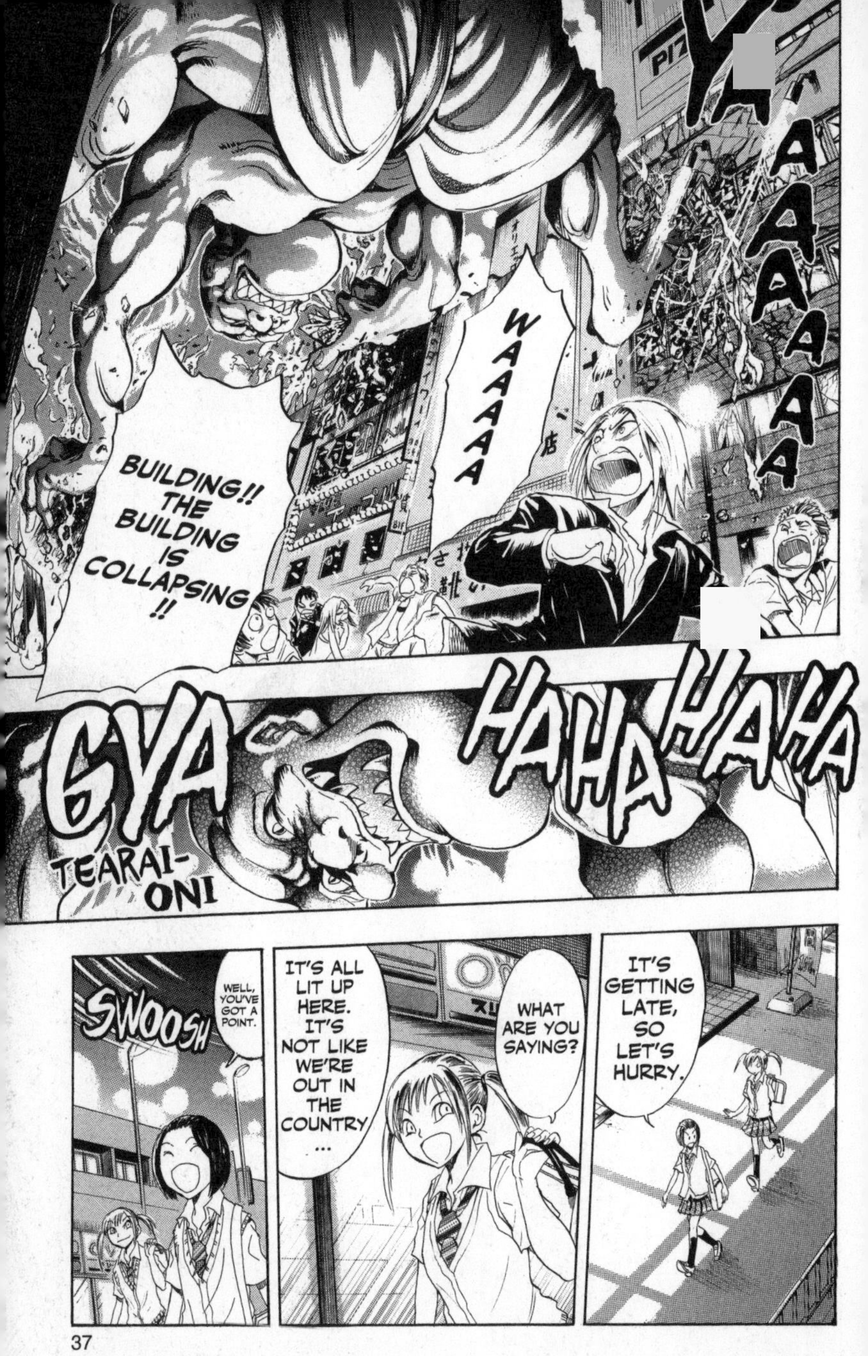
YAAAAAAA
WAAAAAAA
BUILDING!! THE BUILDING IS COLLAPSING!!
GYA HAHAHAHA
TEARAI-ONI
IT'S GETTING LATE, SO LET'S HURRY.
WHAT ARE YOU SAYING?
IT'S ALL LIT UP HERE. IT'S NOT LIKE WE'RE OUT IN THE COUNTRY...
WELL, YOU'VE GOT A POINT.
SWOOSH

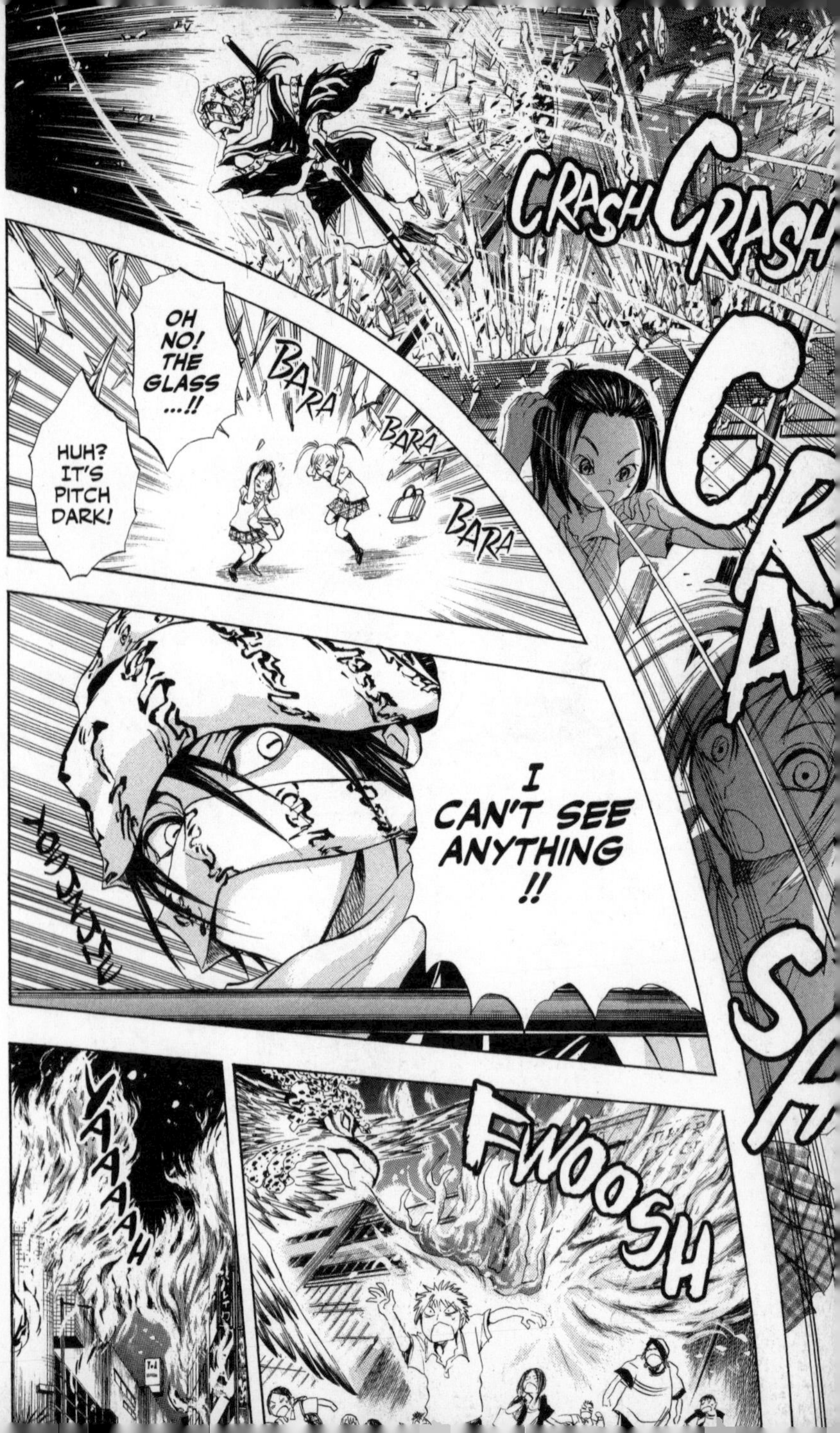
CRASH CRASH
CRASH
OH NO! THE GLASS ...!!
HUH? IT'S PITCH DARK!
BARA
BARA
BARA
I CAN'T SEE ANYTHING !!
FWOOSH
YAAAAAH

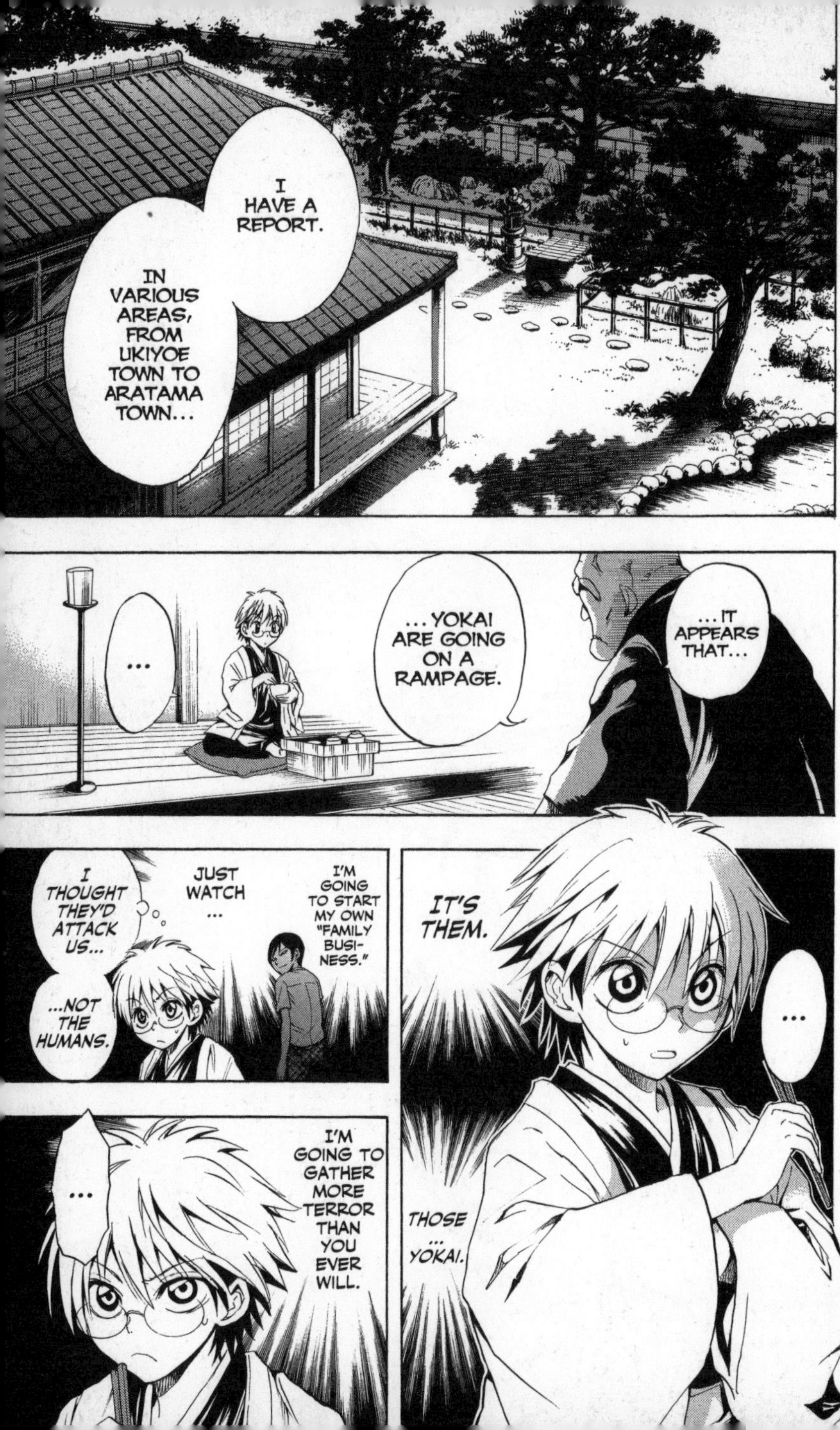
I HAVE A REPORT.
IN VARIOUS AREAS, FROM UKIYOE TOWN TO ARATAMA TOWN...
...IT APPEARS THAT...
...YOKAI ARE GOING ON A RAMPAGE.
...
IT'S THEM.
...
THOSE ... YOKAI.
I'M GOING TO START MY OWN "FAMILY BUSINESS."
JUST WATCH ...
I THOUGHT THEY'D ATTACK US...
...NOT THE HUMANS.
I'M GOING TO GATHER MORE TERROR THAN YOU EVER WILL.
...

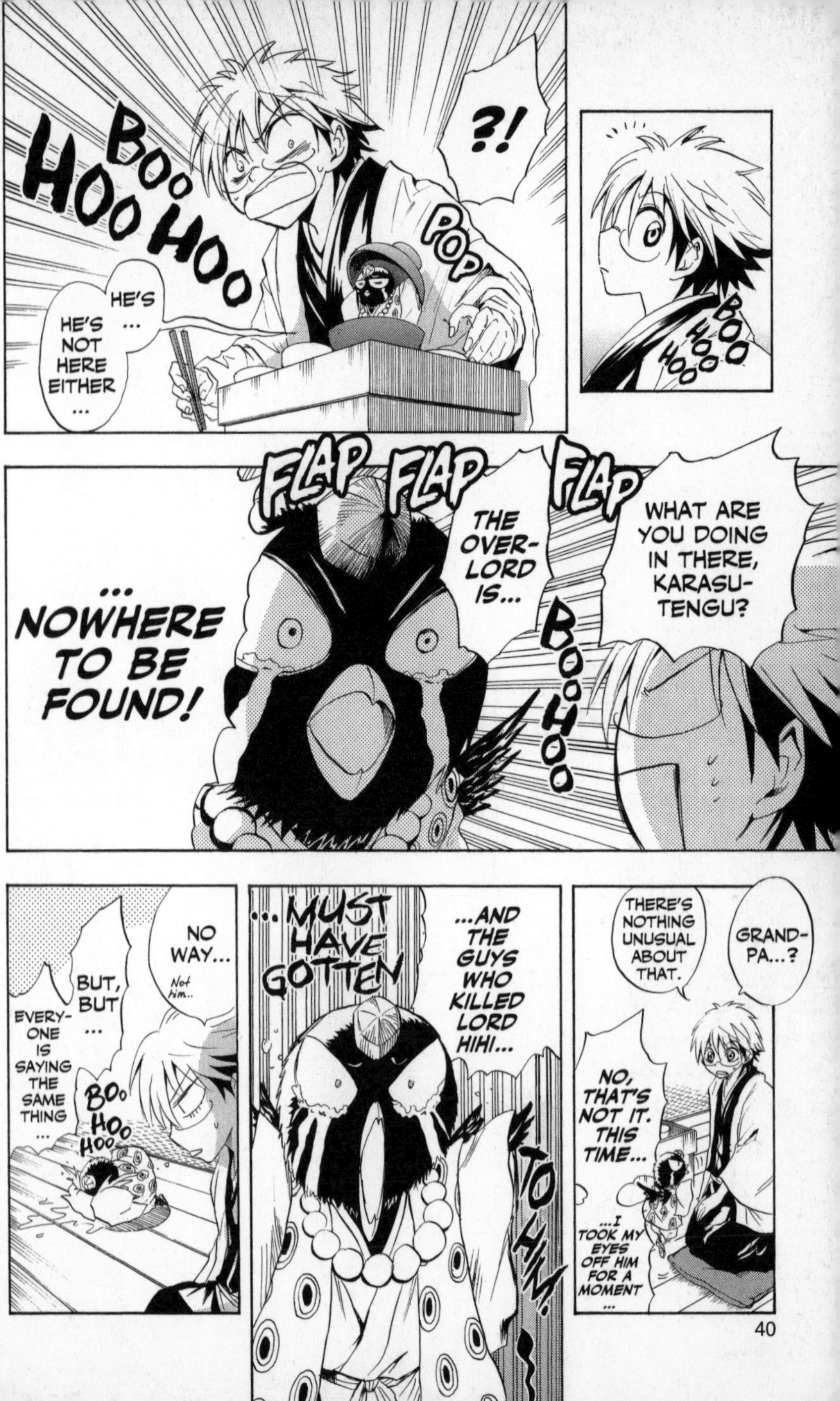
BOO HOO HOO
?!
BOO HOO HOO HOO
POP
HE'S ... HE'S NOT HERE EITHER ...
WHAT ARE YOU DOING IN THERE, KARASU-TENGU?
FLAP FLAP FLAP
THE OVER-LORD IS...
BOO HOO HOO
... NOWHERE TO BE FOUND!
GRAND-PA...?
THERE'S NOTHING UNUSUAL ABOUT THAT.
NO, THAT'S NOT IT. THIS TIME...
...I TOOK MY EYES OFF HIM FOR A MOMENT ...
...AND THE GUYS WHO KILLED LORD HIHI...
...MUST HAVE GOTTEN
TO HIM!
NO WAY...
Not him...
BUT, BUT ...
EVERY-ONE IS SAYING THE SAME THING ...
BOO HOO HOO

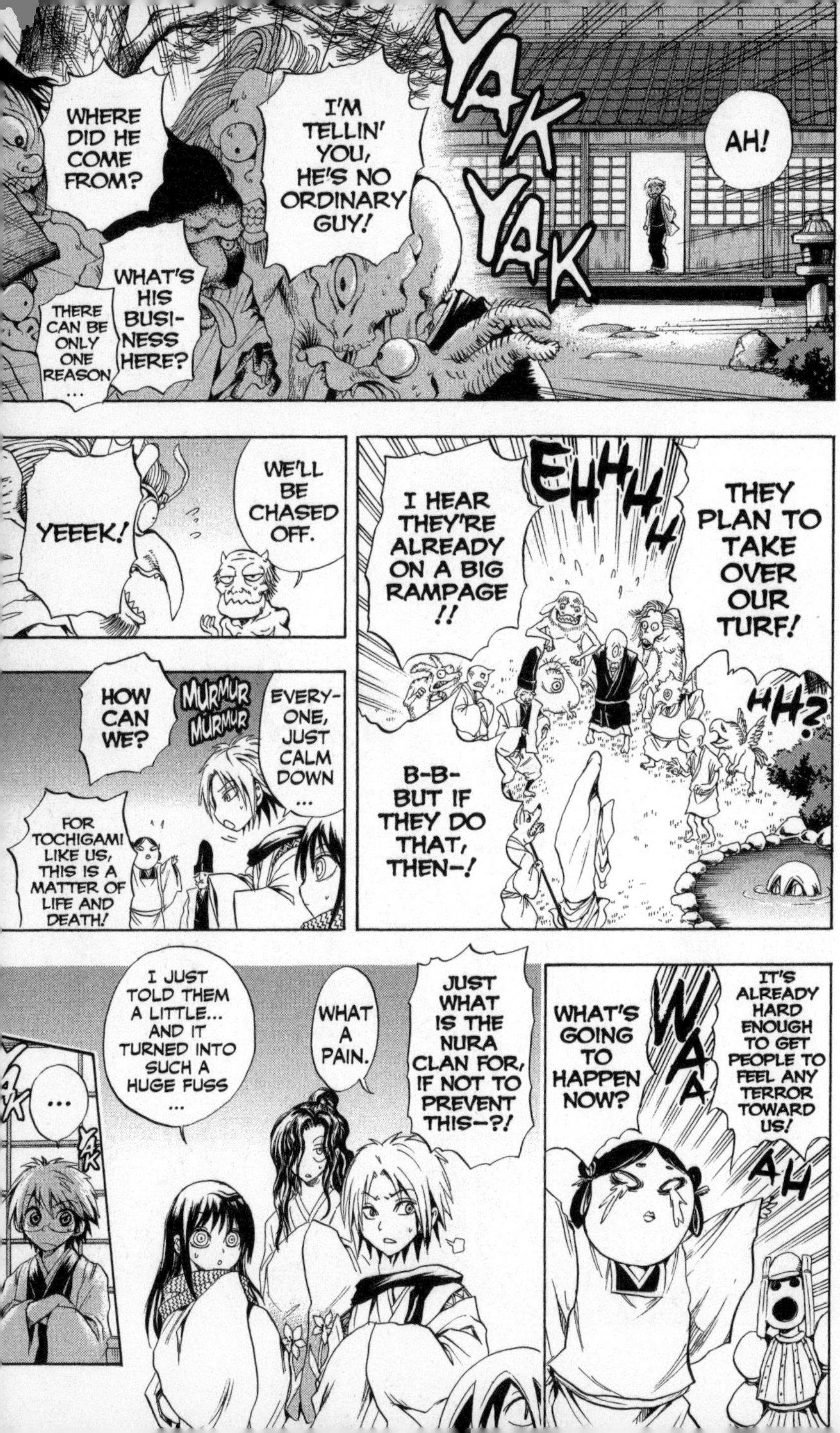
AH!
YAK YAK
I'M TELLIN' YOU, HE'S NO ORDINARY GUY!
WHERE DID HE COME FROM?
WHAT'S HIS BUSI-NESS HERE?
THERE CAN BE ONLY ONE REASON ...
THEY PLAN TO TAKE OVER OUR TURF!
EHHHH
I HEAR THEY'RE ALREADY ON A BIG RAMPAGE!!
HH?
B-B-BUT IF THEY DO THAT, THEN-!
WE'LL BE CHASED OFF.
YEEEK!
EVERY-ONE, JUST CALM DOWN ...
MURMUR MURMUR
HOW CAN WE?
FOR TOCHIGAMI LIKE US, THIS IS A MATTER OF LIFE AND DEATH!
IT'S ALREADY HARD ENOUGH TO GET PEOPLE TO FEEL ANY TERROR TOWARD US!
WAA
AH
WHAT'S GOING TO HAPPEN NOW?
JUST WHAT IS THE NURA CLAN FOR, IF NOT TO PREVENT THIS-?!
WHAT A PAIN.
I JUST TOLD THEM A LITTLE... AND IT TURNED INTO SUCH A HUGE FUSS ...
YAK
...

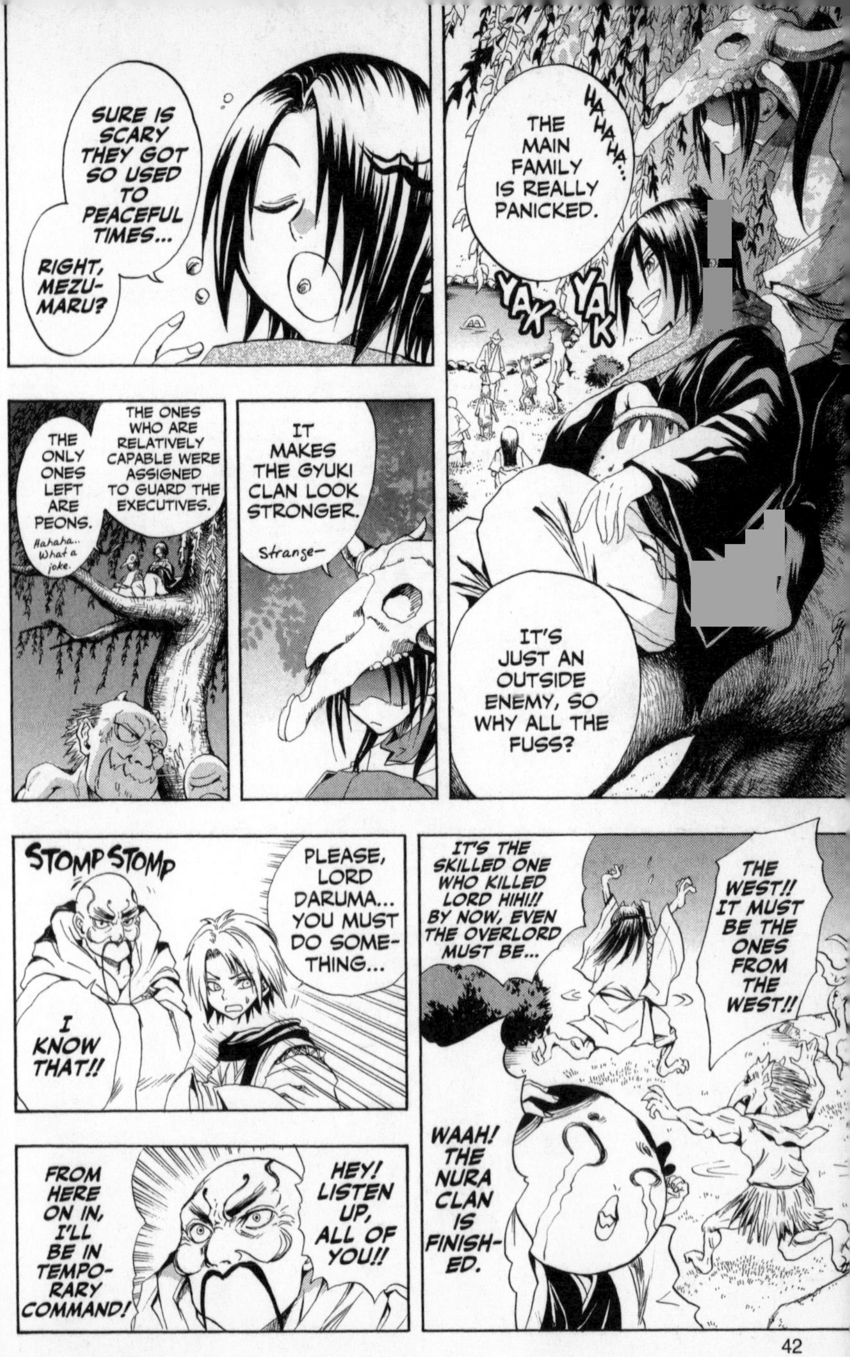
HAHAHA...
THE MAIN FAMILY IS REALLY PANICKED.
YAK YAK
IT'S JUST AN OUTSIDE ENEMY, SO WHY ALL THE FUSS?
SURE IS SCARY THEY GOT SO USED TO PEACEFUL TIMES...
RIGHT, MEZU-MARU?
IT MAKES THE GYUKI CLAN LOOK STRONGER.
Strange—
THE ONES WHO ARE RELATIVELY CAPABLE WERE ASSIGNED TO GUARD THE EXECUTIVES.
THE ONLY ONES LEFT ARE PEONS.
Hahaha.. What a joke.
THE WEST!! IT MUST BE THE ONES FROM THE WEST!!
IT'S THE SKILLED ONE WHO KILLED LORD HIHI!! BY NOW, EVEN THE OVERLORD MUST BE...
WAAH! THE NURA CLAN IS FINISH-ED.
PLEASE, LORD DARUMA... YOU MUST DO SOME-THING...
STOMP STOMP
I KNOW THAT!!
HEY! LISTEN UP, ALL OF YOU!!
FROM HERE ON IN, I'LL BE IN TEMPO-RARY COMMAND!

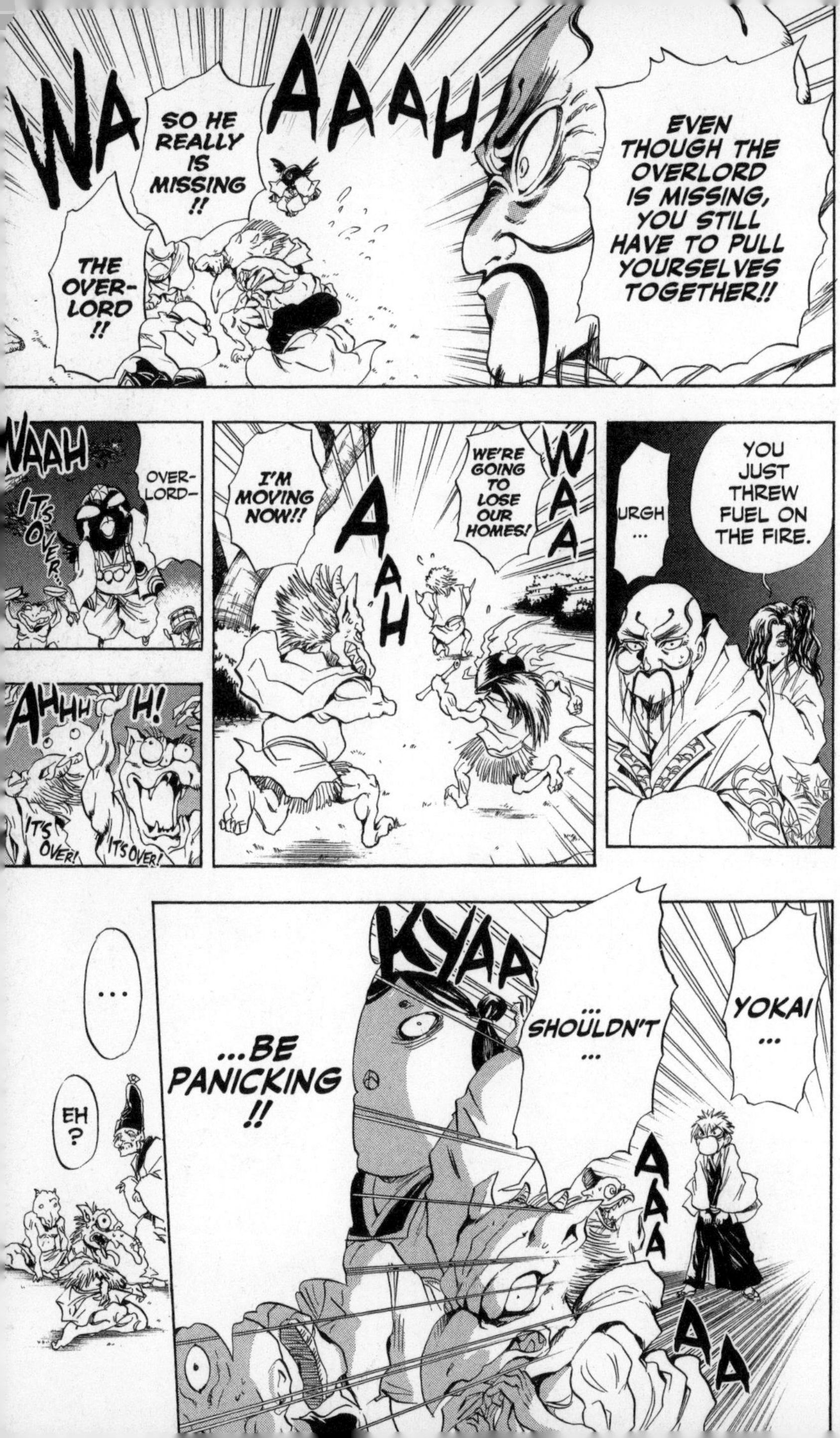
EVEN THOUGH THE OVERLORD IS MISSING, YOU STILL HAVE TO PULL YOURSELVES TOGETHER!!
WA AAAH
SO HE REALLY IS MISSING!!
THE OVER-LORD!!
YOU JUST THREW FUEL ON THE FIRE.
URGH ...
WAA
WE'RE GOING TO LOSE OUR HOMES!
AAH
I'M MOVING NOW!!
WAAH
OVER-LORD-
IT'S OVER...
AHHHH!
IT'S OVER!
IT'S OVER!
YOKAI ...
... SHOULDN'T ...
...BE PANICKING!!
KYAA
AAAAA
...
EH?

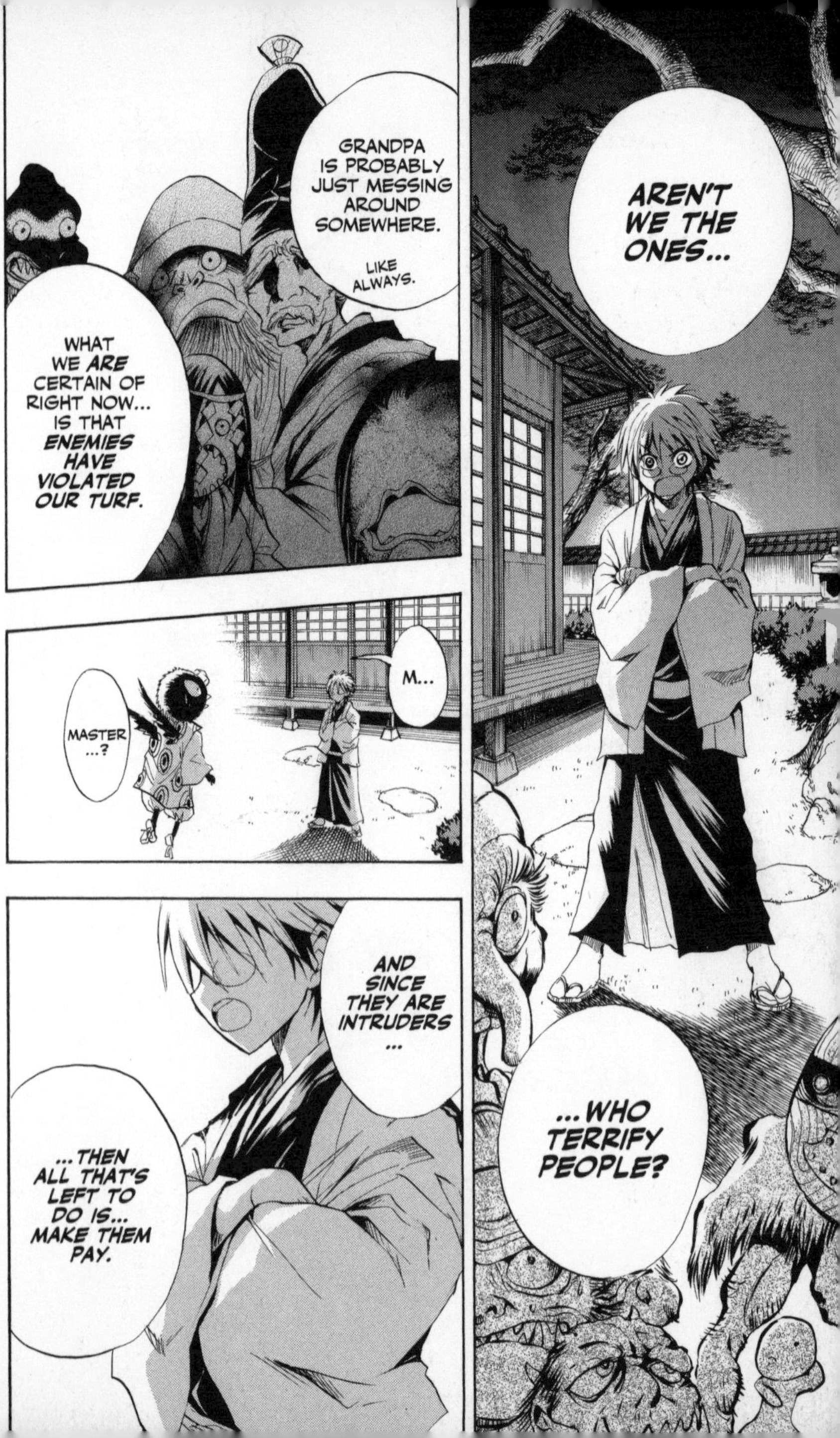
GRANDPA IS PROBABLY JUST MESSING AROUND SOMEWHERE.
LIKE ALWAYS.
WHAT WE *ARE* CERTAIN OF RIGHT NOW... IS THAT *ENEMIES HAVE VIOLATED OUR TURF.*
M...
MASTER ...?
AND SINCE THEY ARE INTRUDERS ...
...THEN ALL THAT'S LEFT TO DO IS... MAKE THEM PAY.
AREN'T WE THE ONES...
...WHO TERRIFY PEOPLE?

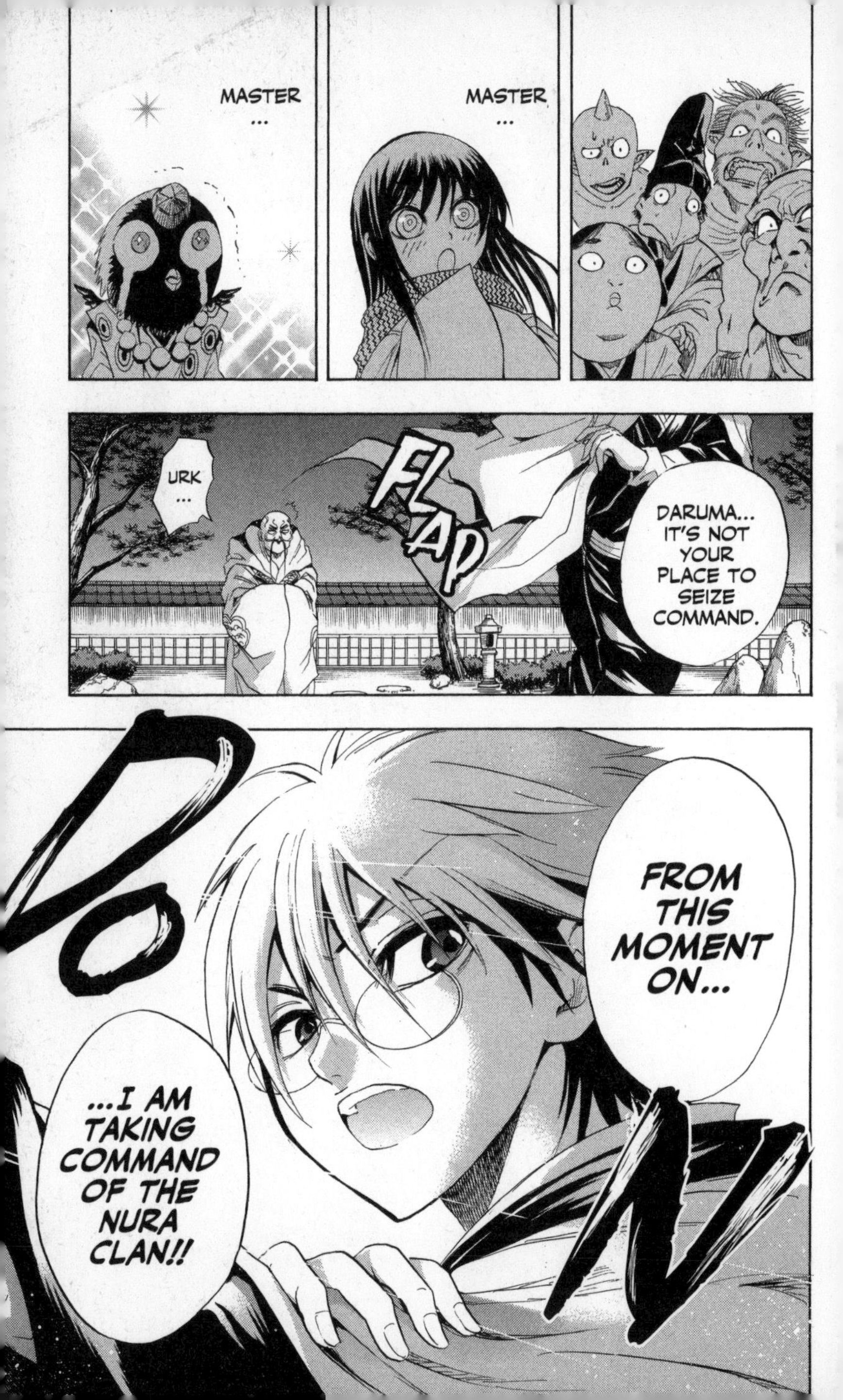
MASTER ...
MASTER ...
DARUMA... IT'S NOT YOUR PLACE TO SEIZE COMMAND.
FLAP
URK ...
FROM THIS MOMENT ON...
...I AM TAKING COMMAND OF THE NURA CLAN!!

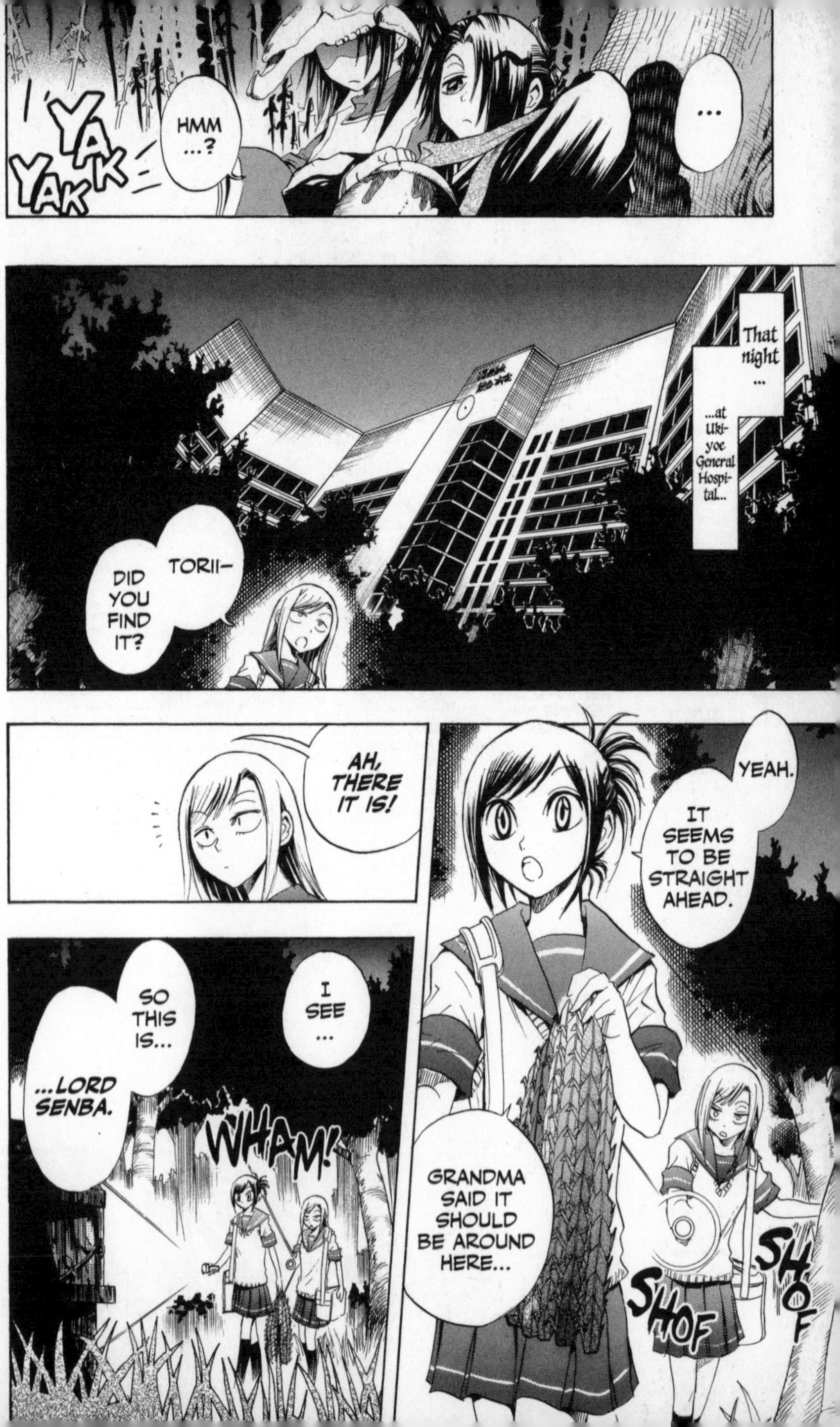
...
HMM ...?
YAK YAK
That night ...
...at Uki-yoe General Hospi-tal...
TORII—
DID YOU FIND IT?
YEAH.
IT SEEMS TO BE STRAIGHT AHEAD.
GRANDMA SAID IT SHOULD BE AROUND HERE...
SHOF SHOF
AH, THERE IT IS!
I SEE ...
SO THIS IS...
...LORD SENBA.
WHAM!

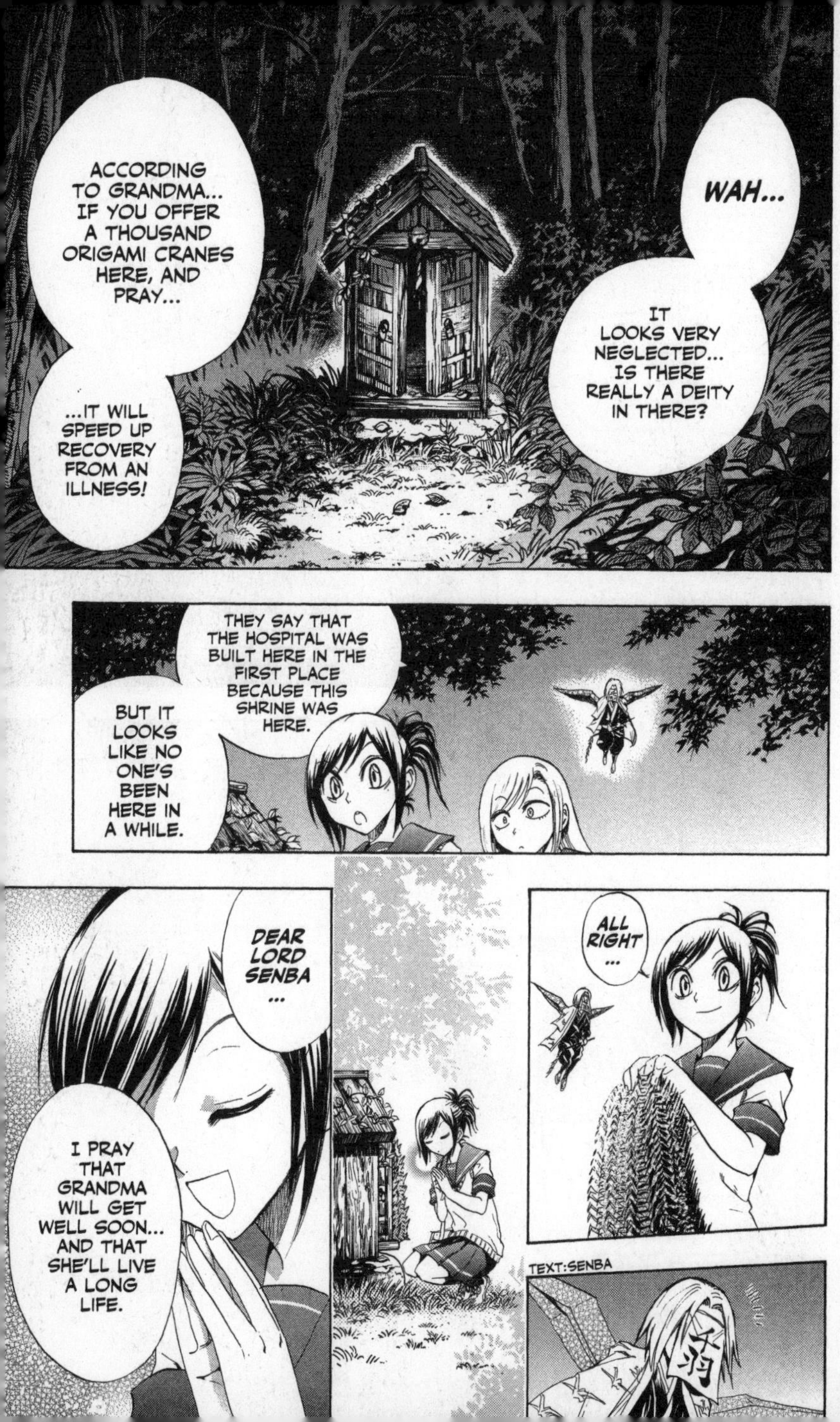
WAH...
IT LOOKS VERY NEGLECTED... IS THERE REALLY A DEITY IN THERE?
ACCORDING TO GRANDMA... IF YOU OFFER A THOUSAND ORIGAMI CRANES HERE, AND PRAY...
...IT WILL SPEED UP RECOVERY FROM AN ILLNESS!
THEY SAY THAT THE HOSPITAL WAS BUILT HERE IN THE FIRST PLACE BECAUSE THIS SHRINE WAS HERE.
BUT IT LOOKS LIKE NO ONE'S BEEN HERE IN A WHILE.
ALL RIGHT ...
千羽
TEXT:SENBA
DEAR LORD SENBA ...
I PRAY THAT GRANDMA WILL GET WELL SOON... AND THAT SHE'LL LIVE A LONG LIFE.

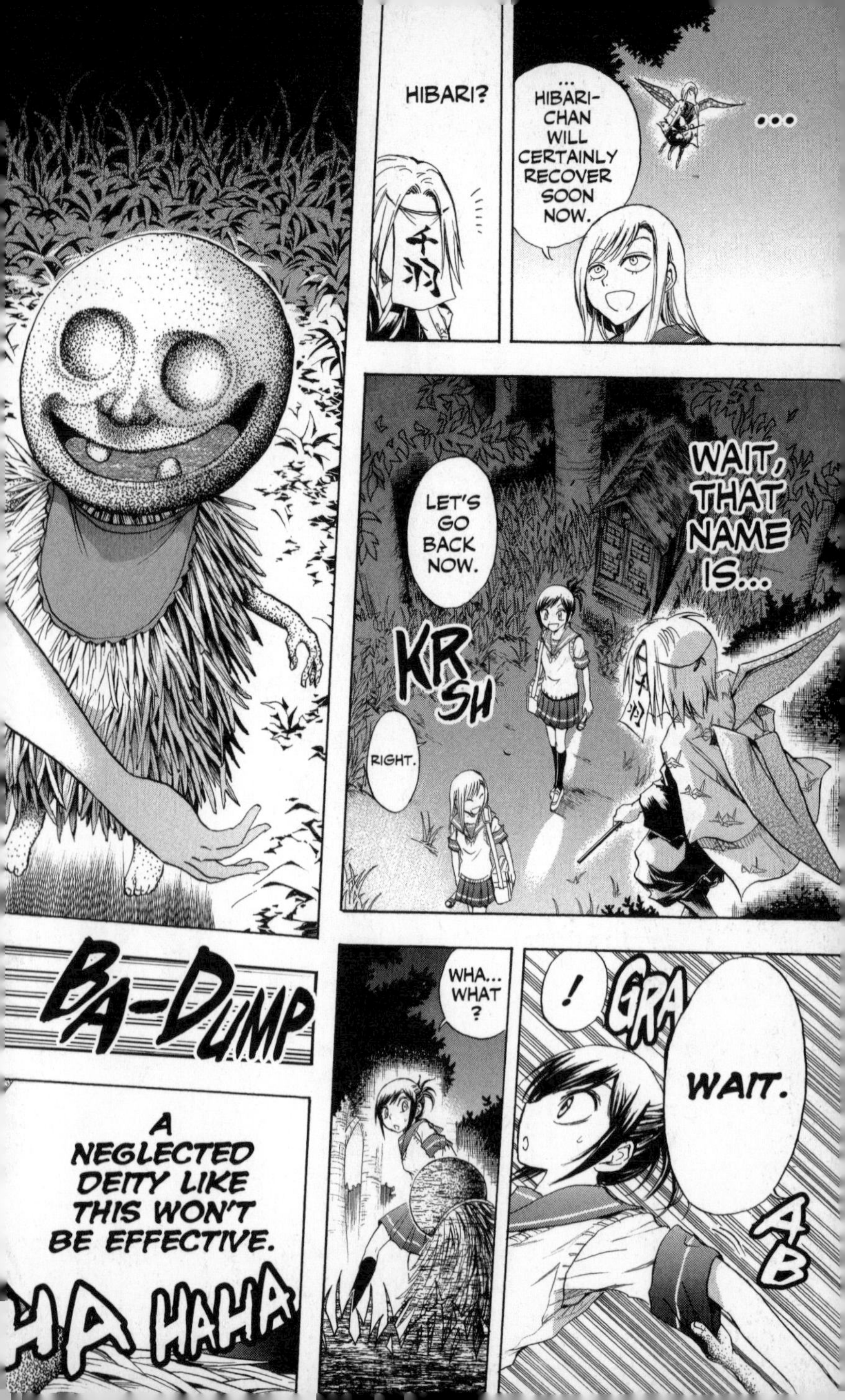
...
... HIBARI-CHAN WILL CERTAINLY RECOVER SOON NOW.
HIBARI?
WAIT, THAT NAME IS...
LET'S GO BACK NOW.
KRSH
RIGHT.
!
GRAB
WAIT.
WHA... WHAT?
BA-DUMP
A NEGLECTED DEITY LIKE THIS WON'T BE EFFECTIVE.
HA HAHA

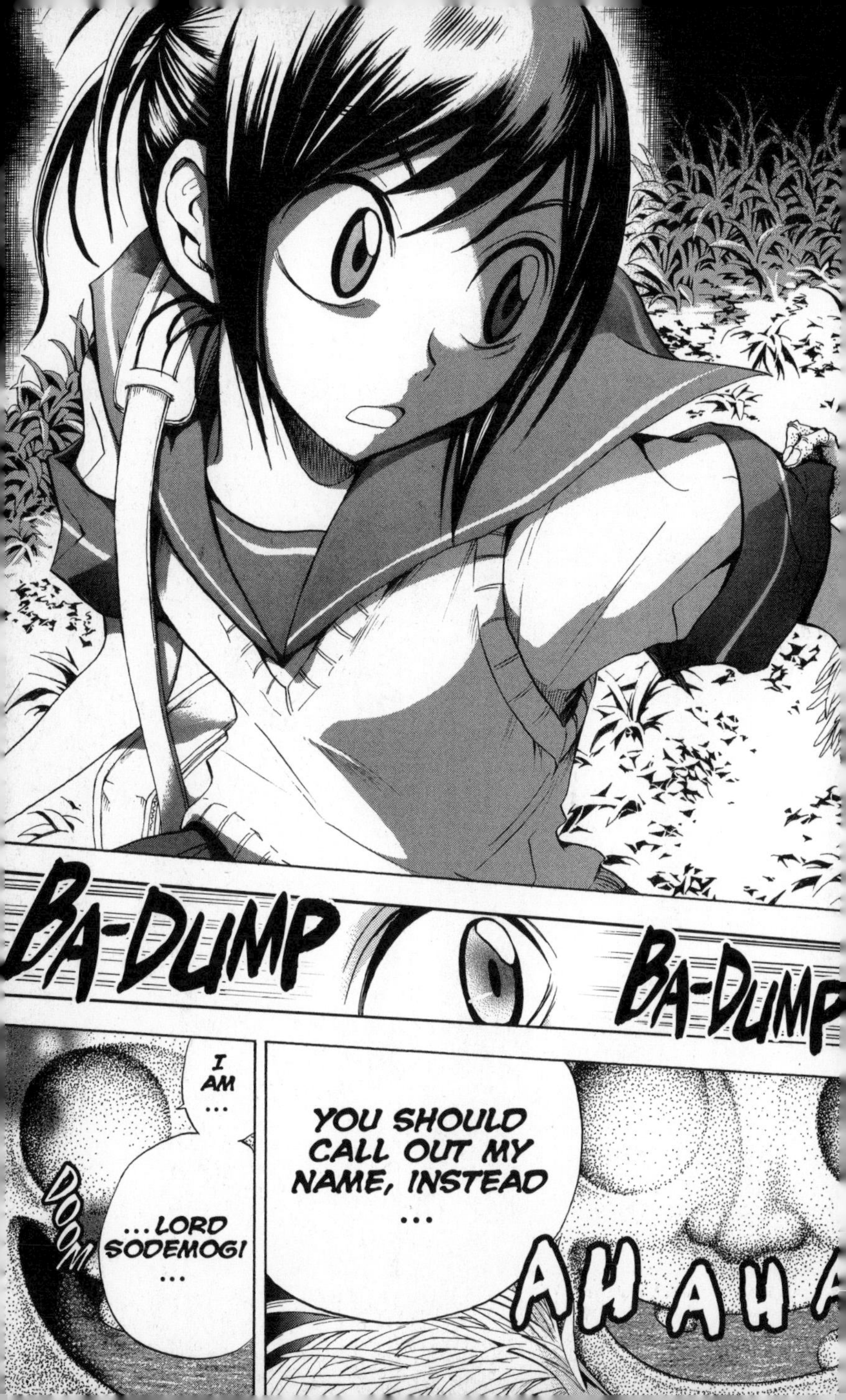
BA-DUMP
BA-DUMP
YOU SHOULD CALL OUT MY NAME, INSTEAD ...
AH AH A
I AM ...
... LORD SODEMOGI ...
DOOM

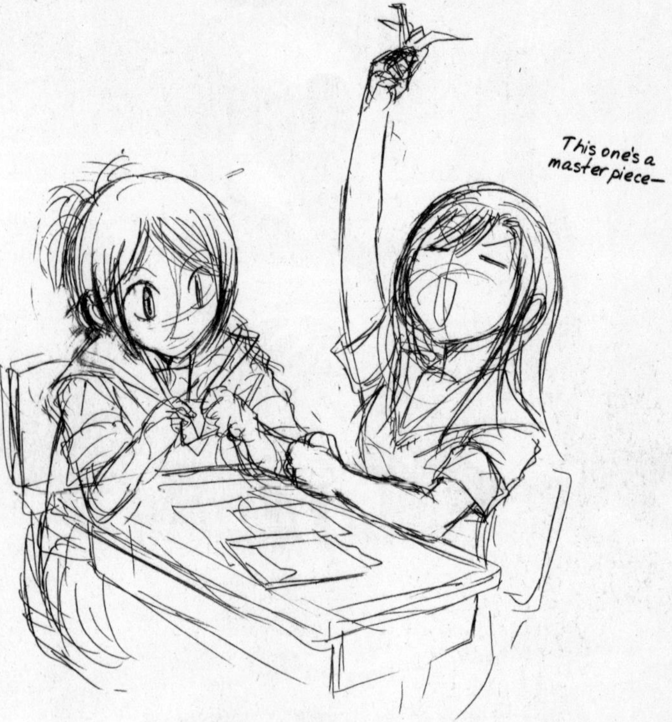
This one's a masterpiece—

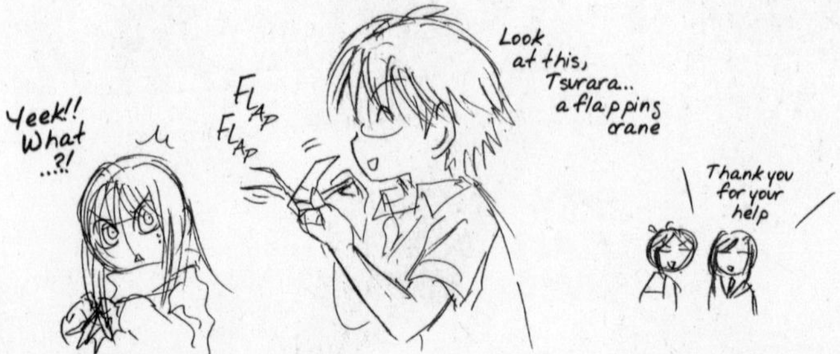
Thank you for your help
Look at this, Tsurara.. a flapping crane
FLAP FLAP
Yeek!! What ...?!

Act 27: Lord Sodemogi

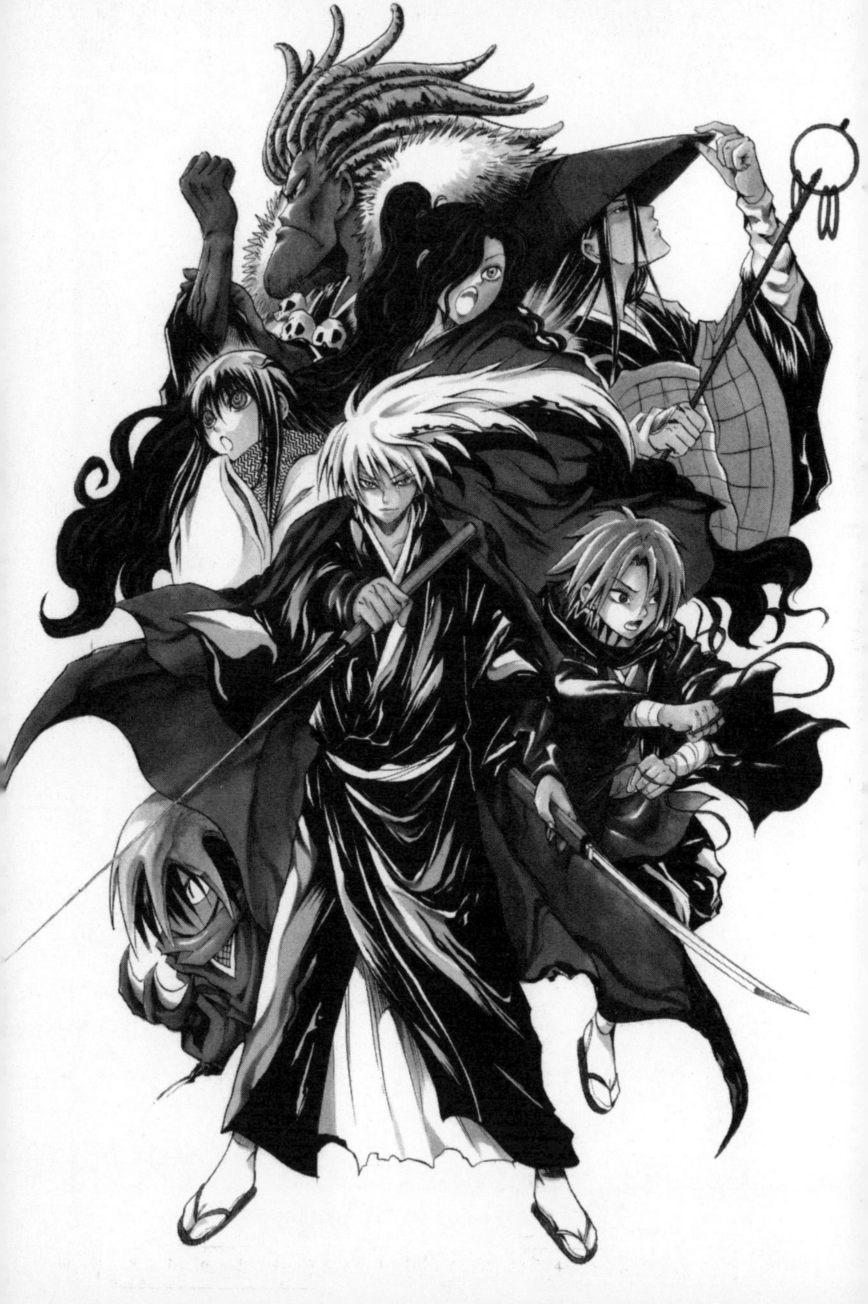

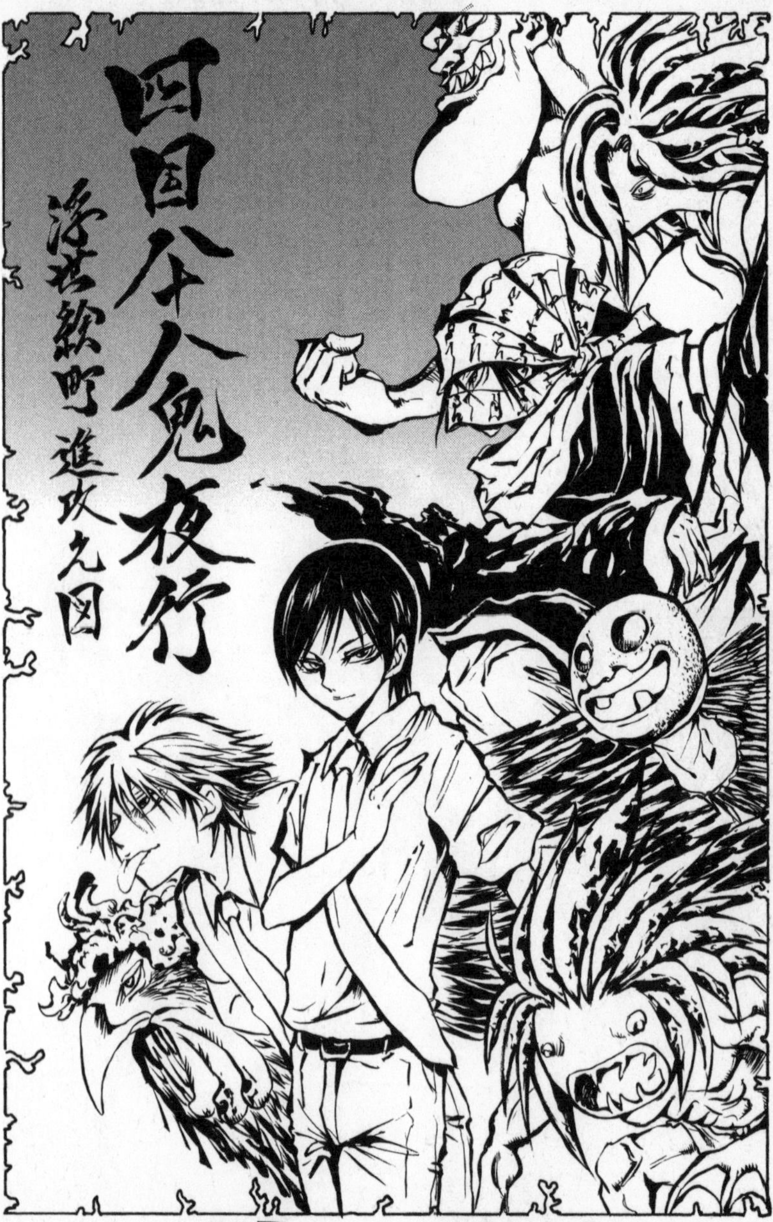
四国八十八鬼夜行
浮世絵町進攻之図

88 Demons of Shikoku
Depiction of the Ukiyoe Town Invasion

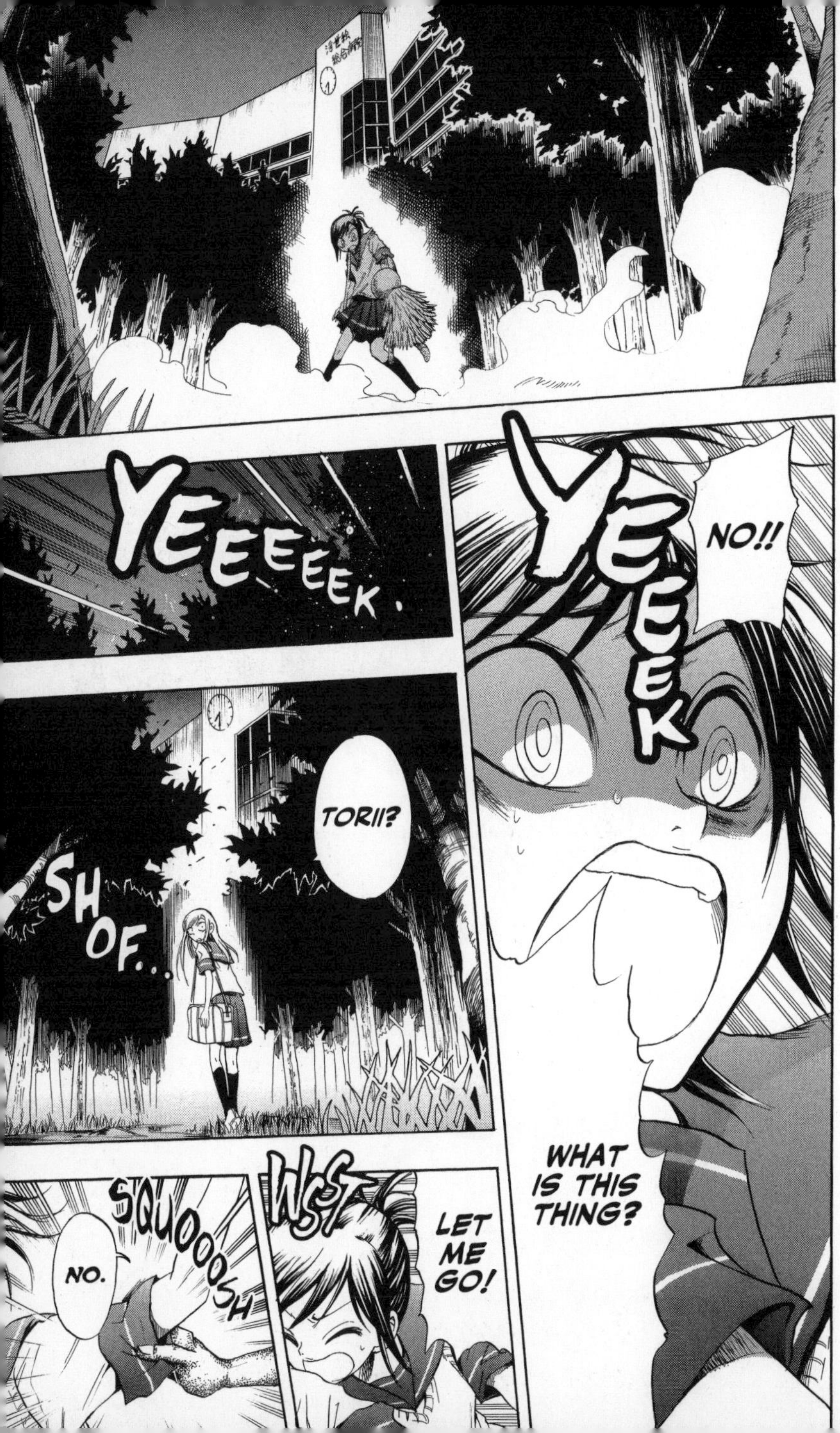
YEEEEK
NO!!
WHAT IS THIS THING?
YEEEEEEK.
TORII?
SHOF...
WST
LET ME GO!
SQUOOOOSH
NO.

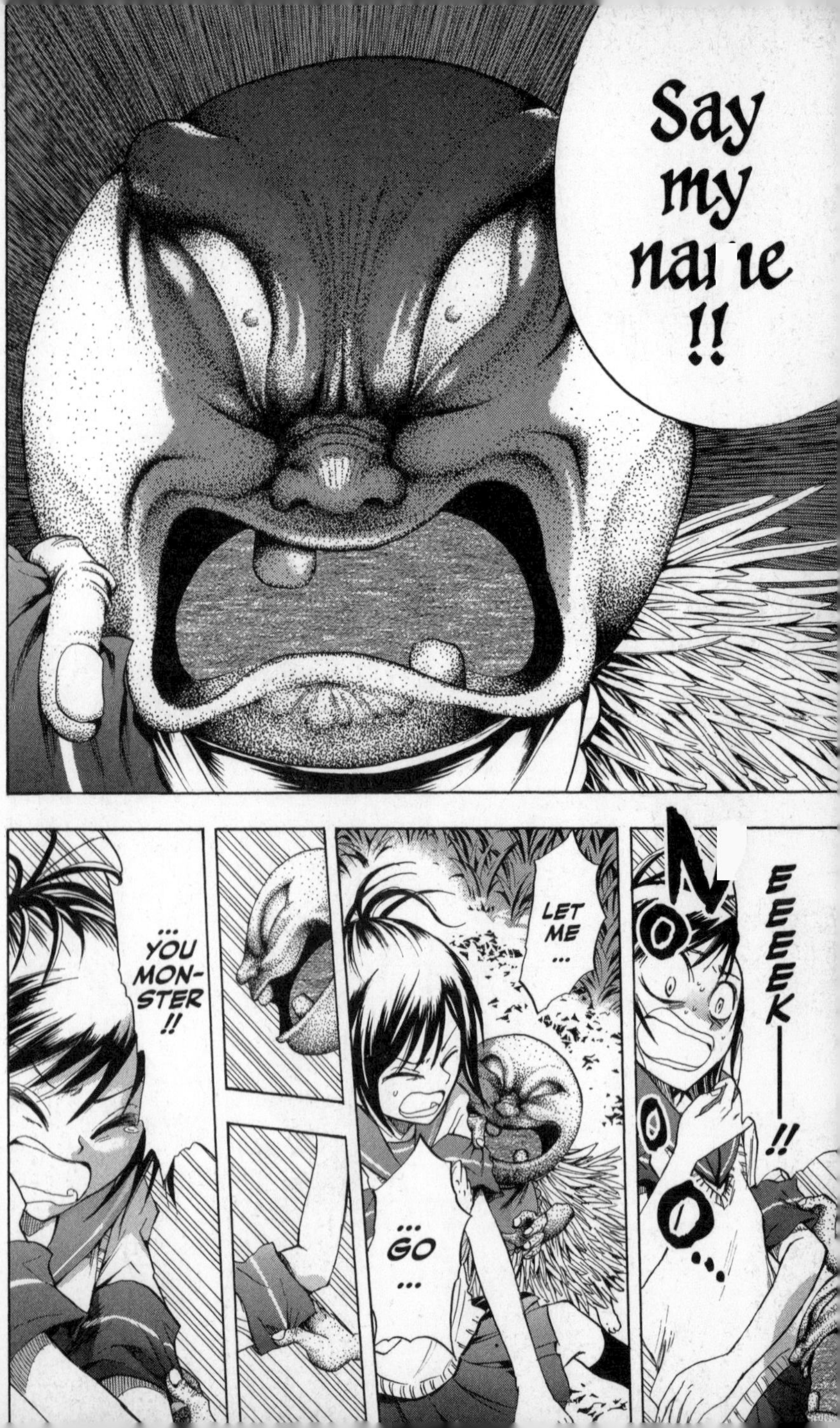
Say my name !!
NOOOO...
EEEEK——!!
LET ME ...
...GO ...
...YOU MON-STER !!

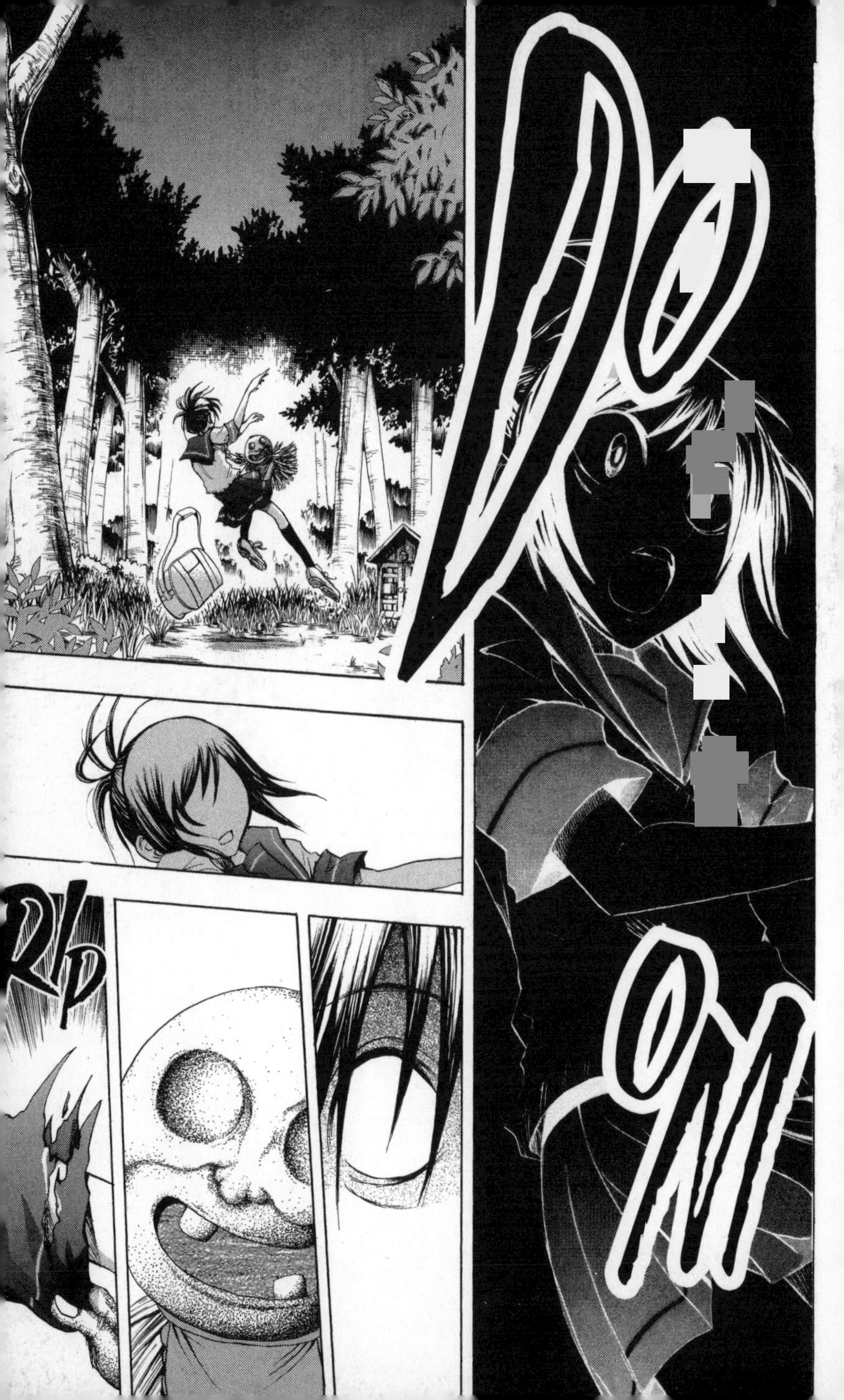
RIP

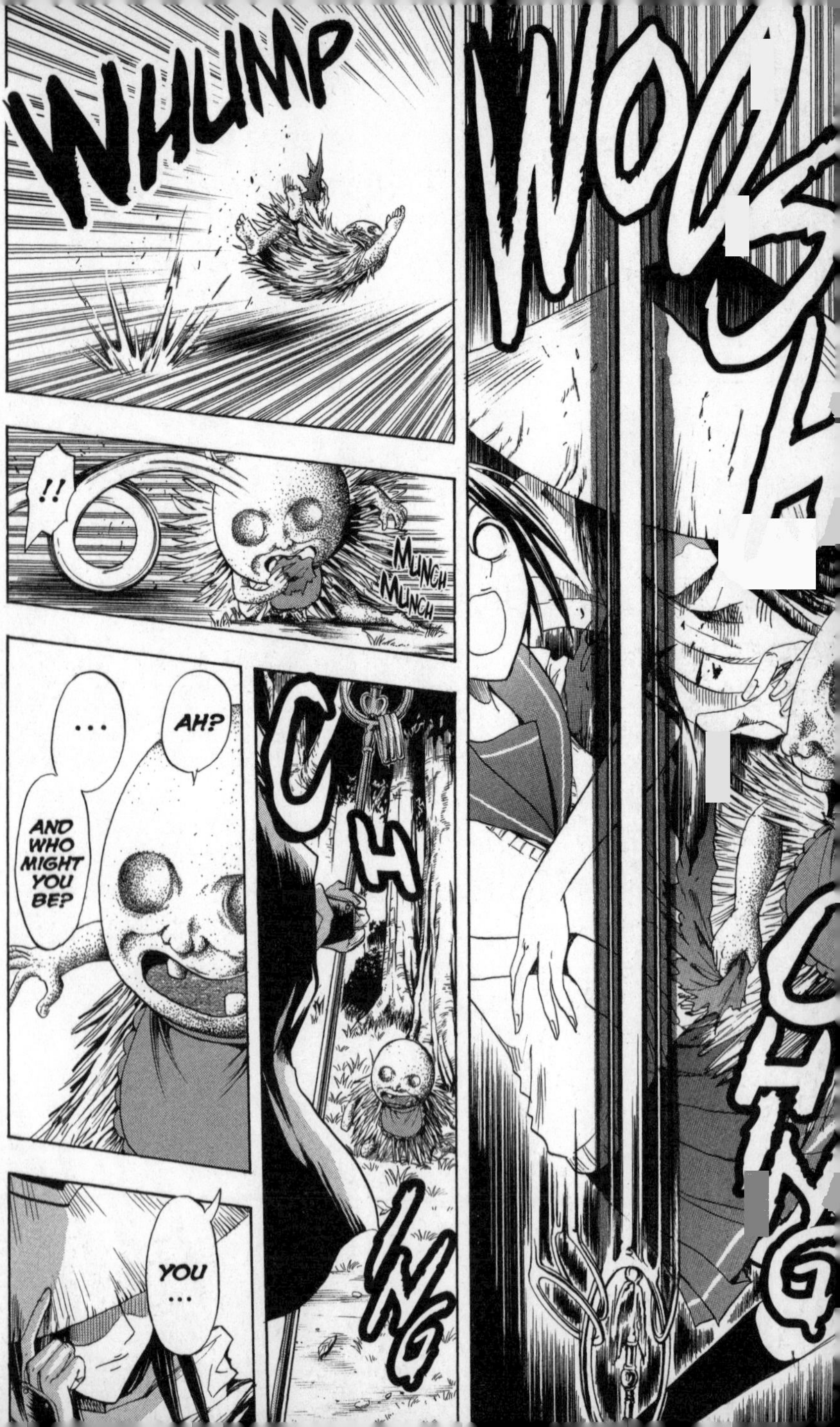
WHUMP
!!
MUNCH MUNCH
CHING
AH?
...
AND WHO MIGHT YOU BE?
YOU ...

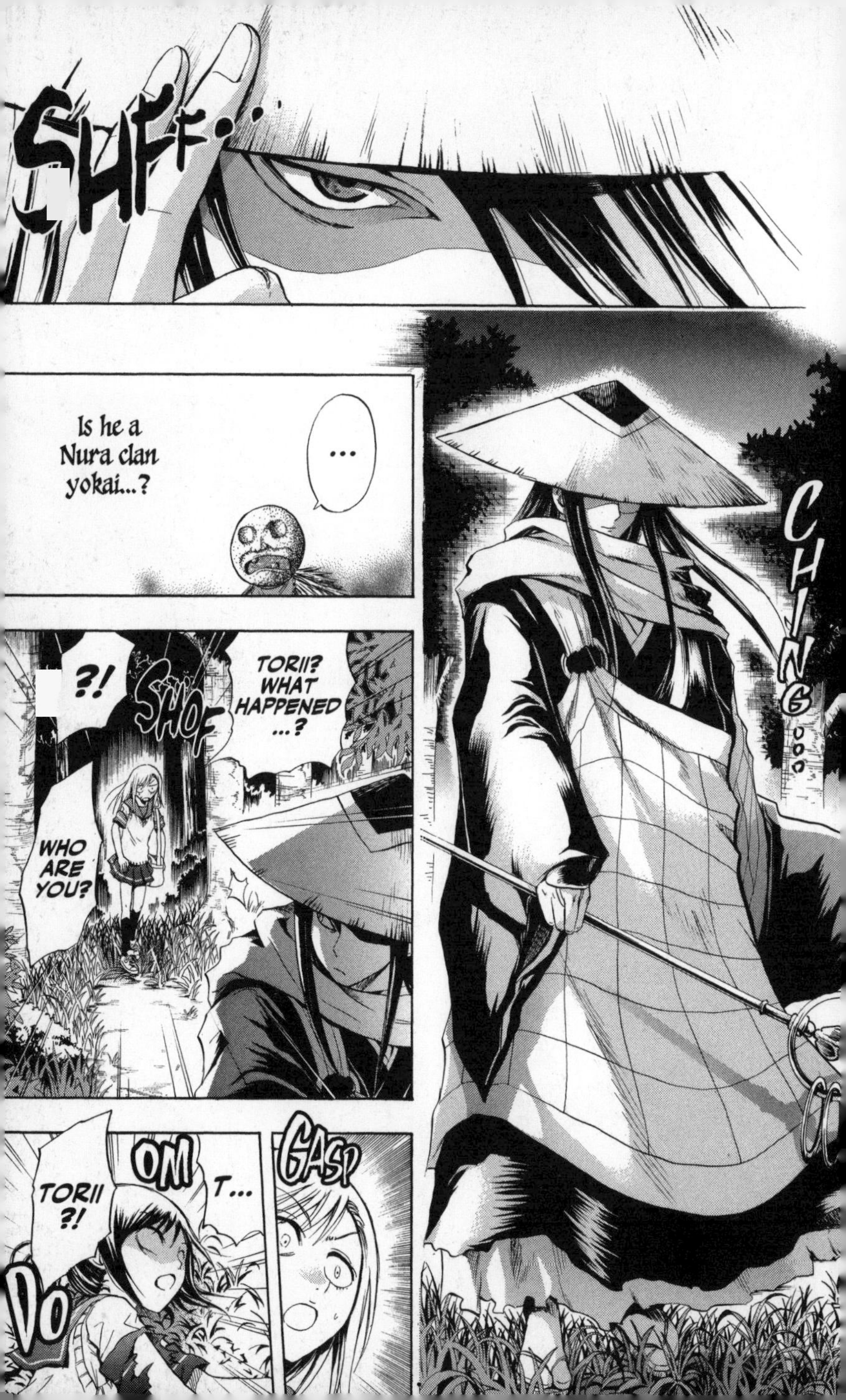
SHFF...
CHING...
...
Is he a Nura clan yokai...?
TORII? WHAT HAPPENED...?
SHOF
?!
WHO ARE YOU?
GASP
T...
OM
TORII?!
DO

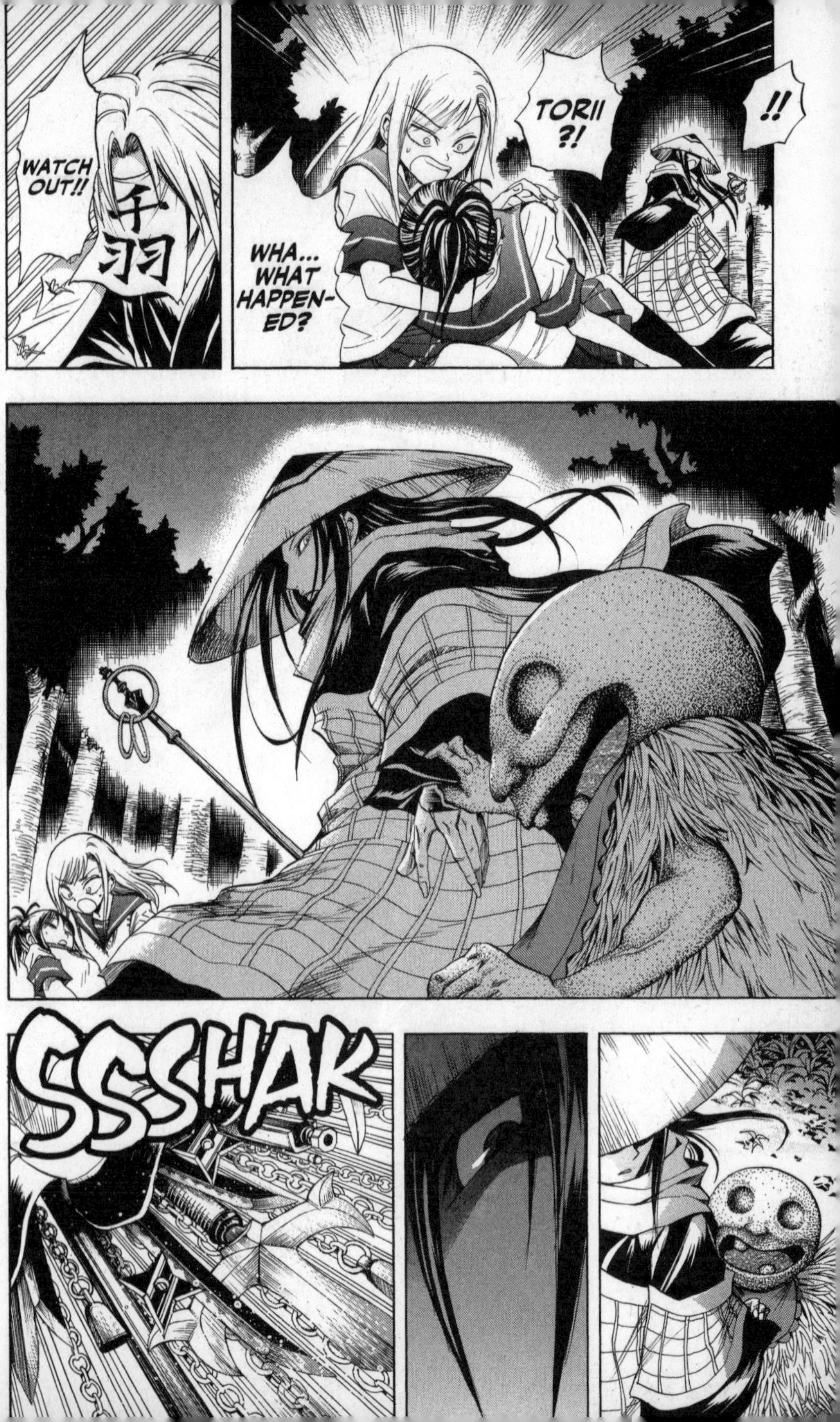
!!
TORII ?!
WHA... WHAT HAPPEN-ED?
WATCH OUT!!
千羽
SSSHAK

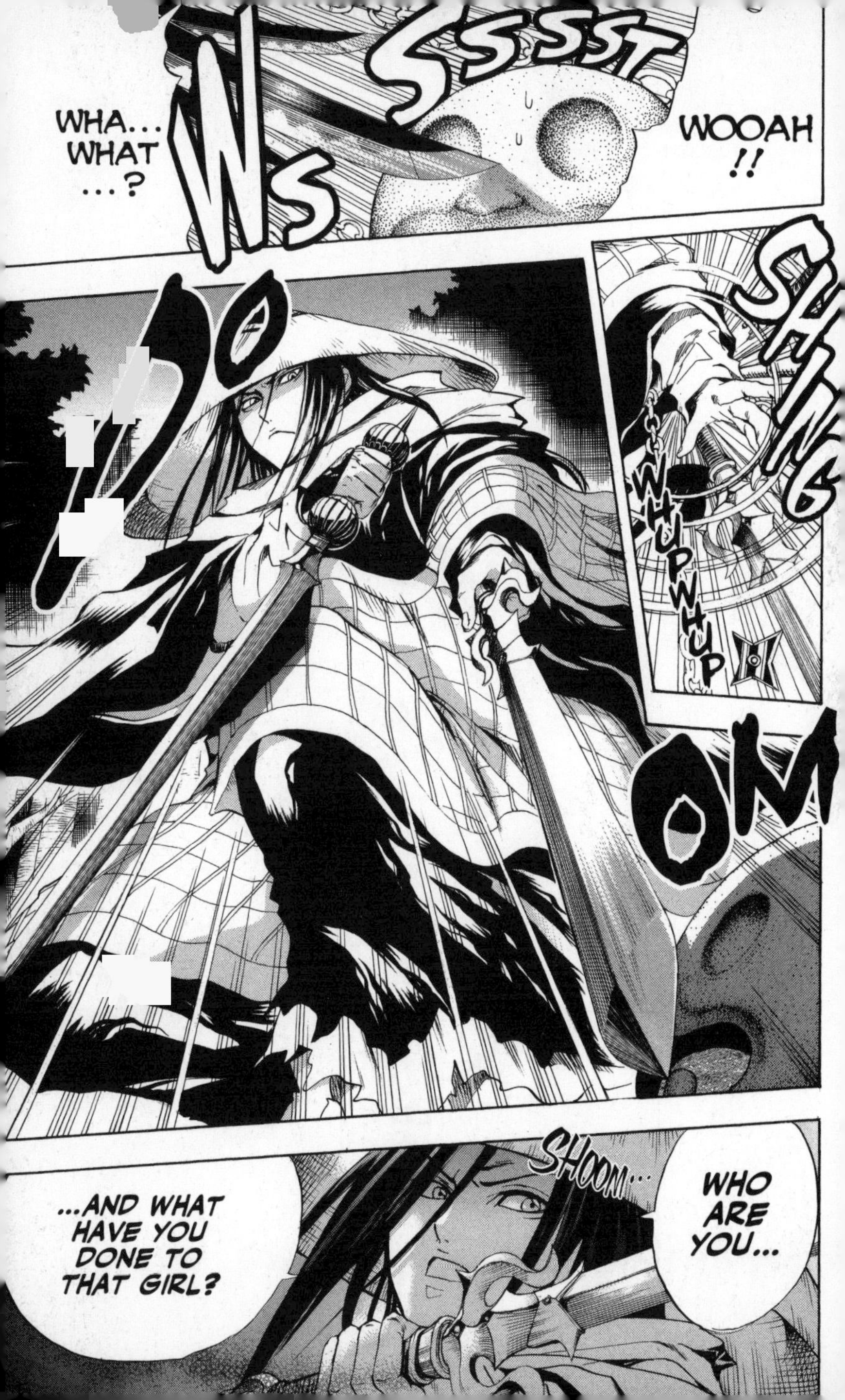
WOOAH !!
SSSST
WS
WHA... WHAT ...?
SHING
WHUP WHUP
OM
WHO ARE YOU...
SHOOM...
...AND WHAT HAVE YOU DONE TO THAT GIRL?

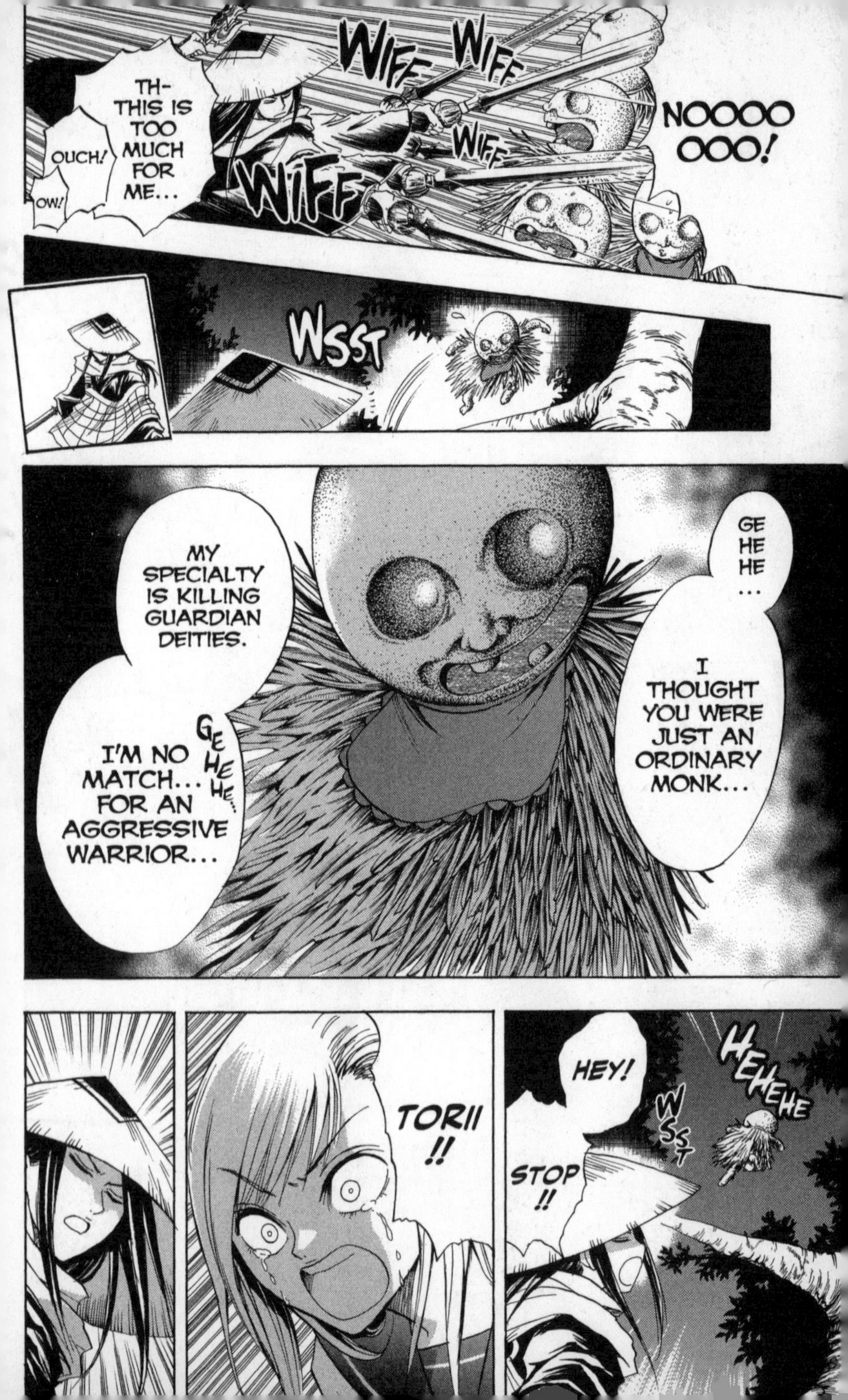
NOOOO OOO!
WIFF WIFF
WIFF
WIFF
TH- THIS IS TOO MUCH FOR ME...
OUCH!
OW!
WSST
GE HE HE ...
I THOUGHT YOU WERE JUST AN ORDINARY MONK...
MY SPECIALTY IS KILLING GUARDIAN DEITIES.
GEHEHE...
I'M NO MATCH... FOR AN AGGRESSIVE WARRIOR...
HEHEHE
WSST
HEY!
STOP !!
TORII !!

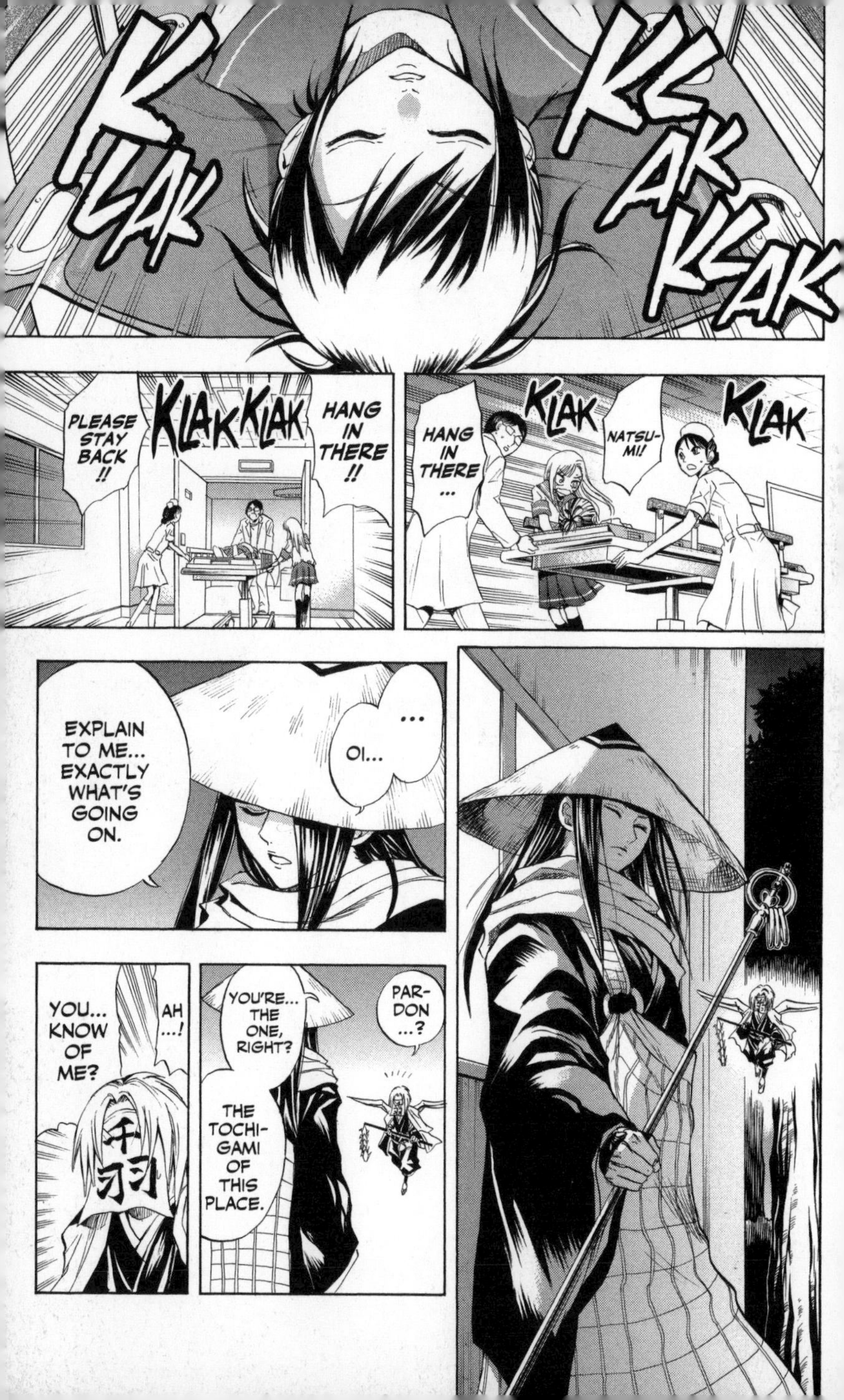
KLAK KLAK
KLAK
KLAK
NATSU-MI!
KLAK
HANG IN THERE ...
HANG IN THERE !!
KLAK KLAK
PLEASE STAY BACK !!
... OI...
EXPLAIN TO ME... EXACTLY WHAT'S GOING ON.
PAR-DON ...?
YOU'RE... THE ONE, RIGHT?
THE TOCHIGAMI OF THIS PLACE.
AH ...!
YOU... KNOW OF ME?
千羽

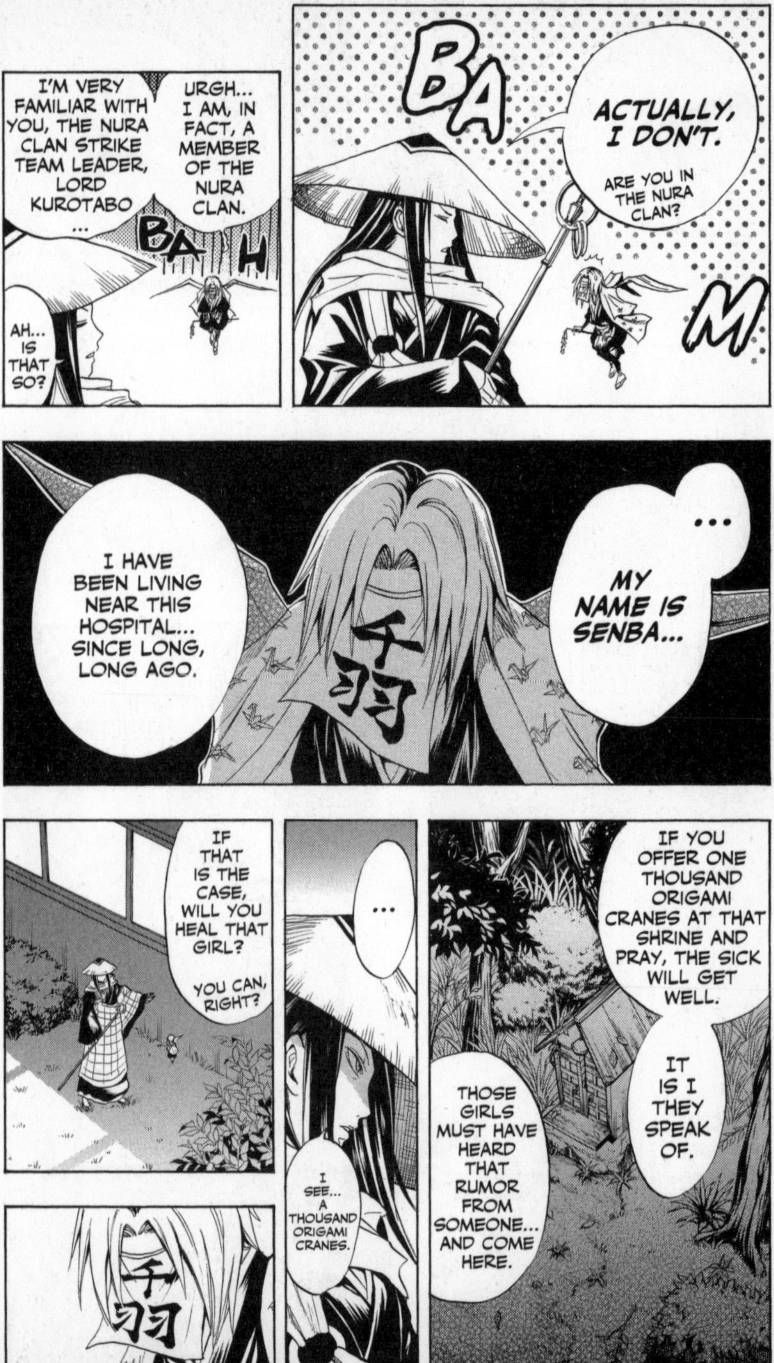
BA
M
ACTUALLY, I DON'T.
ARE YOU IN THE NURA CLAN?
URGH... I AM, IN FACT, A MEMBER OF THE NURA CLAN.
BAH
I'M VERY FAMILIAR WITH YOU, THE NURA CLAN STRIKE TEAM LEADER, LORD KUROTABO ...
AH... IS THAT SO?
...
MY NAME IS SENBA...
I HAVE BEEN LIVING NEAR THIS HOSPITAL... SINCE LONG, LONG AGO.
千羽
IF YOU OFFER ONE THOUSAND ORIGAMI CRANES AT THAT SHRINE AND PRAY, THE SICK WILL GET WELL.
IT IS I THEY SPEAK OF.
THOSE GIRLS MUST HAVE HEARD THAT RUMOR FROM SOMEONE... AND COME HERE.
...
I SEE... A THOUSAND ORIGAMI CRANES.
IF THAT IS THE CASE, WILL YOU HEAL THAT GIRL?
YOU CAN, RIGHT?
千羽

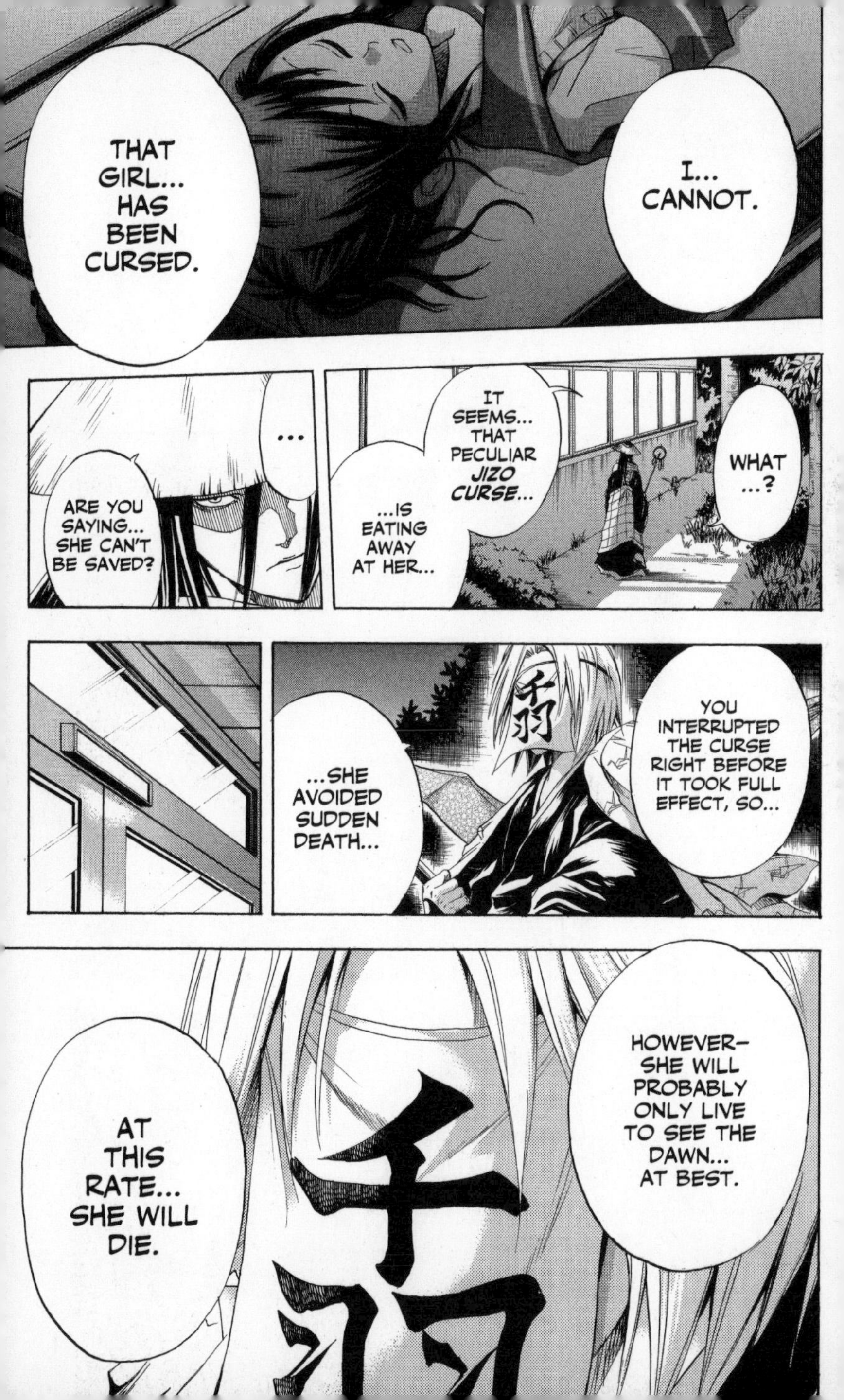
I... CANNOT.
THAT GIRL... HAS BEEN CURSED.
WHAT ...?
IT SEEMS... THAT PECULIAR *JIZO CURSE*...
...IS EATING AWAY AT HER...
...
ARE YOU SAYING... SHE CAN'T BE SAVED?
YOU INTERRUPTED THE CURSE RIGHT BEFORE IT TOOK FULL EFFECT, SO...
...SHE AVOIDED SUDDEN DEATH...
HOWEVER- SHE WILL PROBABLY ONLY LIVE TO SEE THE DAWN... AT BEST.
AT THIS RATE... SHE WILL DIE.

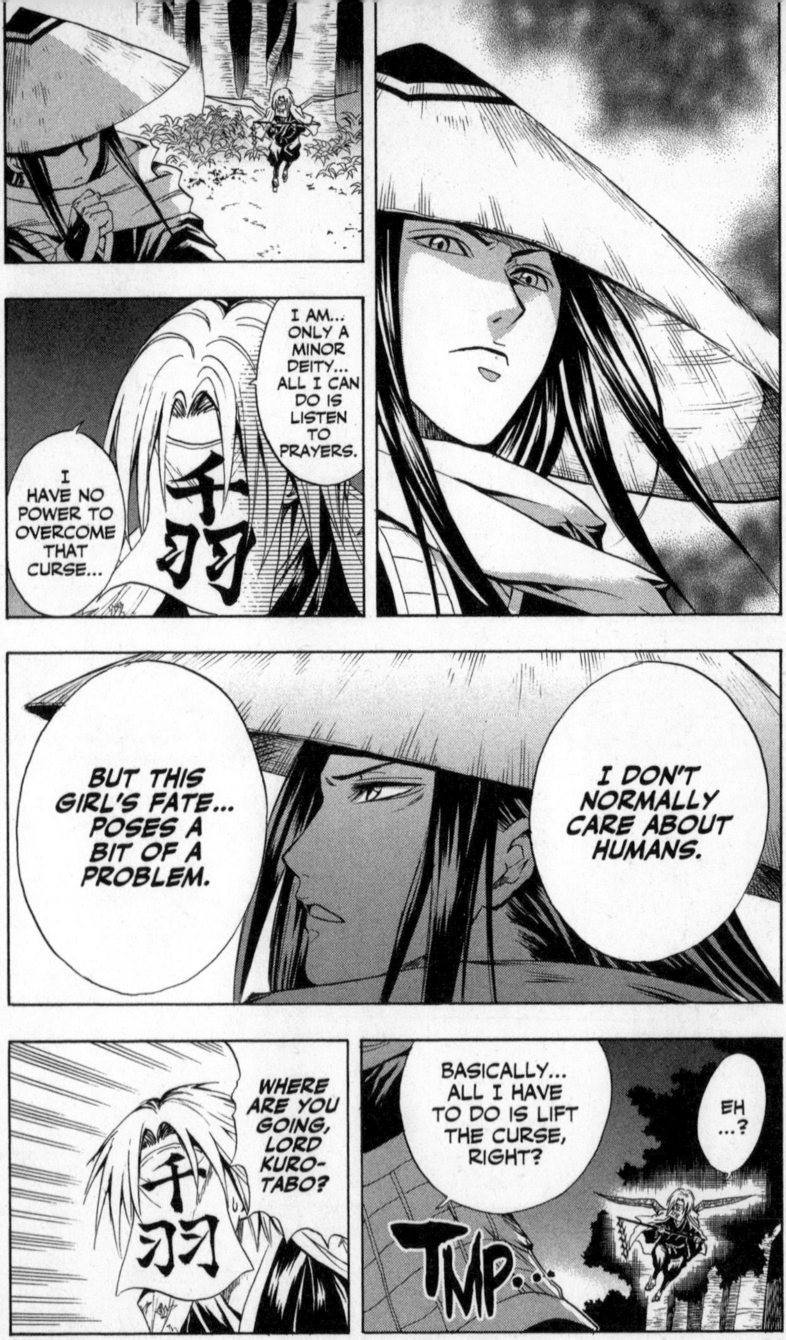
I AM... ONLY A MINOR DEITY... ALL I CAN DO IS LISTEN TO PRAYERS.
I HAVE NO POWER TO OVERCOME THAT CURSE...
I DON'T NORMALLY CARE ABOUT HUMANS.
BUT THIS GIRL'S FATE... POSES A BIT OF A PROBLEM.
BASICALLY... ALL I HAVE TO DO IS LIFT THE CURSE, RIGHT?
EH ...?
TMP...
WHERE ARE YOU GOING, LORD KURO-TABO?

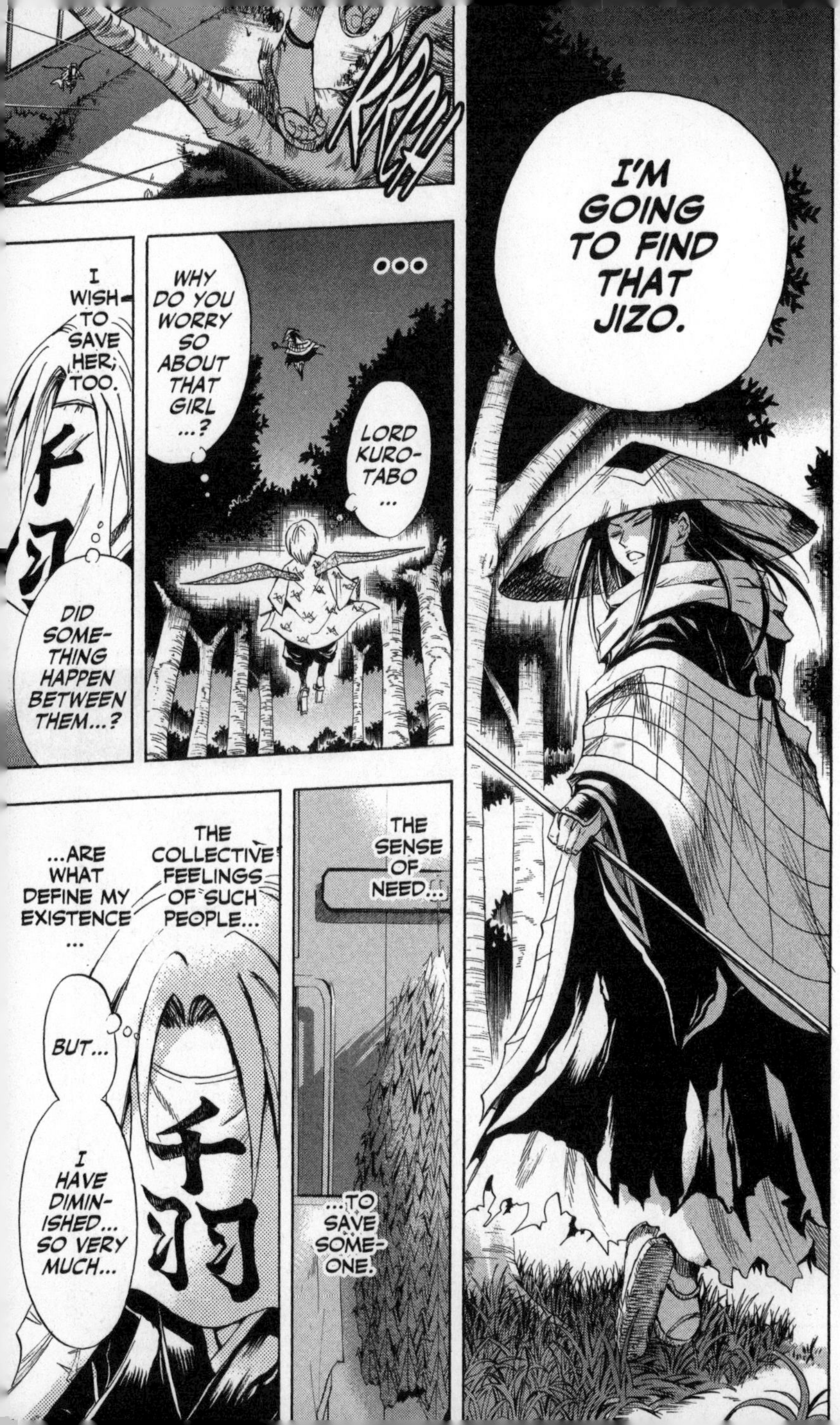
KRACK
...
LORD KURO-TABO...
WHY DO YOU WORRY SO ABOUT THAT GIRL...?
I WISH TO SAVE HER, TOO.
DID SOMETHING HAPPEN BETWEEN THEM...?
THE SENSE OF NEED...
...TO SAVE SOMEONE.
THE COLLECTIVE FEELINGS OF SUCH PEOPLE...
...ARE WHAT DEFINE MY EXISTENCE...
BUT...
I HAVE DIMINISHED... SO VERY MUCH...
I'M GOING TO FIND THAT JIZO.

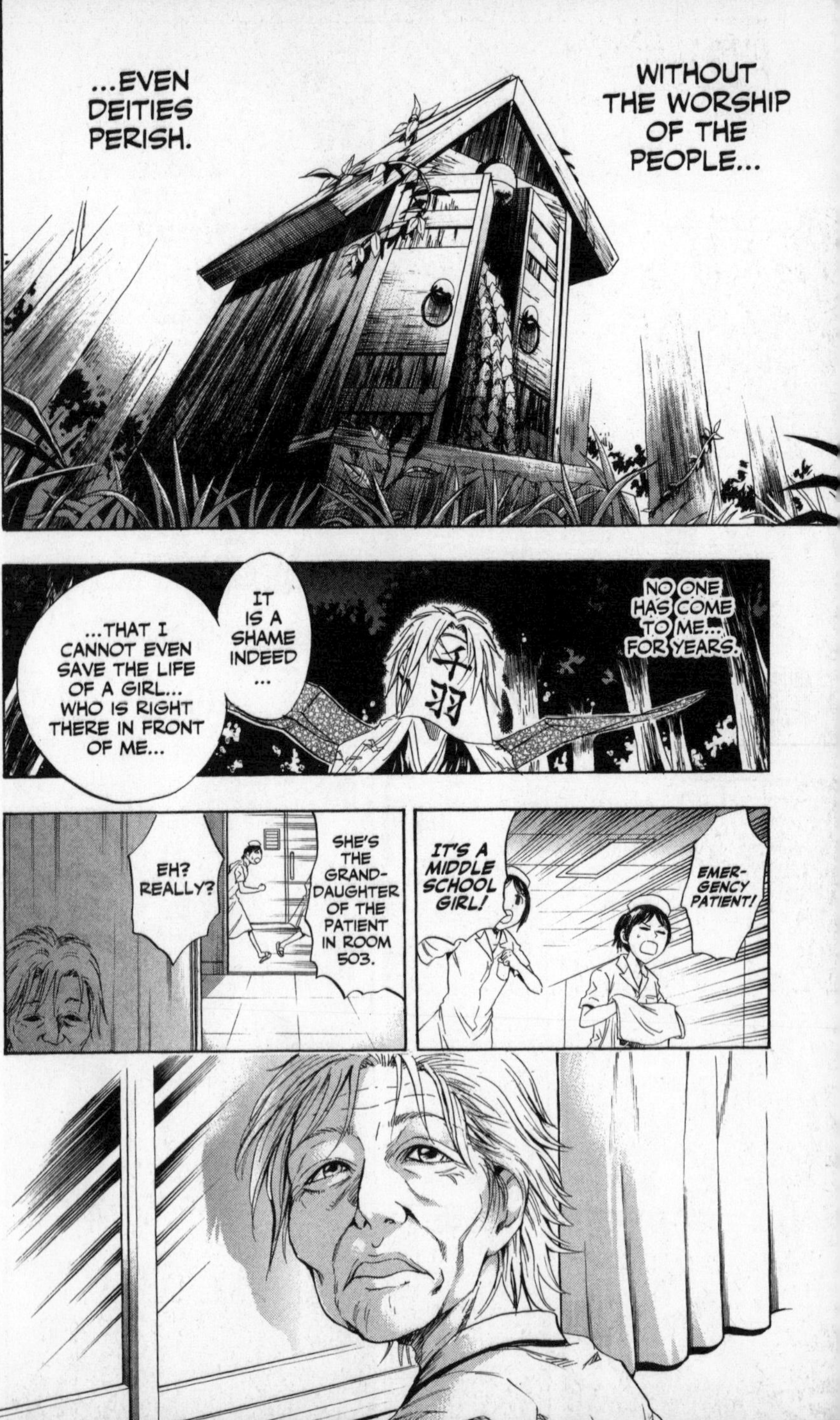
WITHOUT THE WORSHIP OF THE PEOPLE...
...EVEN DEITIES PERISH.
NO ONE HAS COME TO ME... FOR YEARS.
千羽
IT IS A SHAME INDEED...
...THAT I CANNOT EVEN SAVE THE LIFE OF A GIRL... WHO IS RIGHT THERE IN FRONT OF ME...
EMER-GENCY PATIENT!
IT'S A MIDDLE SCHOOL GIRL!
SHE'S THE GRAND-DAUGHTER OF THE PATIENT IN ROOM 503.
EH? REALLY?

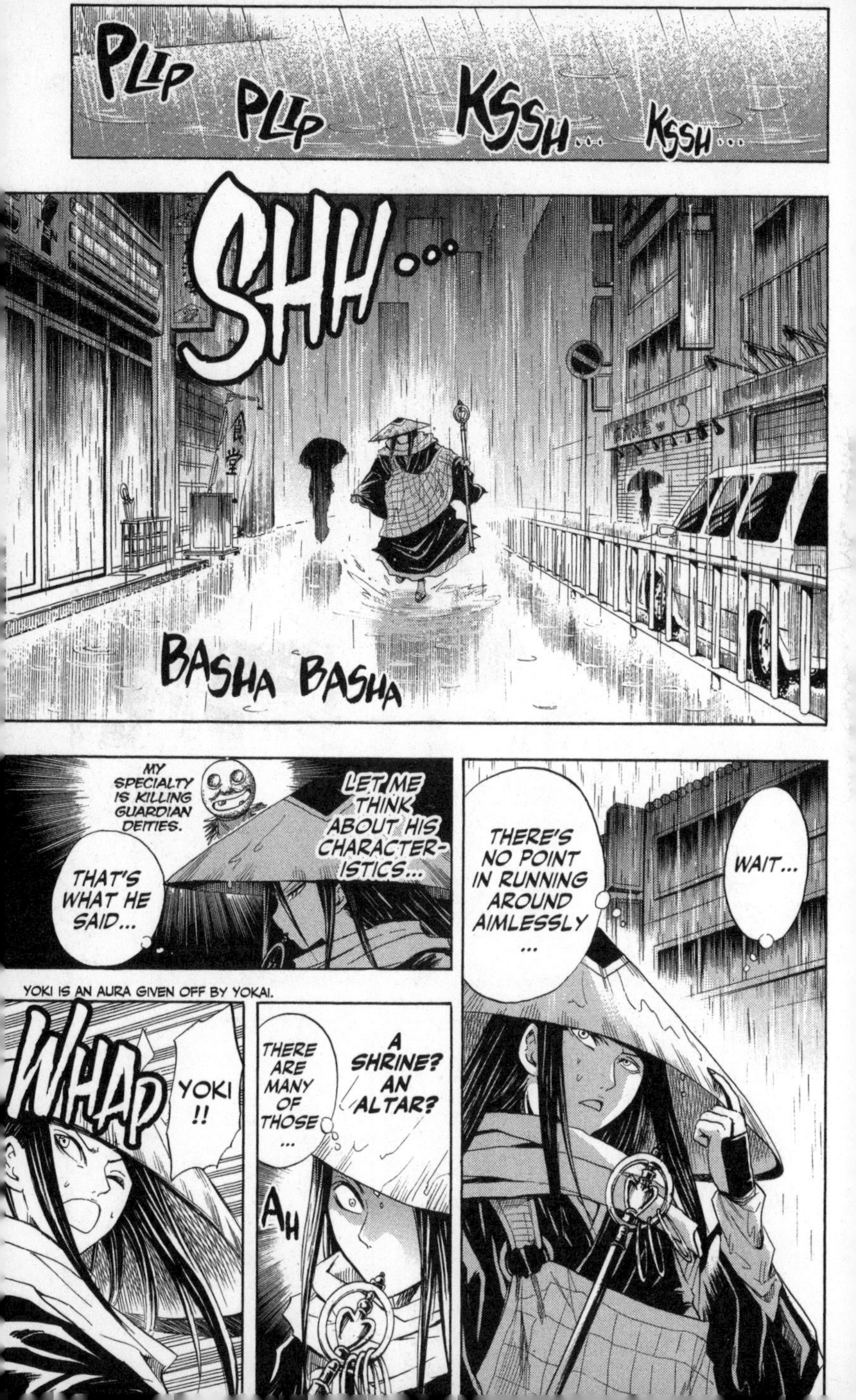
PLIP
PLIP
KSSH...
KSSH...
SHH...
BASHA BASHA
WAIT...
THERE'S NO POINT IN RUNNING AROUND AIMLESSLY...
LET ME THINK ABOUT HIS CHARACTERISTICS...
MY SPECIALTY IS KILLING GUARDIAN DEITIES.
THAT'S WHAT HE SAID...
A SHRINE? AN ALTAR?
THERE ARE MANY OF THOSE...
AH
WHAP
YOKI!!

YOKI IS AN AURA GIVEN OFF BY YOKAI.

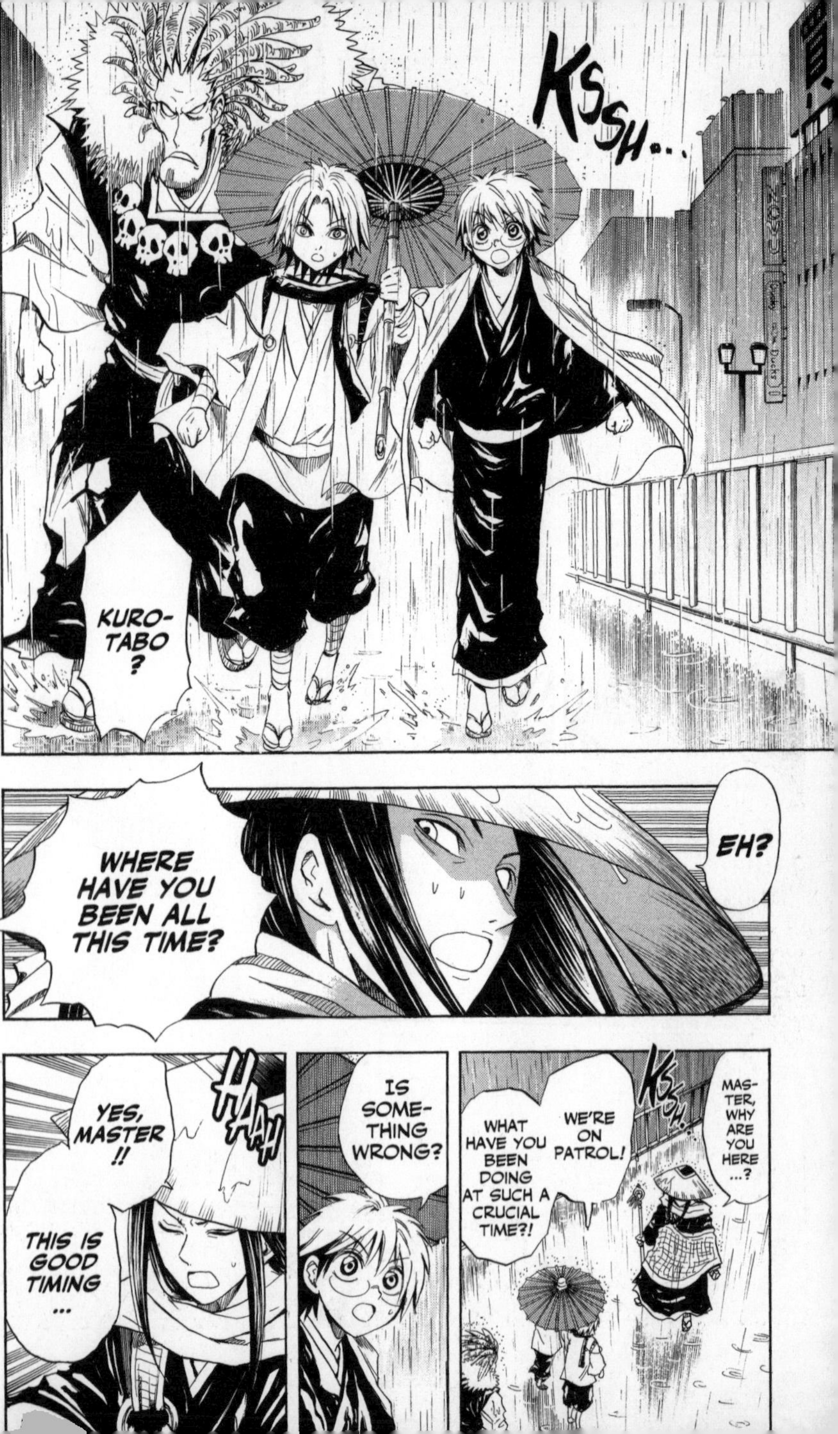
KSSH...
KURO-TABO?
EH?
WHERE HAVE YOU BEEN ALL THIS TIME?
KSSH...
MASTER, WHY ARE YOU HERE...?
WE'RE ON PATROL!
WHAT HAVE YOU BEEN DOING AT SUCH A CRUCIAL TIME?!
IS SOMETHING WRONG?
HAAH
YES, MASTER!!
THIS IS GOOD TIMING...

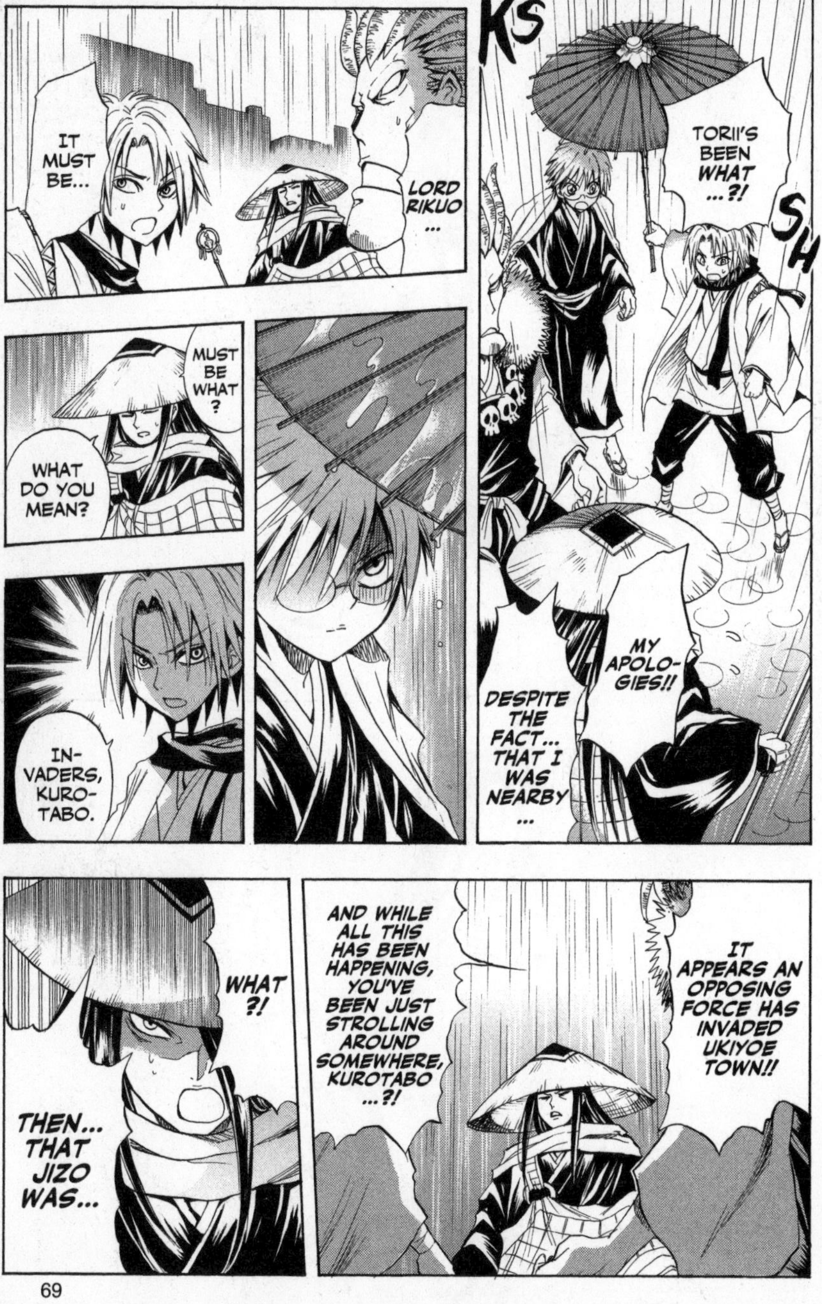
KSSH
TORII'S BEEN WHAT ...?!
MY APOLOGIES!!
DESPITE THE FACT... THAT I WAS NEARBY ...
LORD RIKUO ...
IT MUST BE...
MUST BE WHAT ?
WHAT DO YOU MEAN?
INVADERS, KUROTABO.
IT APPEARS AN OPPOSING FORCE HAS INVADED UKIYOE TOWN!!
AND WHILE ALL THIS HAS BEEN HAPPENING, YOU'VE BEEN JUST STROLLING AROUND SOMEWHERE, KUROTABO ...?!
WHAT ?!
THEN... THAT JIZO WAS...

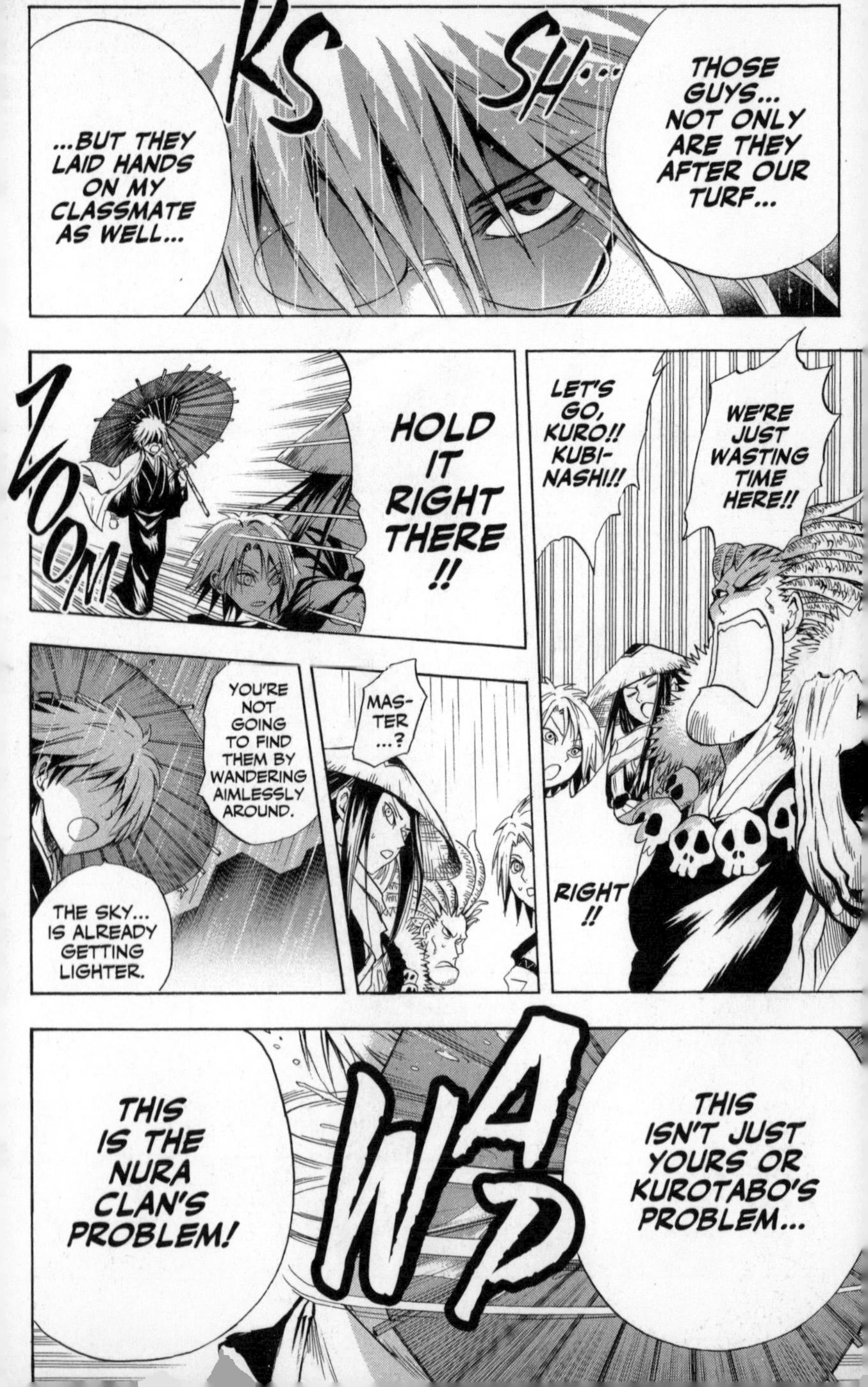
THOSE GUYS... NOT ONLY ARE THEY AFTER OUR TURF...
KSSH...
...BUT THEY LAID HANDS ON MY CLASSMATE AS WELL...
WE'RE JUST WASTING TIME HERE!!
LET'S GO, KURO!! KUBI-NASHI!!
RIGHT!!
HOLD IT RIGHT THERE!!
ZOOM
MAS-TER ...?
YOU'RE NOT GOING TO FIND THEM BY WANDERING AIMLESSLY AROUND.
THE SKY... IS ALREADY GETTING LIGHTER.
THIS ISN'T JUST YOURS OR KUROTABO'S PROBLEM...
WAP
THIS IS THE NURA CLAN'S PROBLEM!

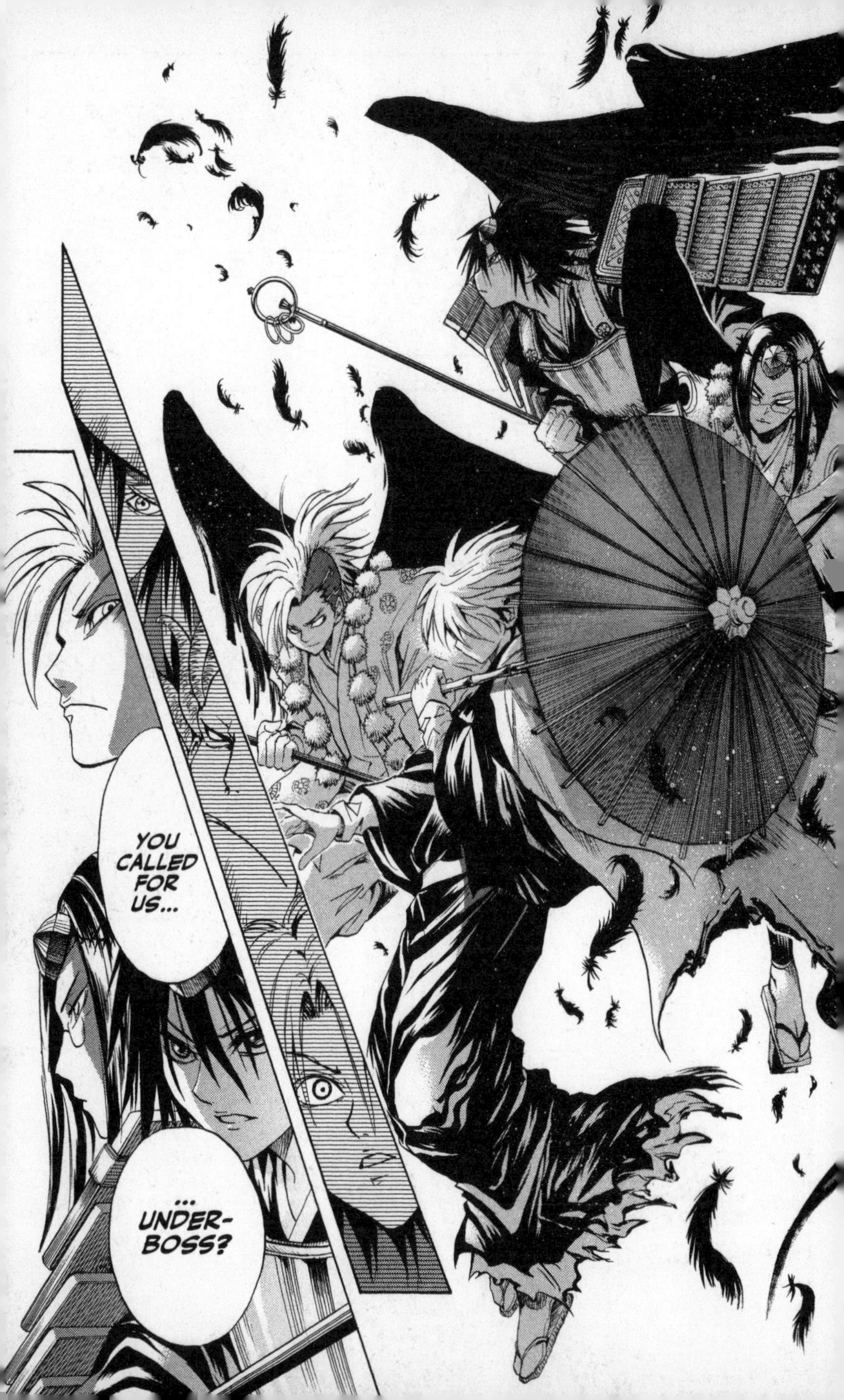
YOU CALLED FOR US...
... UNDER-BOSS?

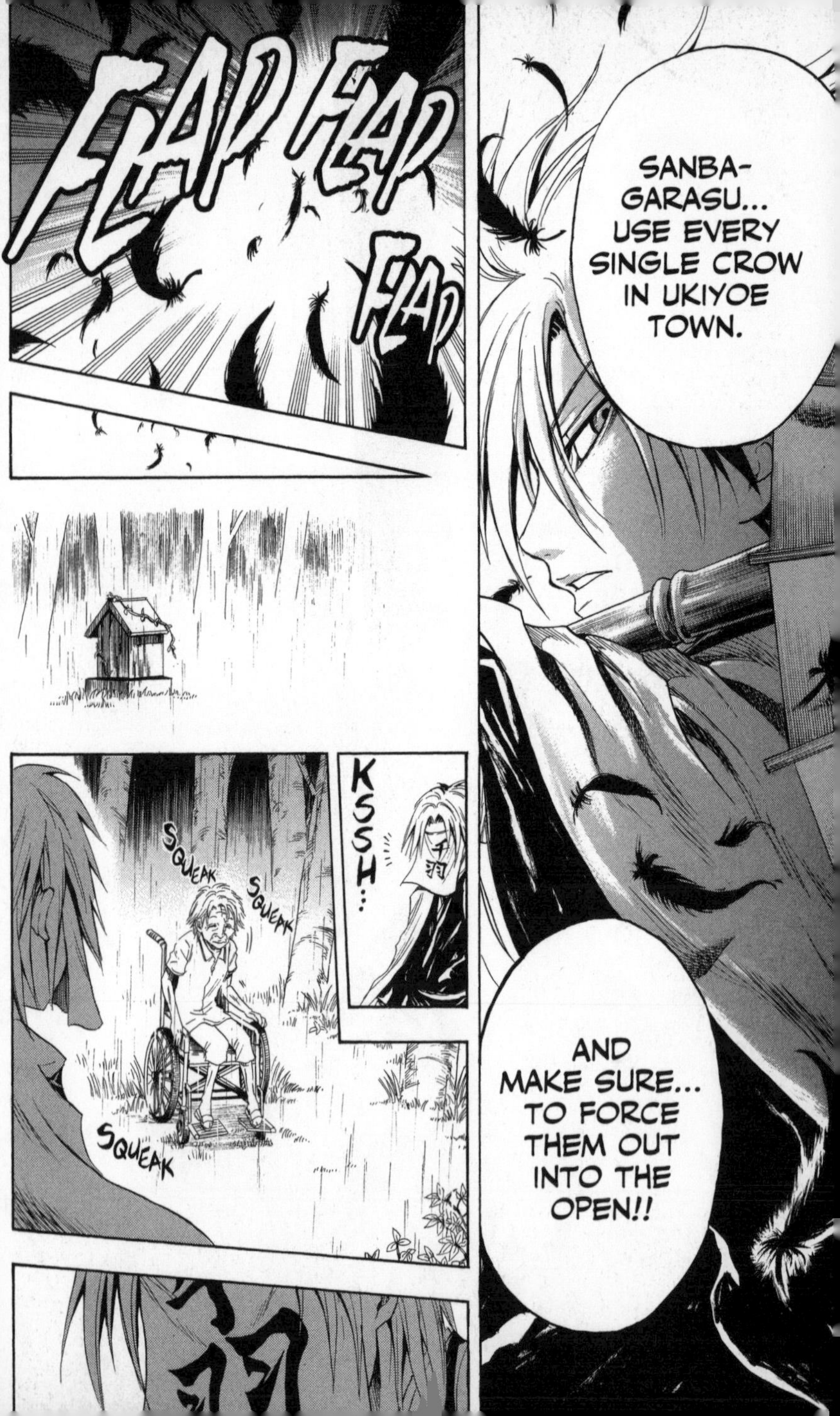
SANBA-GARASU... USE EVERY SINGLE CROW IN UKIYOE TOWN.
AND MAKE SURE... TO FORCE THEM OUT INTO THE OPEN!!
FLAP FLAP
FLAP
KSSH...
SQUEAK
SQUEAK
SQUEAK

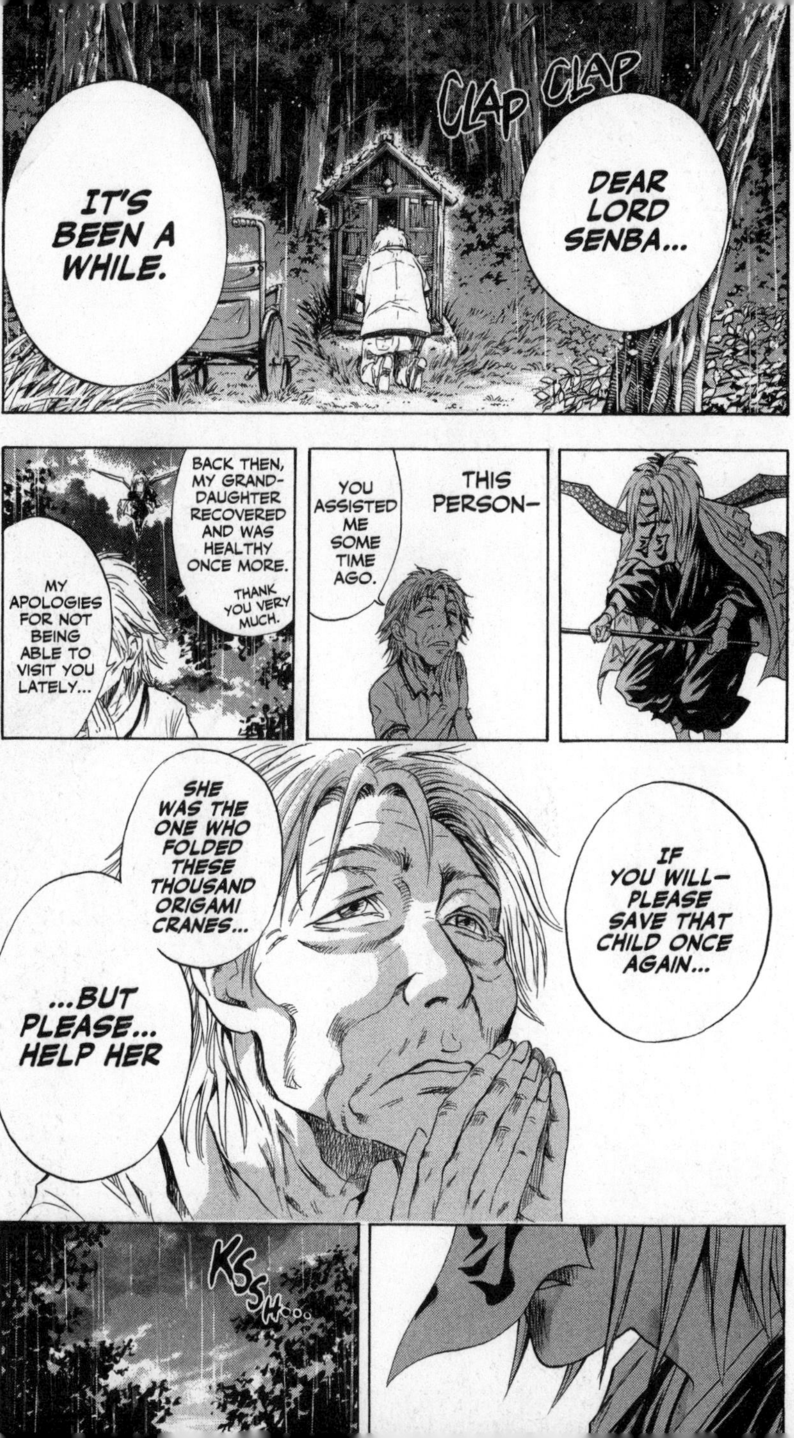
CLAP CLAP
DEAR LORD SENBA...
IT'S BEEN A WHILE.
THIS PERSON—
YOU ASSISTED ME SOME TIME AGO.
BACK THEN, MY GRAND-DAUGHTER RECOVERED AND WAS HEALTHY ONCE MORE.
THANK YOU VERY MUCH.
MY APOLOGIES FOR NOT BEING ABLE TO VISIT YOU LATELY...
IF YOU WILL— PLEASE SAVE THAT CHILD ONCE AGAIN...
SHE WAS THE ONE WHO FOLDED THESE THOUSAND ORIGAMI CRANES...
...BUT PLEASE... HELP HER
KSSH...

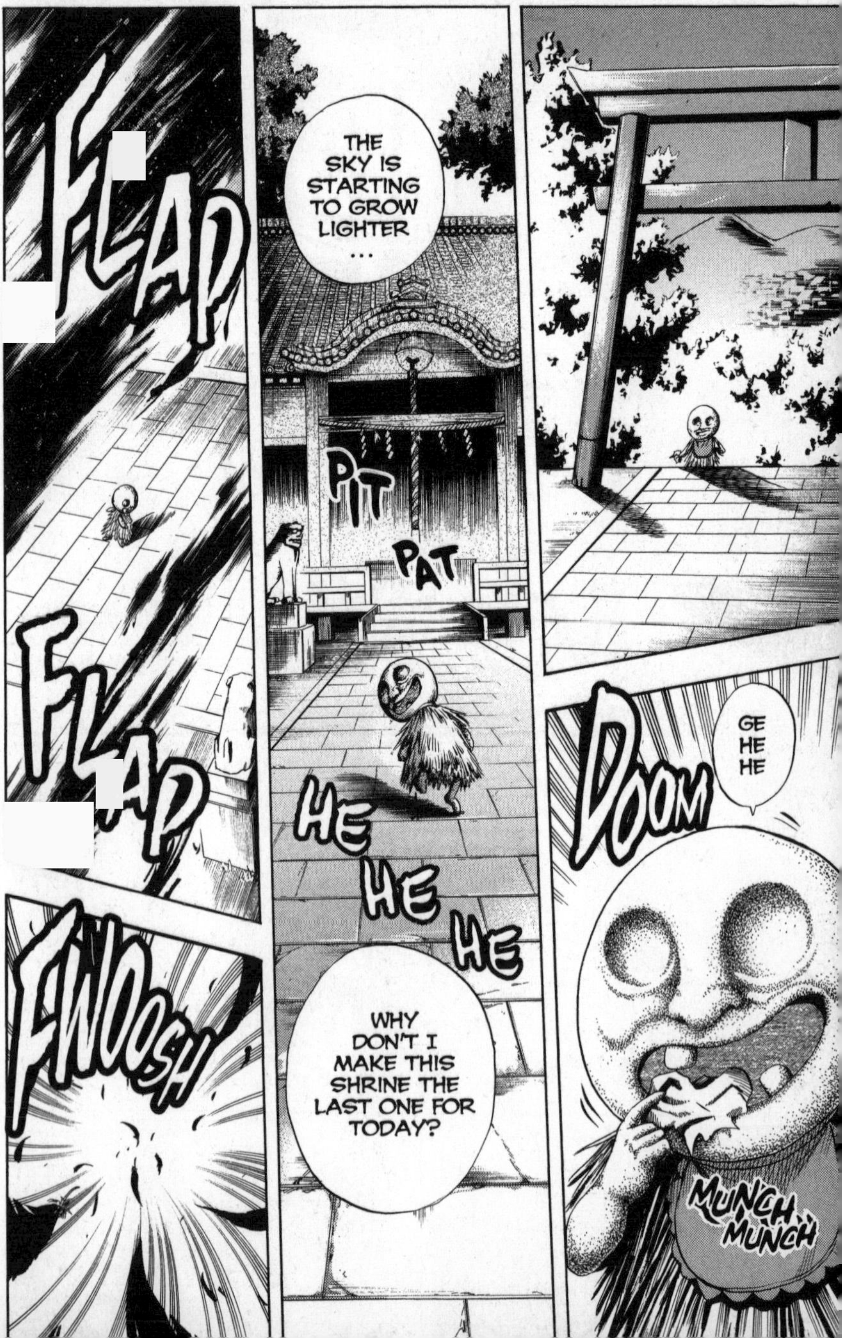
DOOM
GE HE HE
MUNCH MUNCH
THE SKY IS STARTING TO GROW LIGHTER...
PIT PAT
HE HE HE
WHY DON'T I MAKE THIS SHRINE THE LAST ONE FOR TODAY?
FLAP
FLAP
FWOOSH

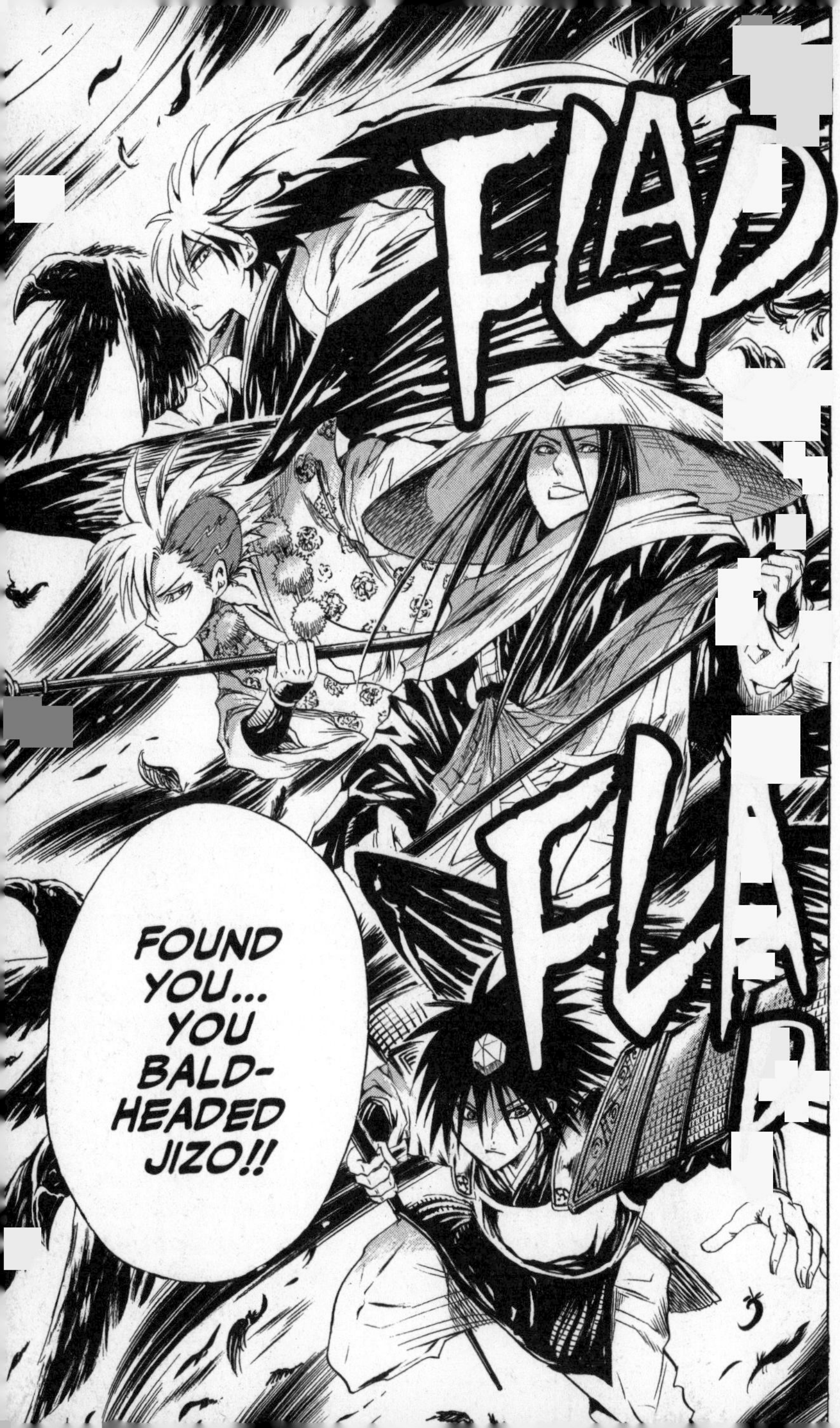
FLAP
FLAP
FOUND YOU... YOU BALD-HEADED JIZO!!

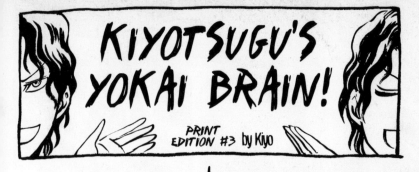

KIYOTSUGU'S YOKAI BRAIN!
PRINT EDITION #3 by Kiyo

After school on a certain day, as usual, the Kiyojuji Paranormal Patrol members gather one by one in the (recently acquired) meeting room.

Vnnn Vnnn

Gzz Klik Klak

Kiyotsugu's laptop begins to emit a weird sound. Even before Kiyotsugu arrived, there were numerous posts being made on the Yokai Brain site.

Kiyo: So, let us begin another day of great research on yokai!! Wow!! There are so many posts here!! Let's see...

Kiyotsugu reads them carefully, but his enthusiasm slowly wanes.

Rikuo: What's wrong, Kiyotsugu?

Kiyotsugu: Nura, take a look at this.

Rikuo looks at the laptop screen.

Rikuo: Gah!! These questions are mostly about..."Nura clan yokai"?!

Kiyo: I don't understand any of this... I guess I still have a lot more studying to do!! Augh!! I'm so ashamed of myself!!

Rikuo: This isn't good... I can't just leave this alone... Well, for now, perhaps I should reply to them?

Question 1: "Are Kurotabo and Aotabo the same kind of yokai?" —*Shiotabo, X Prefecture*

Rikuo: I wonder... They've both been around as long as I can remember, but I've never talked to them about that... I think they mentioned that they were human monks long ago...? I don't know the details. Hm, sorry, Shiotabo...is that good enough?

Question 2: "Yuki-Onna and Karasu-Tengu have cell phones, but are there other yokai that have one as well?" —*Chinami Takada, Tomiyama Prefecture*

Rikuo: Oh, I think our family is renting about a hundred of them on a group plan. I don't think they carry individual ones, so I guess they just take one along when necessary. Is that kind of response okay...? I'm not used to this, so I wonder if it's actually going through?

Question 3: "This is a question for Rikuo!! Is there any other career you'd like to take on, other than being Supreme Commander?" —*Chachamaru, Shizuoka Prefecture*

Rikuo: Eh—? Let's see... If I could, I'd want a job where I can be of assistance to people. It's been my dream to do volunteer work overseas...

Kiyo: Nura-kun, what are you doing—? (creeps up on him)

Rikuo: Waah... Waaah... Not good! Th-there are questions for Kiyotsugu, too!!

Kiyo: Hmmm...?

(continued on page 158)

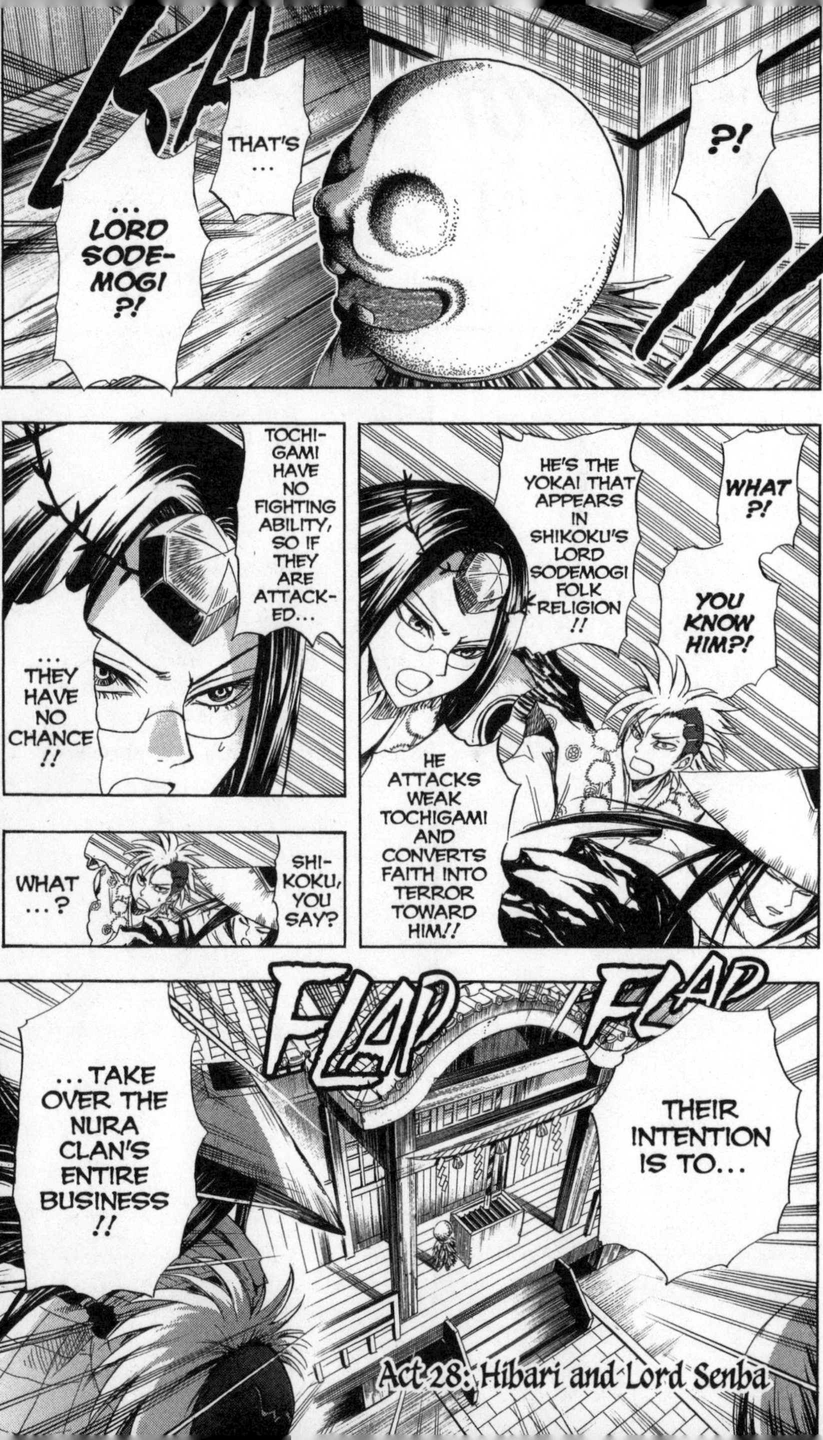
?!
THAT'S ...
... LORD SODE-MOGI ?!
WHAT ?!
YOU KNOW HIM?!
HE'S THE YOKAI THAT APPEARS IN SHIKOKU'S LORD SODEMOGI FOLK RELIGION !!
HE ATTACKS WEAK TOCHIGAMI AND CONVERTS FAITH INTO TERROR TOWARD HIM!!
TOCHIGAMI HAVE NO FIGHTING ABILITY, SO IF THEY ARE ATTACKED...
... THEY HAVE NO CHANCE !!
SHIKOKU, YOU SAY?
WHAT ... ?
FLAP FLAP
THEIR INTENTION IS TO...
... TAKE OVER THE NURA CLAN'S ENTIRE BUSINESS !!
Act 28: Hibari and Lord Senba

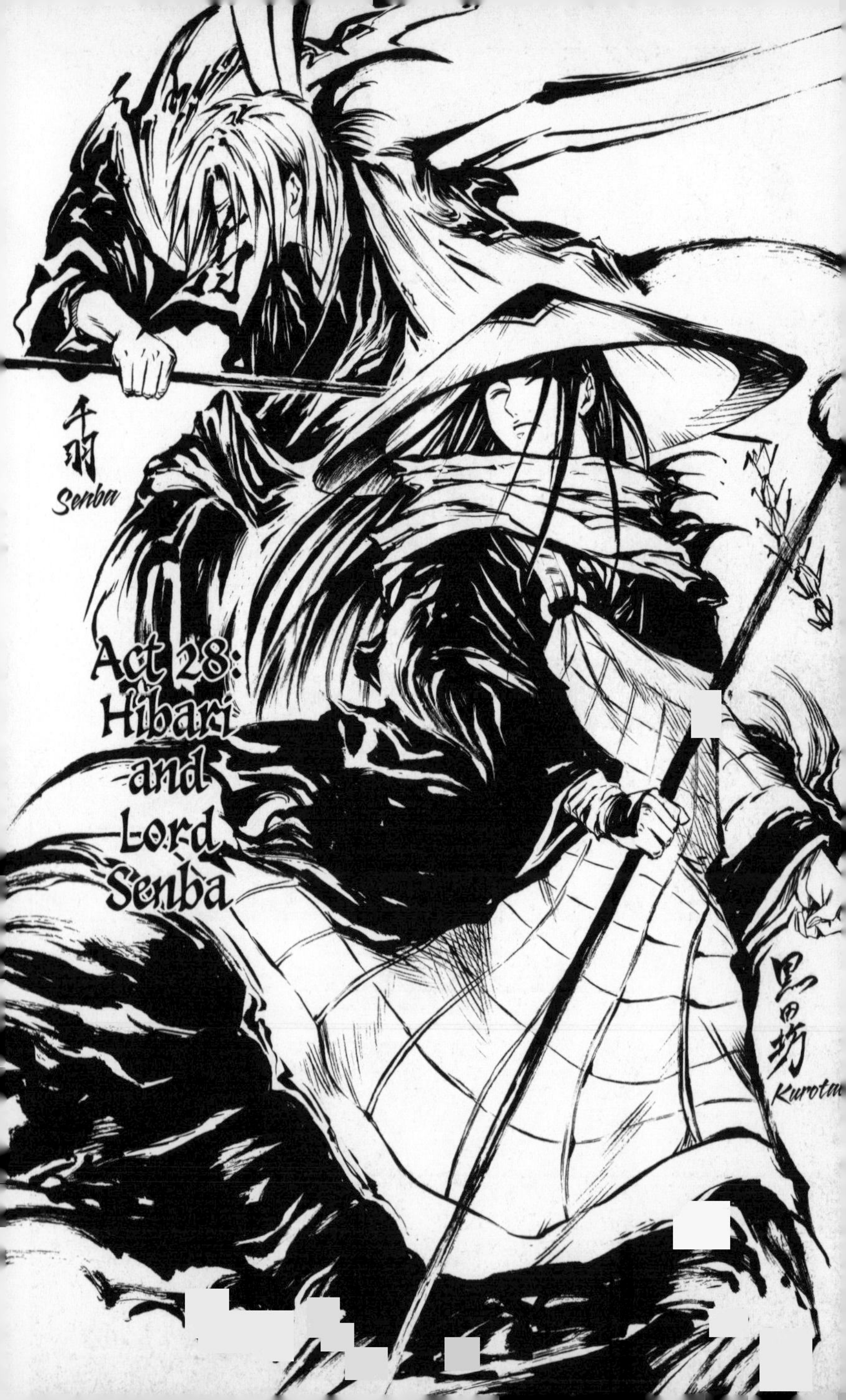
千羽
Senba
Act 28: Hibari and Lord Senba
黒田坊
Kurota

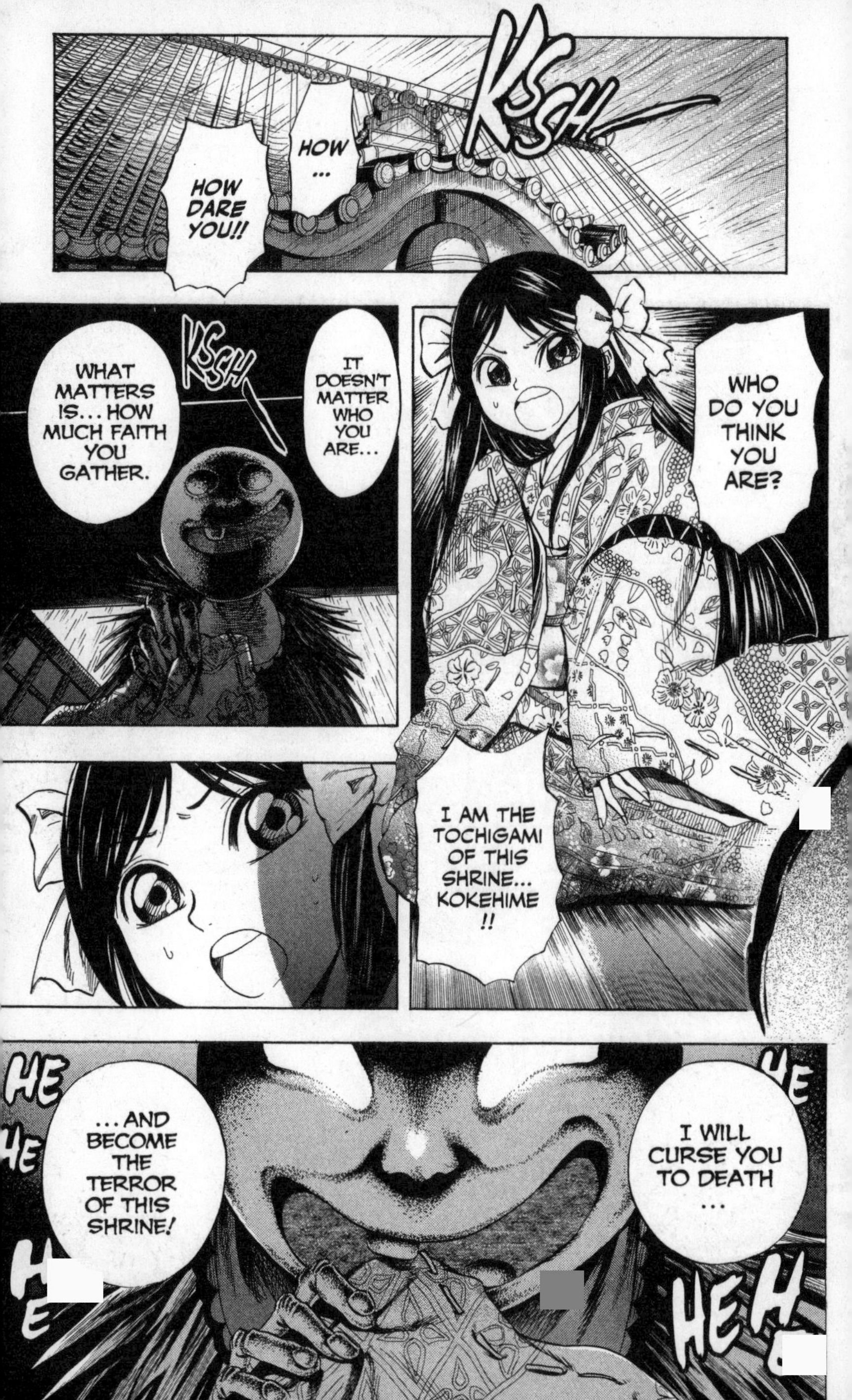
KSSH
HOW ...
HOW DARE YOU!!
WHO DO YOU THINK YOU ARE?
IT DOESN'T MATTER WHO YOU ARE...
KSSH
WHAT MATTERS IS... HOW MUCH FAITH YOU GATHER.
I AM THE TOCHIGAMI OF THIS SHRINE... KOKEHIME !!
HE
I WILL CURSE YOU TO DEATH ...
HE H
HE
HE
...AND BECOME THE TERROR OF THIS SHRINE!
HE

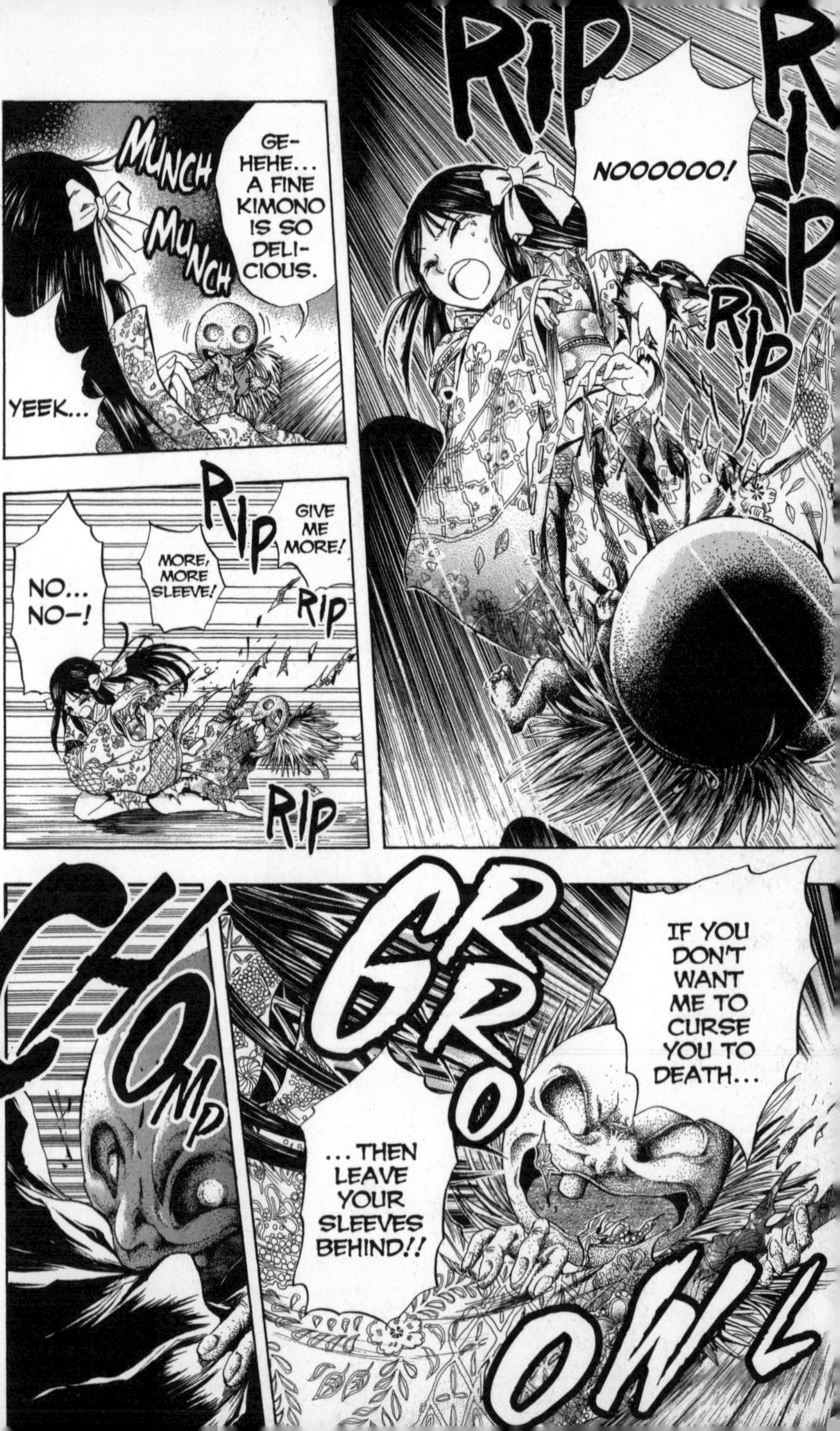
RIP
RIP
NOOOOOO!
RIP
RIP
MUNCH
MUNCH
GE-HEHE... A FINE KIMONO IS SO DELI-CIOUS.
YEEK...
RIP
GIVE ME MORE!
MORE, MORE SLEEVE!
NO... NO–!
RIP
RIP
GROWL
IF YOU DON'T WANT ME TO CURSE YOU TO DEATH...
...THEN LEAVE YOUR SLEEVES BEHIND!!
CHOMP

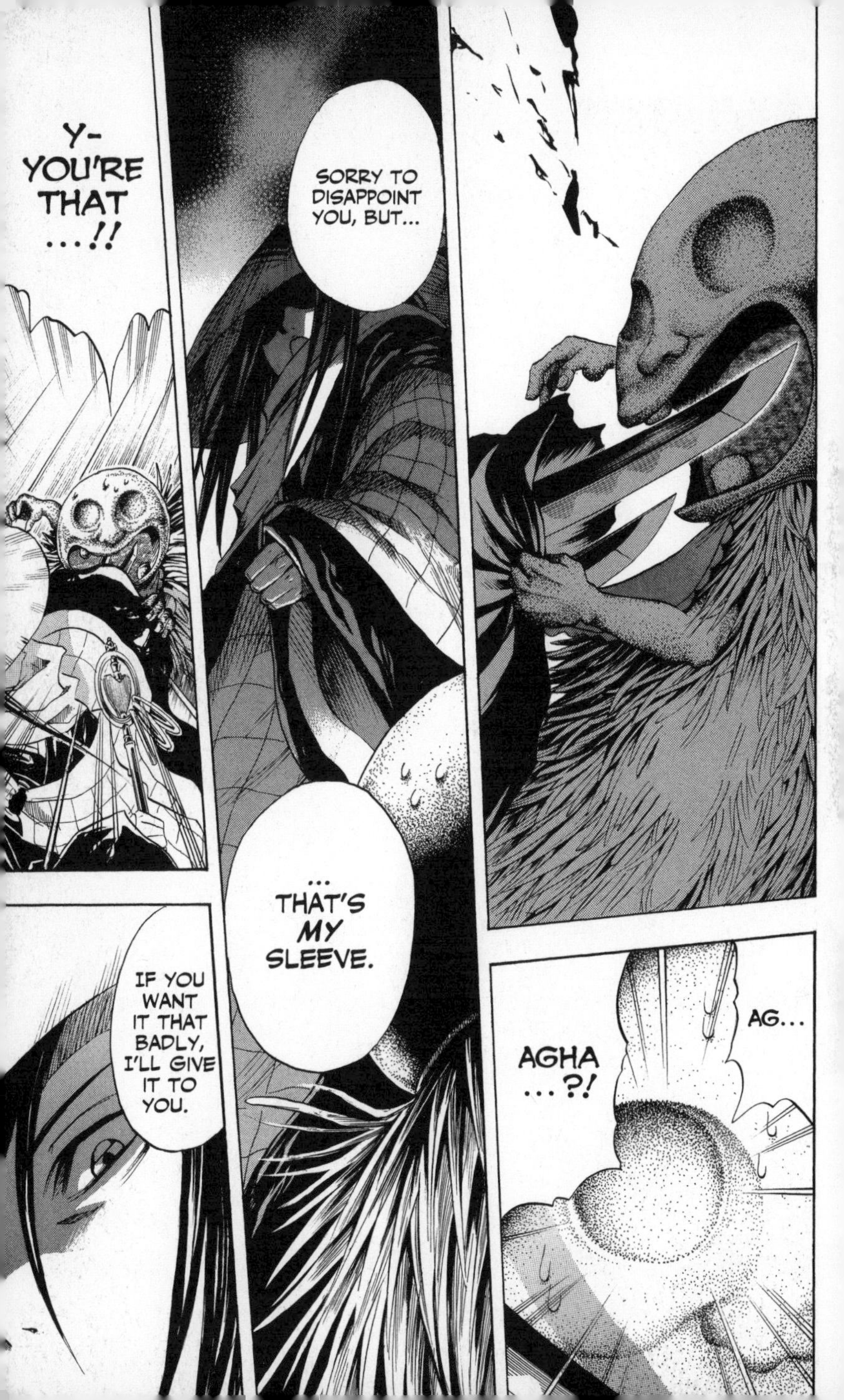
SORRY TO DISAPPOINT YOU, BUT...
... THAT'S MY SLEEVE.
Y- YOU'RE THAT ...!!
AG...
AGHA ...?!
IF YOU WANT IT THAT BADLY, I'LL GIVE IT TO YOU.

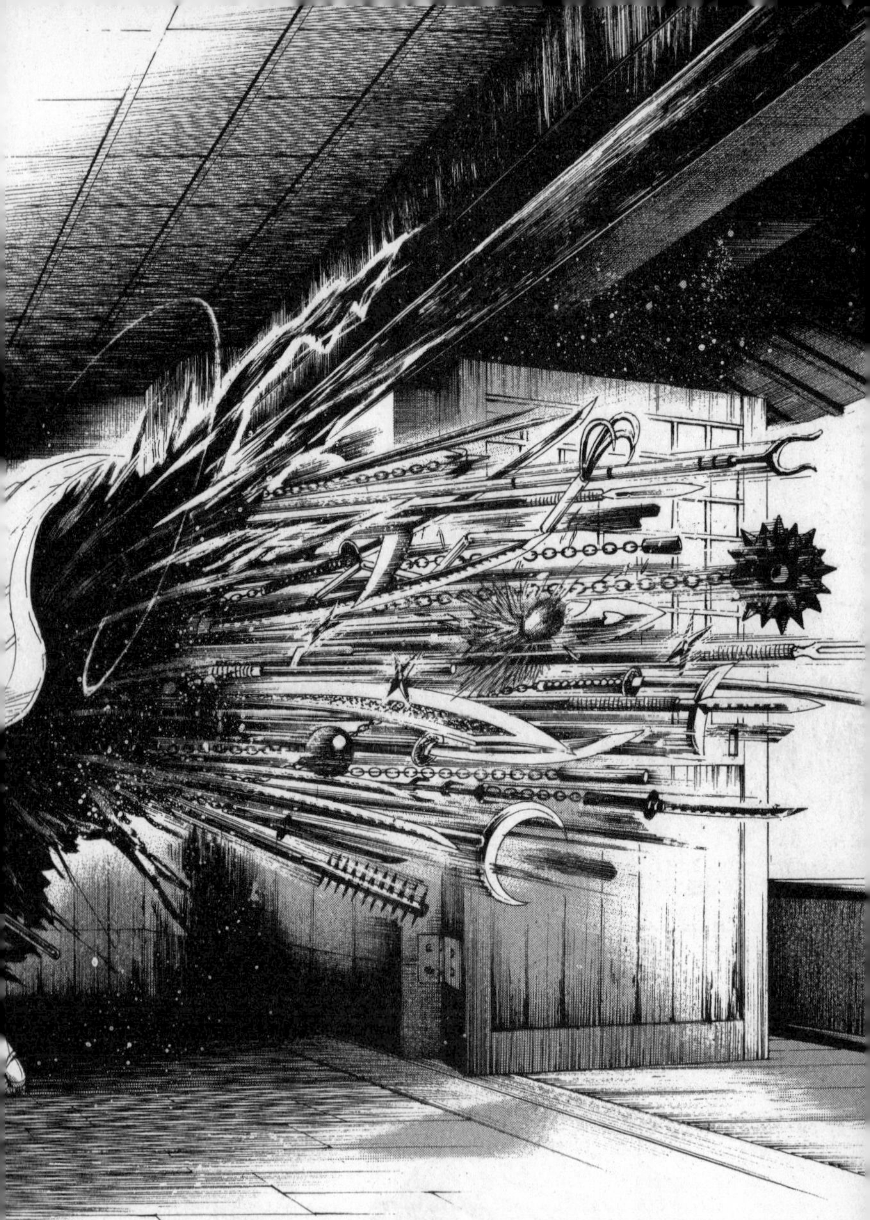

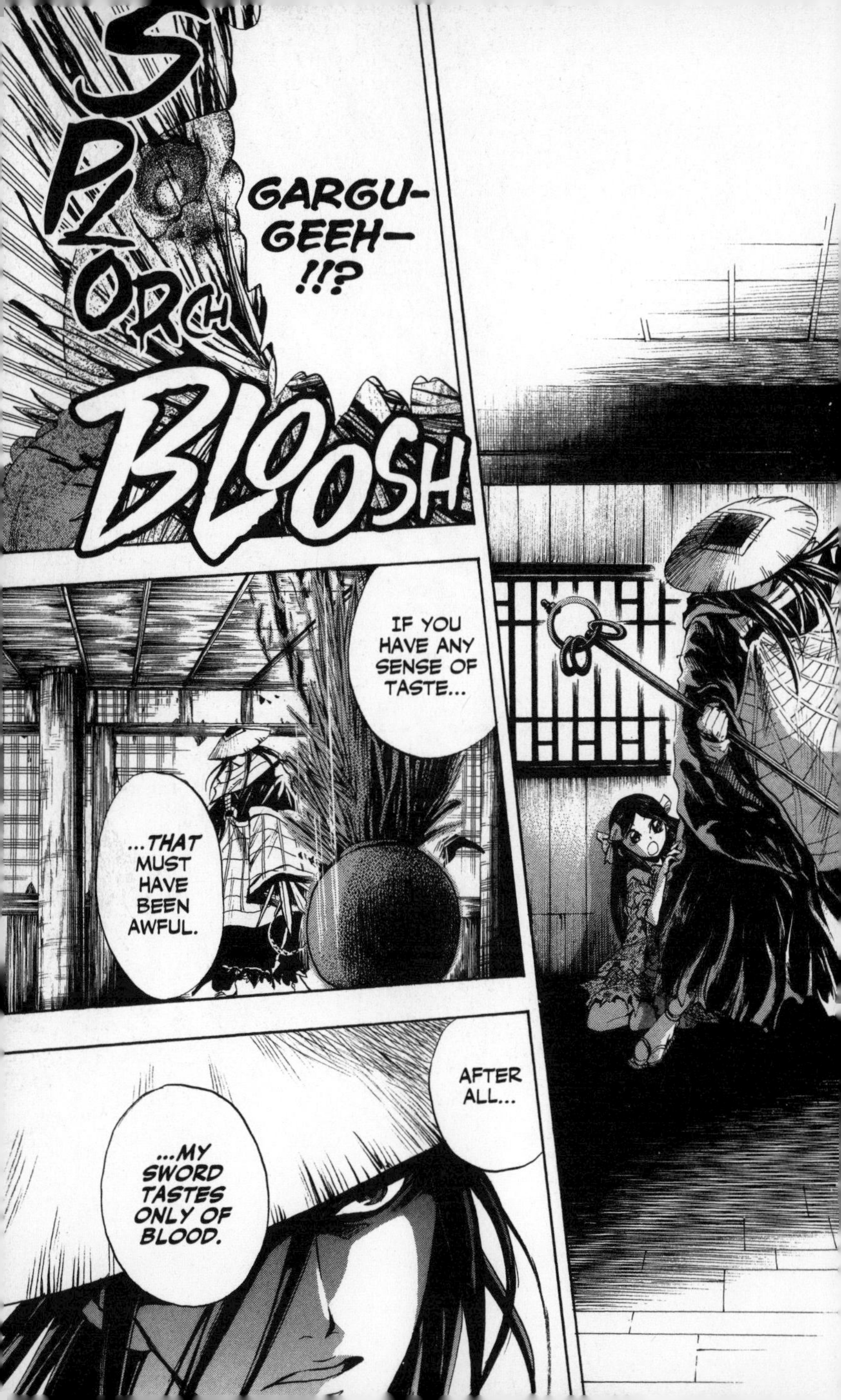
SPLORCH
GARGU-GEEH—!!?
BLOOSH
IF YOU HAVE ANY SENSE OF TASTE...
...THAT MUST HAVE BEEN AWFUL.
AFTER ALL...
...MY SWORD TASTES ONLY OF BLOOD.

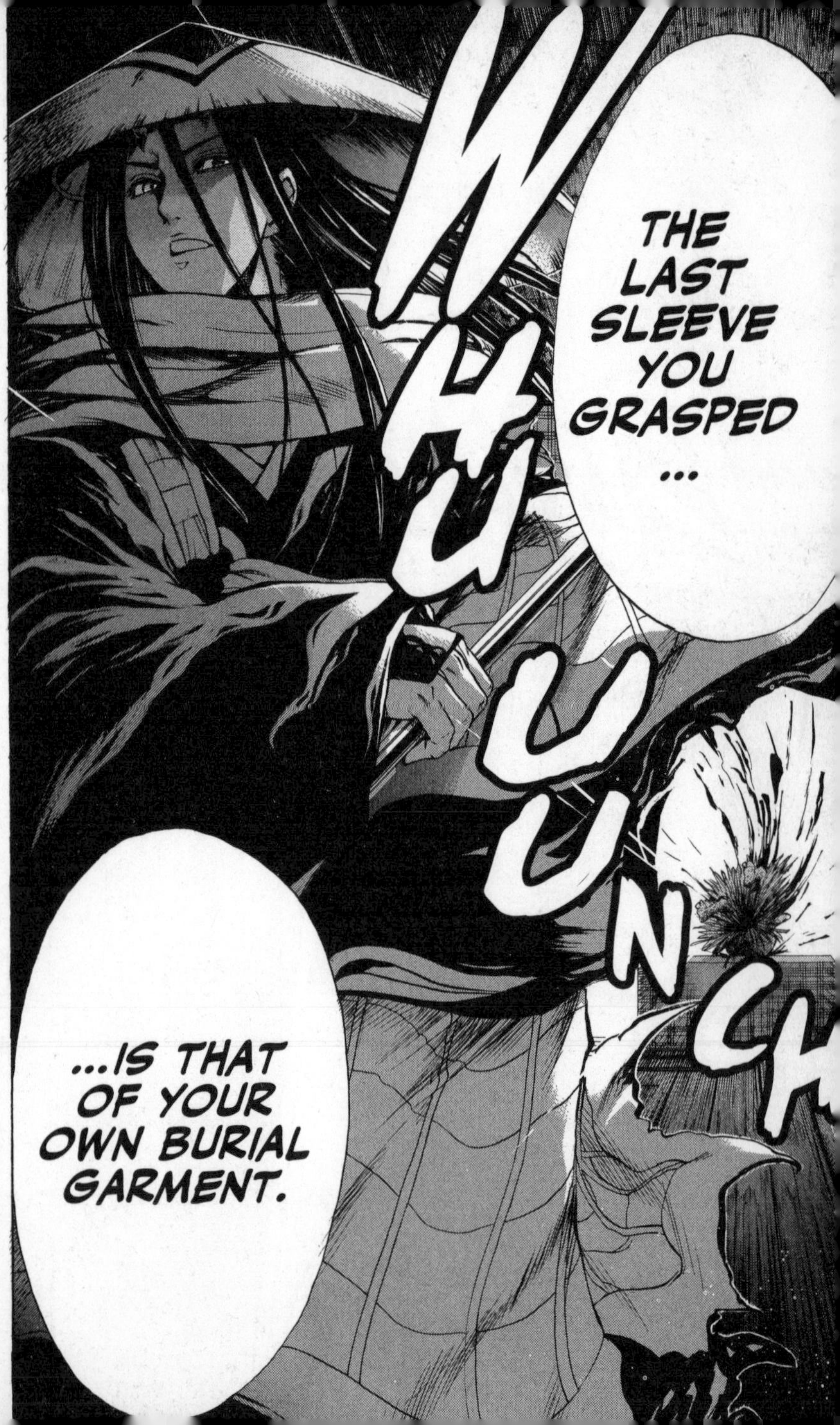
THE LAST SLEEVE YOU GRASPED ...
WHUUUNCH
...IS THAT OF YOUR OWN BURIAL GARMENT.

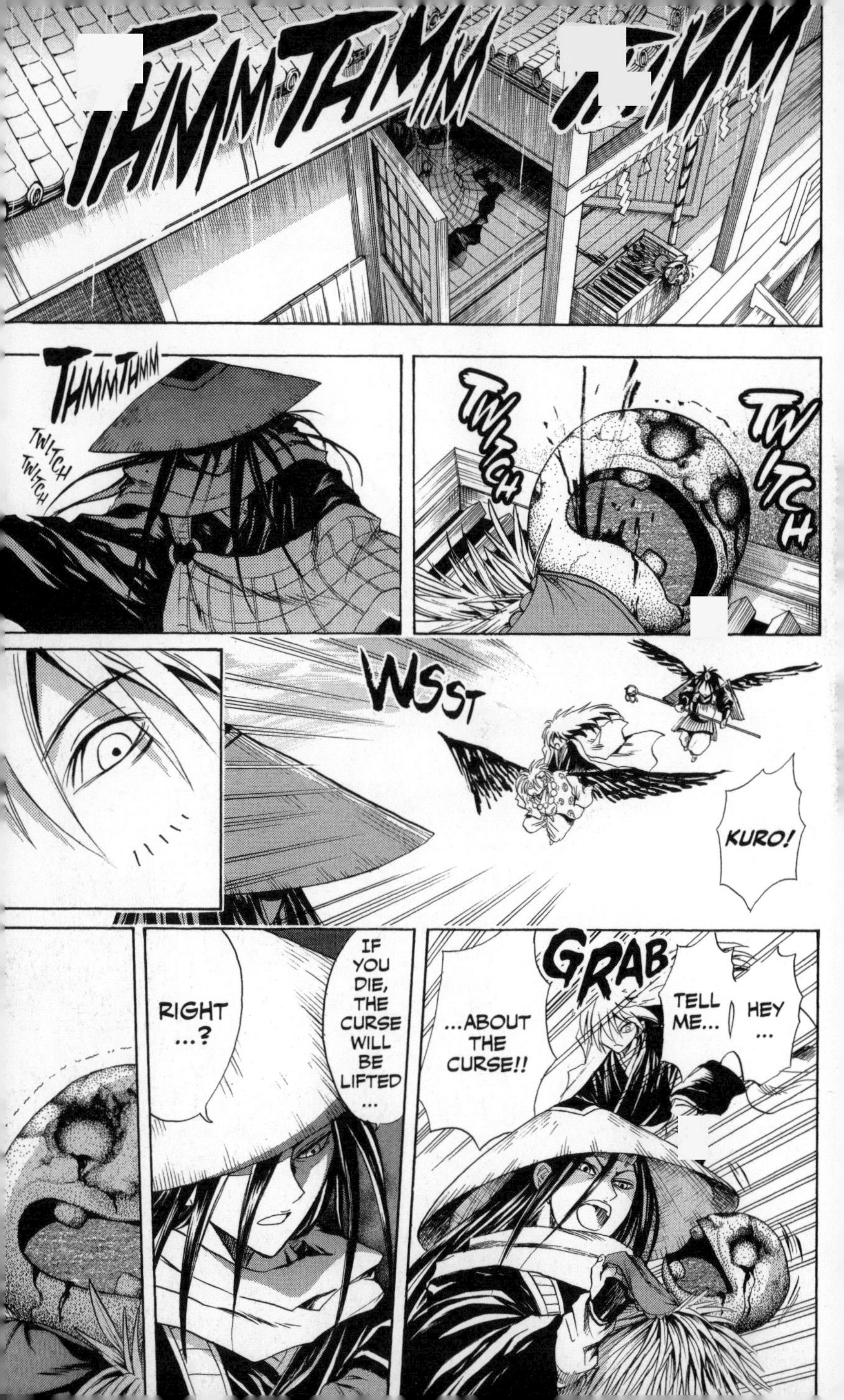
THMMTHMM
TWITCH
TWITCH
THMMTHMM
TWITCH TWITCH
WSST
KURO!
HEY...
TELL ME...
GRAB
...ABOUT THE CURSE!!
IF YOU DIE, THE CURSE WILL BE LIFTED...
RIGHT...?

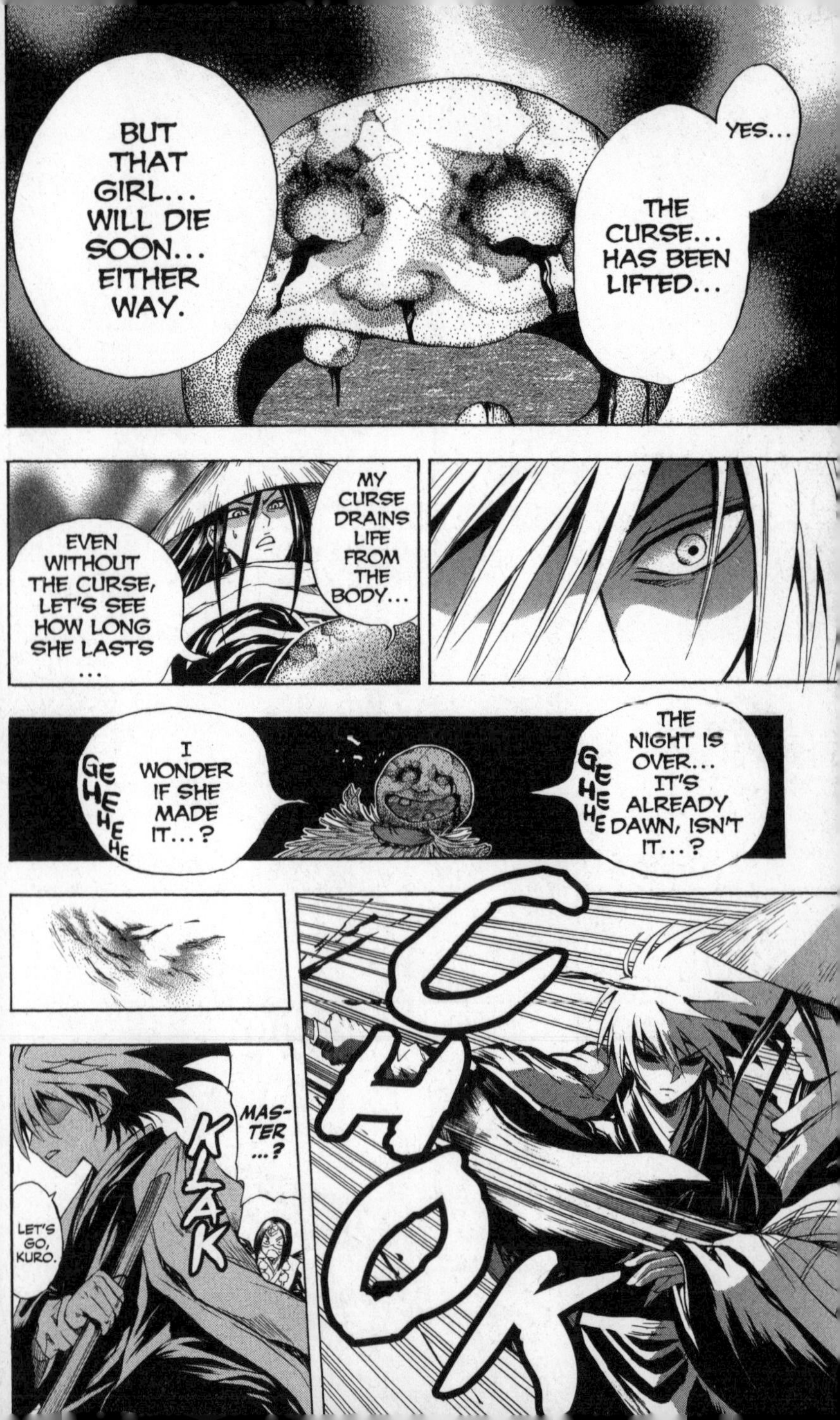
YES...
THE CURSE... HAS BEEN LIFTED...
BUT THAT GIRL... WILL DIE SOON... EITHER WAY.
MY CURSE DRAINS LIFE FROM THE BODY...
EVEN WITHOUT THE CURSE, LET'S SEE HOW LONG SHE LASTS...
GEHEHEHE
THE NIGHT IS OVER... IT'S ALREADY DAWN, ISN'T IT...?
GEHEHEHEHE
I WONDER IF SHE MADE IT...?
CHOK
MAS-TER...?
KLAK
LET'S GO, KURO.

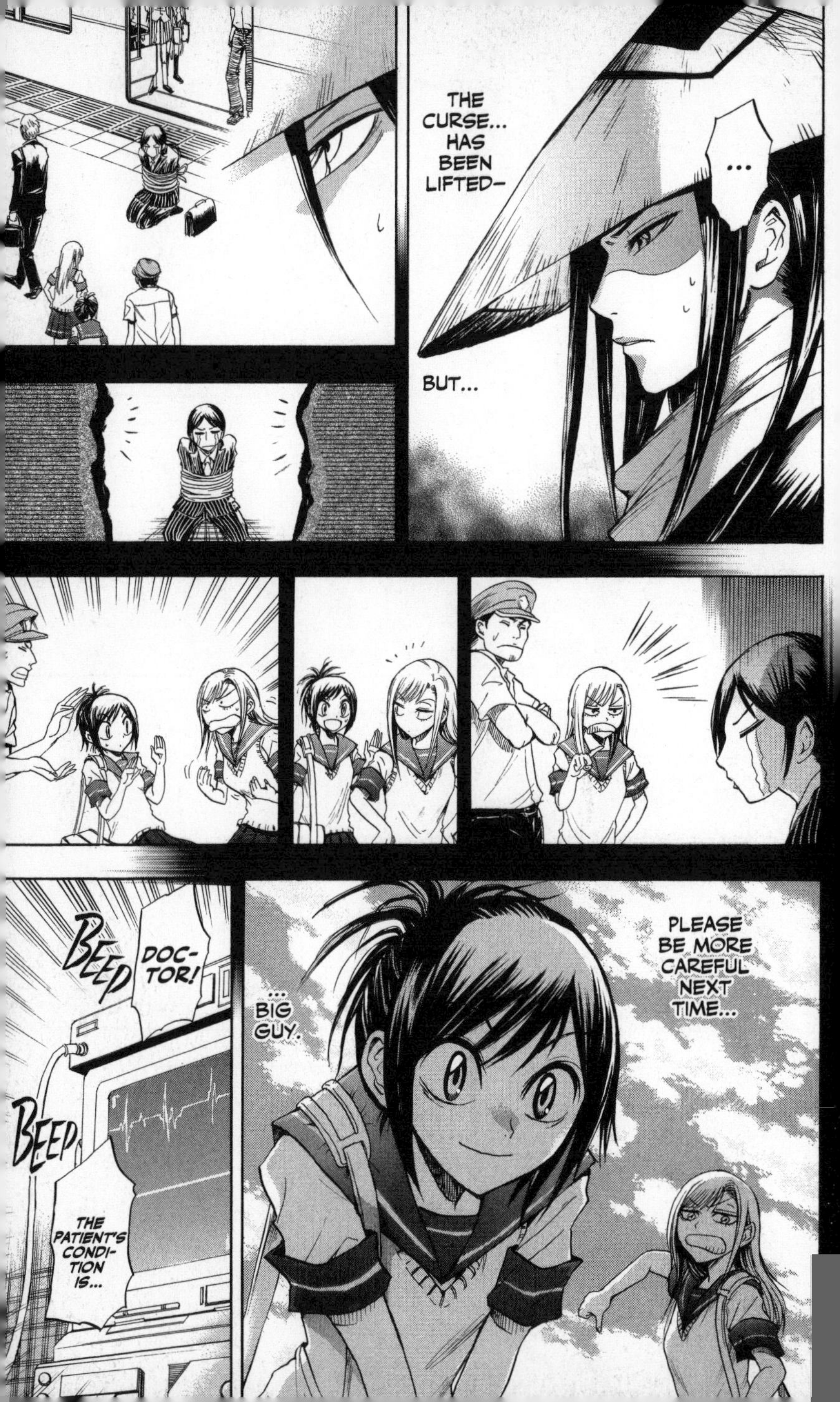
THE CURSE... HAS BEEN LIFTED—
...
BUT...
PLEASE BE MORE CAREFUL NEXT TIME...
... BIG GUY.
BEEP
DOC-TOR!
BEEP
THE PATIENT'S CONDI-TION IS...

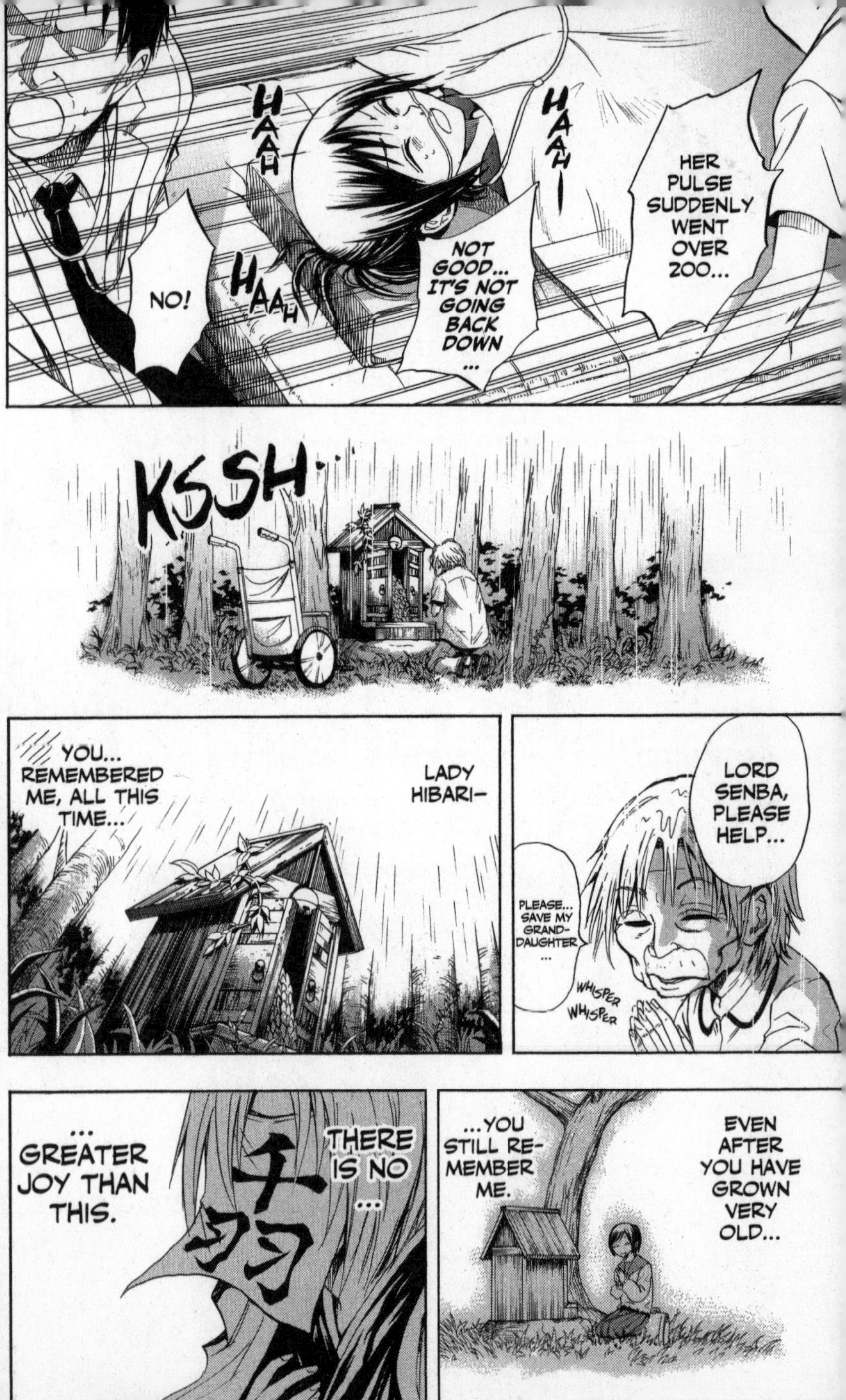
HAAH
HAAH
HER PULSE SUDDENLY WENT OVER 200...
NOT GOOD... IT'S NOT GOING BACK DOWN...
HAAH
NO!
KSSH
LORD SENBA, PLEASE HELP...
PLEASE... SAVE MY GRAND-DAUGHTER...
WHISPER WHISPER
LADY HIBARI–
YOU... REMEMBERED ME, ALL THIS TIME...
EVEN AFTER YOU HAVE GROWN VERY OLD...
...YOU STILL RE-MEMBER ME.
THERE IS NO...
...GREATER JOY THAN THIS.

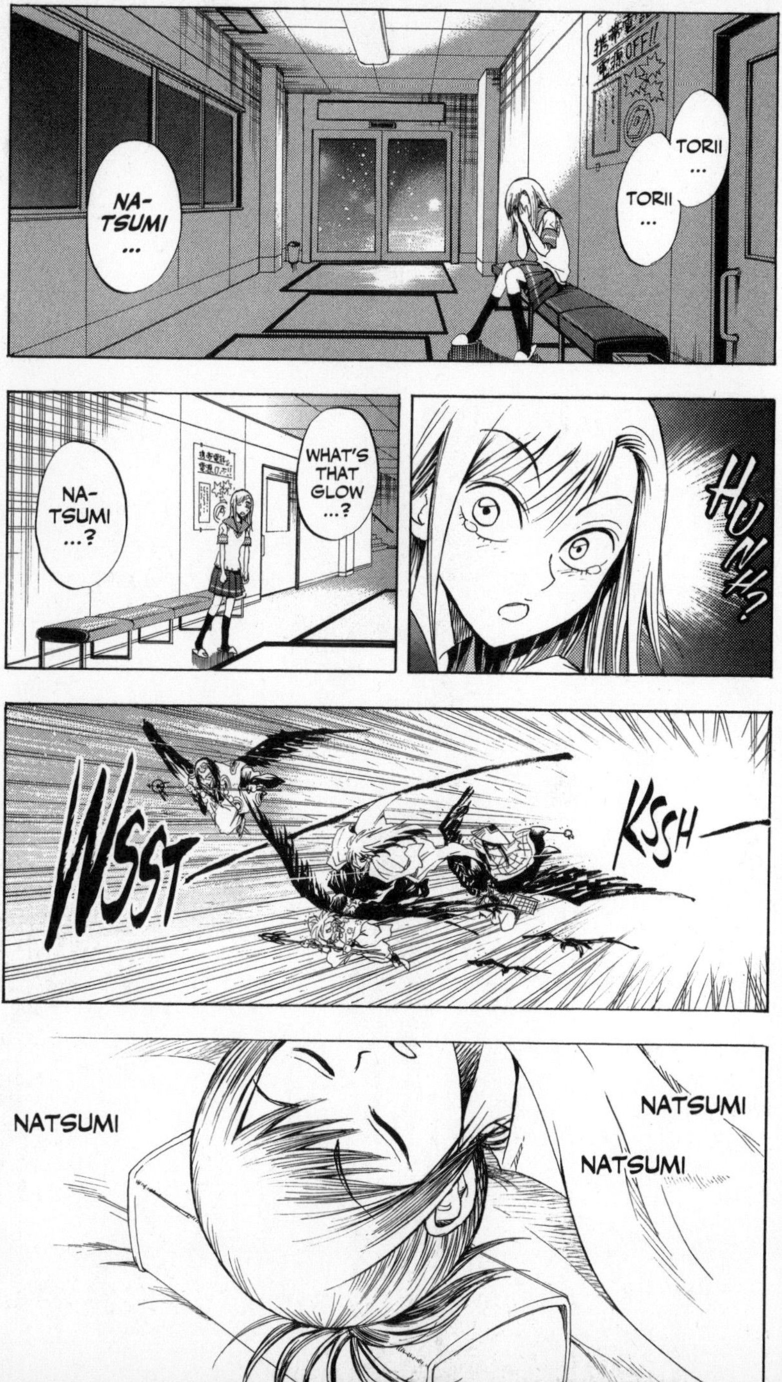
TORII ...
TORII ...
NA-TSUMI ...
HUNH?
WHAT'S THAT GLOW ...?
NA-TSUMI ...?
KSSH
WSST
NATSUMI
NATSUMI
NATSUMI

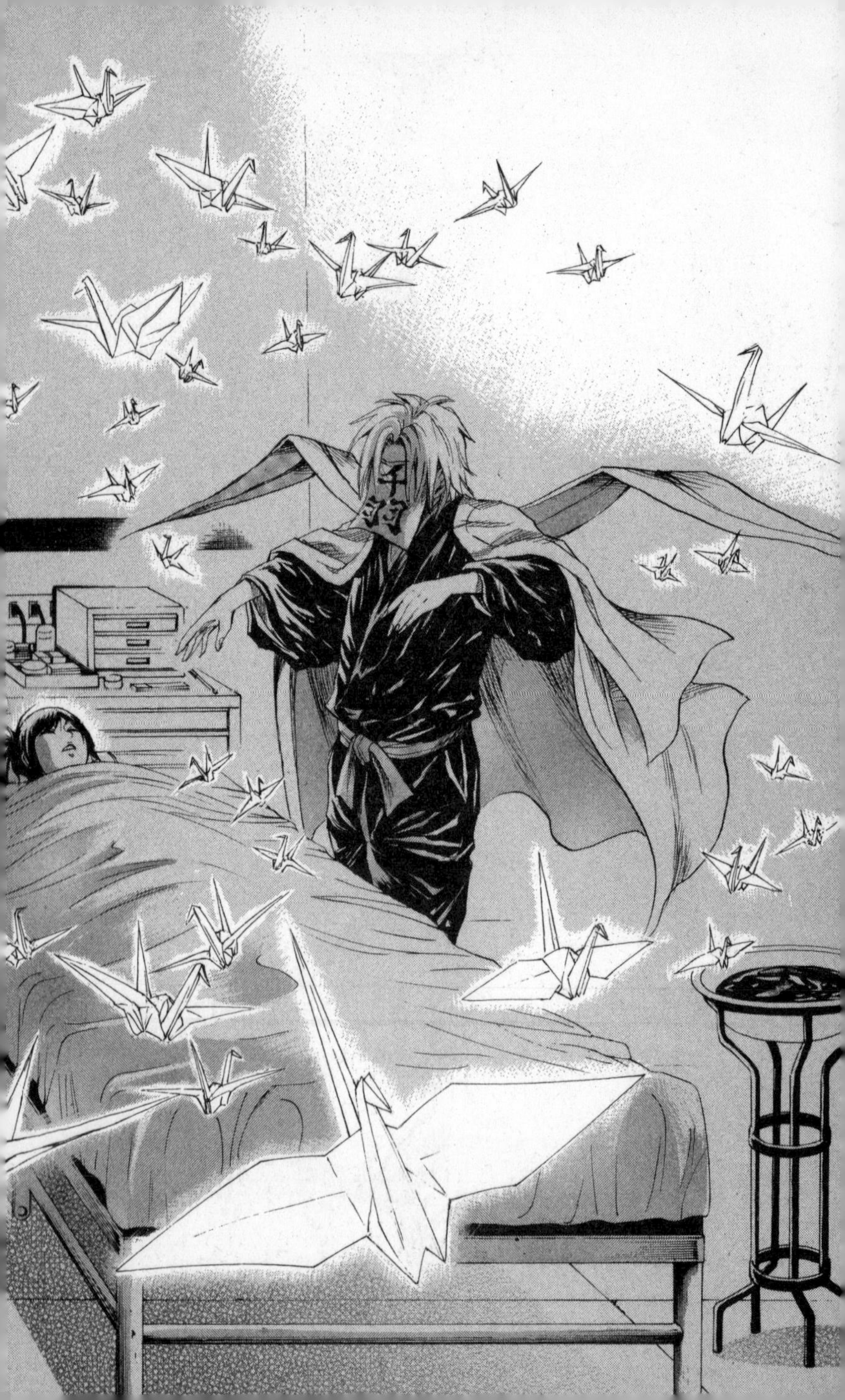

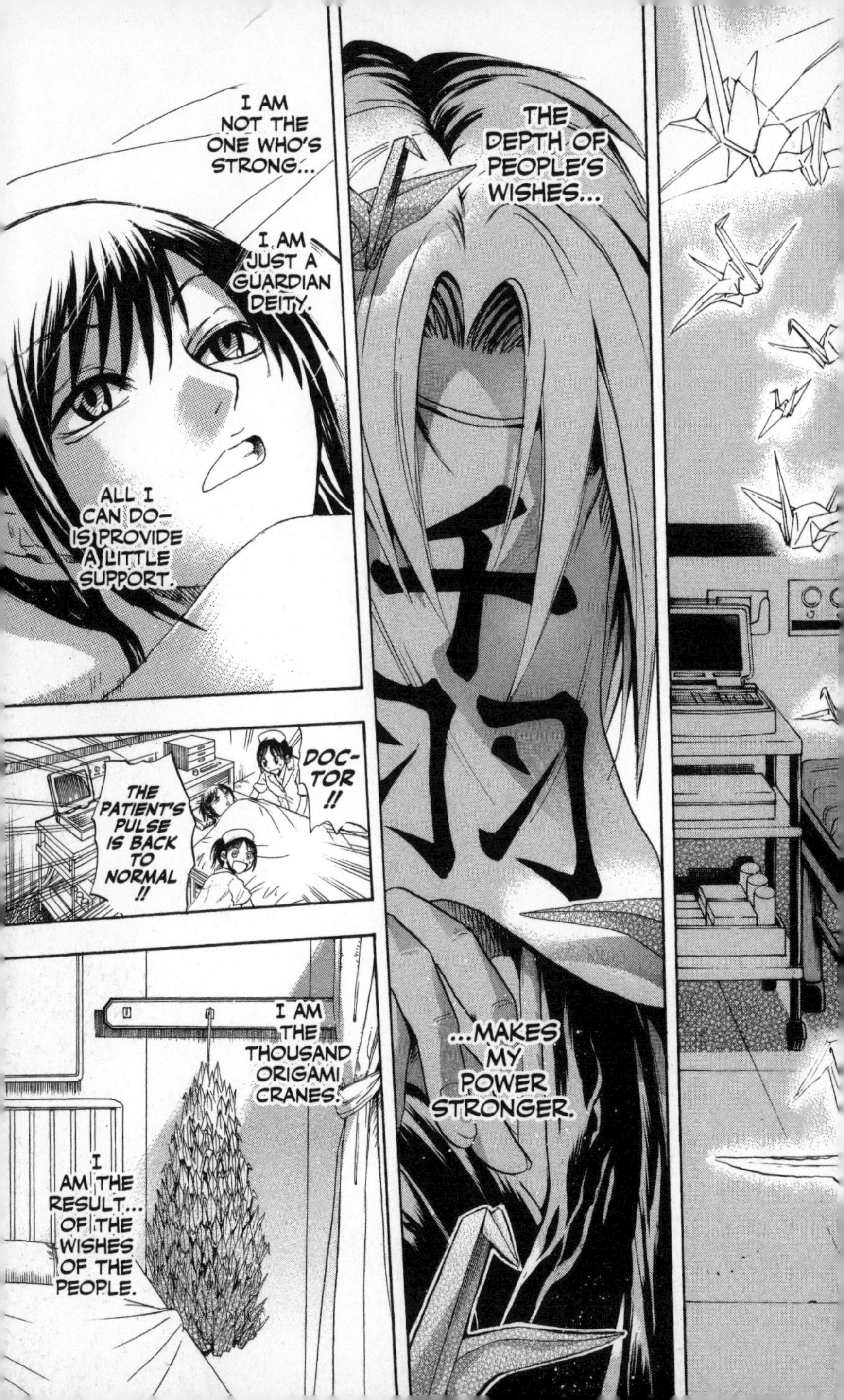
THE DEPTH OF PEOPLE'S WISHES...
...MAKES MY POWER STRONGER.
I AM NOT THE ONE WHO'S STRONG...
I AM JUST A GUARDIAN DEITY.
ALL I CAN DO—IS PROVIDE A LITTLE SUPPORT.
DOCTOR!!
THE PATIENT'S PULSE IS BACK TO NORMAL!!
I AM THE THOUSAND ORIGAMI CRANES.
I AM THE RESULT... OF THE WISHES OF THE PEOPLE.

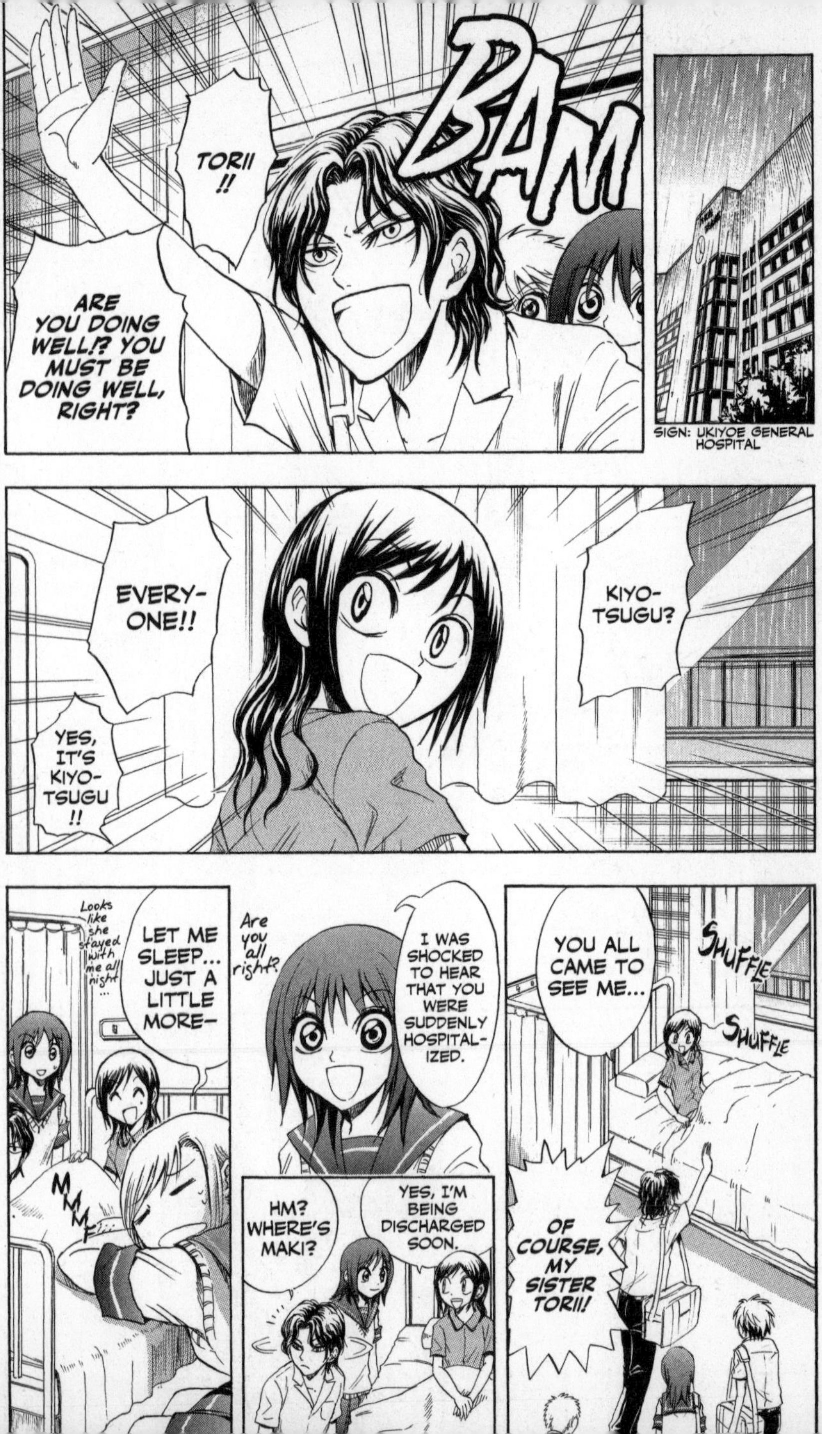
SIGN: UKIYOE GENERAL HOSPITAL
BAM
TORII !!
ARE YOU DOING WELL!? YOU MUST BE DOING WELL, RIGHT?
KIYO-TSUGU?
EVERY-ONE!!
YES, IT'S KIYO-TSUGU !!
YOU ALL CAME TO SEE ME...
SHUFFLE
SHUFFLE
OF COURSE, MY SISTER TORII!
I WAS SHOCKED TO HEAR THAT YOU WERE SUDDENLY HOSPITAL-IZED.
Are you all right?
YES, I'M BEING DISCHARGED SOON.
HM? WHERE'S MAKI?
LET ME SLEEP... JUST A LITTLE MORE–
Looks like she stayed with me all night...
MMMF

READ THIS WAY

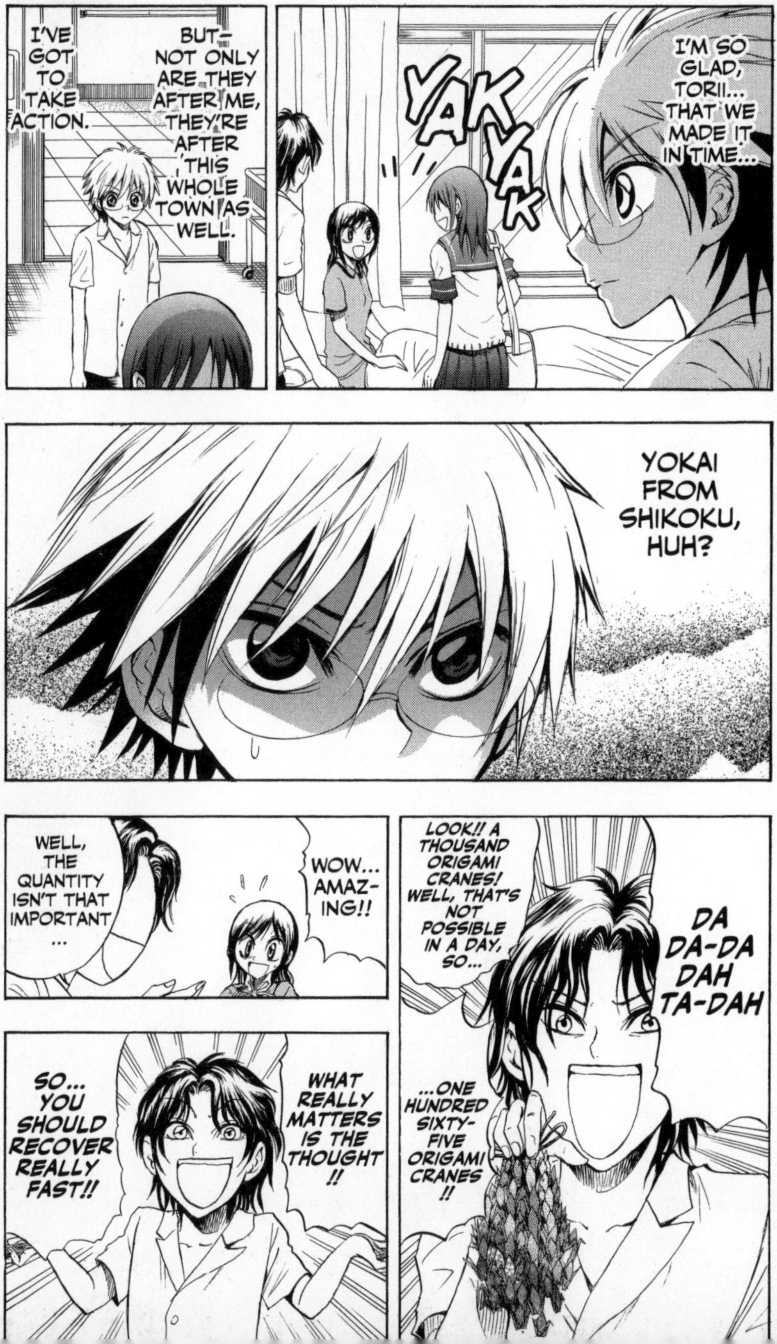
I'M SO GLAD, TORII... THAT WE MADE IT IN TIME...
YAK YAK
BUT— NOT ONLY ARE THEY AFTER ME, THEY'RE AFTER THIS WHOLE TOWN AS WELL.
I'VE GOT TO TAKE ACTION.
YOKAI FROM SHIKOKU, HUH?
DA DA-DA DAH TA-DAH
LOOK!! A THOUSAND ORIGAMI CRANES! WELL, THAT'S NOT POSSIBLE IN A DAY, SO...
...ONE HUNDRED SIXTY-FIVE ORIGAMI CRANES!!
WOW... AMAZING!!
WELL, THE QUANTITY ISN'T THAT IMPORTANT...
WHAT REALLY MATTERS IS THE THOUGHT!!
SO... YOU SHOULD RECOVER REALLY FAST!!

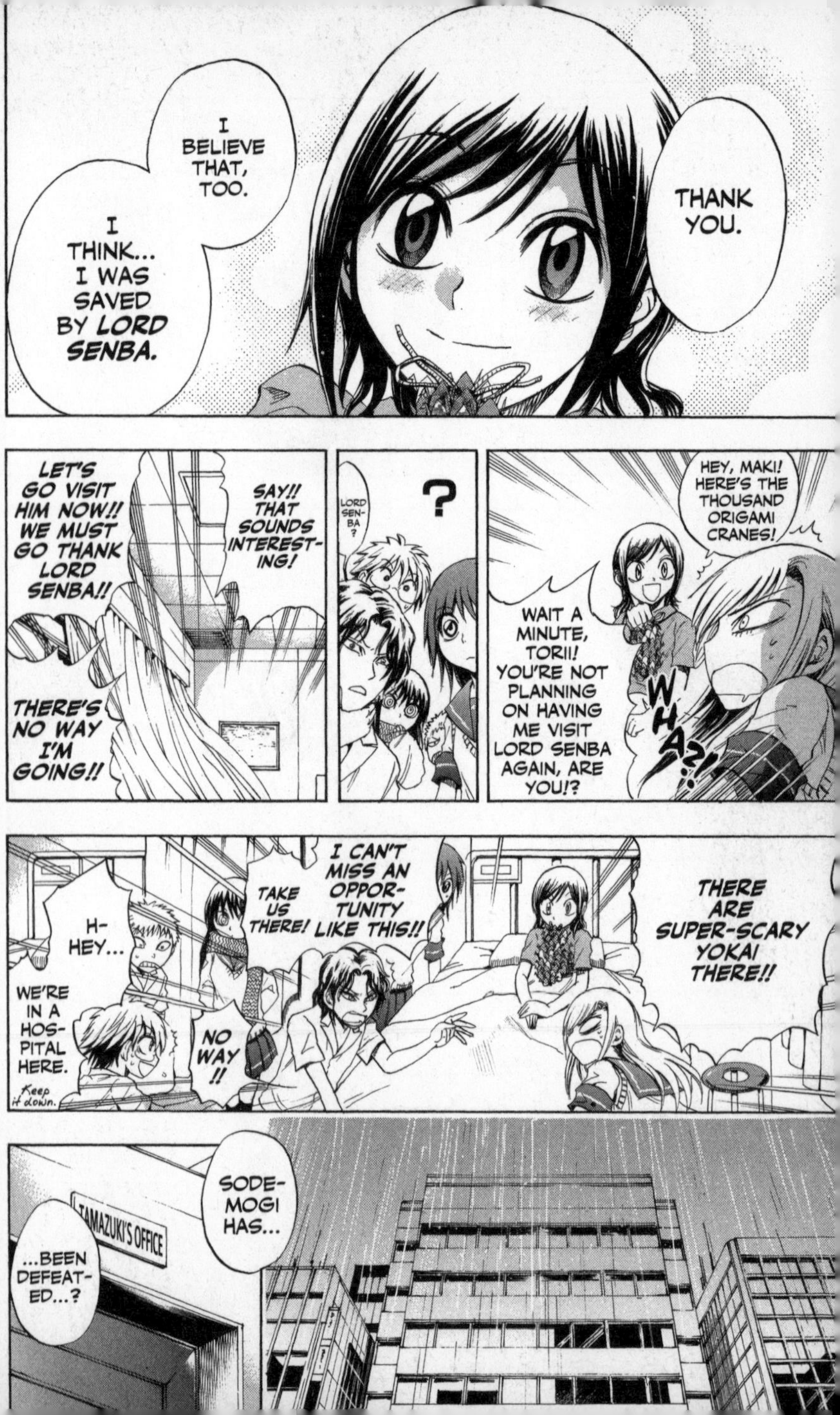
THANK YOU.
I BELIEVE THAT, TOO.
I THINK... I WAS SAVED BY LORD SENBA.
HEY, MAKI! HERE'S THE THOUSAND ORIGAMI CRANES!
WHA?!
WAIT A MINUTE, TORII! YOU'RE NOT PLANNING ON HAVING ME VISIT LORD SENBA AGAIN, ARE YOU!?
?
LORD SENBA?
SAY!! THAT SOUNDS INTERESTING!
LET'S GO VISIT HIM NOW!! WE MUST GO THANK LORD SENBA!!
THERE'S NO WAY I'M GOING!!
THERE ARE SUPER-SCARY YOKAI THERE!!
I CAN'T MISS AN OPPORTUNITY LIKE THIS!!
TAKE US THERE!
NO WAY!!
H-HEY...
WE'RE IN A HOSPITAL HERE.
Keep it down.
SODEMOGI HAS...
TAMAZUKI'S OFFICE
...BEEN DEFEATED...?

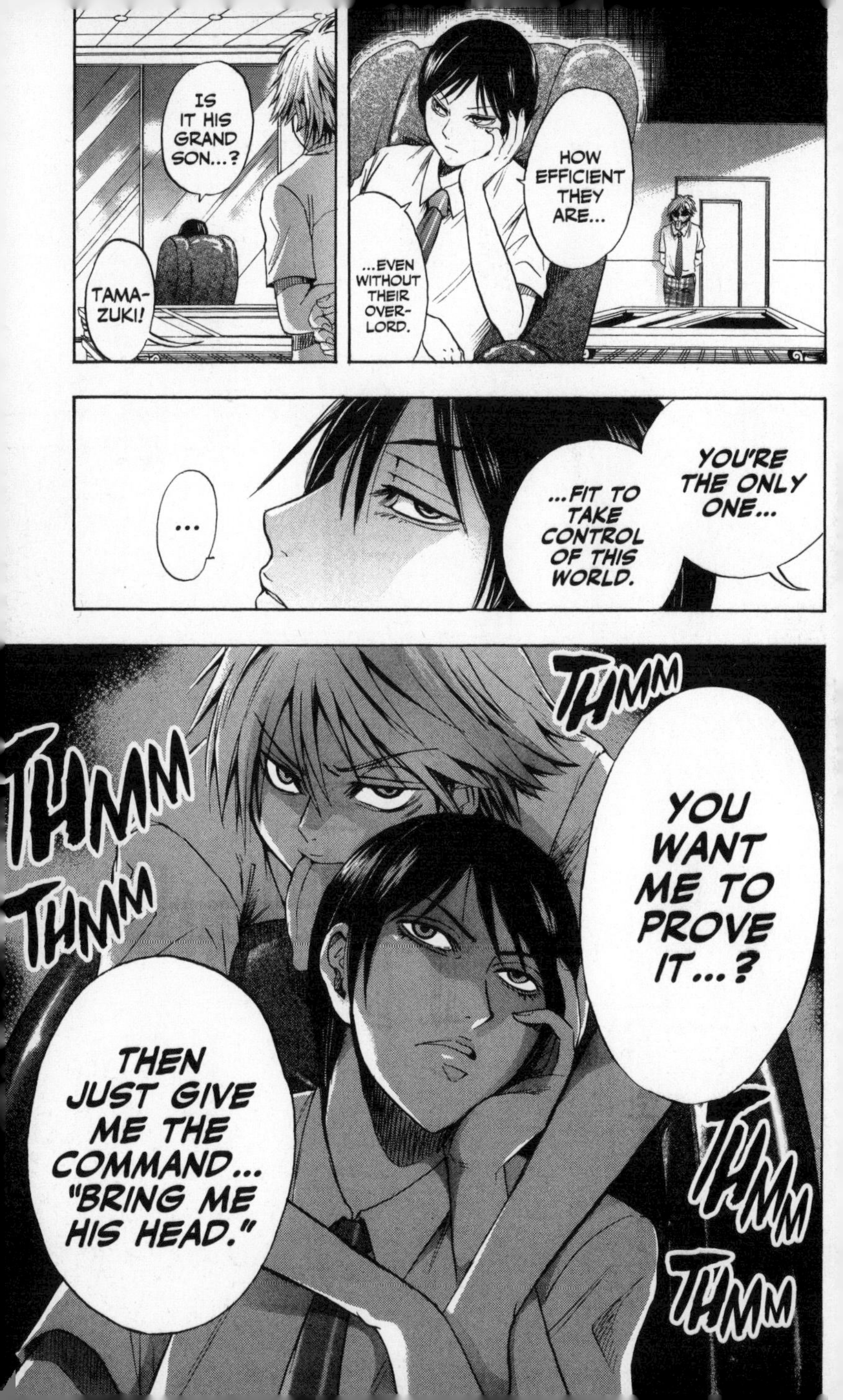
HOW EFFICIENT THEY ARE...
...EVEN WITHOUT THEIR OVER-LORD.
IS IT HIS GRAND SON...?
TAMA-ZUKI!
YOU'RE THE ONLY ONE...
...FIT TO TAKE CONTROL OF THIS WORLD.
...
THMM
YOU WANT ME TO PROVE IT...?
THMM
THMM
THEN JUST GIVE ME THE COMMAND... "BRING ME HIS HEAD."
THMM
THMM

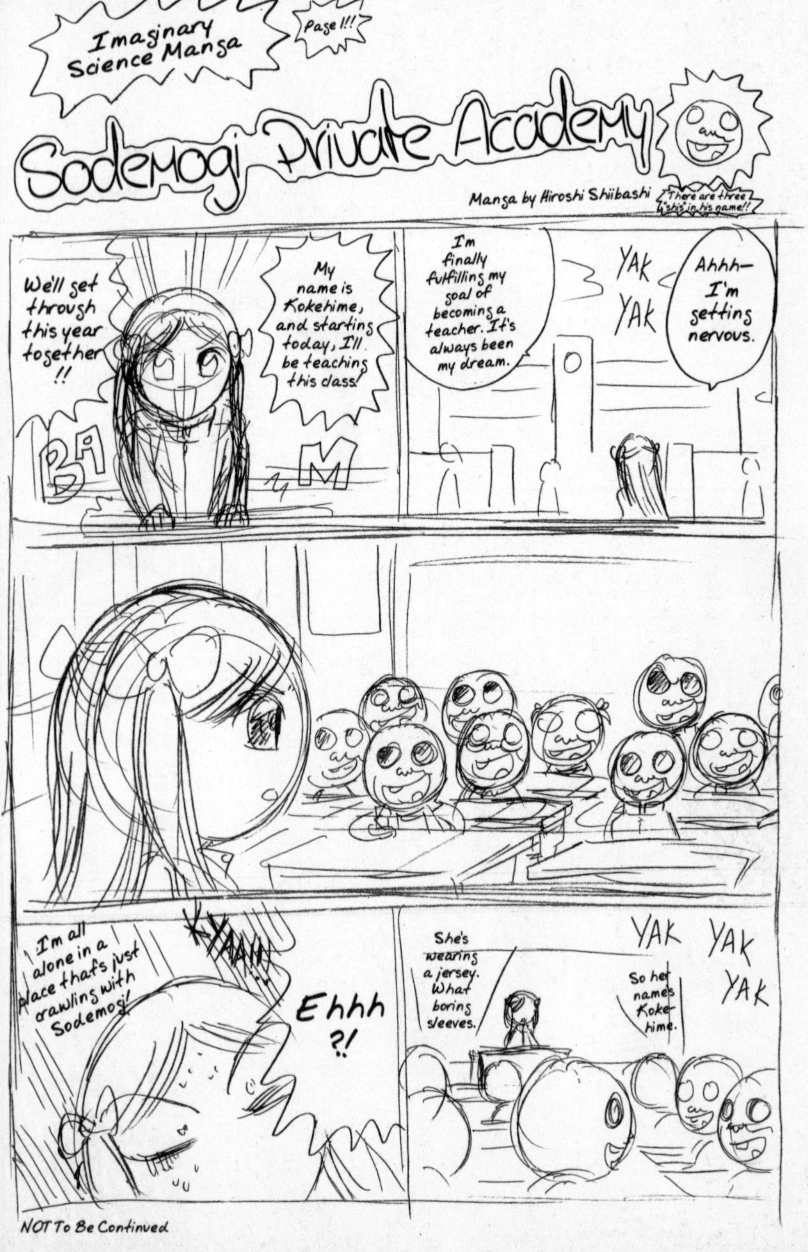
Imaginary Science Manga
Page!!!
Sodemogi Private Academy
Manga by Hiroshi Shiibashi
There are three "shi"s in his name!!
Ahhh— I'm getting nervous.
YAK YAK
I'm finally fulfilling my goal of becoming a teacher. It's always been my dream.
My name is Kokehime, and starting today, I'll be teaching this class!
We'll get through this year together!!
BAM
YAK YAK
YAK
So her name's Kokehime.
She's wearing a jersey. What boring sleeves.
Ehhh ?!
KYAAH
I'm all alone in a place that's just crawling with Sodemogi!
NOT To Be Continued

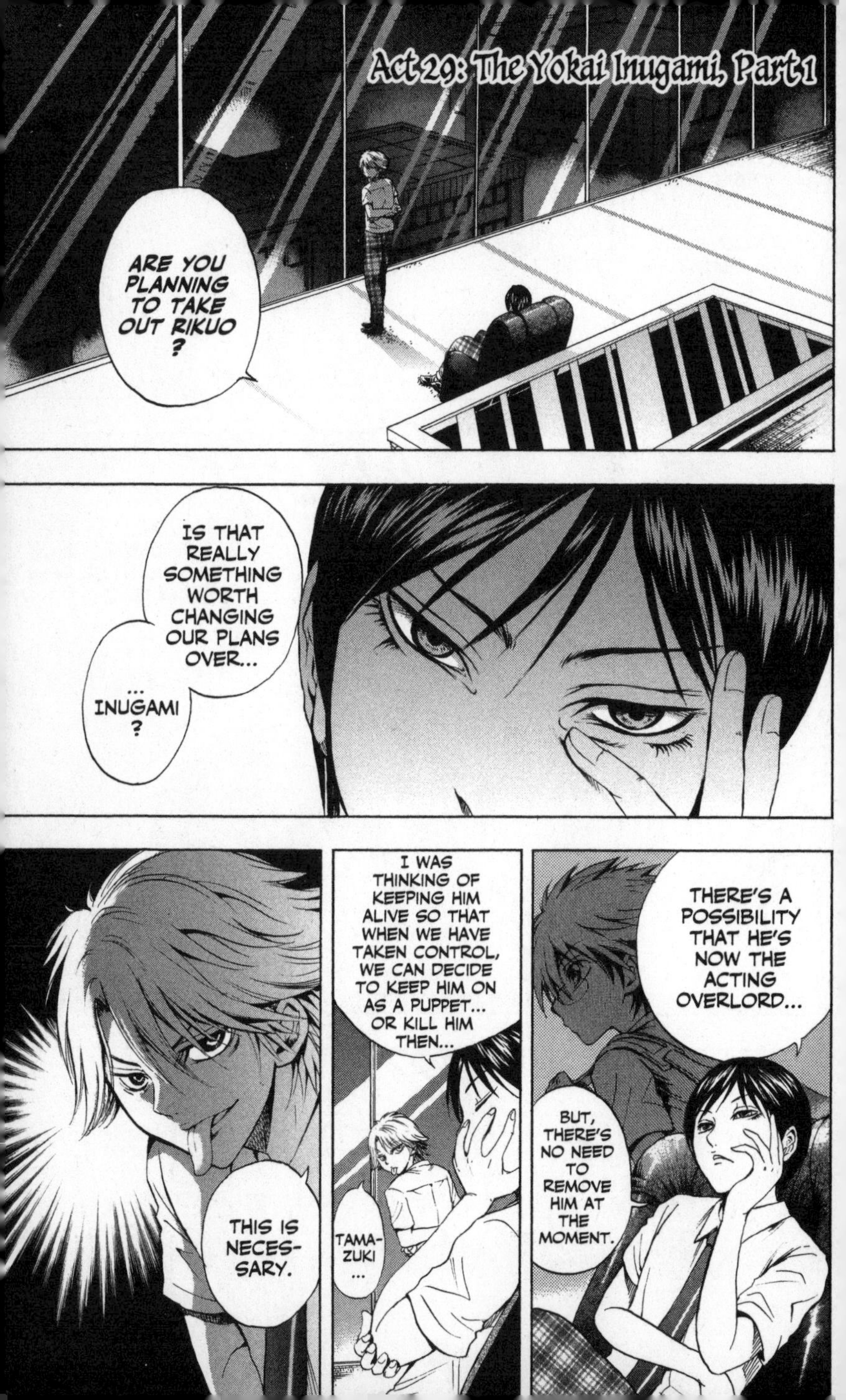
Act 29: The Yokai Inugami, Part 1
ARE YOU PLANNING TO TAKE OUT RIKUO?
IS THAT REALLY SOMETHING WORTH CHANGING OUR PLANS OVER...
...INUGAMI?
THERE'S A POSSIBILITY THAT HE'S NOW THE ACTING OVERLORD...
BUT, THERE'S NO NEED TO REMOVE HIM AT THE MOMENT.
I WAS THINKING OF KEEPING HIM ALIVE SO THAT WHEN WE HAVE TAKEN CONTROL, WE CAN DECIDE TO KEEP HIM ON AS A PUPPET... OR KILL HIM THEN...
TAMAZUKI...
THIS IS NECESSARY.

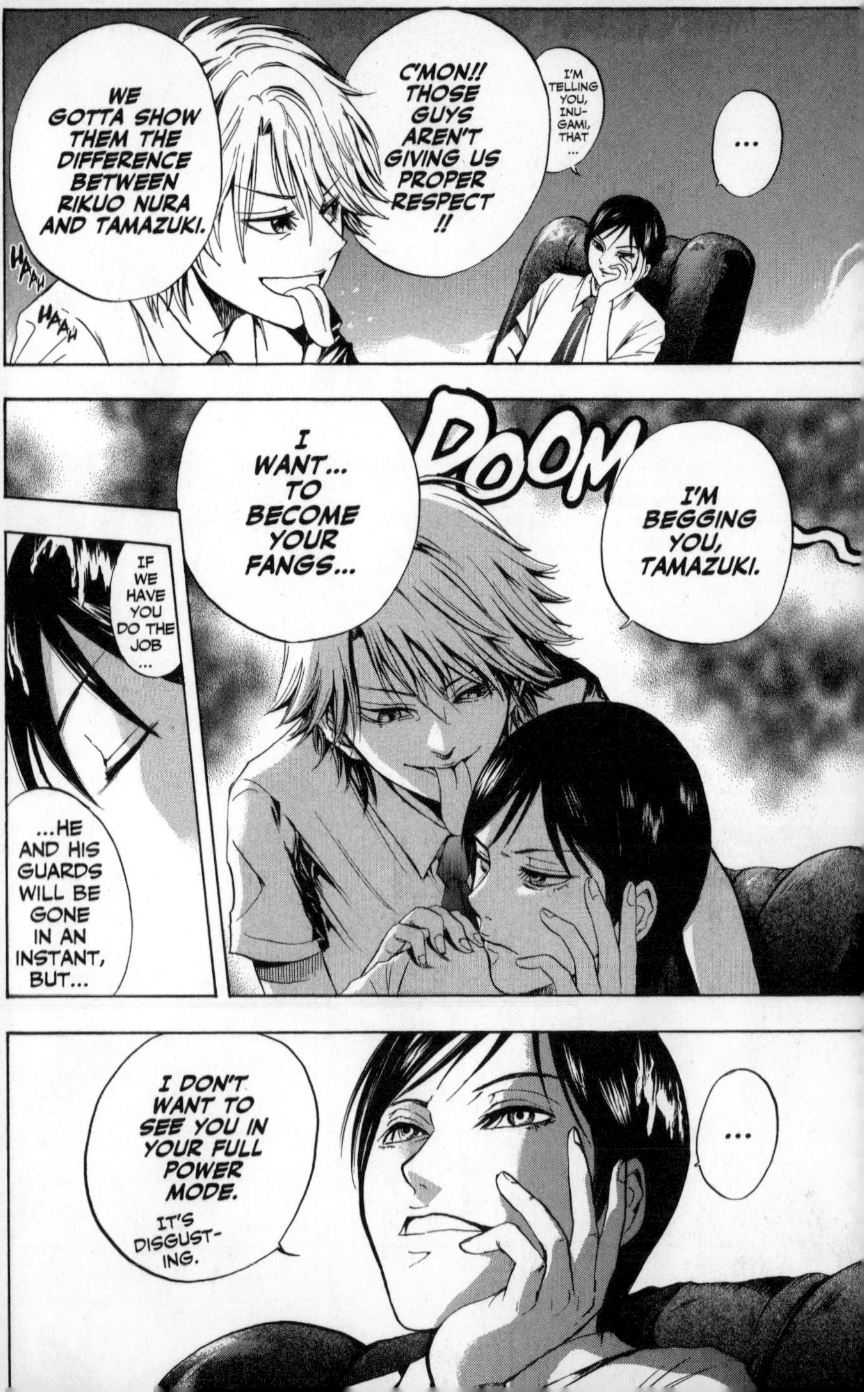
...
I'M TELLING YOU, INUGAMI, THAT ...
C'MON!! THOSE GUYS AREN'T GIVING US PROPER RESPECT !!
WE GOTTA SHOW THEM THE DIFFERENCE BETWEEN RIKUO NURA AND TAMAZUKI.
HAAH
HAAH
DOOM
I'M BEGGING YOU, TAMAZUKI.
I WANT... TO BECOME YOUR FANGS...
IF WE HAVE YOU DO THE JOB ...
...HE AND HIS GUARDS WILL BE GONE IN AN INSTANT, BUT...
...
I DON'T WANT TO SEE YOU IN YOUR FULL POWER MODE.
IT'S DISGUSTING.

Act 29: The Yokai Inugami, Part 1

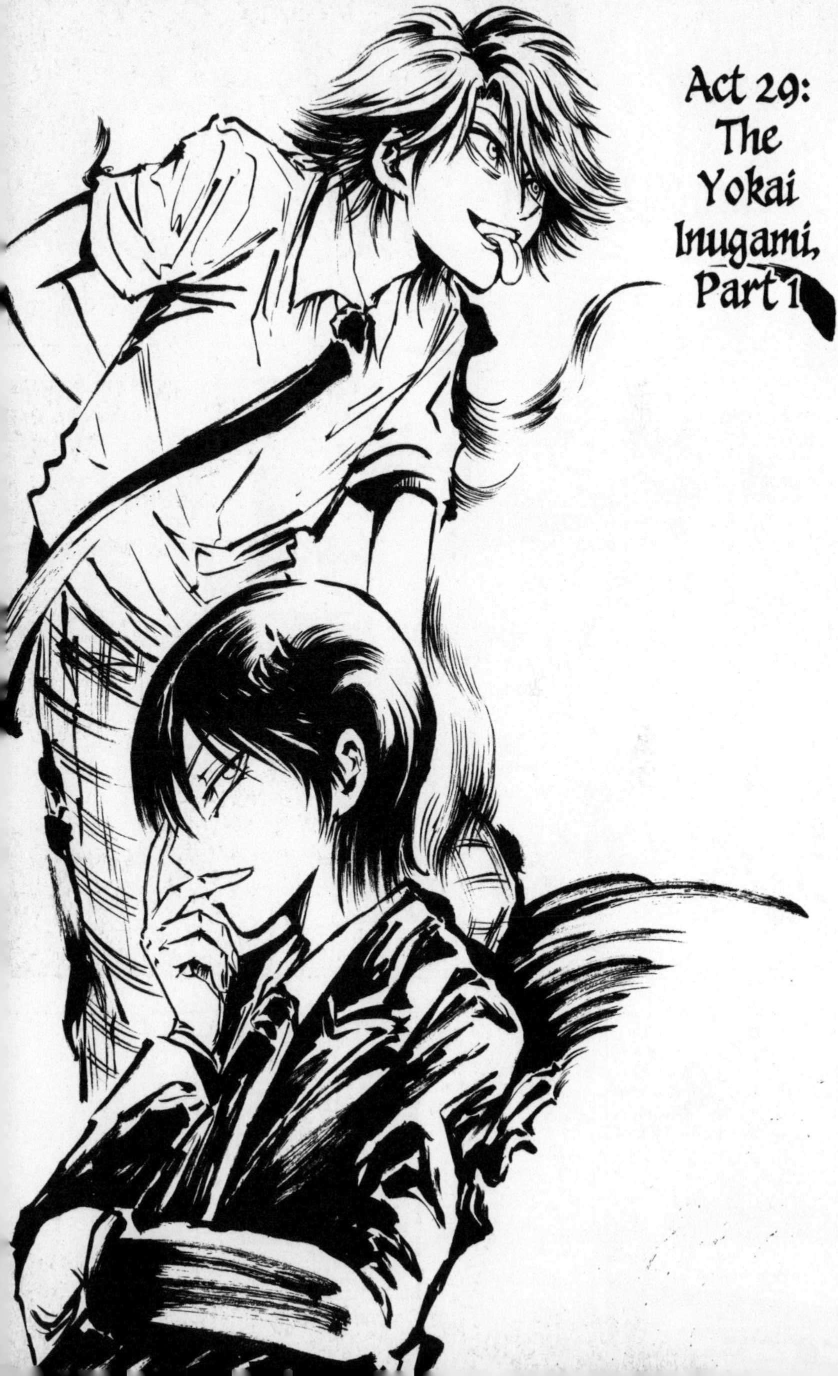

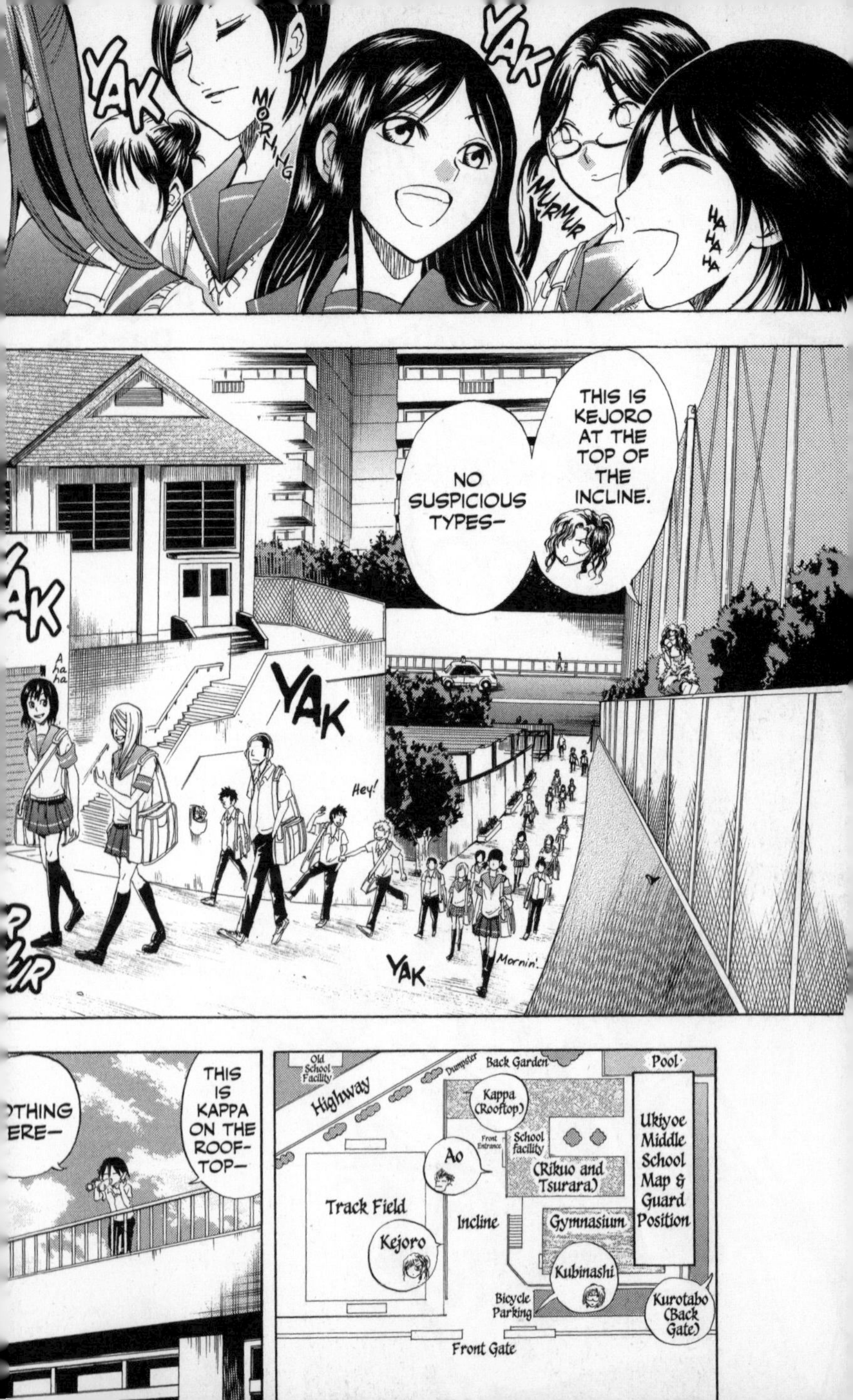
HA HA HA HA
MURMUR
YAK
MORNING
YAK
THIS IS KEJORO AT THE TOP OF THE INCLINE.
NO SUSPICIOUS TYPES—
YAK
Hey!
A ha ha
YAK
Mornin'.
Pool
Back Garden
Dumpster
Old School Facility
Highway
Ukiyoe Middle School Map & Guard Position
Kappa (Rooftop)
School facility
Front Entrance
Ao
(Rikuo and Tsurara)
Track Field
Incline
Gymnasium
Kejoro
Kubinashi
Kurotabo (Back Gate)
Bicycle Parking
Front Gate
THIS IS KAPPA ON THE ROOF-TOP—

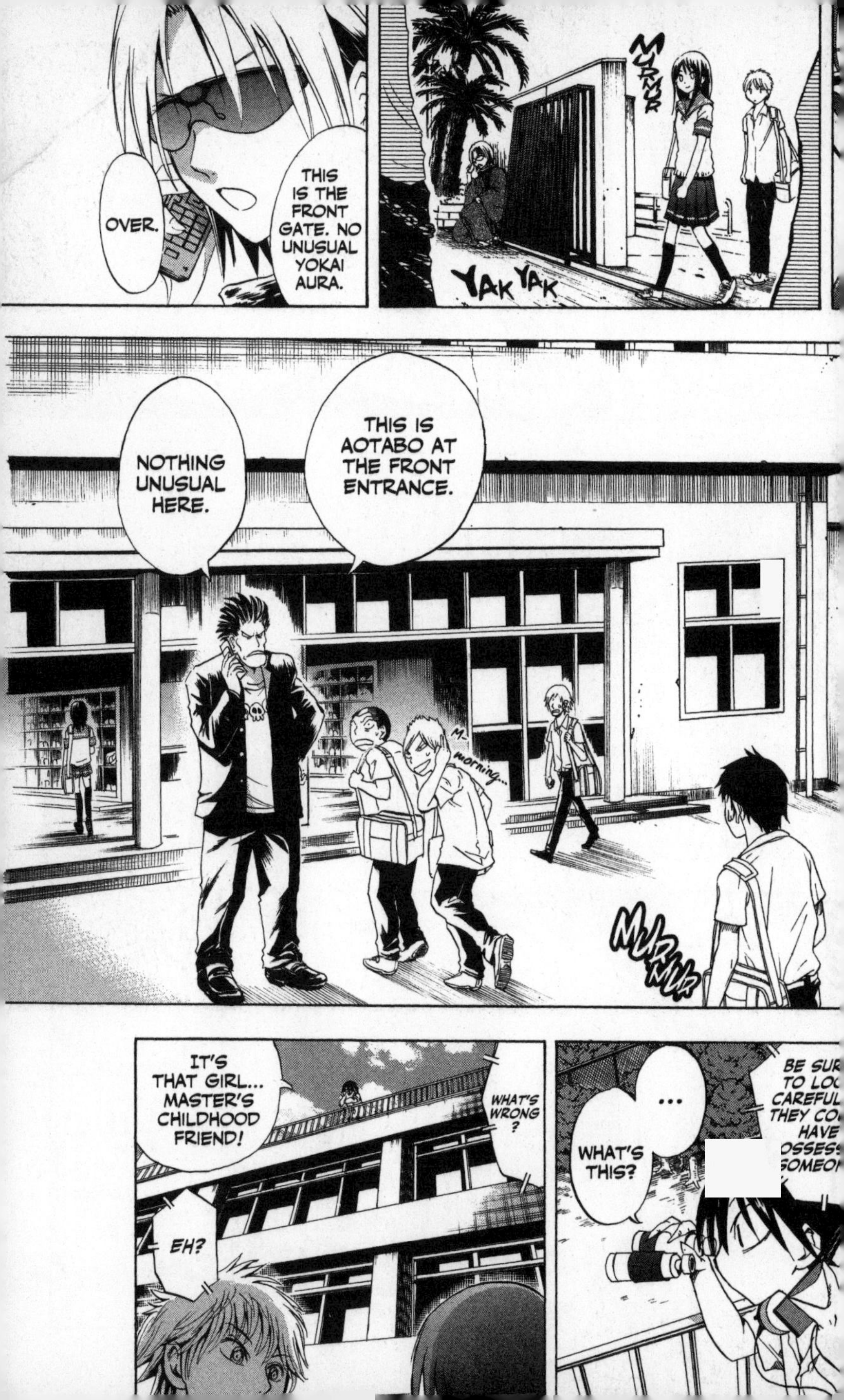
MURMUR
YAK YAK
THIS IS THE FRONT GATE. NO UNUSUAL YOKAI AURA.
OVER.
THIS IS AOTABO AT THE FRONT ENTRANCE.
NOTHING UNUSUAL HERE.
M-morning...
MURMUR
BE SUR TO LOC CAREFUL THEY CO HAVE OSSES SOMEO
...
WHAT'S THIS?
WHAT'S WRONG?
IT'S THAT GIRL... MASTER'S CHILDHOOD FRIEND!
EH?

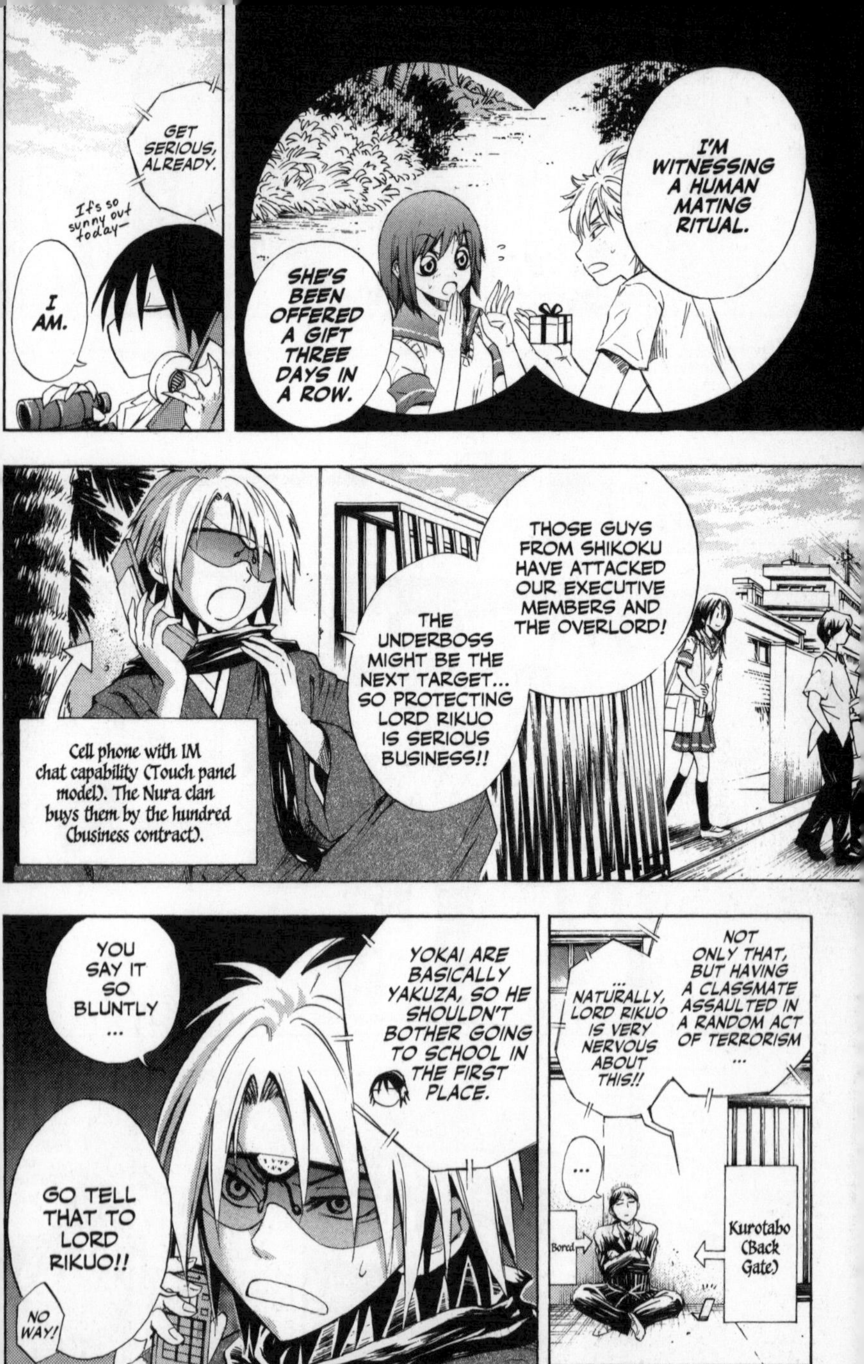
I'M WITNESSING A HUMAN MATING RITUAL.
SHE'S BEEN OFFERED A GIFT THREE DAYS IN A ROW.
GET SERIOUS, ALREADY.
It's so sunny out today—
I AM.
THOSE GUYS FROM SHIKOKU HAVE ATTACKED OUR EXECUTIVE MEMBERS AND THE OVERLORD!
THE UNDERBOSS MIGHT BE THE NEXT TARGET... SO PROTECTING LORD RIKUO IS SERIOUS BUSINESS!!
Cell phone with IM chat capability (Touch panel model). The Nura clan buys them by the hundred (business contract).
NOT ONLY THAT, BUT HAVING A CLASSMATE ASSAULTED IN A RANDOM ACT OF TERRORISM ...
... NATURALLY, LORD RIKUO IS VERY NERVOUS ABOUT THIS!!
...
Bored
Kurotabo (Back Gate)
YOKAI ARE BASICALLY YAKUZA, SO HE SHOULDN'T BOTHER GOING TO SCHOOL IN THE FIRST PLACE.
YOU SAY IT SO BLUNTLY ...
GO TELL THAT TO LORD RIKUO!!
NO WAY!

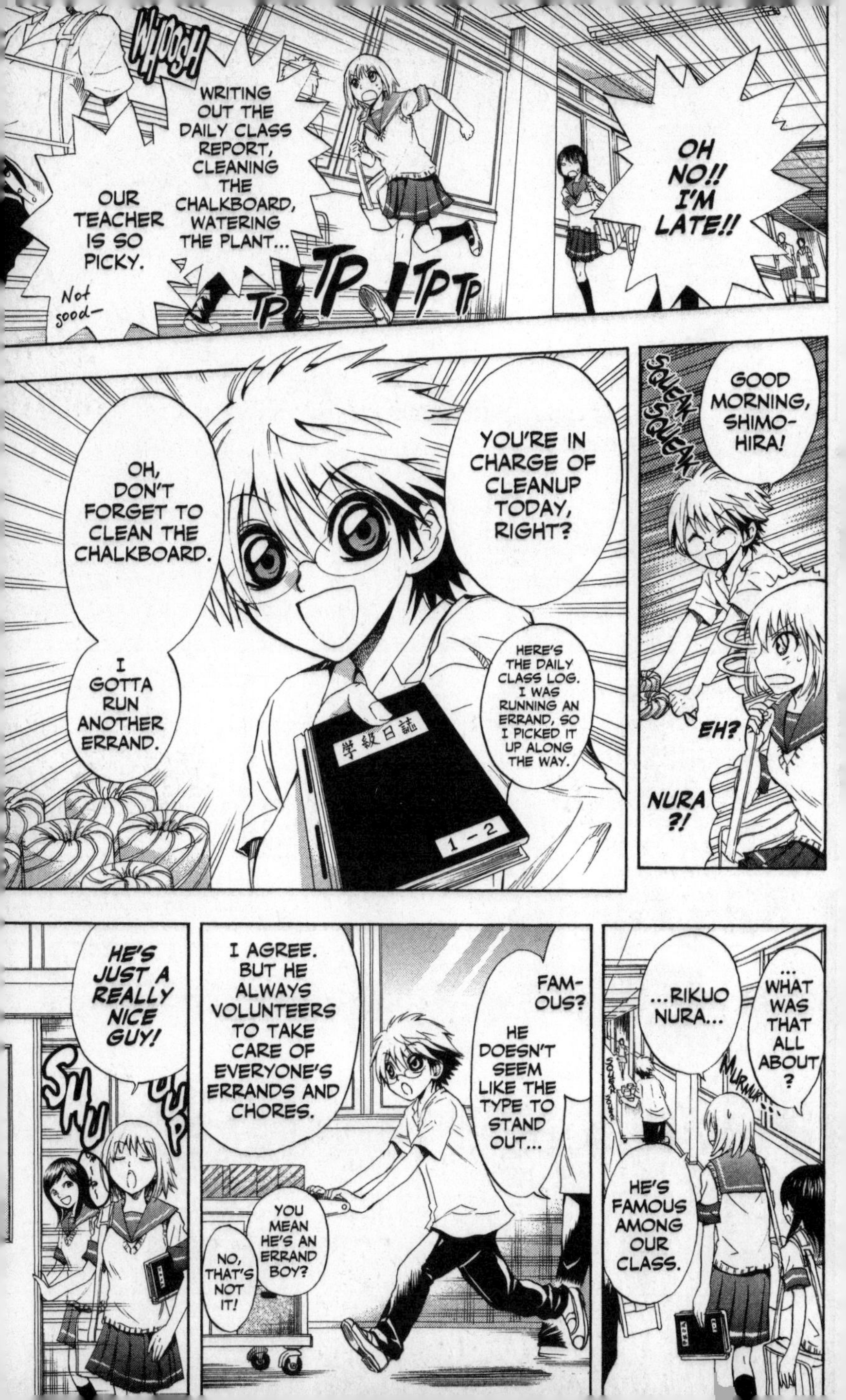
OH NO!! I'M LATE!!
WHOOSH
WRITING OUT THE DAILY CLASS REPORT, CLEANING THE CHALKBOARD, WATERING THE PLANT...
OUR TEACHER IS SO PICKY.
Not good—
TP TP TP TP
SQUEAK SQUEAK
GOOD MORNING, SHIMOHIRA!
EH?
NURA?!
YOU'RE IN CHARGE OF CLEANUP TODAY, RIGHT?
HERE'S THE DAILY CLASS LOG. I WAS RUNNING AN ERRAND, SO I PICKED IT UP ALONG THE WAY.
学級日誌
1-2
OH, DON'T FORGET TO CLEAN THE CHALKBOARD.
I GOTTA RUN ANOTHER ERRAND.
... WHAT WAS THAT ALL ABOUT?
MURMUR
...RIKUO NURA...
HE'S FAMOUS AMONG OUR CLASS.
FAMOUS?
HE DOESN'T SEEM LIKE THE TYPE TO STAND OUT...
I AGREE. BUT HE ALWAYS VOLUNTEERS TO TAKE CARE OF EVERYONE'S ERRANDS AND CHORES.
YOU MEAN HE'S AN ERRAND BOY?
NO, THAT'S NOT IT!
HE'S JUST A REALLY NICE GUY!

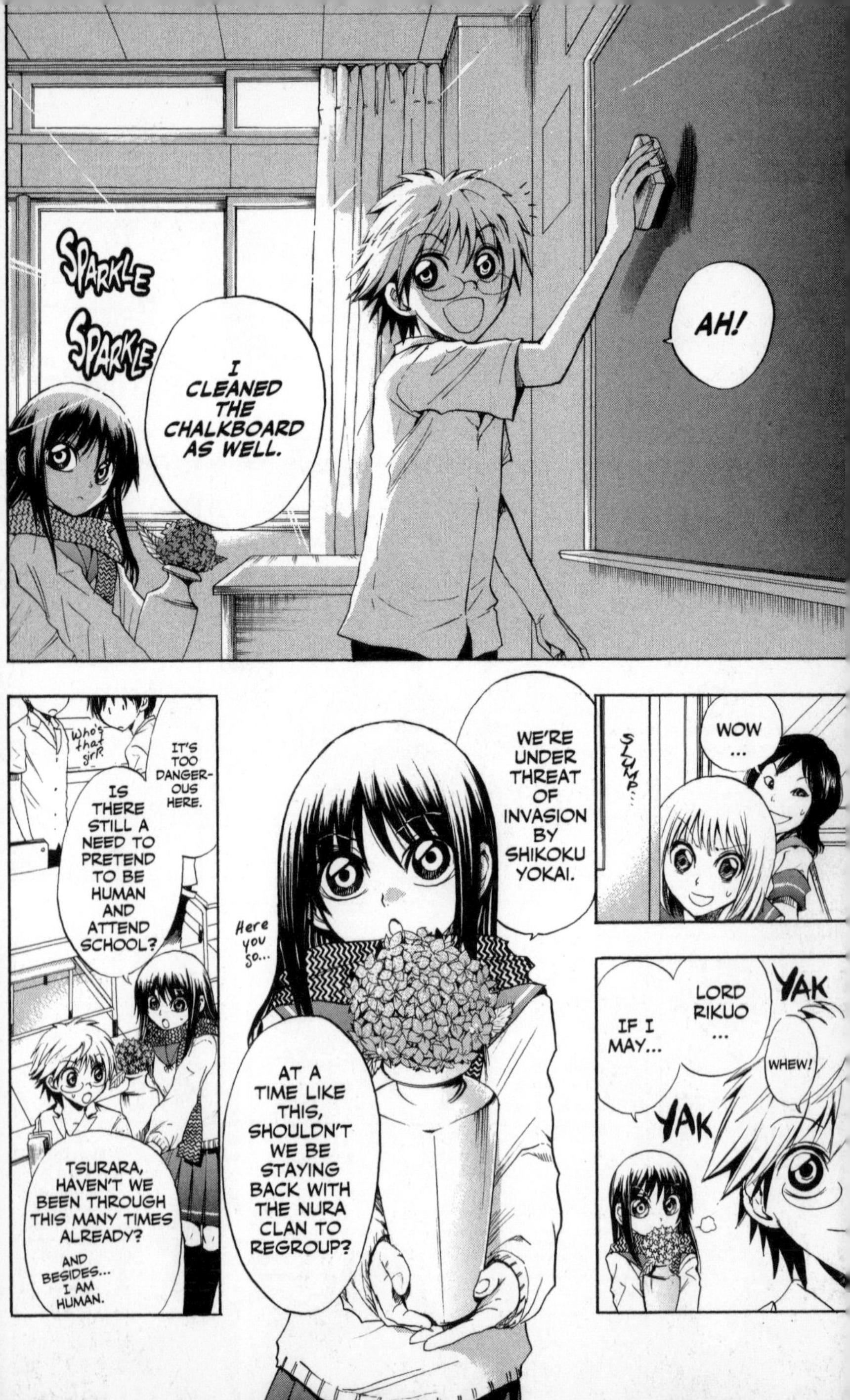
AH!
I CLEANED THE CHALKBOARD AS WELL.
SPARKLE
SPARKLE
WOW...
SLUMP...
YAK
LORD RIKUO...
WHEW!
IF I MAY...
YAK
WE'RE UNDER THREAT OF INVASION BY SHIKOKU YOKAI.
Here you go...
AT A TIME LIKE THIS, SHOULDN'T WE BE STAYING BACK WITH THE NURA CLAN TO REGROUP?
IT'S TOO DANGEROUS HERE.
Who's that girl?
IS THERE STILL A NEED TO PRETEND TO BE HUMAN AND ATTEND SCHOOL?
TSURARA, HAVEN'T WE BEEN THROUGH THIS MANY TIMES ALREADY?
AND BESIDES... I AM HUMAN.

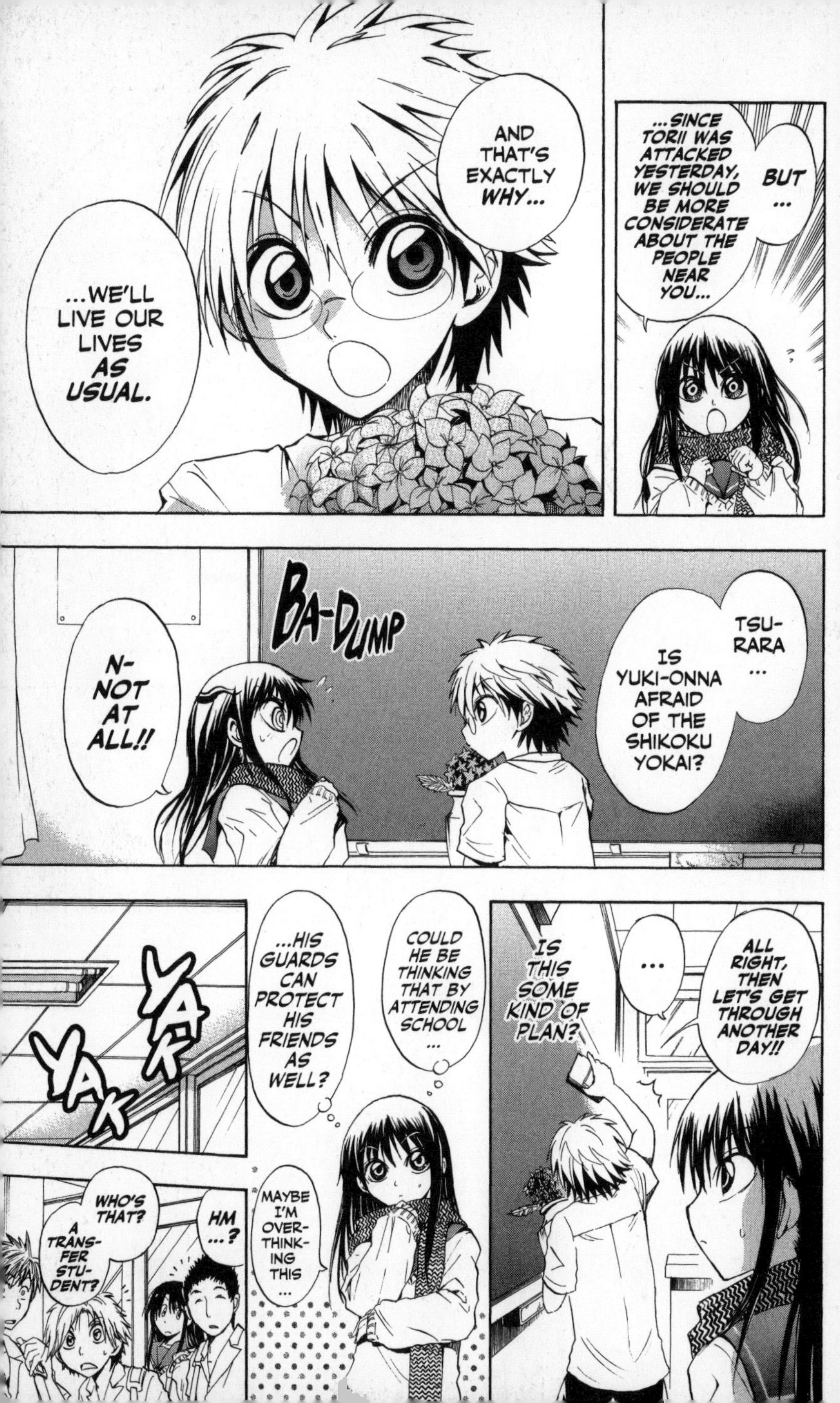
BUT...
...SINCE TORII WAS ATTACKED YESTERDAY, WE SHOULD BE MORE CONSIDERATE ABOUT THE PEOPLE NEAR YOU...
AND THAT'S EXACTLY WHY...
...WE'LL LIVE OUR LIVES AS USUAL.
TSU-RARA...
IS YUKI-ONNA AFRAID OF THE SHIKOKU YOKAI?
BA-DUMP
N-NOT AT ALL!!
ALL RIGHT, THEN LET'S GET THROUGH ANOTHER DAY!!
...
IS THIS SOME KIND OF PLAN?
COULD HE BE THINKING THAT BY ATTENDING SCHOOL...
...HIS GUARDS CAN PROTECT HIS FRIENDS AS WELL?
MAYBE I'M OVER-THINK-ING THIS...
YAK YAK
HM...?
WHO'S THAT?
A TRANS-FER STU-DENT?

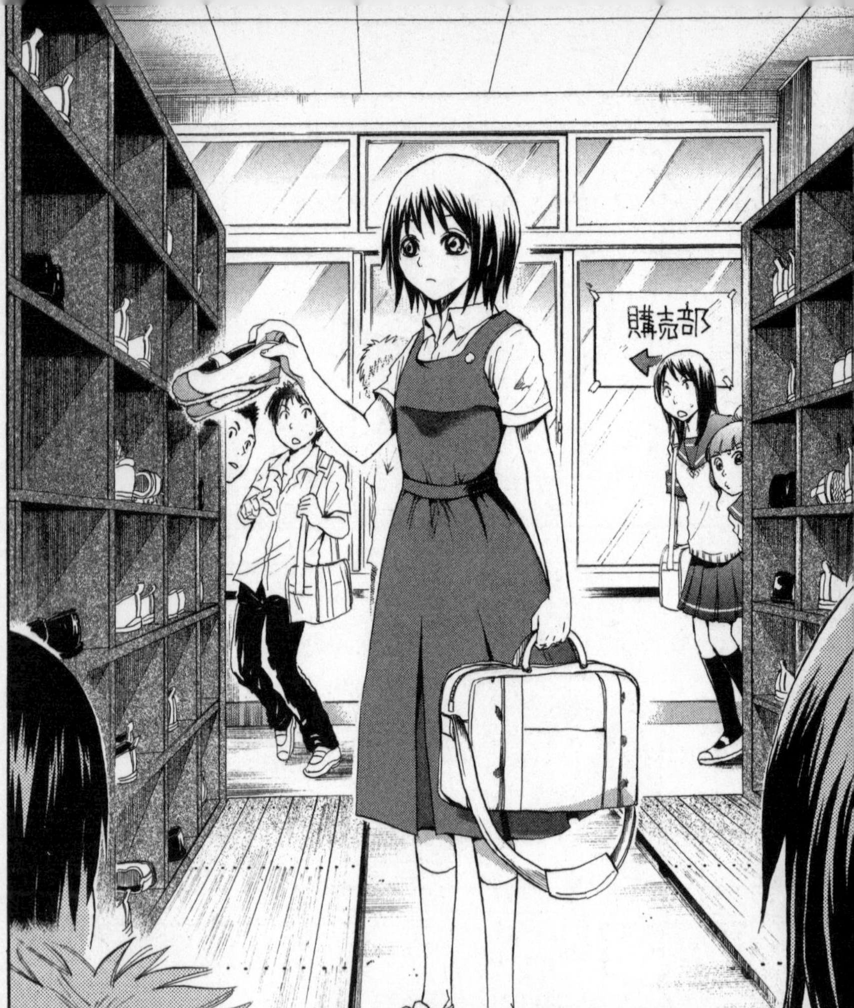
購売部
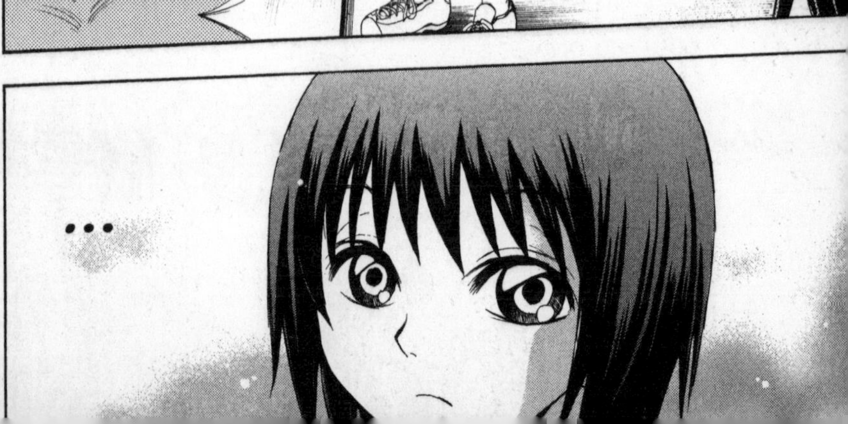
...

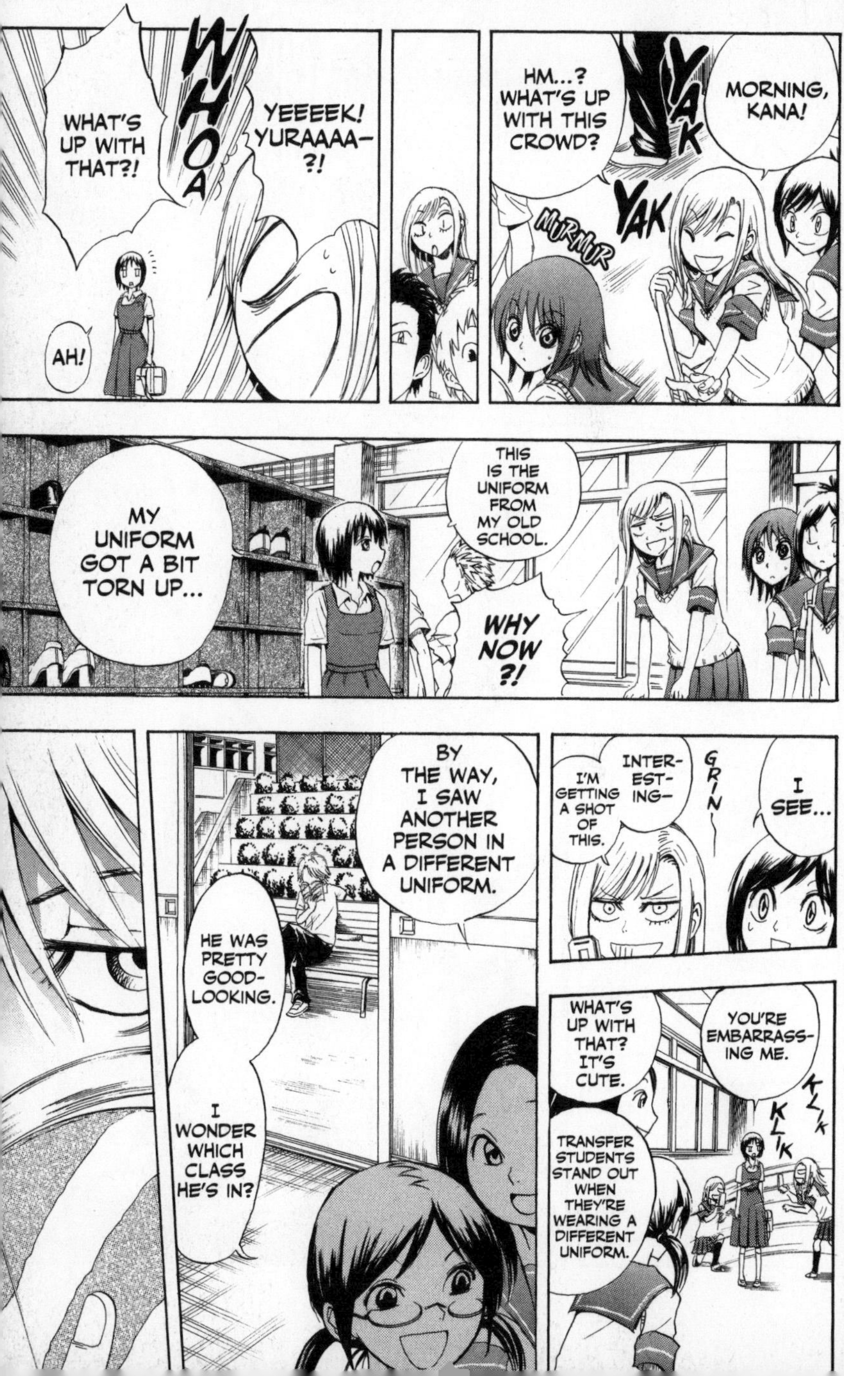
MORNING, KANA!
YAK
YAK
HM...? WHAT'S UP WITH THIS CROWD?
MURMUR
YEEEEK! YURAAAA—?!
WHOA
WHAT'S UP WITH THAT?!
AH!
THIS IS THE UNIFORM FROM MY OLD SCHOOL.
WHY NOW?!
MY UNIFORM GOT A BIT TORN UP...
I SEE...
GRIN
INTER-EST-ING—
I'M GETTING A SHOT OF THIS.
YOU'RE EMBARRASS-ING ME.
WHAT'S UP WITH THAT? IT'S CUTE.
KLIK
KLIK
TRANSFER STUDENTS STAND OUT WHEN THEY'RE WEARING A DIFFERENT UNIFORM.
BY THE WAY, I SAW ANOTHER PERSON IN A DIFFERENT UNIFORM.
HE WAS PRETTY GOOD-LOOKING.
I WONDER WHICH CLASS HE'S IN?

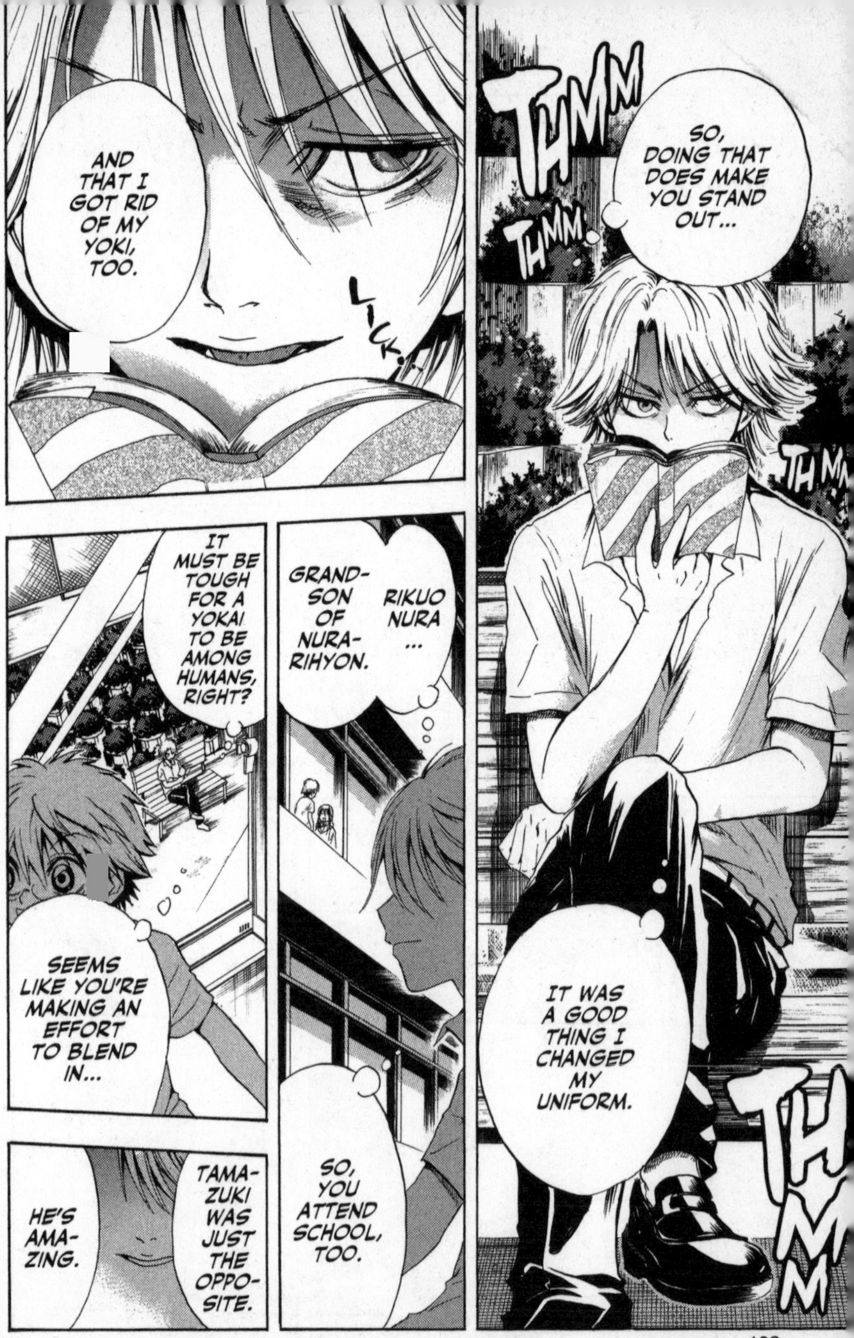
THMM
SO, DOING THAT DOES MAKE YOU STAND OUT...
THMM
THMM
IT WAS A GOOD THING I CHANGED MY UNIFORM.
THMM
AND THAT I GOT RID OF MY YOKI, TOO.
LICK...
RIKUO NURA...
GRAND-SON OF NURA-RIHYON.
SO, YOU ATTEND SCHOOL, TOO.
IT MUST BE TOUGH FOR A YOKAI TO BE AMONG HUMANS, RIGHT?
SEEMS LIKE YOU'RE MAKING AN EFFORT TO BLEND IN...
TAMA-ZUKI WAS JUST THE OPPO-SITE.
HE'S AMA-ZING.

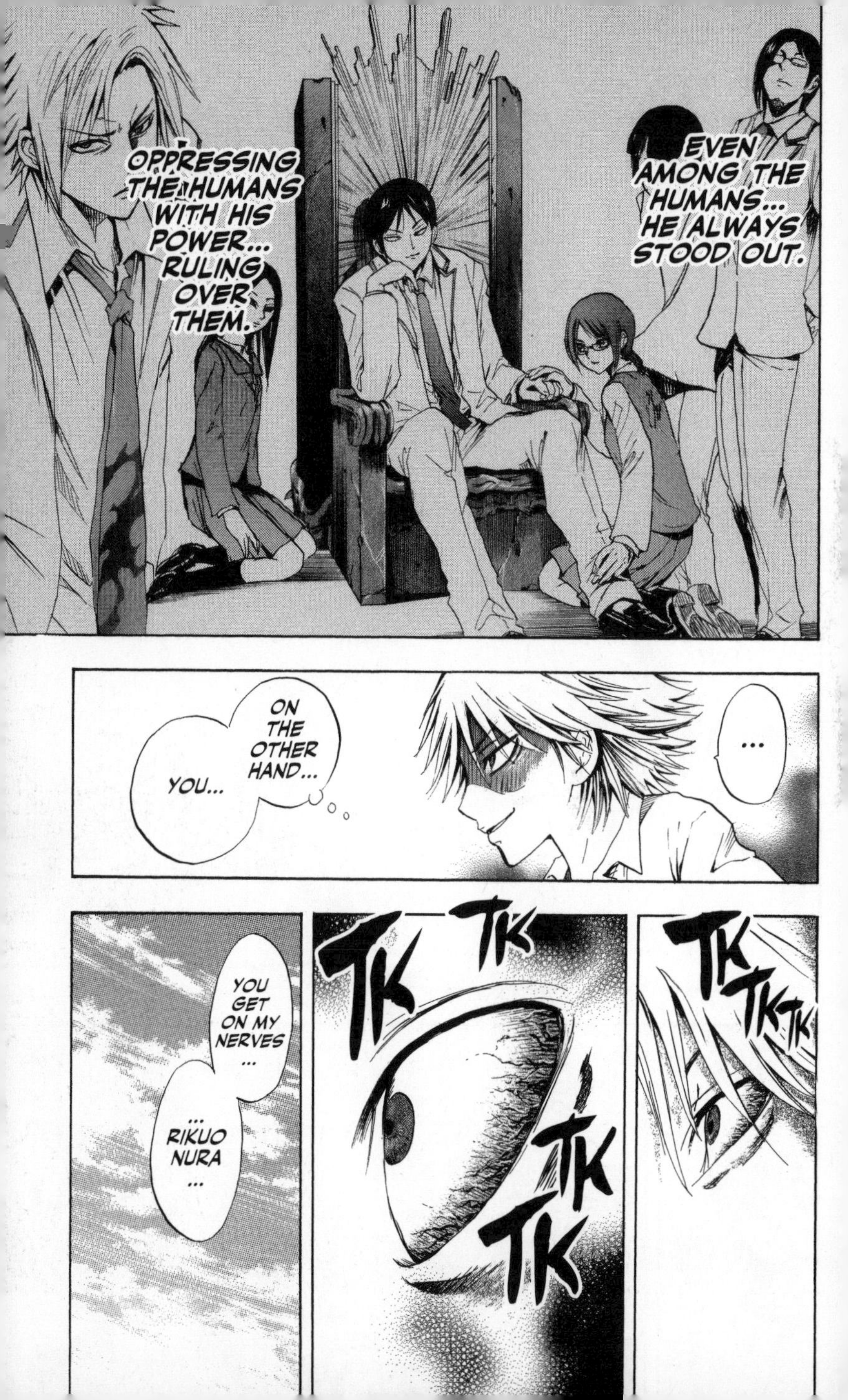
EVEN AMONG THE HUMANS... HE ALWAYS STOOD OUT.
OPPRESSING THE HUMANS WITH HIS POWER... RULING OVER THEM.
...
ON THE OTHER HAND... YOU...
TK TK TK-TK
TK TK TK TK
YOU GET ON MY NERVES...
...RIKUO NURA...

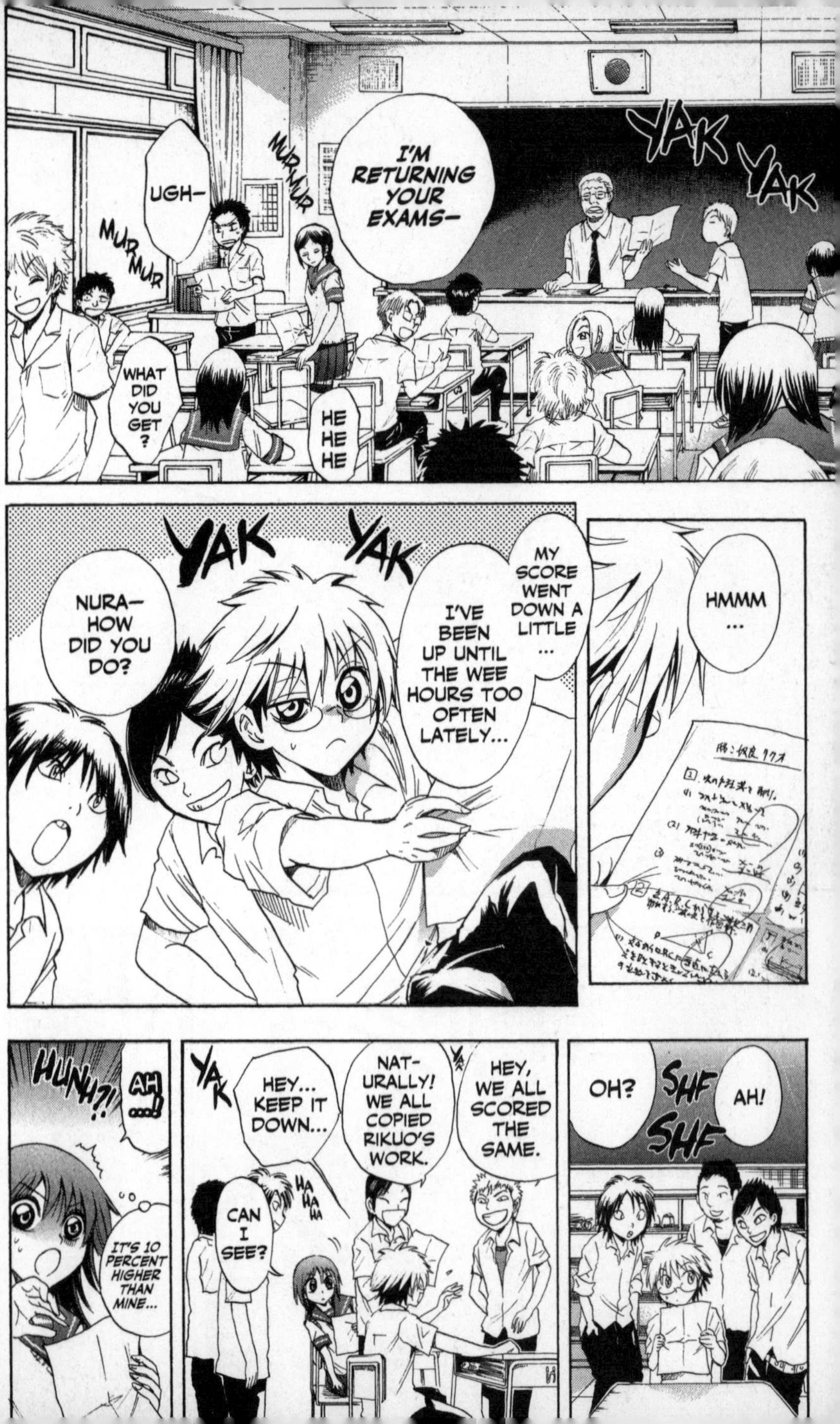
YAK YAK
I'M RETURNING YOUR EXAMS—
MURMUR
UGH—
MURMUR
HE HE HE
WHAT DID YOU GET?
HMMM...
MY SCORE WENT DOWN A LITTLE...
I'VE BEEN UP UNTIL THE WEE HOURS TOO OFTEN LATELY...
YAK YAK
NURA— HOW DID YOU DO?
AH!
SHF SHF
OH?
HEY, WE ALL SCORED THE SAME.
YAK
NAT-URALLY! WE ALL COPIED RIKUO'S WORK.
HEY... KEEP IT DOWN...
YAK
HA HA HA
CAN I SEE?
AH...!
HUNH?!
IT'S 10 PERCENT HIGHER THAN MINE...

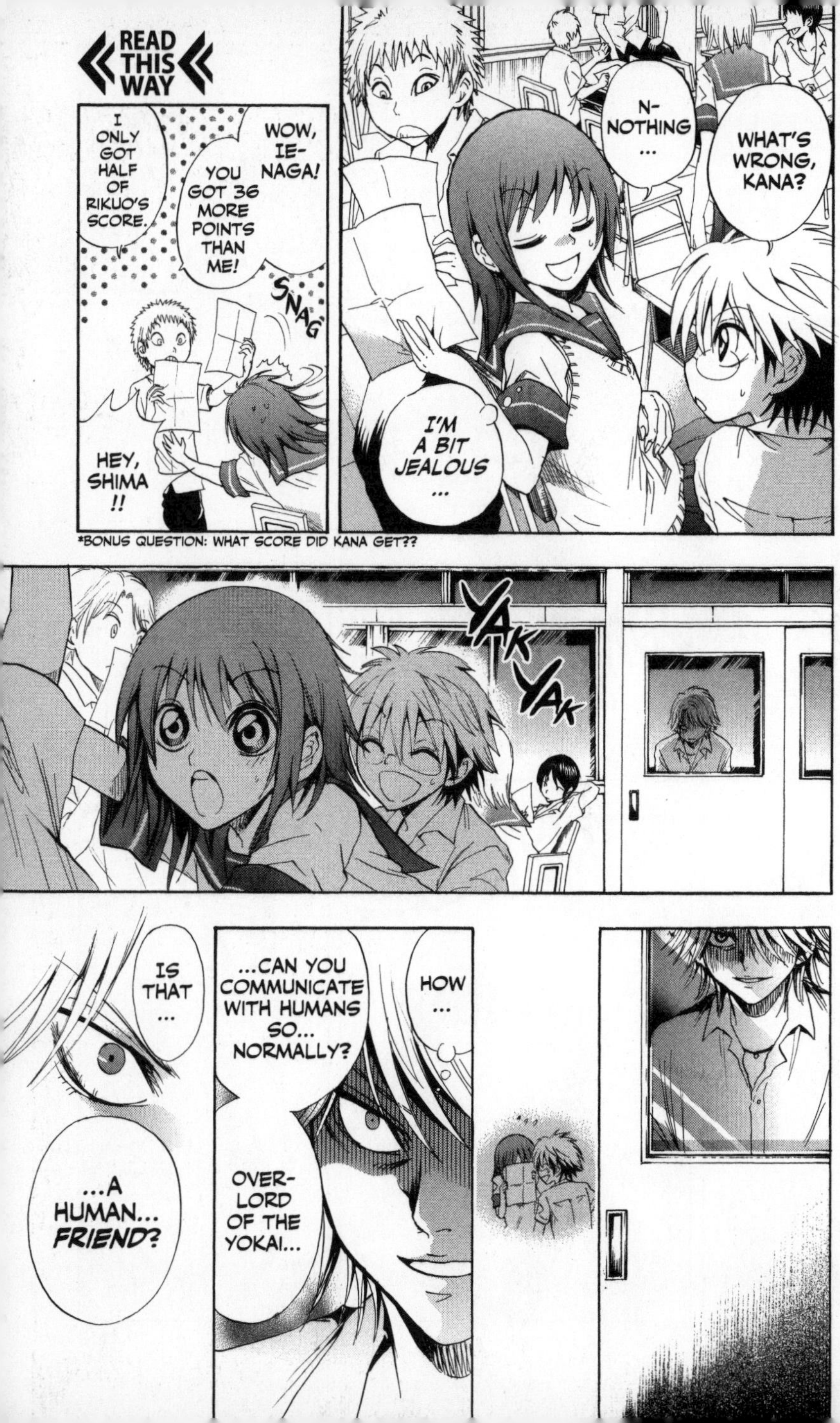
READ THIS WAY
WHAT'S WRONG, KANA?
N-NOTHING...
I'M A BIT JEALOUS...
WOW, IE-NAGA! YOU GOT 36 MORE POINTS THAN ME!
I ONLY GOT HALF OF RIKUO'S SCORE.
SNAG
HEY, SHIMA!!
*BONUS QUESTION: WHAT SCORE DID KANA GET??
YAK YAK
HOW...
...CAN YOU COMMUNICATE WITH HUMANS SO... NORMALLY?
OVER-LORD OF THE YOKAI...
IS THAT...
...A HUMAN... FRIEND?

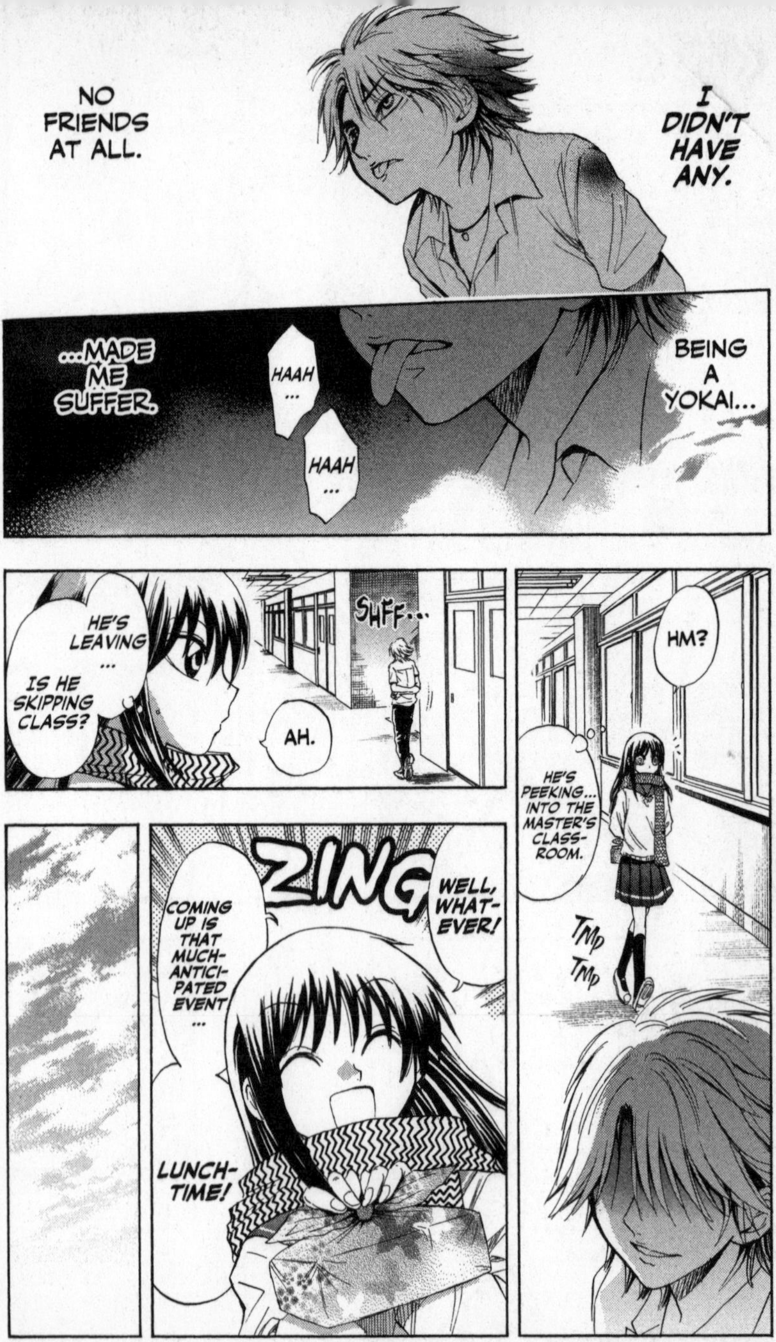
I DIDN'T HAVE ANY.
NO FRIENDS AT ALL.
BEING A YOKAI...
HAAH ...
HAAH ...
...MADE ME SUFFER.
HM?
HE'S PEEKING... INTO THE MASTER'S CLASS-ROOM.
TMP TMP
SHFF...
HE'S LEAVING ... IS HE SKIPPING CLASS?
AH.
WELL, WHAT-EVER!
ZING
COMING UP IS THAT MUCH-ANTICI-PATED EVENT ...
LUNCH-TIME!

READ THIS WAY

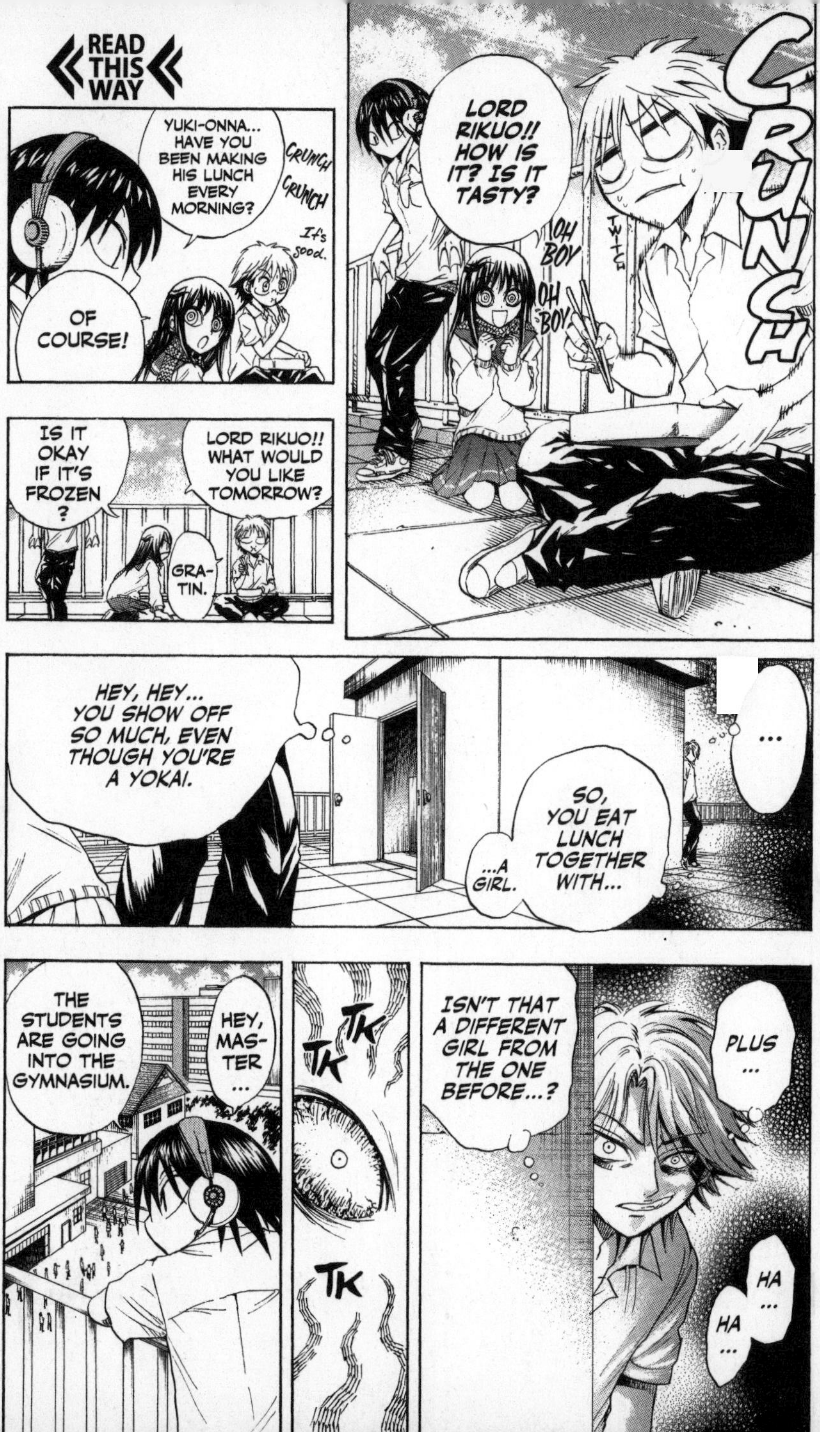
CRUNCH
LORD RIKUO!! HOW IS IT? IS IT TASTY?
TWITCH
OH BOY
OH BOY
YUKI-ONNA... HAVE YOU BEEN MAKING HIS LUNCH EVERY MORNING?
CRUNCH
CRUNCH
It's good.
OF COURSE!
LORD RIKUO!! WHAT WOULD YOU LIKE TOMORROW?
IS IT OKAY IF IT'S FROZEN?
GRA-TIN.
...
SO, YOU EAT LUNCH TOGETHER WITH...
...A GIRL.
HEY, HEY... YOU SHOW OFF SO MUCH, EVEN THOUGH YOU'RE A YOKAI.
PLUS...
ISN'T THAT A DIFFERENT GIRL FROM THE ONE BEFORE...?
HA...
HA...
TK
TK
TK
HEY, MASTER...
THE STUDENTS ARE GOING INTO THE GYMNASIUM.

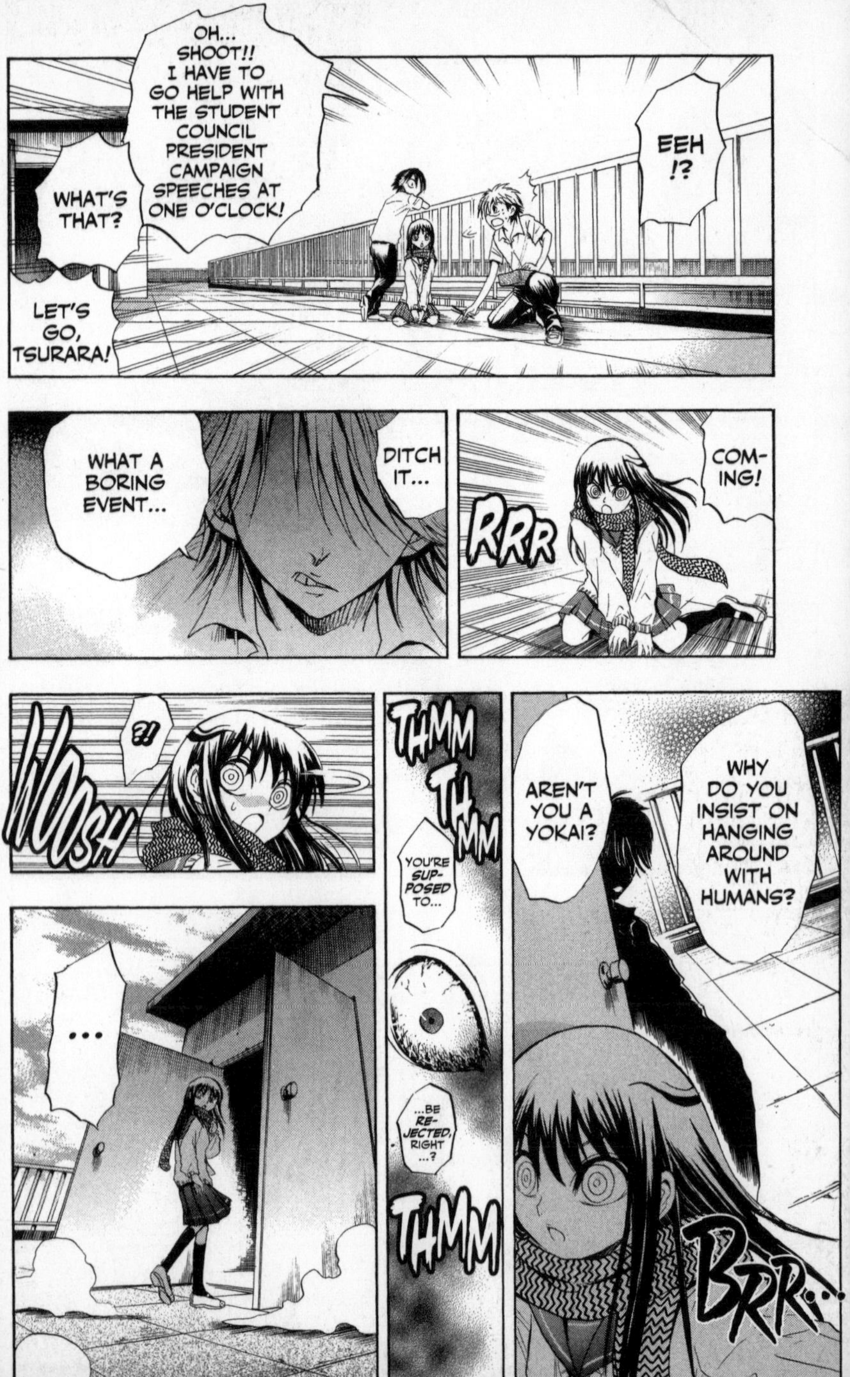
OH... SHOOT!! I HAVE TO GO HELP WITH THE STUDENT COUNCIL PRESIDENT CAMPAIGN SPEECHES AT ONE O'CLOCK!
EEH !?
WHAT'S THAT?
LET'S GO, TSURARA!
COM-ING!
RRR
DITCH IT...
WHAT A BORING EVENT...
WHY DO YOU INSIST ON HANGING AROUND WITH HUMANS?
AREN'T YOU A YOKAI?
BRR...
THMM
THMM
YOU'RE SUP-POSED TO...
...BE RE-JECTED, RIGHT ...?
THMM
?!
WOOSH
...

READ THIS WAY

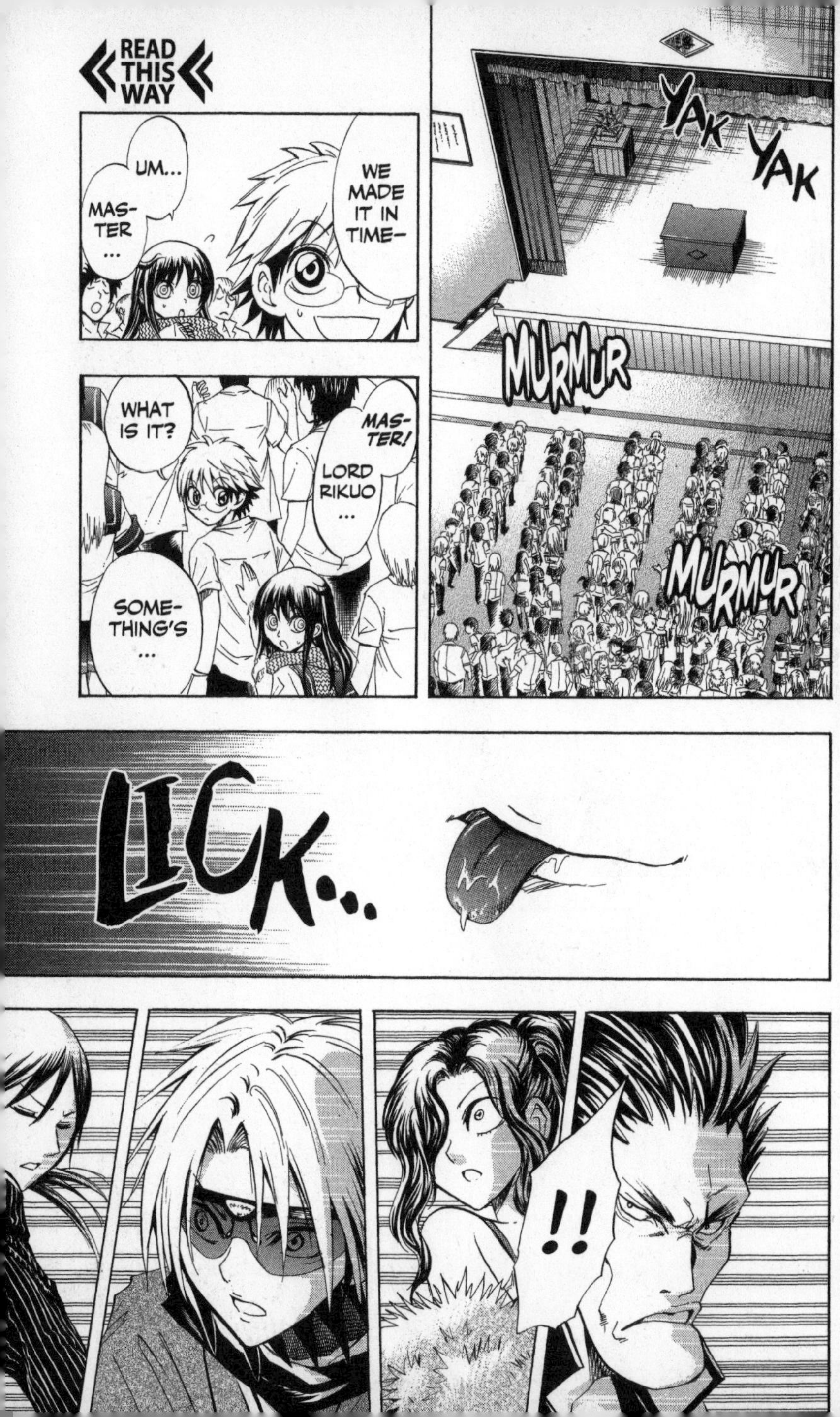
YAK YAK
MURMUR
MURMUR
WE MADE IT IN TIME—
UM...
MASTER ...
MASTER! LORD RIKUO ...
WHAT IS IT?
SOMETHING'S ...
LICK...
!!

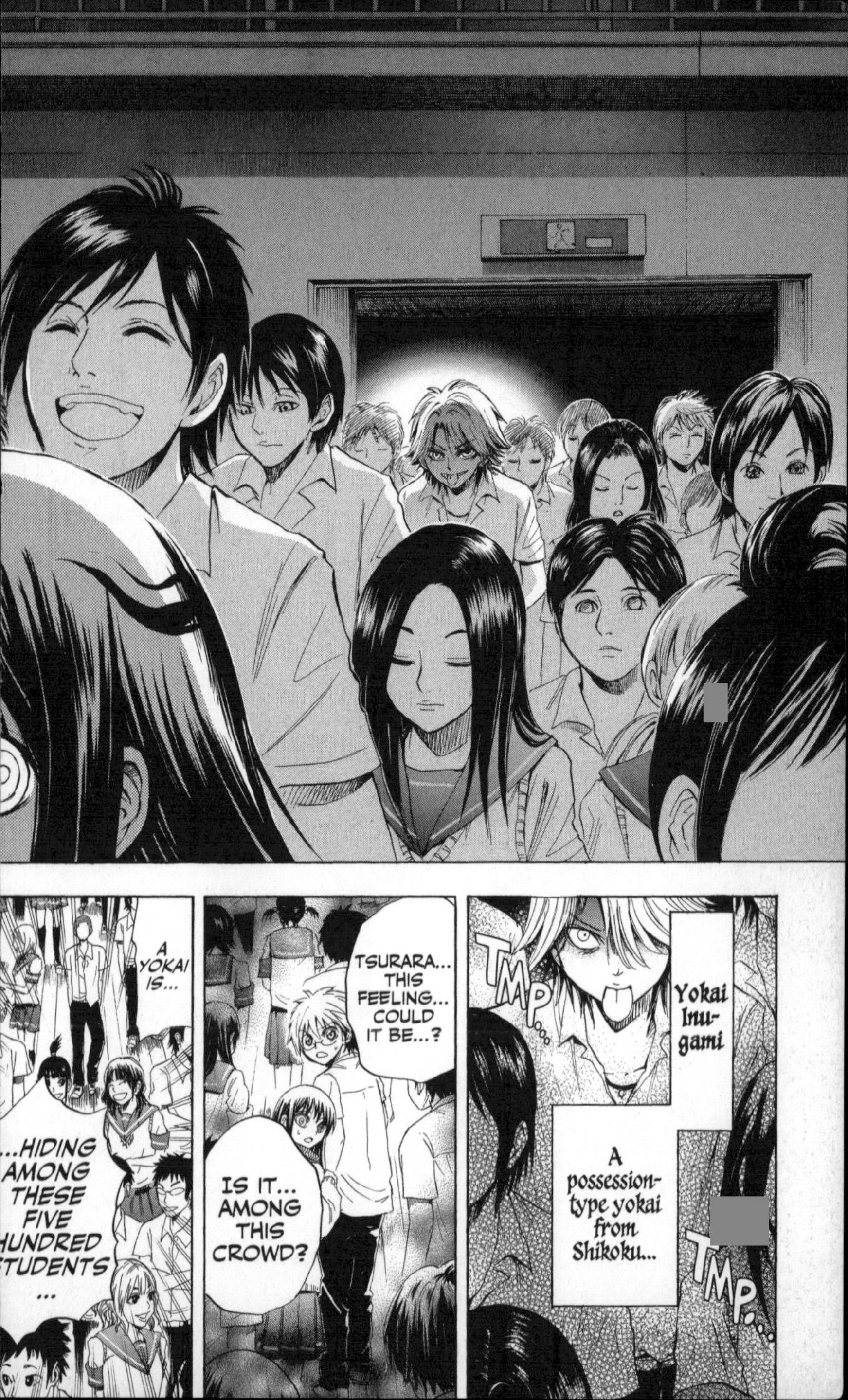
TMP...
Yokai Inugami
A possession-type yokai from Shikoku...
TMP...
TSURARA... THIS FEELING... COULD IT BE...?
IS IT... AMONG THIS CROWD?
A YOKAI IS...
...HIDING AMONG THESE FIVE HUNDRED STUDENTS...

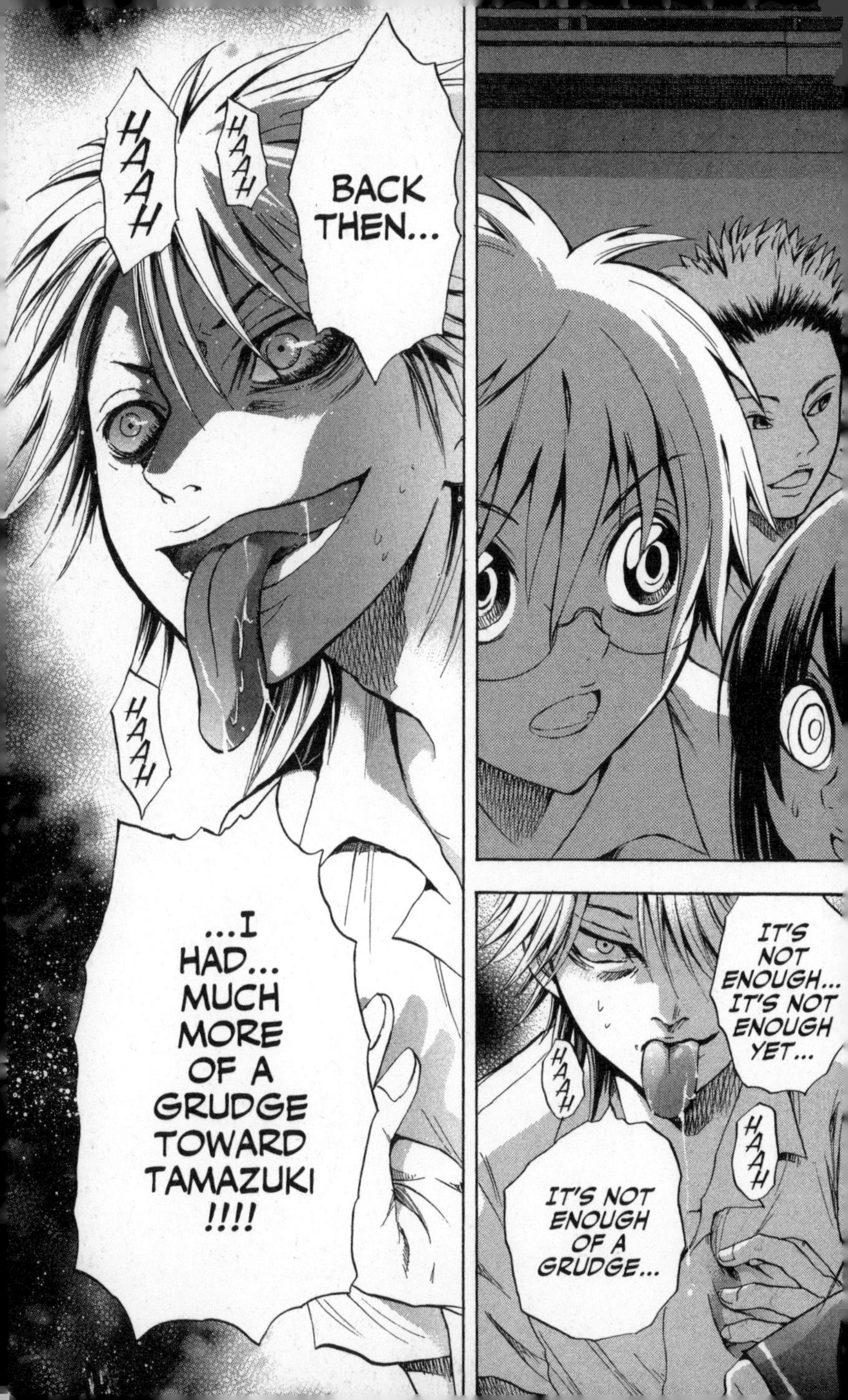
IT'S NOT ENOUGH... IT'S NOT ENOUGH YET...
HAAH
HAAH
IT'S NOT ENOUGH OF A GRUDGE...
HAAH
HAAH
BACK THEN...
HAAH
...I HAD... MUCH MORE OF A GRUDGE TOWARD TAMAZUKI !!!!

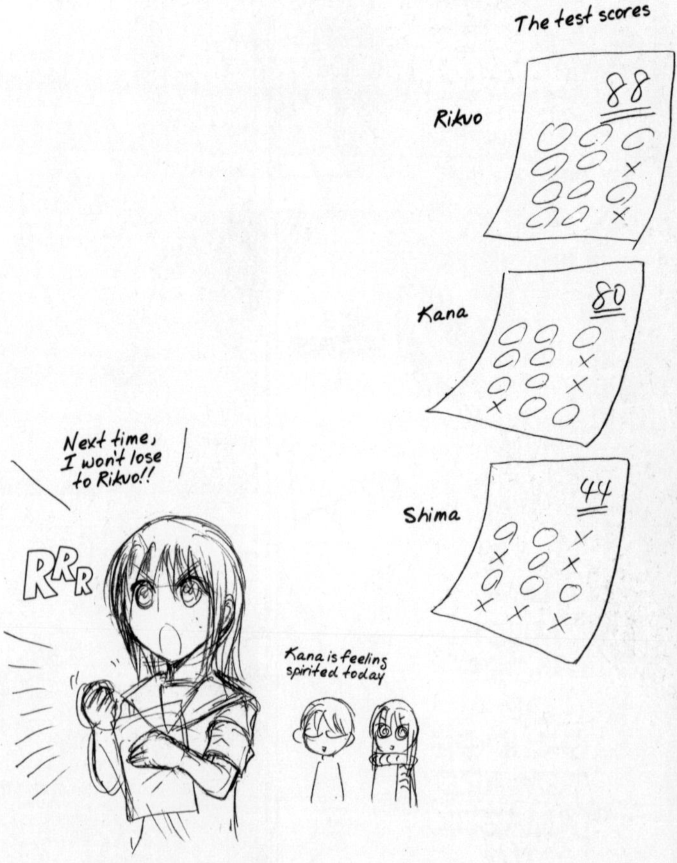

The test scores
Rikuo
88
Kana
80
Shima
44
Next time, I won't lose to Rikuo!!
RRR
Kana is feeling spirited today

Act 30: The Yokai Inugami, Part 2

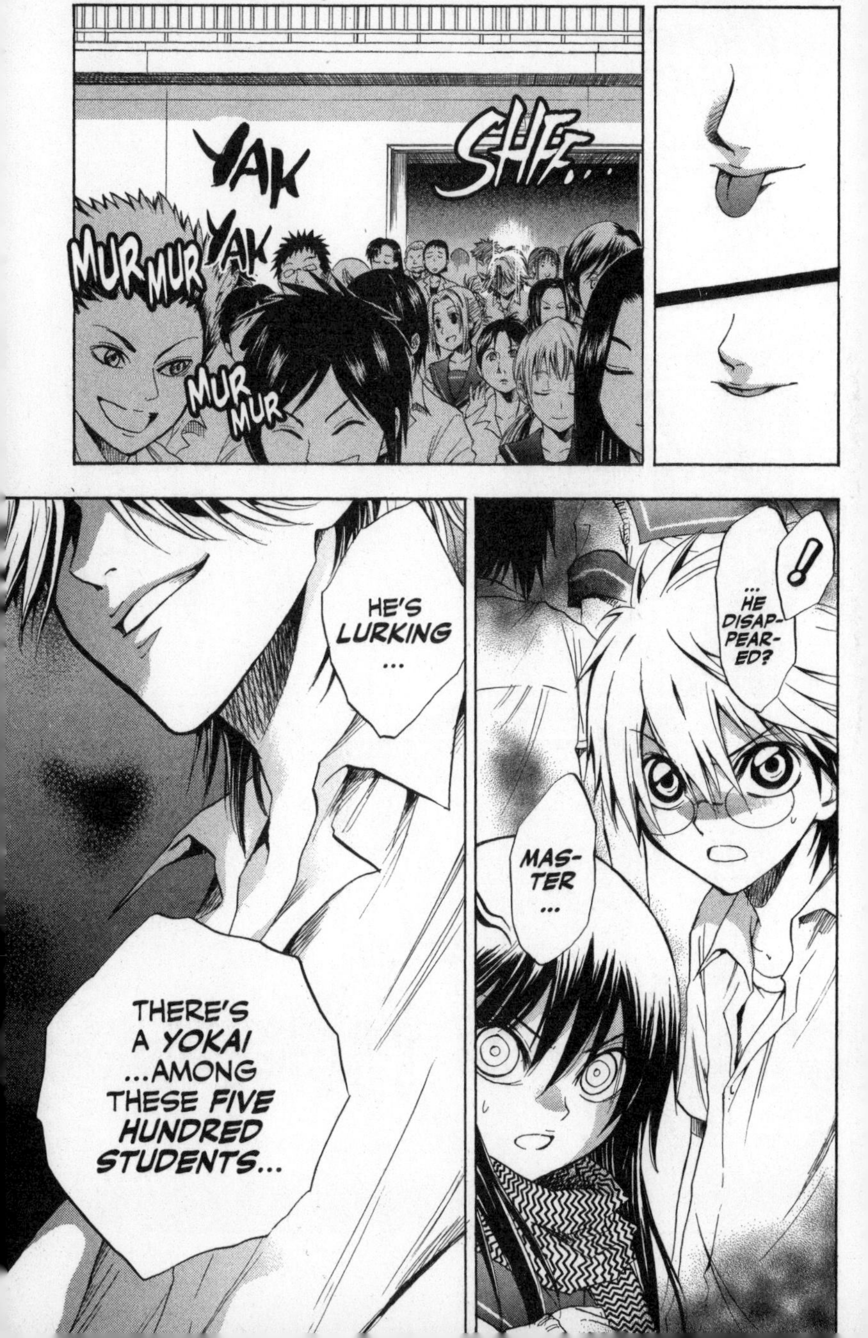
SHFF...
YAK
YAK
MUR MUR
MUR MUR
!
...HE DISAPPEARED?
MASTER...
HE'S LURKING...
THERE'S A YOKAI ...AMONG THESE FIVE HUNDRED STUDENTS...

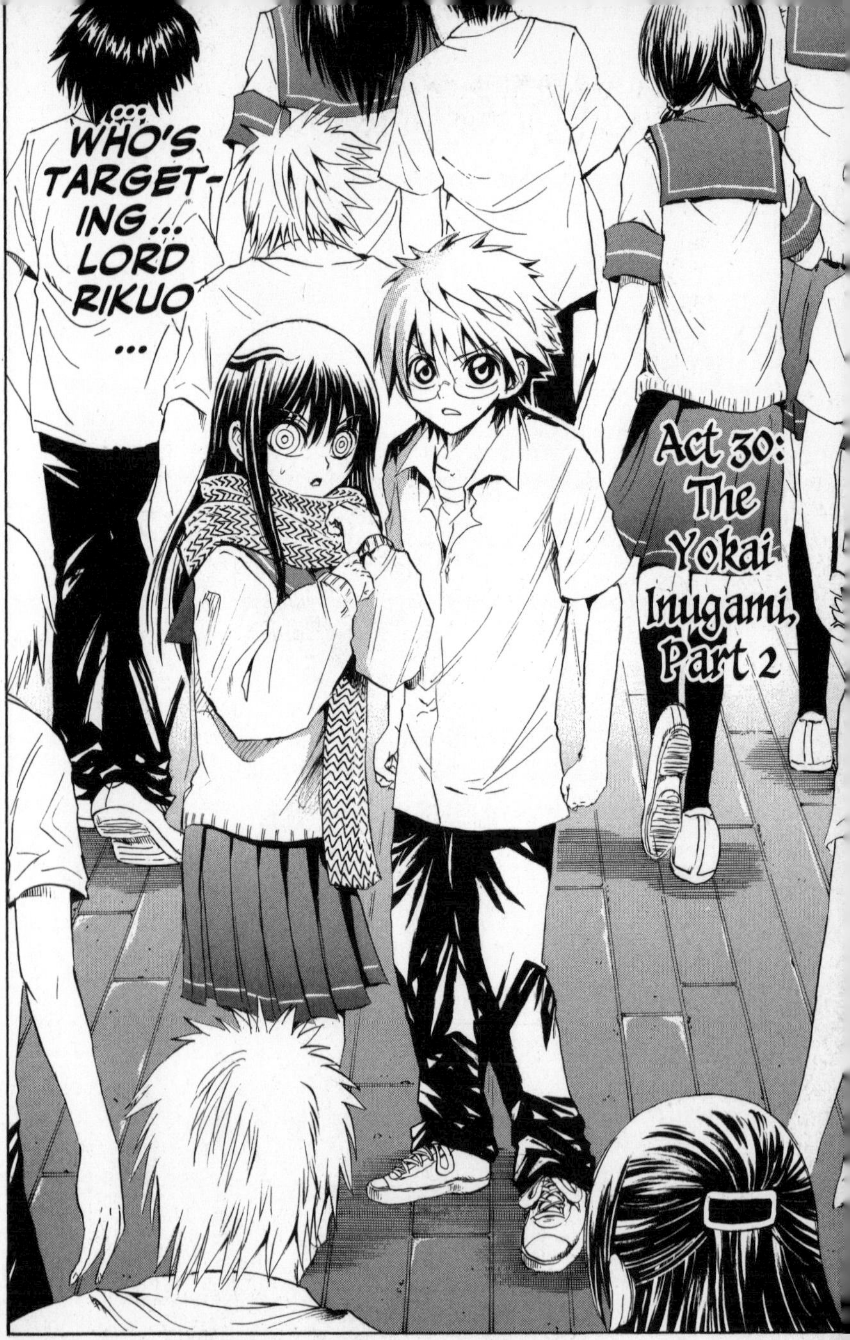
...?!
WHO'S TARGET-ING... LORD RIKUO ...
Act 30: The Yokai Inugami, Part 2

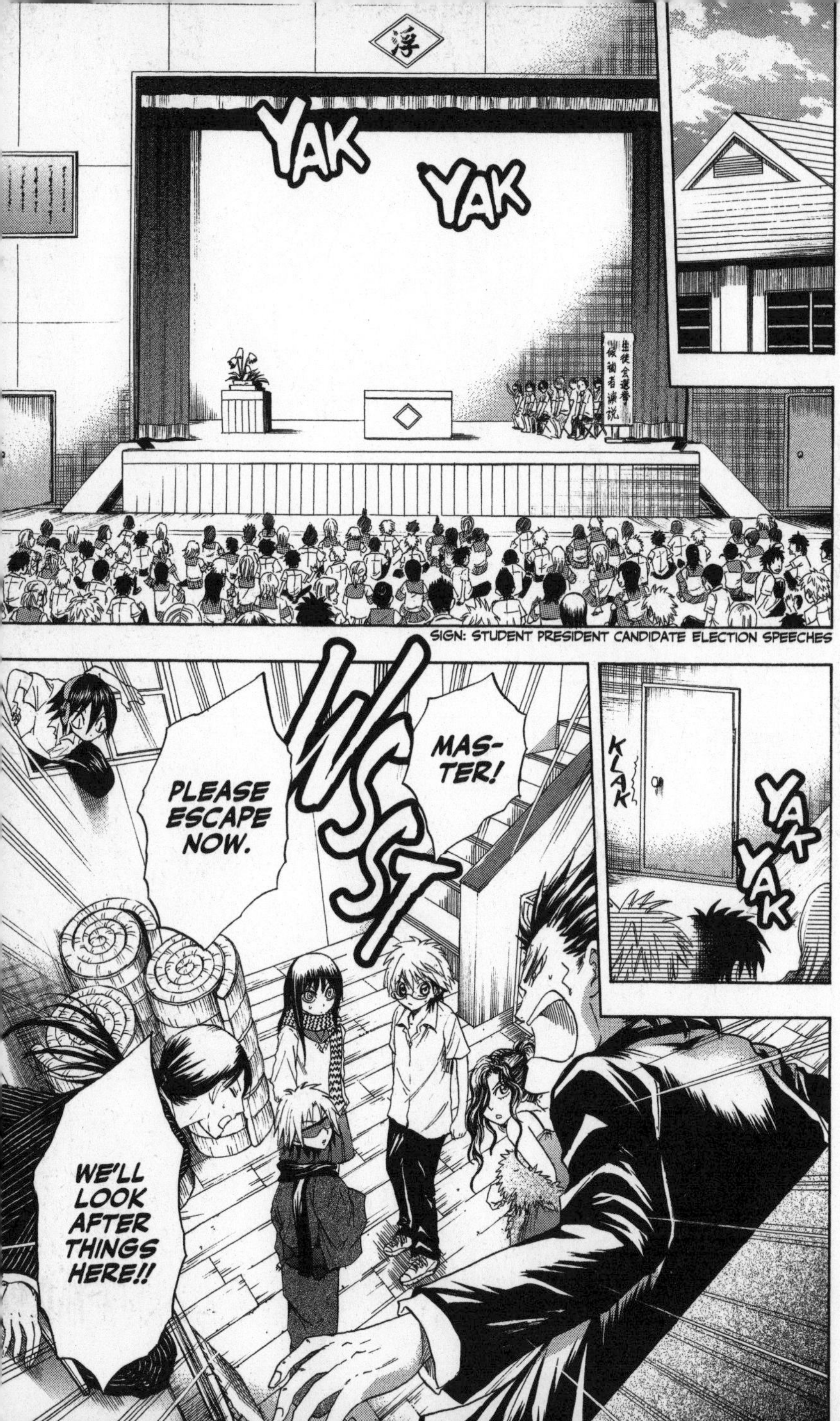
YAK
YAK
SIGN: STUDENT PRESIDENT CANDIDATE ELECTION SPEECHES
KLAK
YAK
YAK
WSST
MAS-TER!
PLEASE ESCAPE NOW.
WE'LL LOOK AFTER THINGS HERE!!

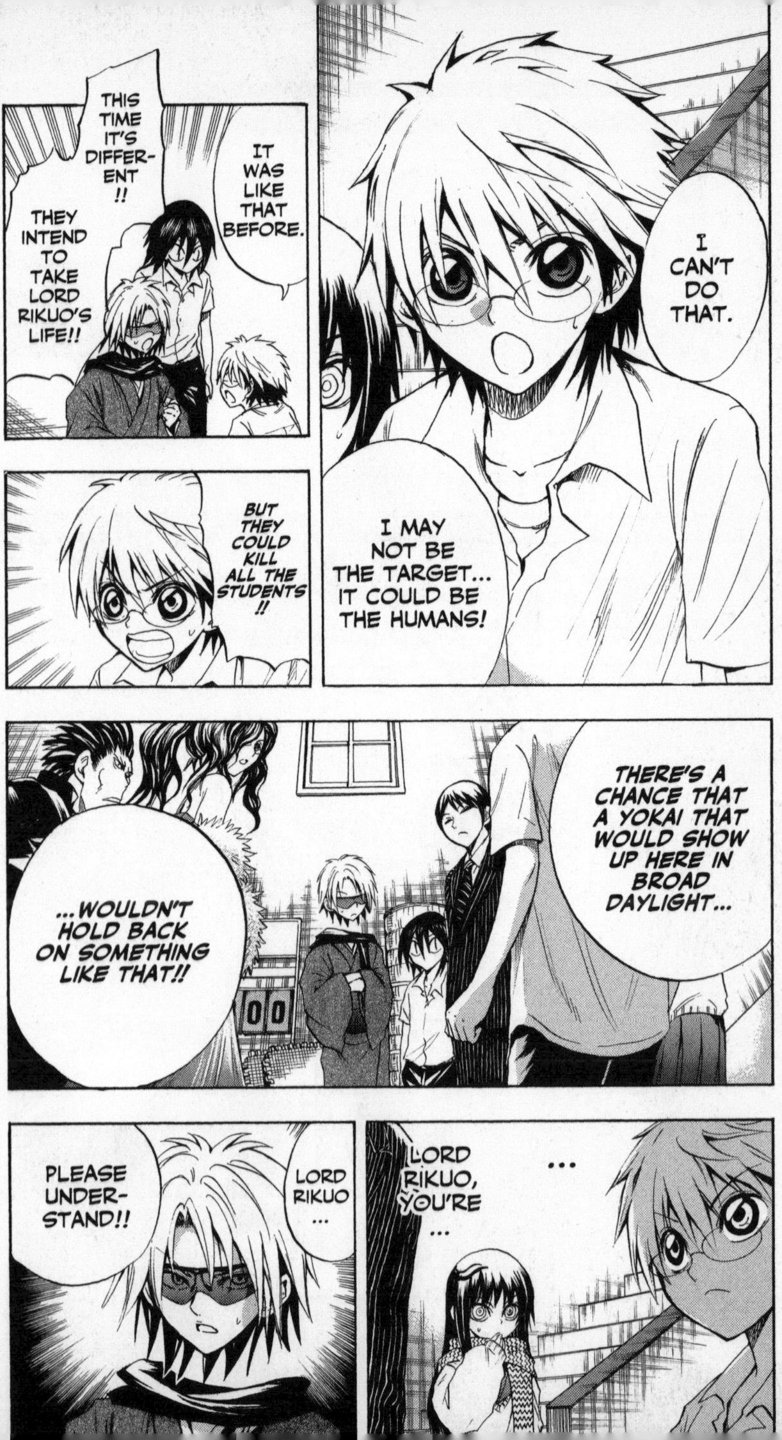
I CAN'T DO THAT.
I MAY NOT BE THE TARGET... IT COULD BE THE HUMANS!
IT WAS LIKE THAT BEFORE.
THIS TIME IT'S DIFFER-ENT!!
THEY INTEND TO TAKE LORD RIKUO'S LIFE!!
BUT THEY COULD KILL ALL THE STUDENTS!!
THERE'S A CHANCE THAT A YOKAI THAT WOULD SHOW UP HERE IN BROAD DAYLIGHT...
...WOULDN'T HOLD BACK ON SOMETHING LIKE THAT!!
...
LORD RIKUO, YOU'RE ...
LORD RIKUO ...
PLEASE UNDER-STAND!!

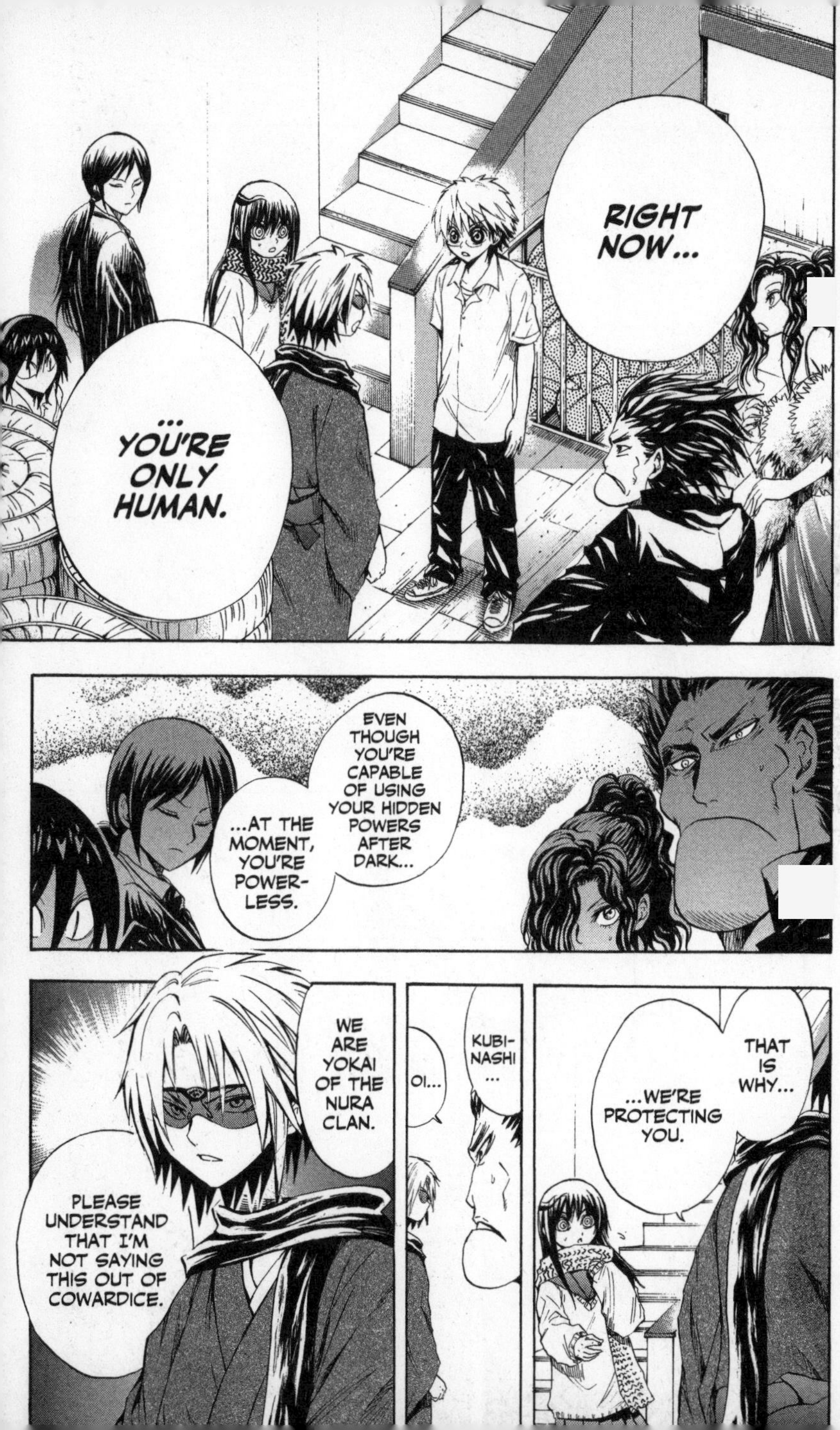
RIGHT NOW...
...YOU'RE ONLY HUMAN.
EVEN THOUGH YOU'RE CAPABLE OF USING YOUR HIDDEN POWERS AFTER DARK...
...AT THE MOMENT, YOU'RE POWERLESS.
THAT IS WHY...
...WE'RE PROTECTING YOU.
KUBINASHI...
OI...
WE ARE YOKAI OF THE NURA CLAN.
PLEASE UNDERSTAND THAT I'M NOT SAYING THIS OUT OF COWARDICE.

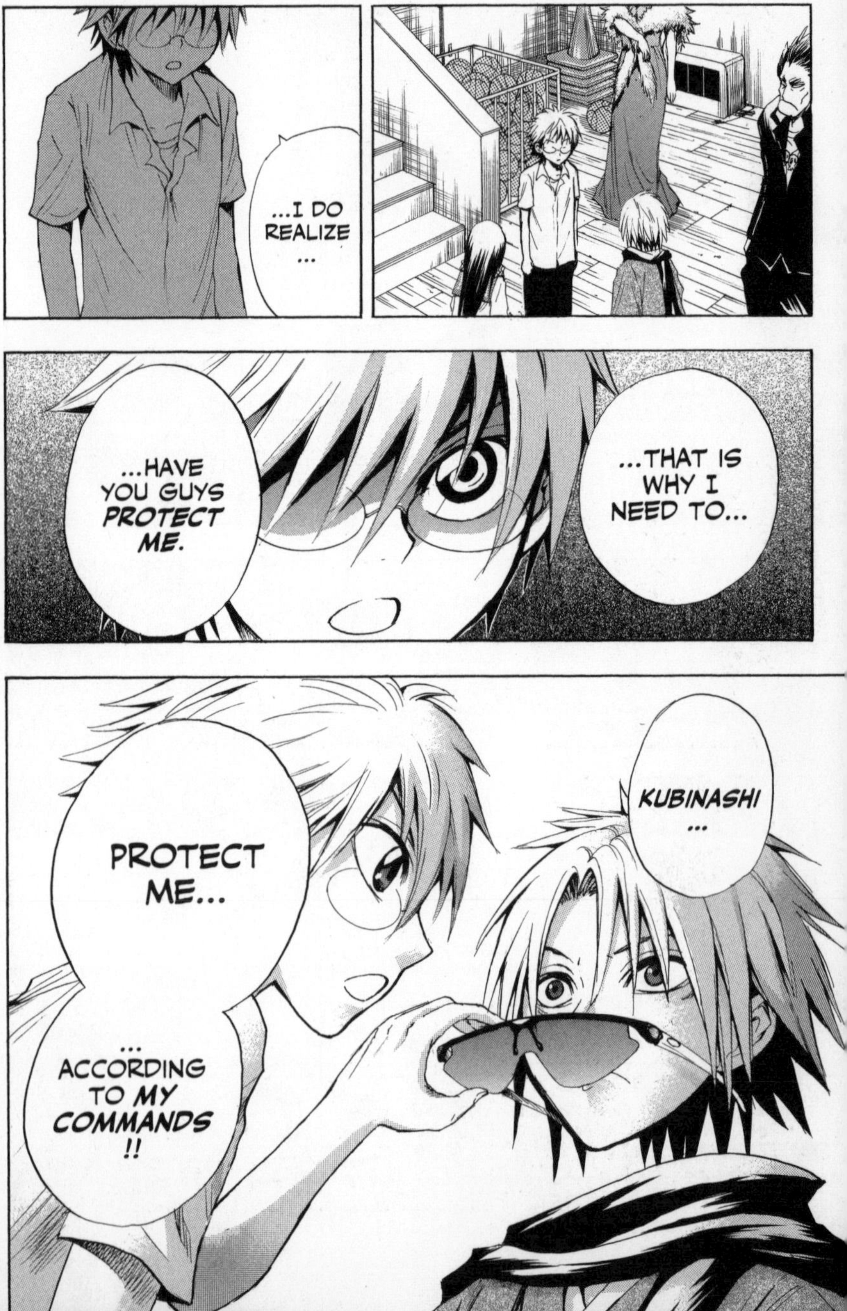
...I DO REALIZE ...
...THAT IS WHY I NEED TO...
...HAVE YOU GUYS *PROTECT ME*.
KUBINASHI ...
PROTECT ME...
... ACCORDING TO *MY COMMANDS* !!

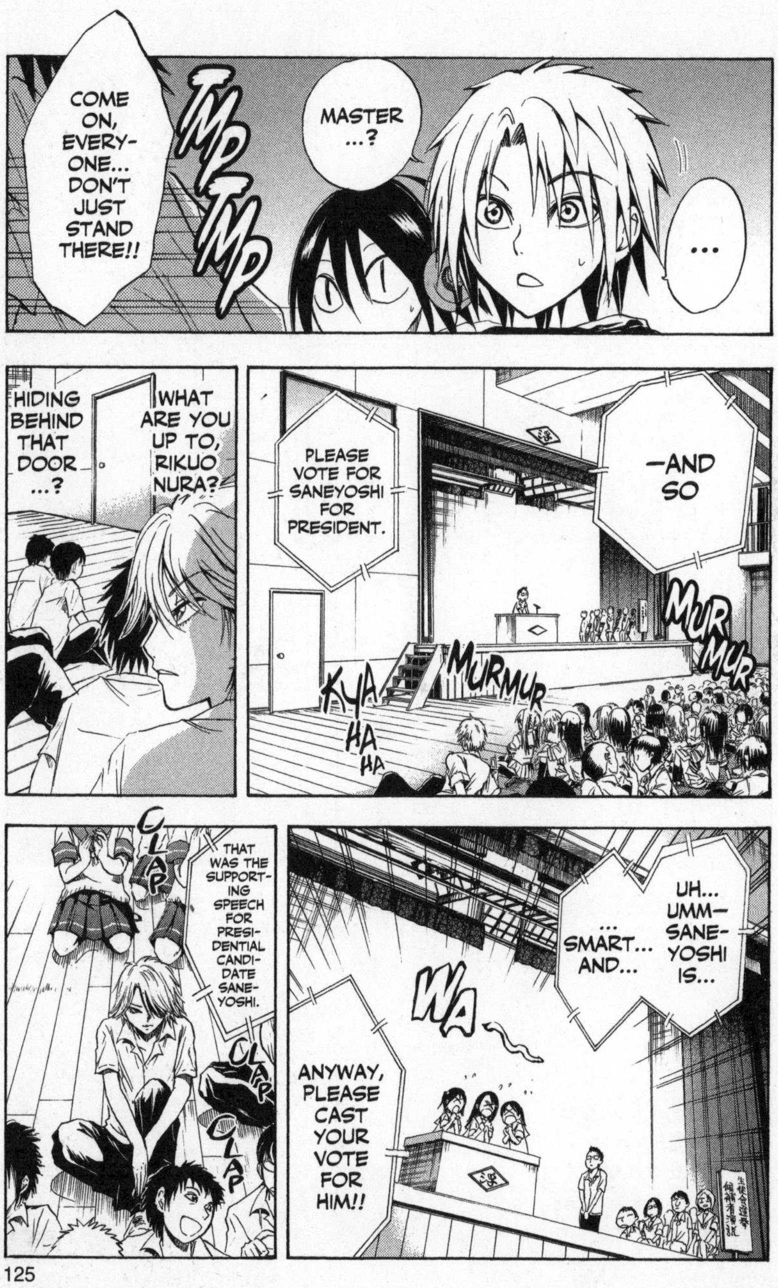
...
MASTER ...?
TMP TMP
COME ON, EVERY-ONE... DON'T JUST STAND THERE!!
—AND SO
PLEASE VOTE FOR SANEYOSHI FOR PRESIDENT.
MURMUR
MURMUR
KYA HA HA HA
WHAT ARE YOU UP TO, RIKUO NURA?
HIDING BEHIND THAT DOOR ...?
UH... UMM— SANE-YOSHI IS...
... SMART... AND...
WA
ANYWAY, PLEASE CAST YOUR VOTE FOR HIM!!
THAT WAS THE SUPPORT-ING SPEECH FOR PRESI-DENTIAL CANDI-DATE SANE-YOSHI.
CLAP
CLAP
CLAP
CLAP

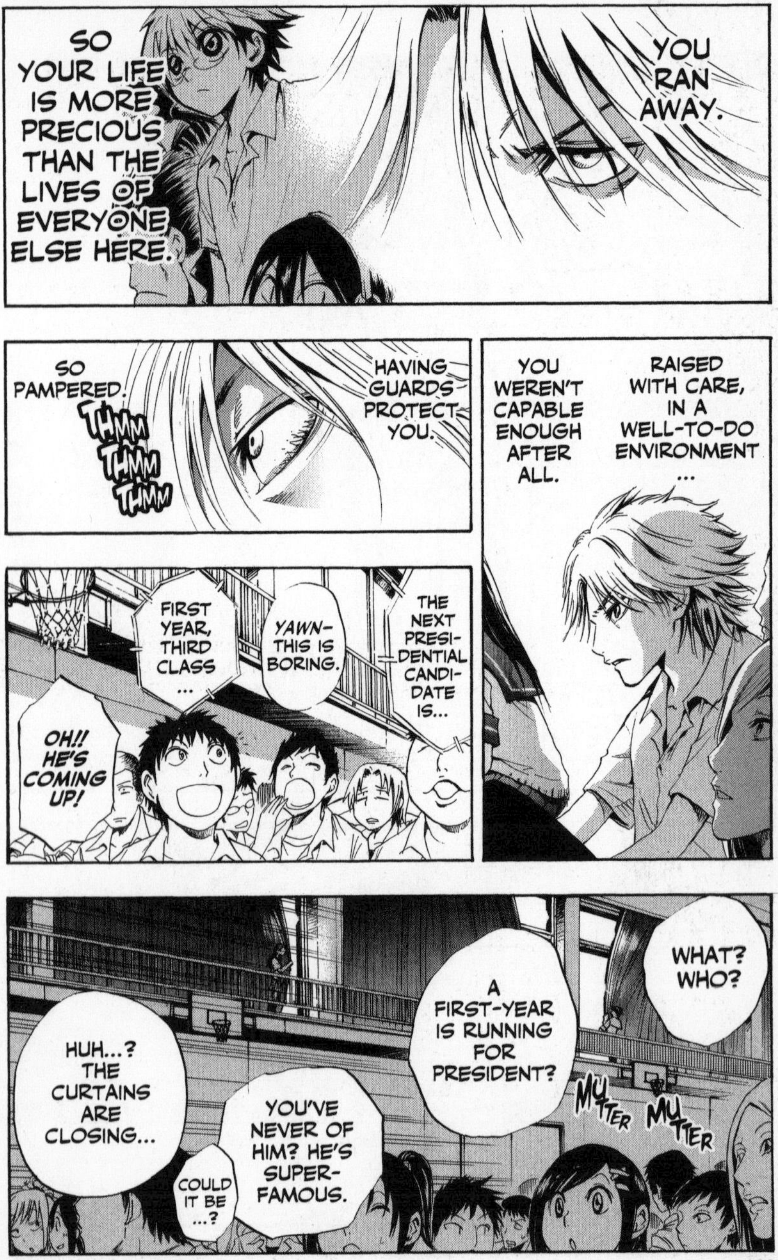
YOU RAN AWAY.
SO YOUR LIFE IS MORE PRECIOUS THAN THE LIVES OF EVERYONE ELSE HERE.
RAISED WITH CARE, IN A WELL-TO-DO ENVIRONMENT ...
YOU WEREN'T CAPABLE ENOUGH AFTER ALL.
HAVING GUARDS PROTECT YOU.
SO PAMPERED.
THMM THMM THMM
THE NEXT PRESIDENTIAL CANDIDATE IS...
YAWN- THIS IS BORING.
FIRST YEAR, THIRD CLASS ...
OH!! HE'S COMING UP!
WHAT? WHO?
A FIRST-YEAR IS RUNNING FOR PRESIDENT?
MUTTER MUTTER
YOU'VE NEVER OF HIM? HE'S SUPER-FAMOUS.
HUH...? THE CURTAINS ARE CLOSING...
COULD IT BE ...?

READ THIS WAY

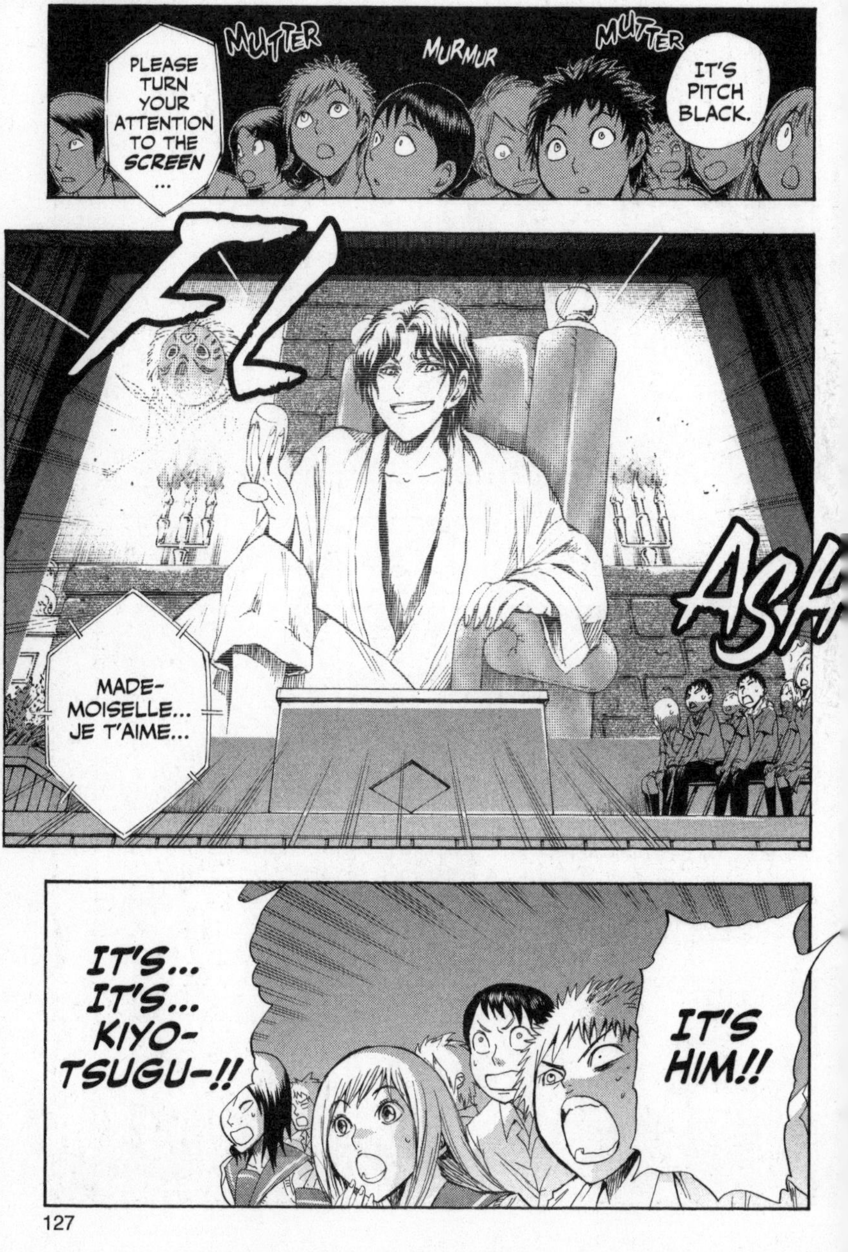

IT'S PITCH BLACK.
MUTTER
MURMUR
MUTTER
PLEASE TURN YOUR ATTENTION TO THE SCREEN...
FL
ASH
MADE-MOISELLE... JE T'AIME...
IT'S HIM!!
IT'S... IT'S... KIYO-TSUGU-!!

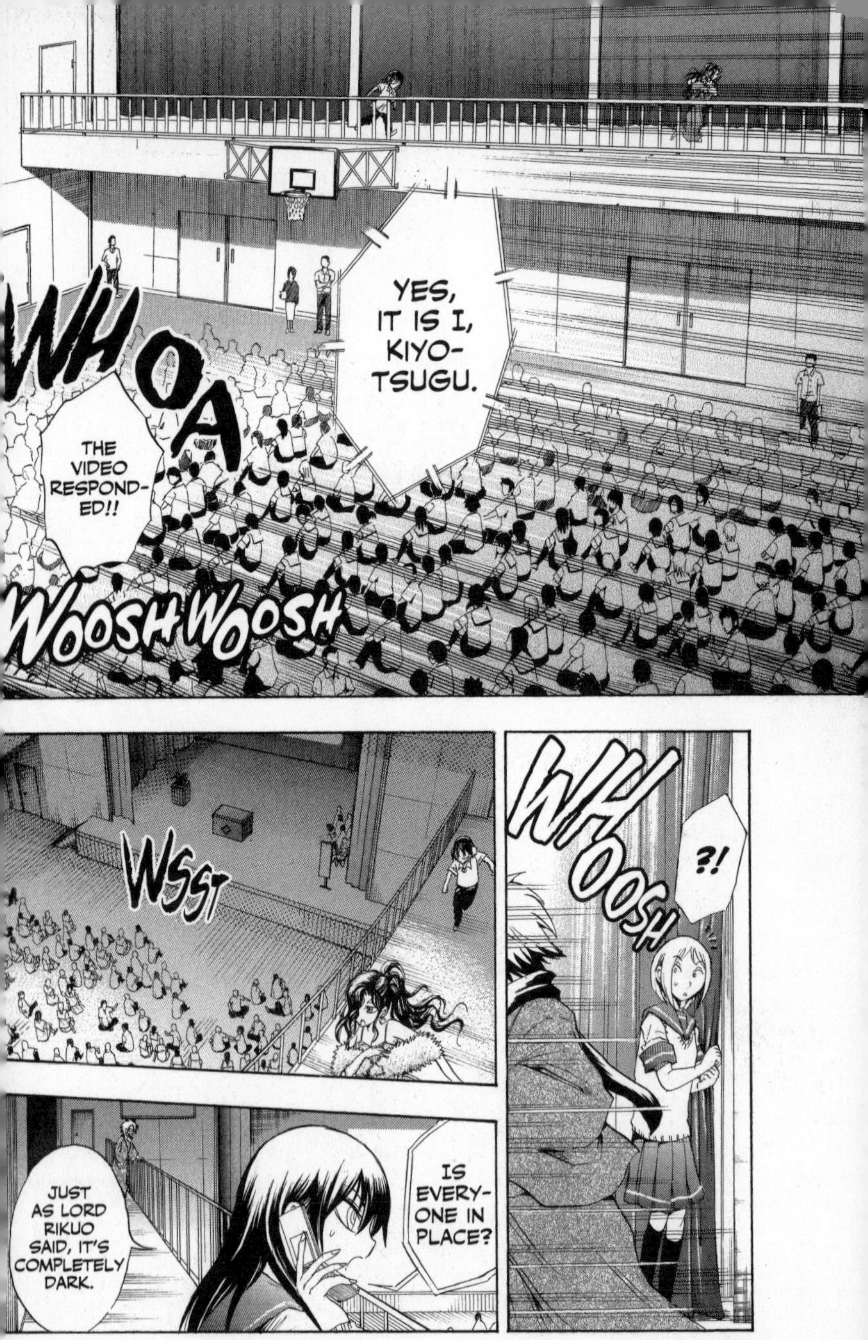
YES, IT IS I, KIYO-TSUGU.
WHOA
THE VIDEO RESPOND-ED!!
WOOSH WOOSH
WHOOSH
?!
WSST
IS EVERY-ONE IN PLACE?
JUST AS LORD RIKUO SAID, IT'S COMPLETELY DARK.

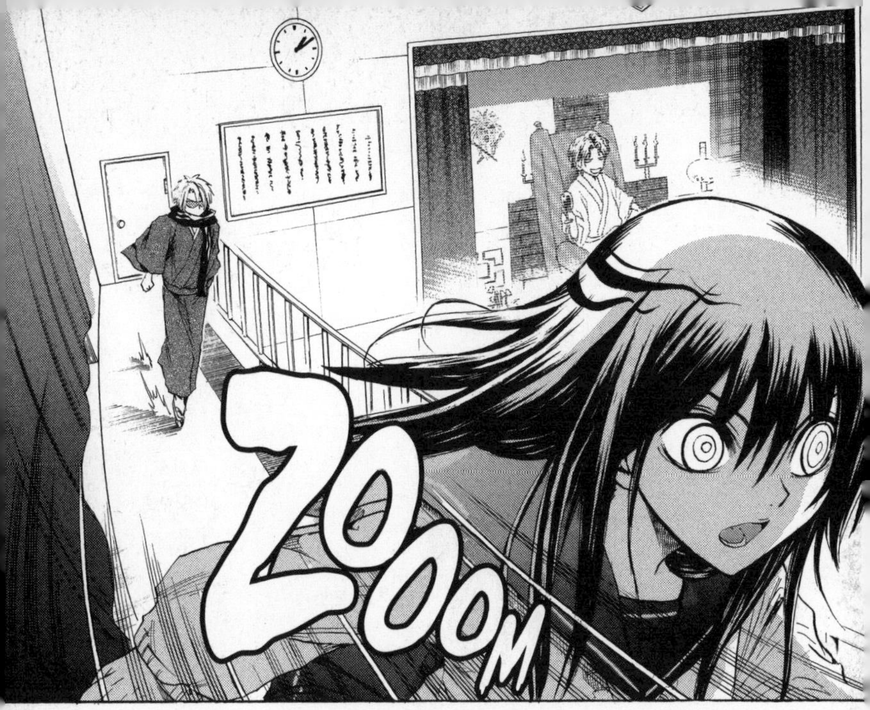
ZOOOM

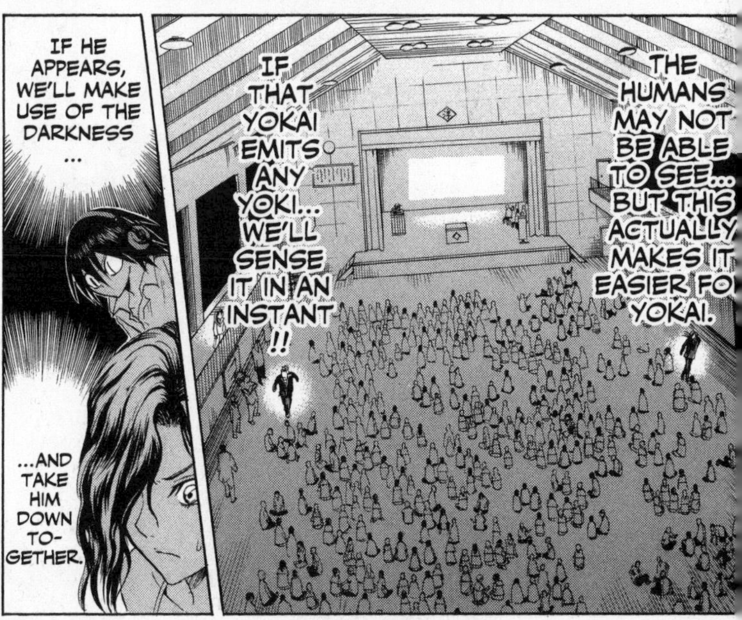
THE HUMANS MAY NOT BE ABLE TO SEE... BUT THIS ACTUALLY MAKES IT EASIER FO YOKAI.
IF THAT YOKAI EMITS ANY YOKI... WE'LL SENSE IT IN AN INSTANT!!
IF HE APPEARS, WE'LL MAKE USE OF THE DARKNESS...
...AND TAKE HIM DOWN TO-GETHER.

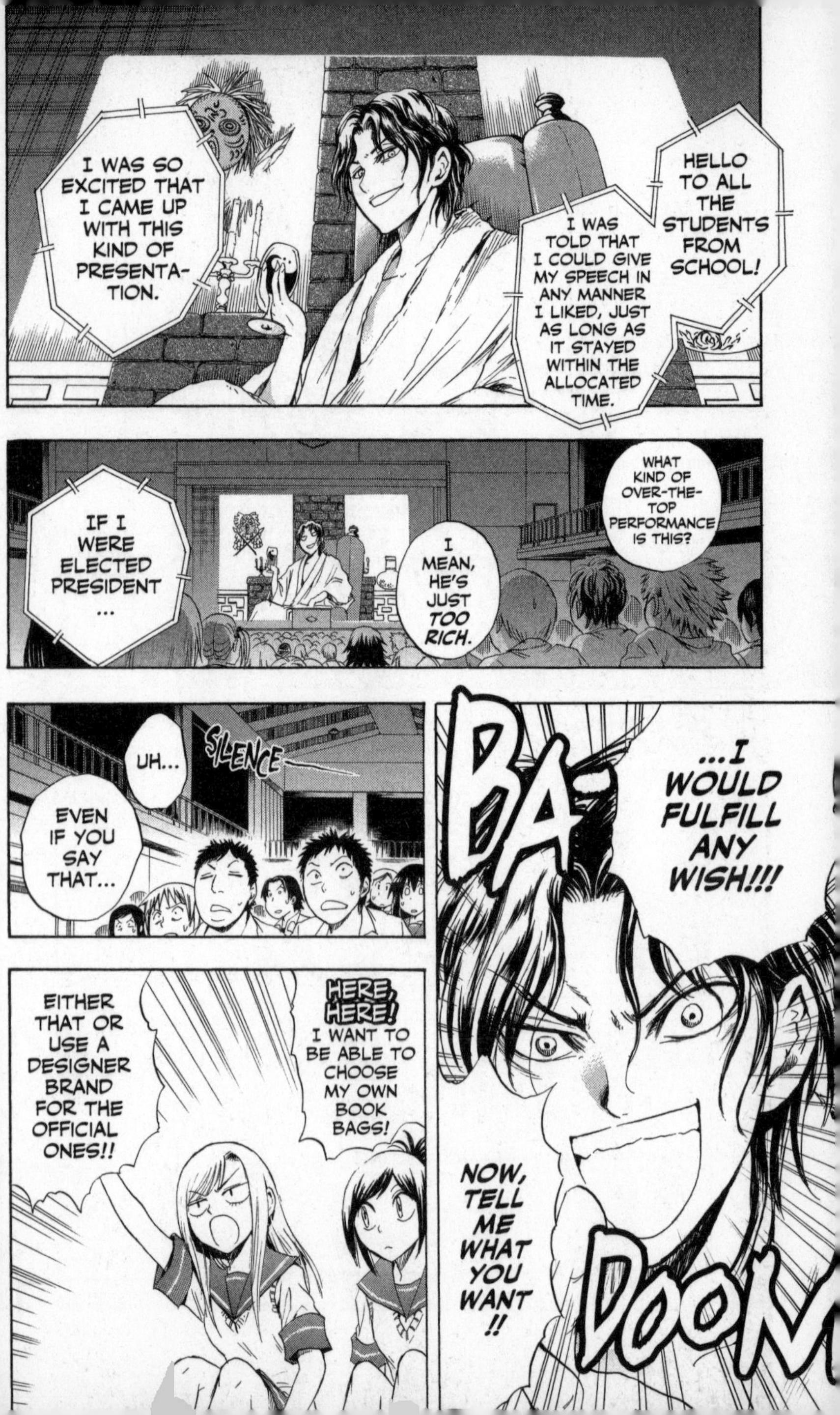
HELLO TO ALL THE STUDENTS FROM SCHOOL!
I WAS TOLD THAT I COULD GIVE MY SPEECH IN ANY MANNER I LIKED, JUST AS LONG AS IT STAYED WITHIN THE ALLOCATED TIME.
I WAS SO EXCITED THAT I CAME UP WITH THIS KIND OF PRESENTATION.
WHAT KIND OF OVER-THE-TOP PERFORMANCE IS THIS?
I MEAN, HE'S JUST *TOO RICH*.
IF I WERE ELECTED PRESIDENT ...
BA-
...I WOULD FULFILL ANY WISH!!!
NOW, TELL ME WHAT YOU WANT!!
DOOM
SILENCE
UH...
EVEN IF YOU SAY THAT...
HERE, HERE! I WANT TO BE ABLE TO CHOOSE MY OWN BOOK BAGS!
EITHER THAT OR USE A DESIGNER BRAND FOR THE OFFICIAL ONES!!

READ THIS WAY

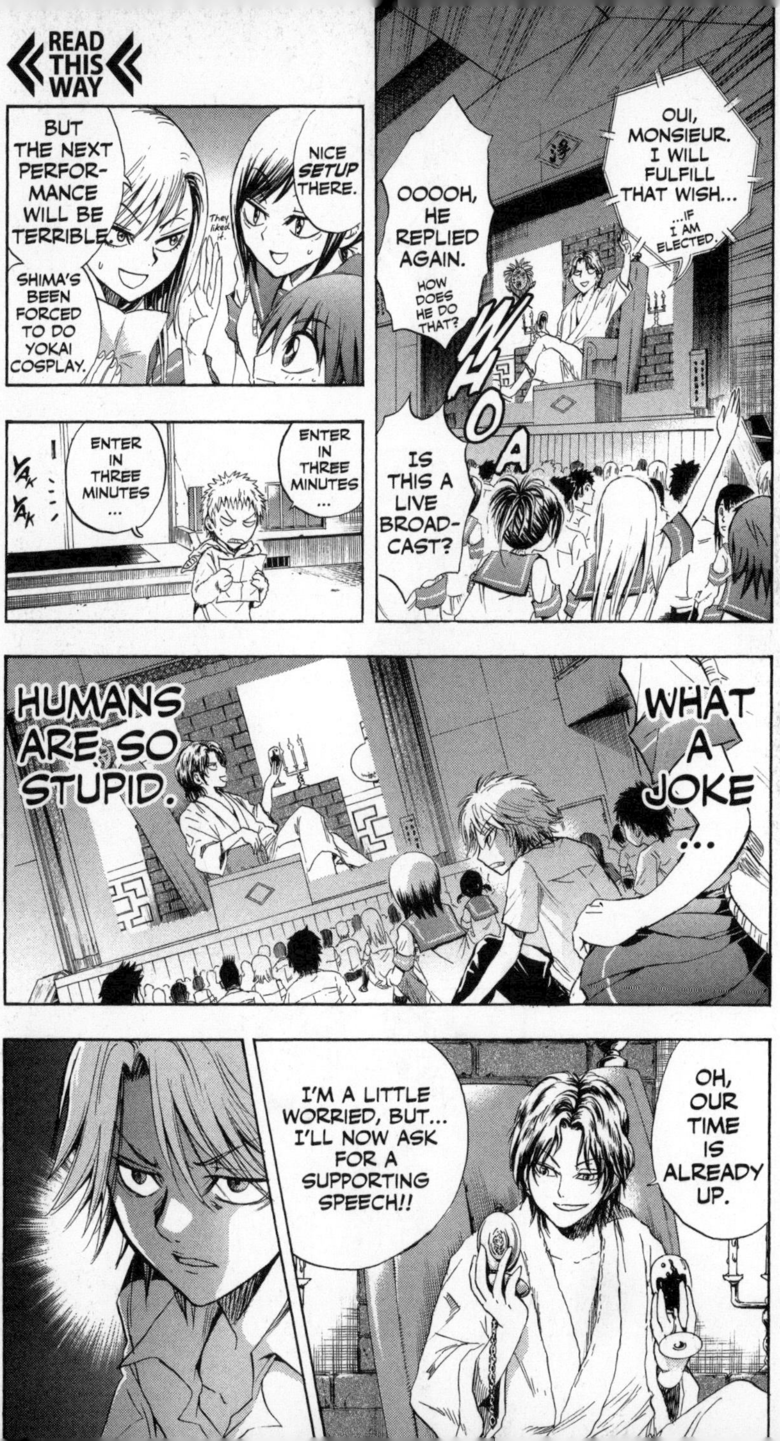
OUI, MONSIEUR. I WILL FULFILL THAT WISH...
...IF I AM ELECTED.
OOOOH, HE REPLIED AGAIN.
HOW DOES HE DO THAT?
WHOA
IS THIS A LIVE BROADCAST?
NICE SETUP THERE.
They liked it.
BUT THE NEXT PERFORMANCE WILL BE TERRIBLE.
SHIMA'S BEEN FORCED TO DO YOKAI COSPLAY.
ENTER IN THREE MINUTES...
ENTER IN THREE MINUTES...
YAK YAK
WHAT A JOKE...
HUMANS ARE SO STUPID.
OH, OUR TIME IS ALREADY UP.
I'M A LITTLE WORRIED, BUT... I'LL NOW ASK FOR A SUPPORTING SPEECH!!

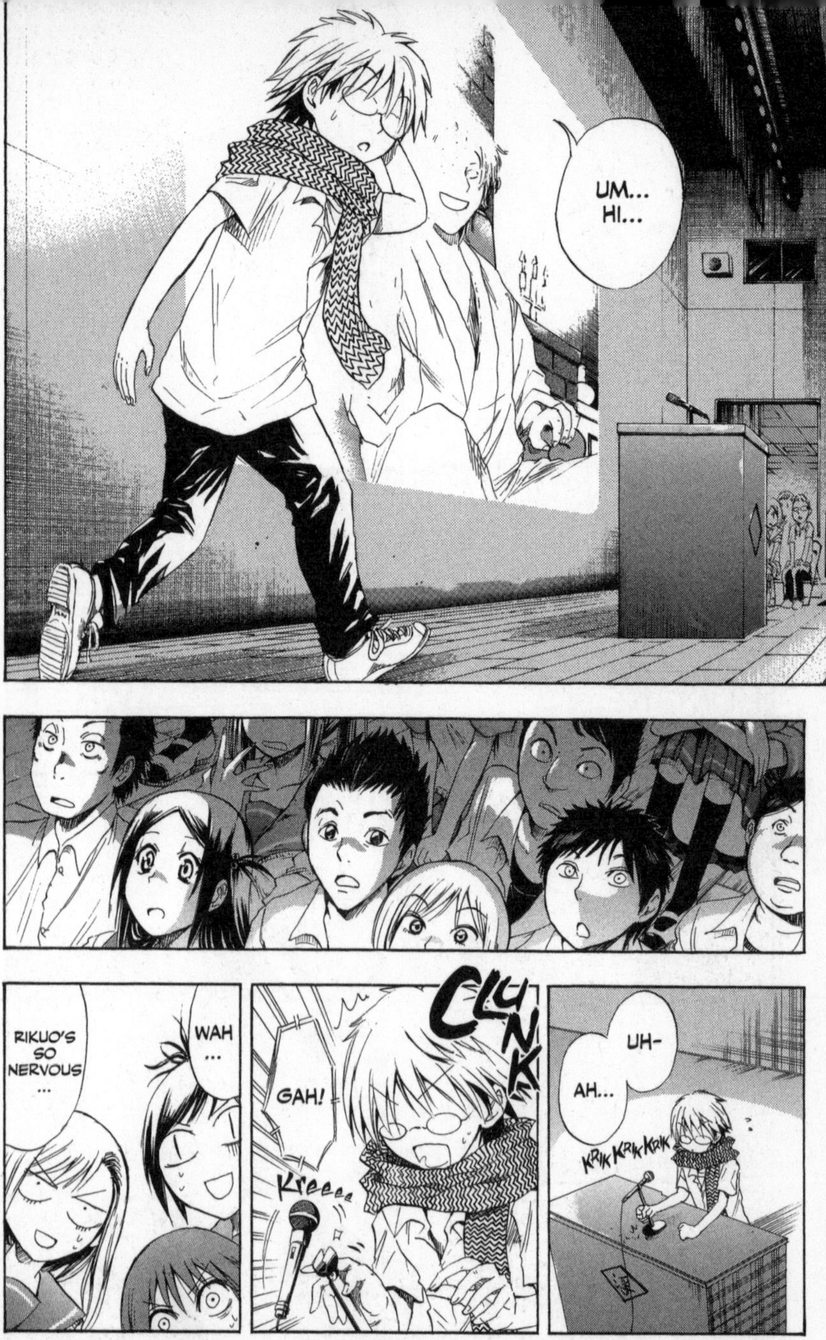
UM... HI...
UH- AH...
KRIK KRIK KRIK KRIK
CLUNK
GAH!
Kreeee
WAH ...
RIKUO'S SO NERVOUS ...

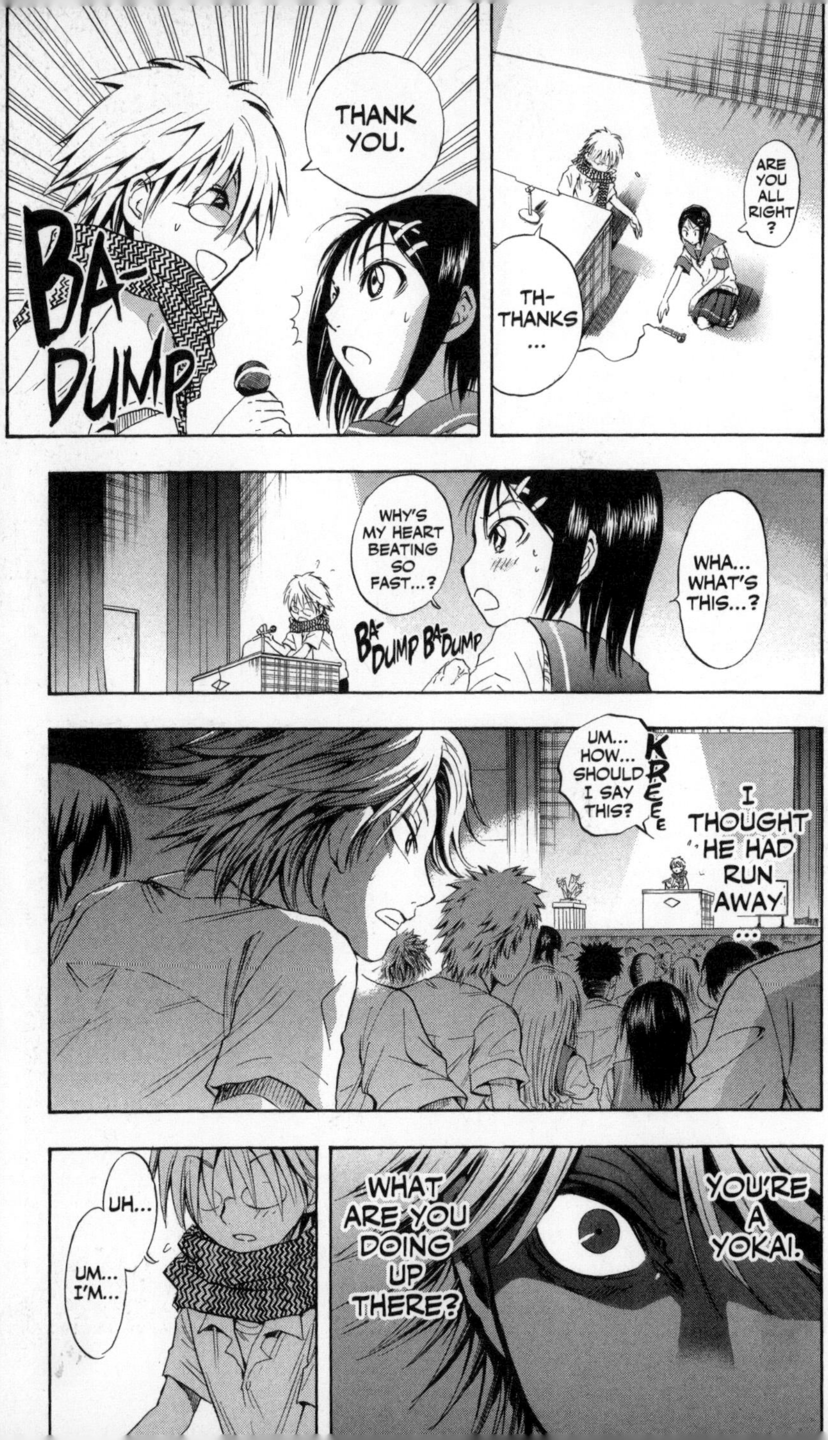
ARE YOU ALL RIGHT?
TH-THANKS...
THANK YOU.
BA-DUMP
WHA... WHAT'S THIS...?
WHY'S MY HEART BEATING SO FAST...?
BA-DUMP BA-DUMP
I THOUGHT HE HAD RUN AWAY...
UM... HOW... SHOULD I SAY THIS?
KREEE
YOU'RE A YOKAI.
WHAT ARE YOU DOING UP THERE?
UH...
UM... I'M...

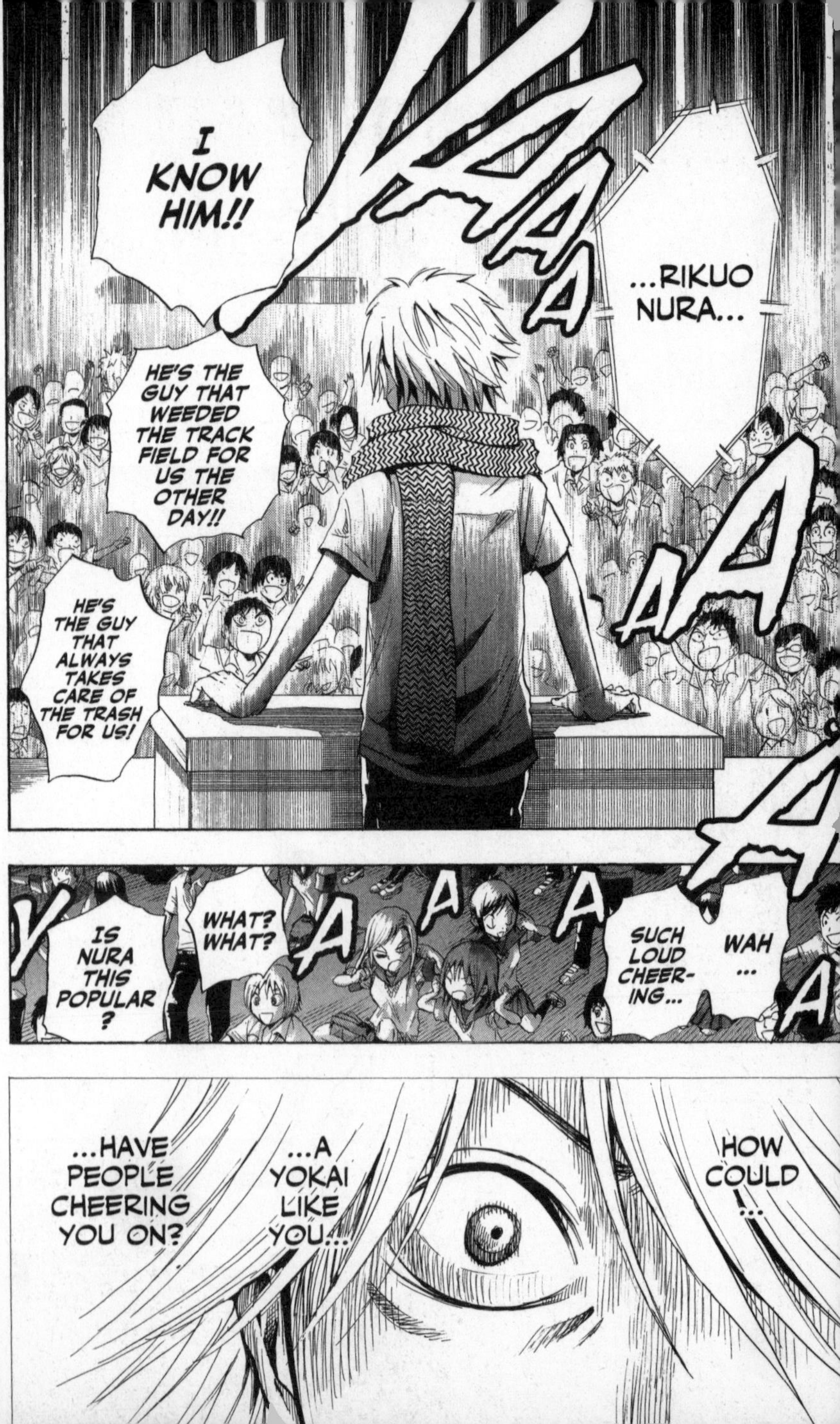
...RIKUO NURA...
I KNOW HIM!!
HE'S THE GUY THAT WEEDED THE TRACK FIELD FOR US THE OTHER DAY!!
HE'S THE GUY THAT ALWAYS TAKES CARE OF THE TRASH FOR US!
WAH...
SUCH LOUD CHEERING...
WHAT? WHAT?
IS NURA THIS POPULAR?
HOW COULD...
...A YOKAI LIKE YOU...
...HAVE PEOPLE CHEERING YOU ON?

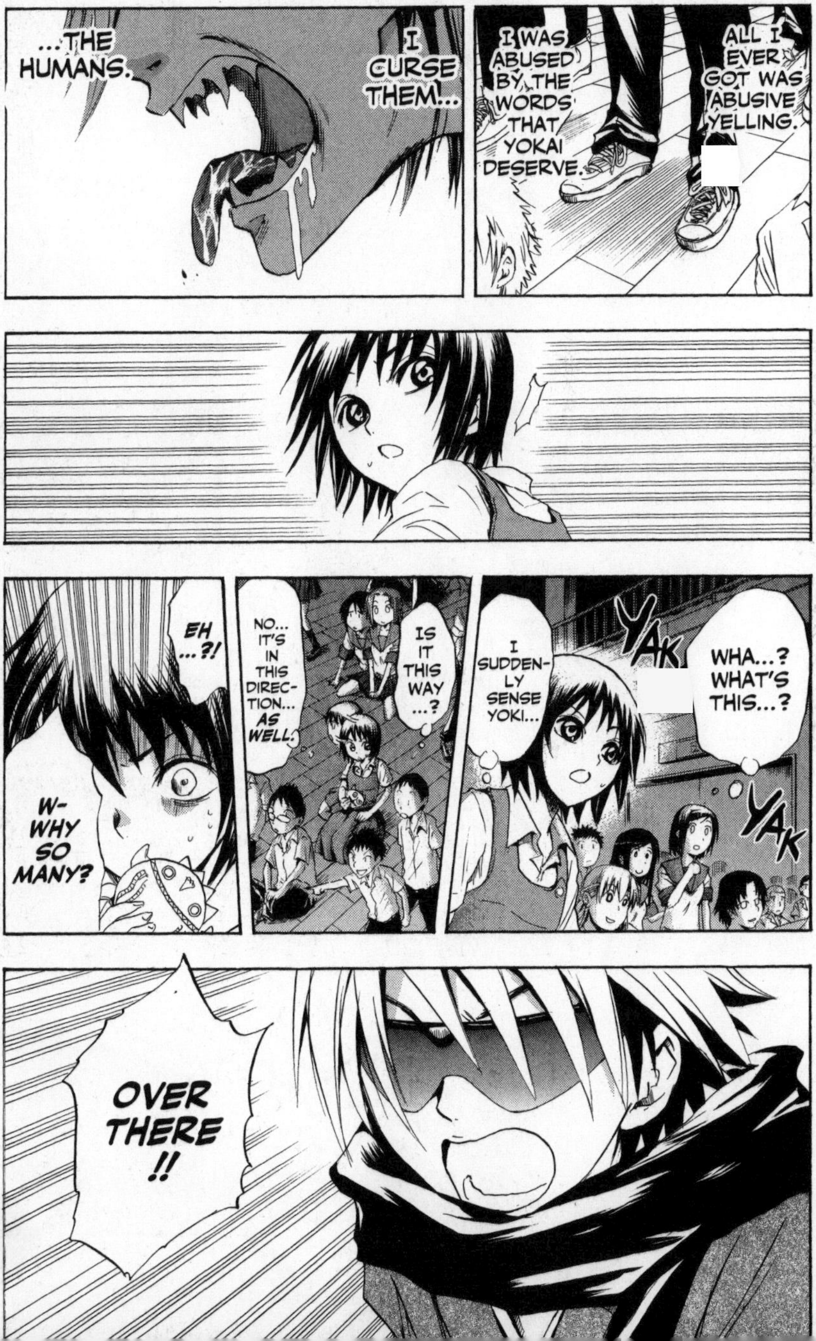
ALL I EVER GOT WAS ABUSIVE YELLING.
I WAS ABUSED BY THE WORDS THAT YOKAI DESERVE.
I CURSE THEM...
...THE HUMANS.
YAK
WHA...? WHAT'S THIS...?
YAK
I SUDDEN-LY SENSE YOKI...
IS IT THIS WAY...?
NO... IT'S IN THIS DIREC-TION... AS WELL.
EH ...?!
W-WHY SO MANY?
OVER THERE !!

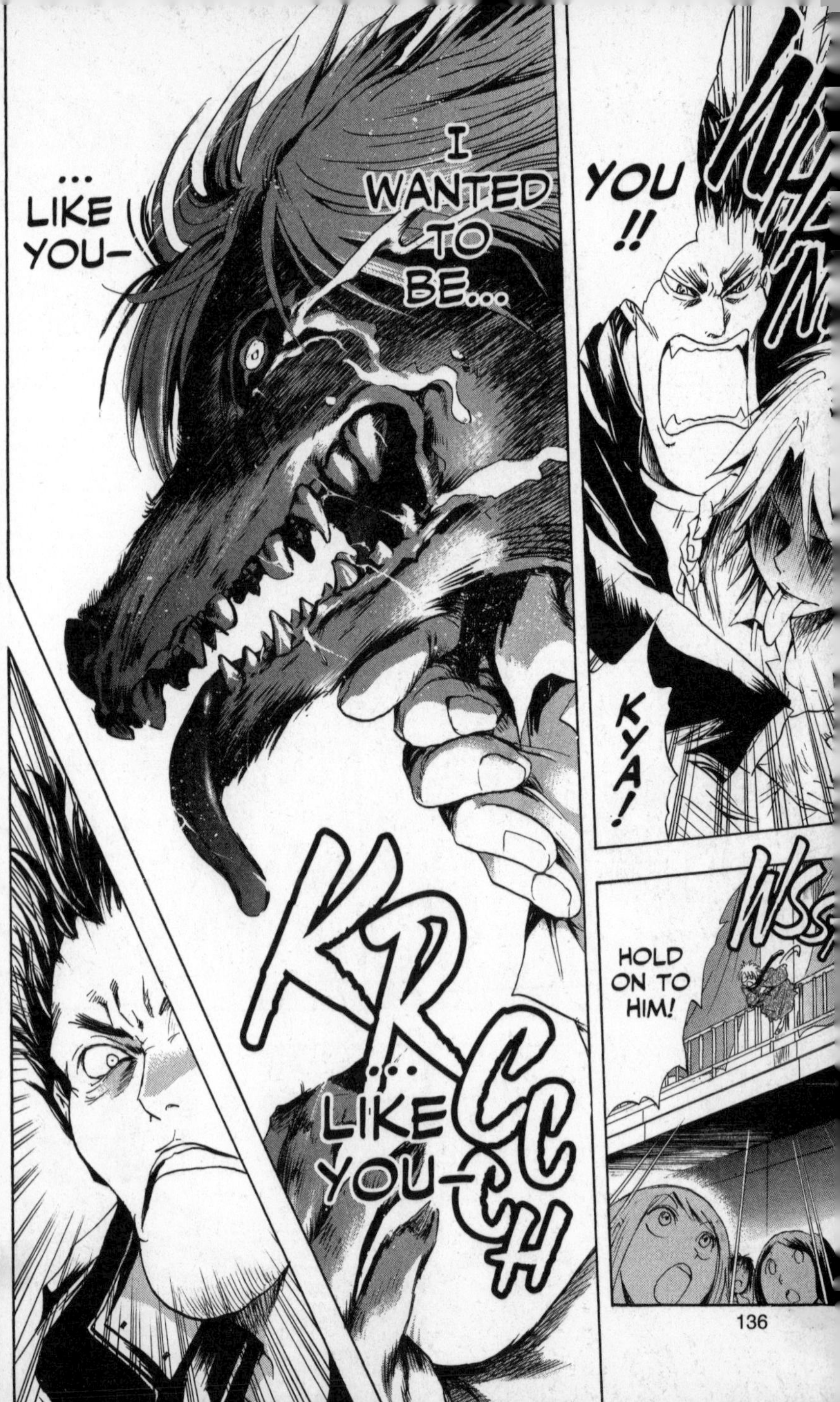
YOU!!
KYA!
HOLD ON TO HIM!
I WANTED TO BE...
... LIKE YOU—
... LIKE YOU—
KRCCH

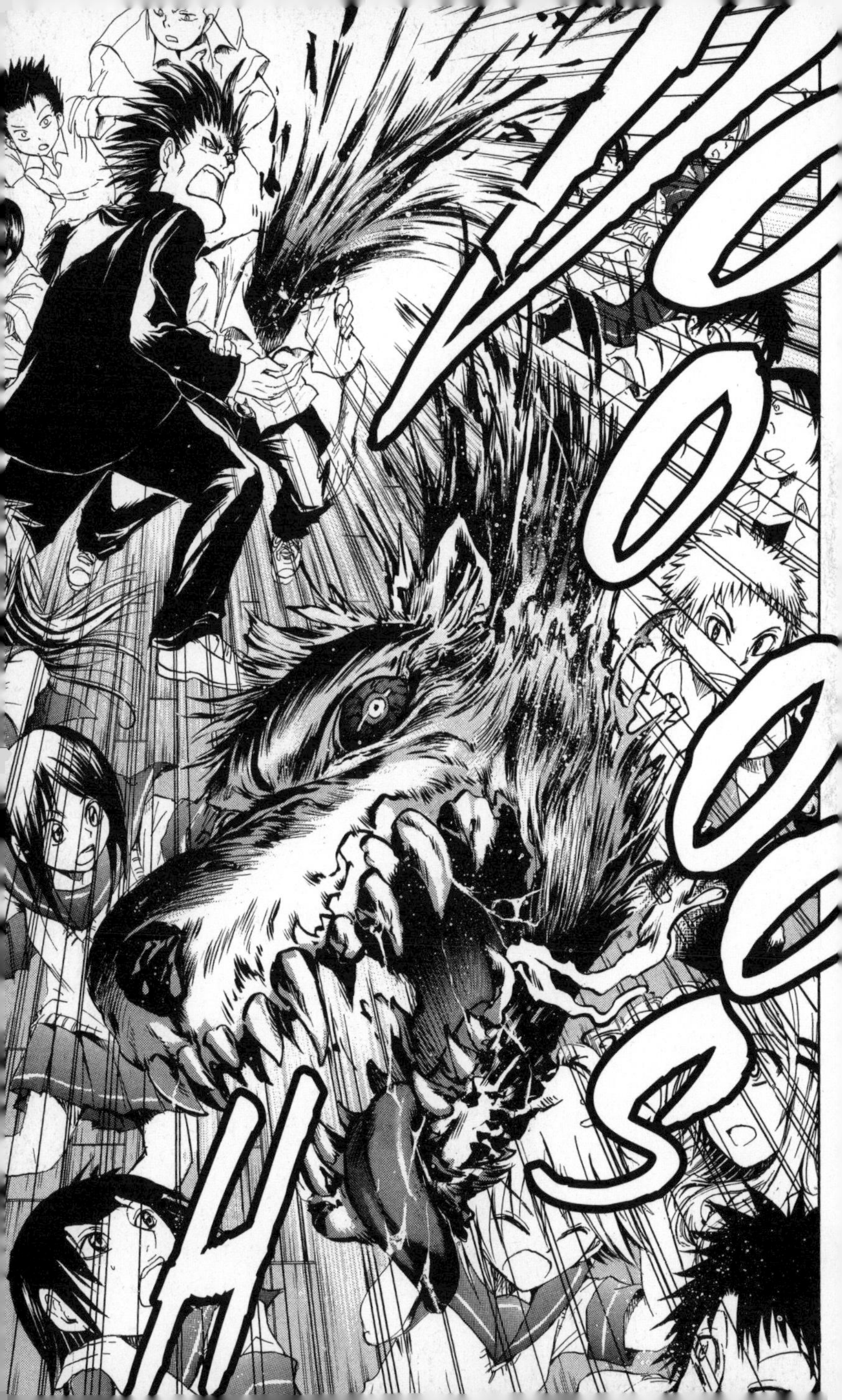
WOOOSH

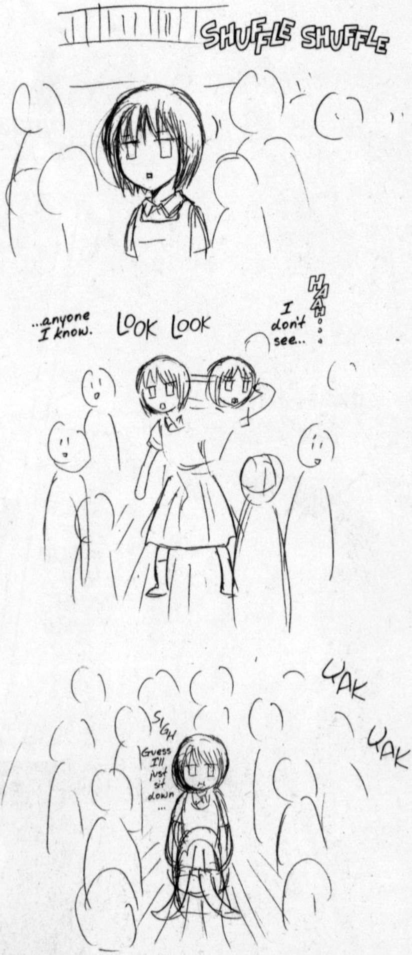
SHUFFLE SHUFFLE
HAAH...
I don't see...
LOOK LOOK
...anyone I know.
WAK
WAK
SIGH
Guess I'll just sit down...

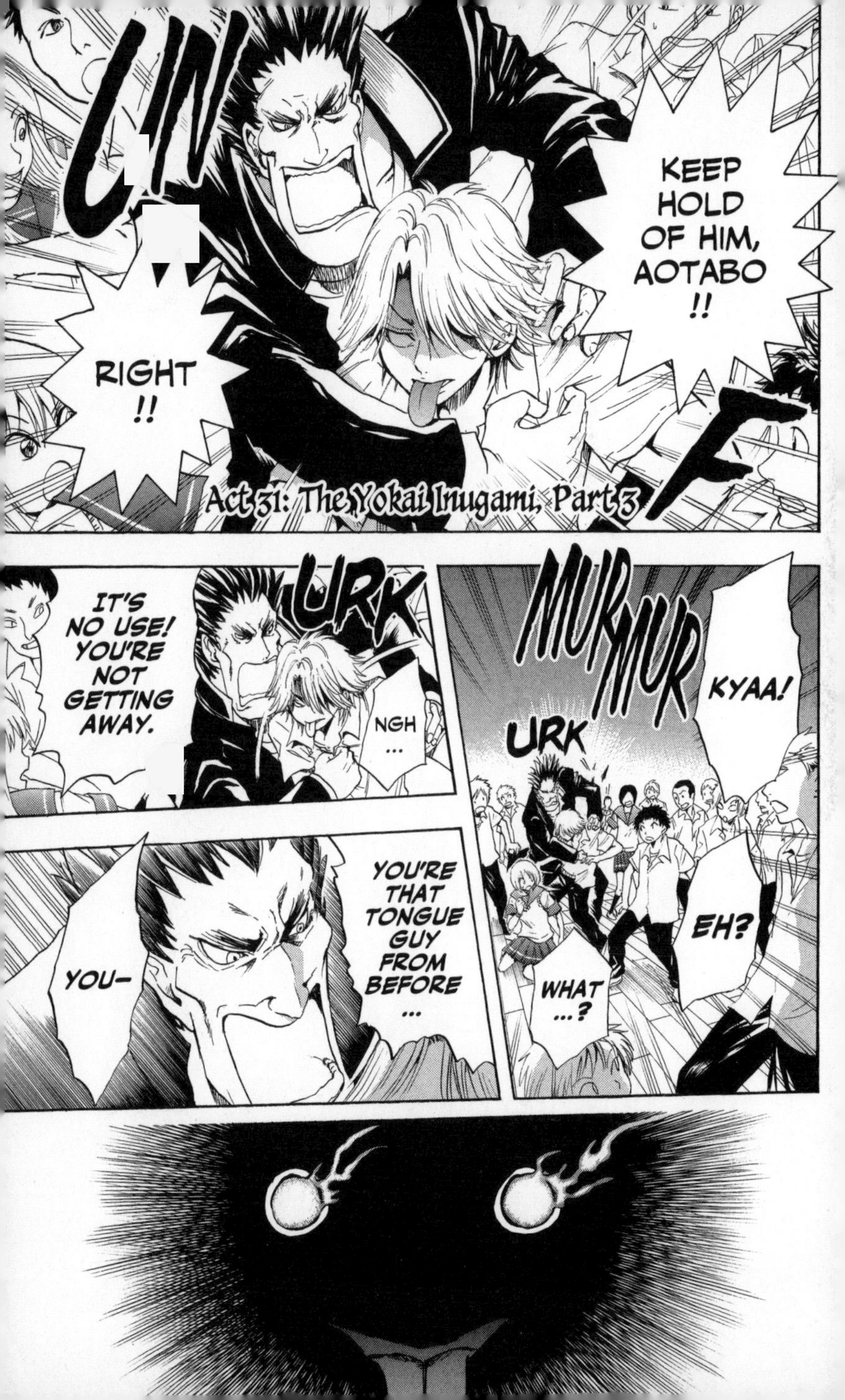
KEEP HOLD OF HIM, AOTABO !!
RIGHT !!
Act 31: The Yokai Inugami, Part 3
MURMUR
KYAA!
URK
EH?
WHAT ...?
URK
NGH ...
IT'S NO USE! YOU'RE NOT GETTING AWAY.
YOU'RE THAT TONGUE GUY FROM BEFORE ...
YOU-

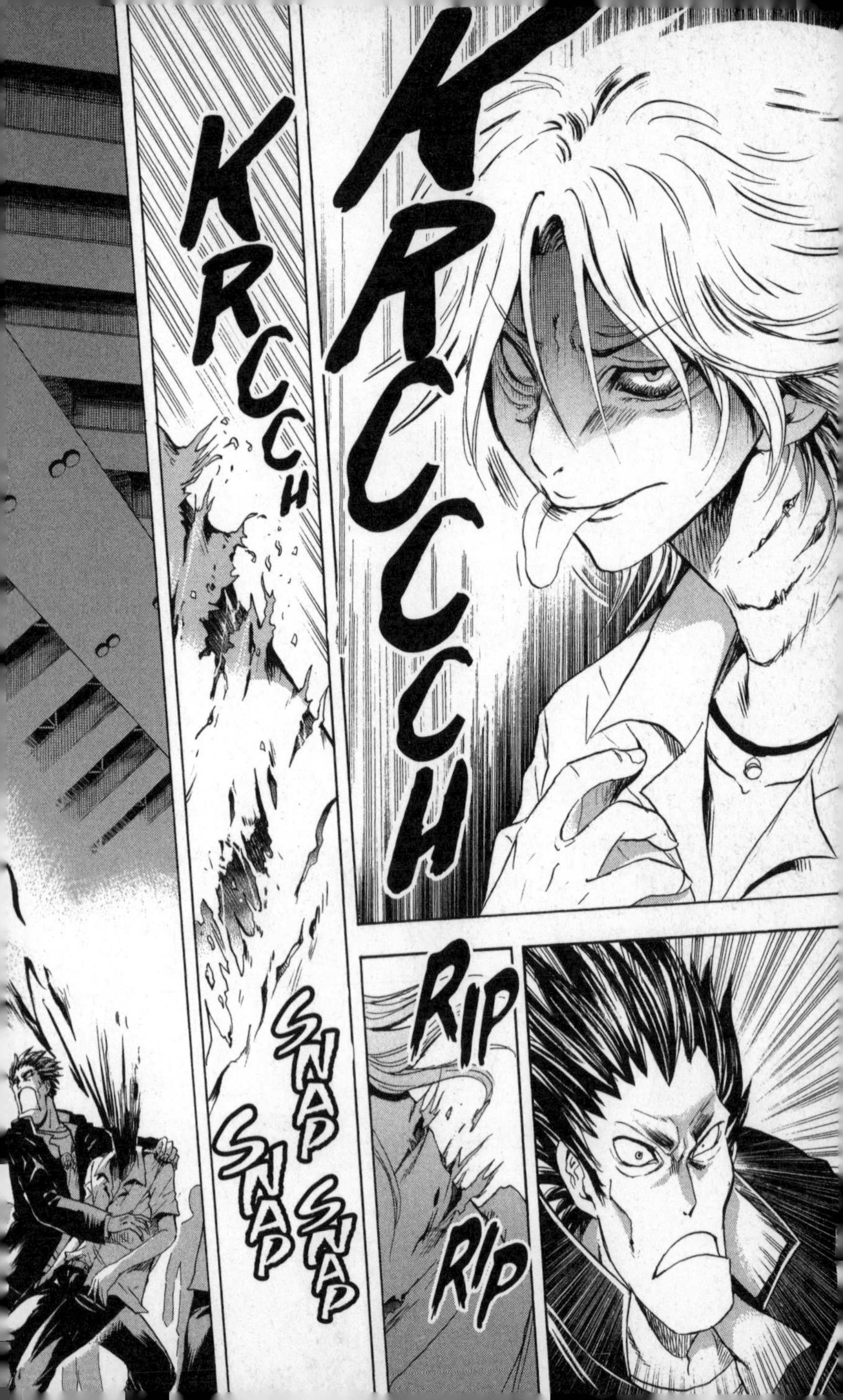
KRCCCH
KRCCH
RIP
RIP
SNAP SNAP
SNAP SNAP

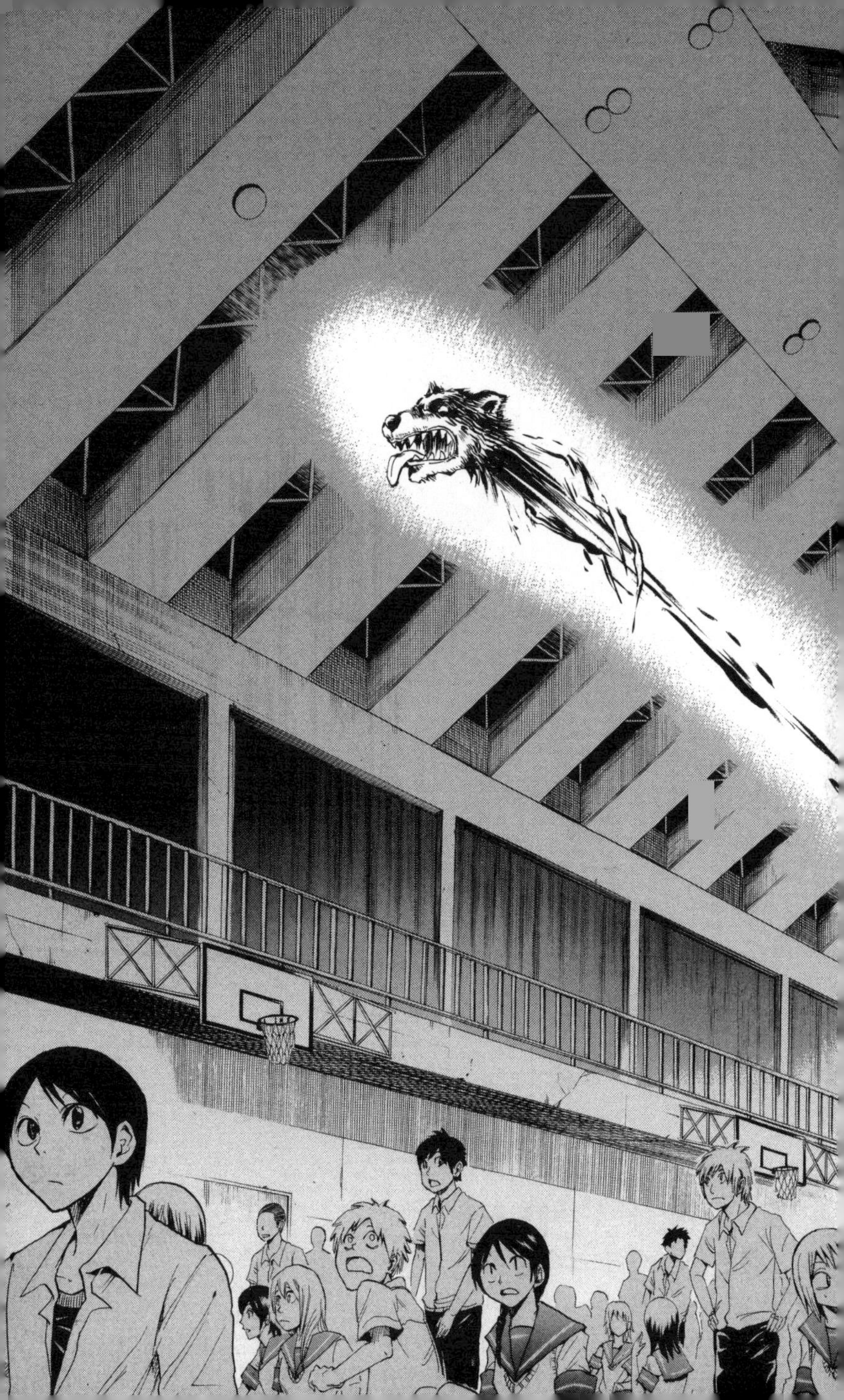

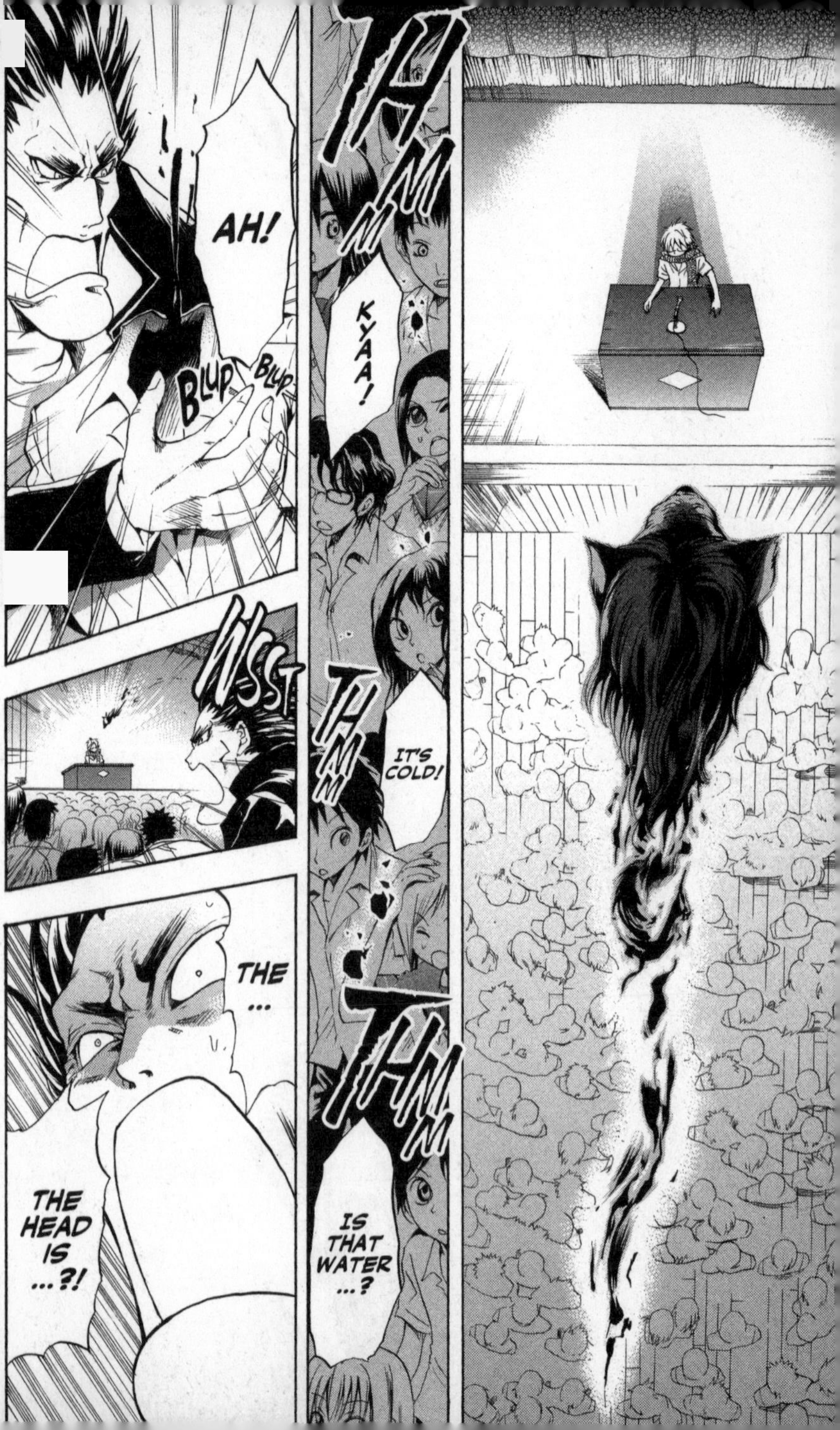
THMM
KYAAA!
THMM
IT'S COLD!
THMM
IS THAT WATER ...?
AH!
BLUP
BLUP
WSST
THE ...
THE HEAD IS ...?!

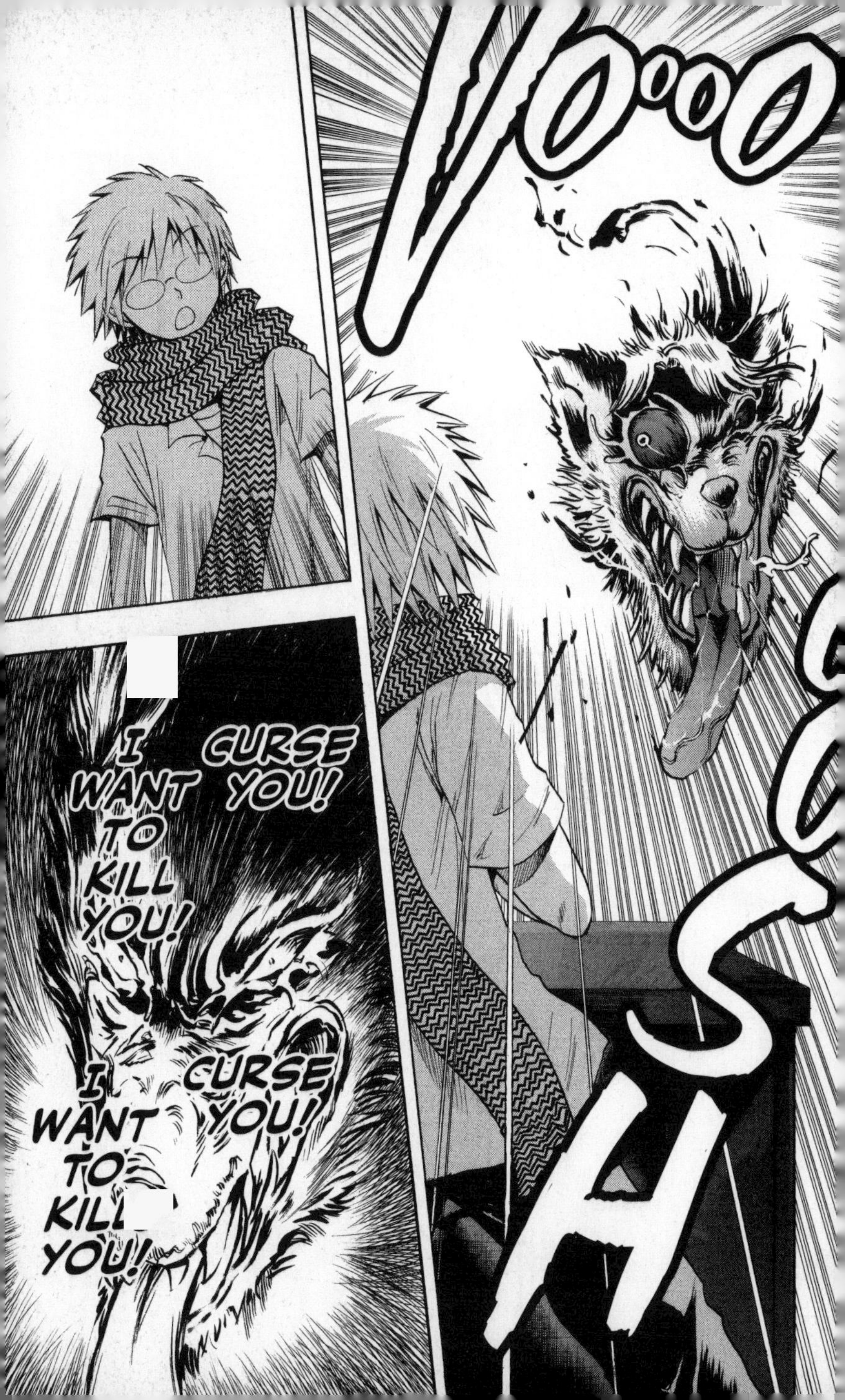
VOOOO
CURSE YOU!
I WANT TO KILL YOU!
CURSE YOU!
I WANT TO KILL YOU!

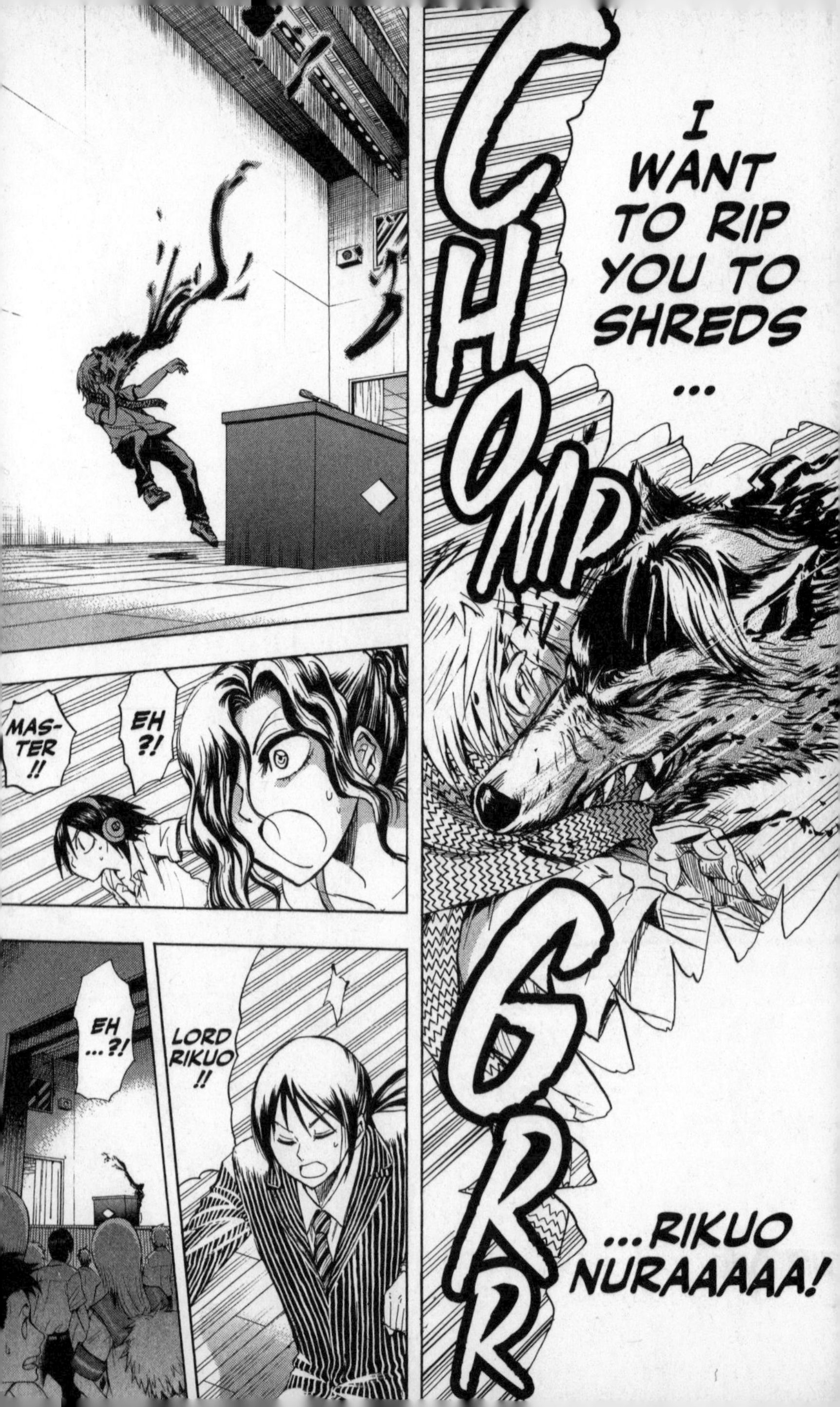
I WANT TO RIP YOU TO SHREDS ...
CHOMP
GRR
...RIKUO NURAAAAA!
EH ?!
MAS-TER !!
LORD RIKUO !!
EH ...?!

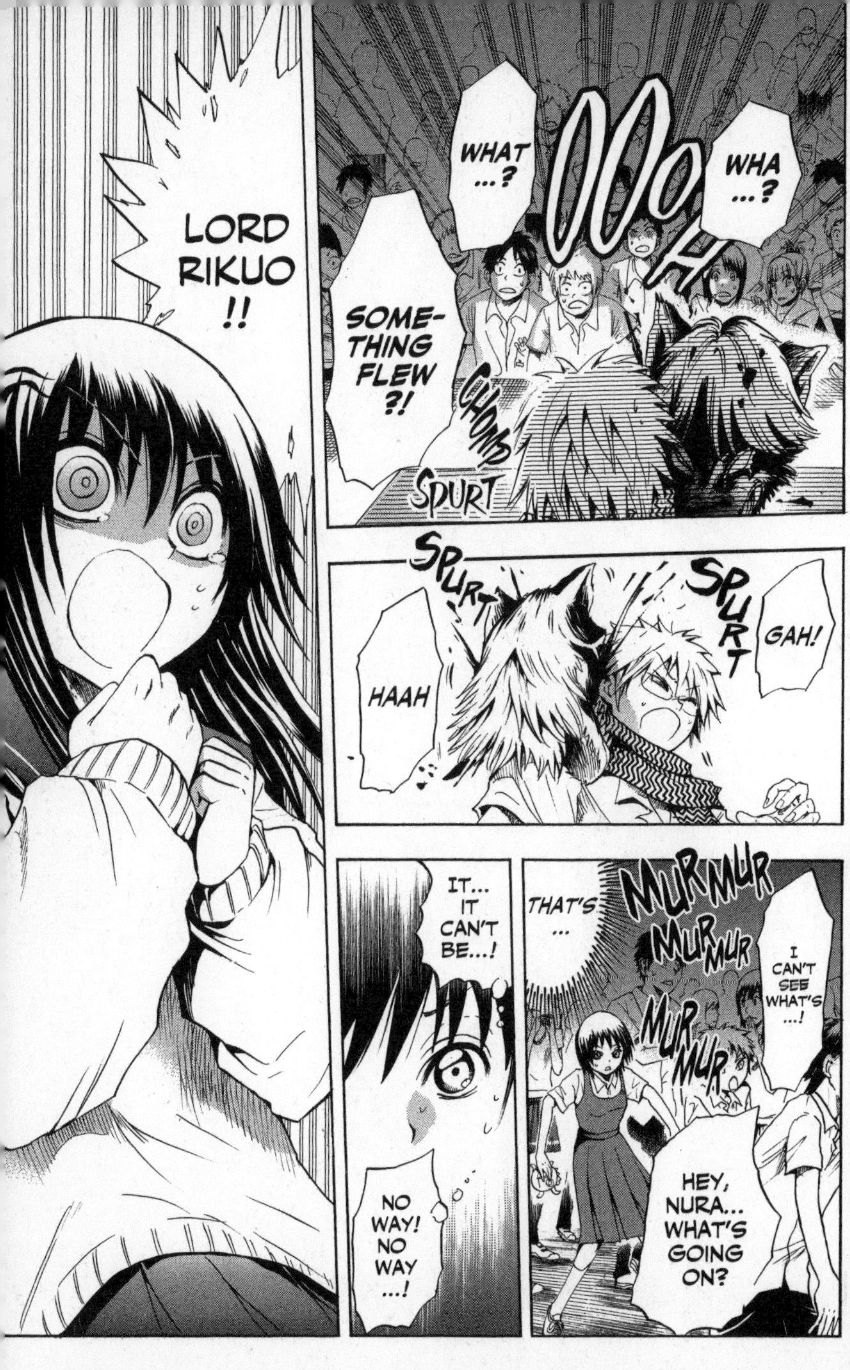
WHA ...?
OOOOH
WHAT ...?
SOME-THING FLEW ?!
CHOMP
SPURT
GAH!
SPURT
SPURT
HAAH
MURMUR
MURMUR
I CAN'T SEE WHAT'S ...!
THAT'S ...
MURMUR
HEY, NURA... WHAT'S GOING ON?
IT... IT CAN'T BE...!
NO WAY! NO WAY ...!
LORD RIKUO !!

Act 31: The Yokai Inugami, Part 3

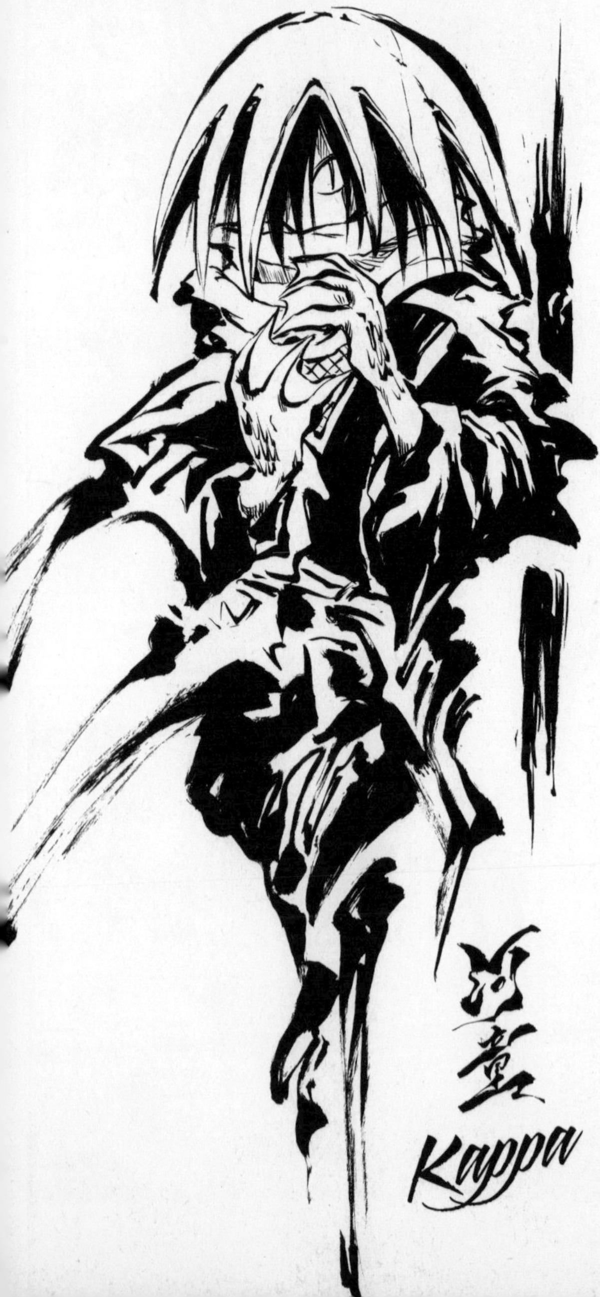
Kappa

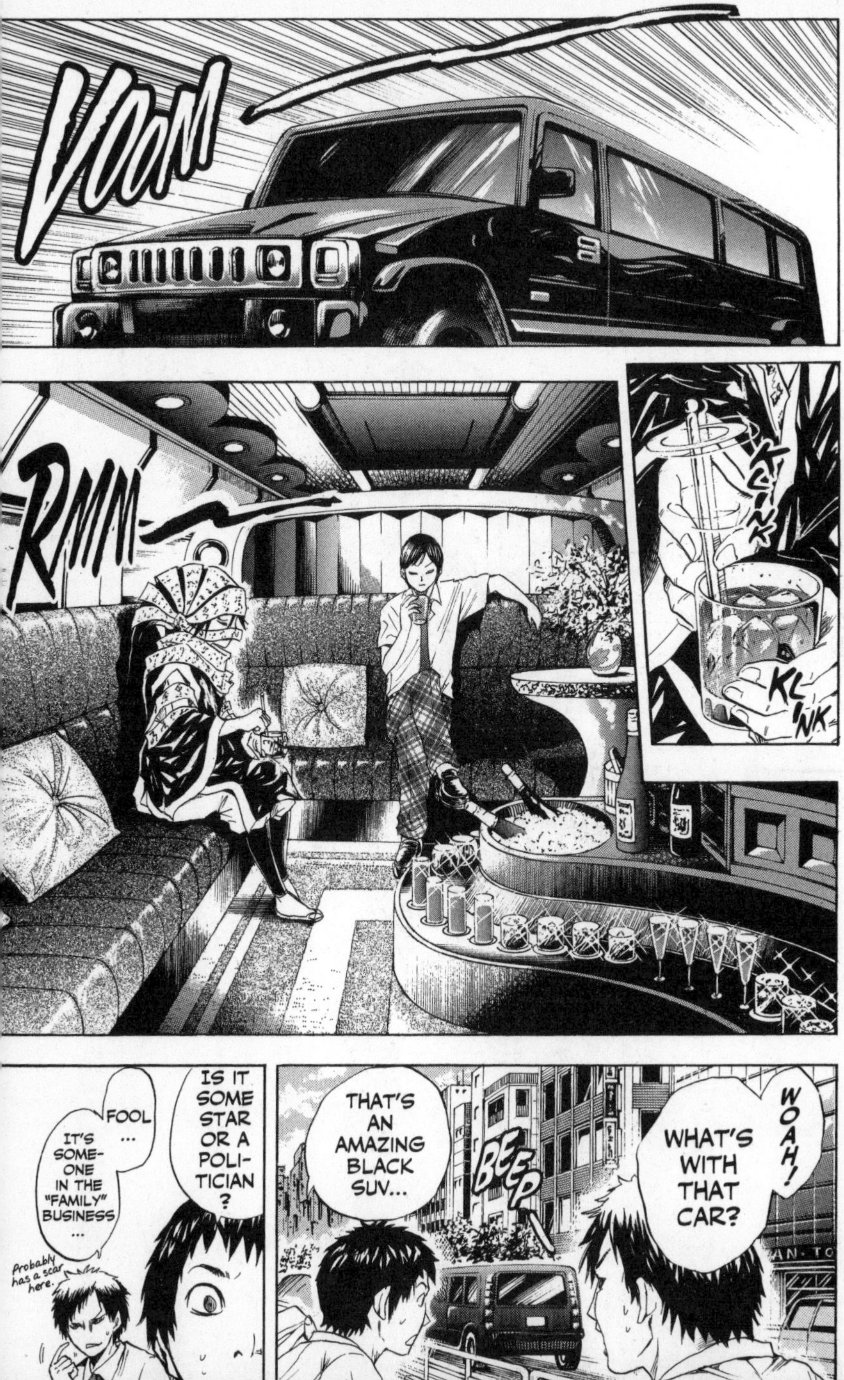
VROOM
KLINK
KLINK
RMM
WOAH!
WHAT'S WITH THAT CAR?
THAT'S AN AMAZING BLACK SUV...
BEEP
IS IT SOME STAR OR A POLITICIAN?
FOOL...
IT'S SOMEONE IN THE "FAMILY" BUSINESS...
Probably has a scar here.

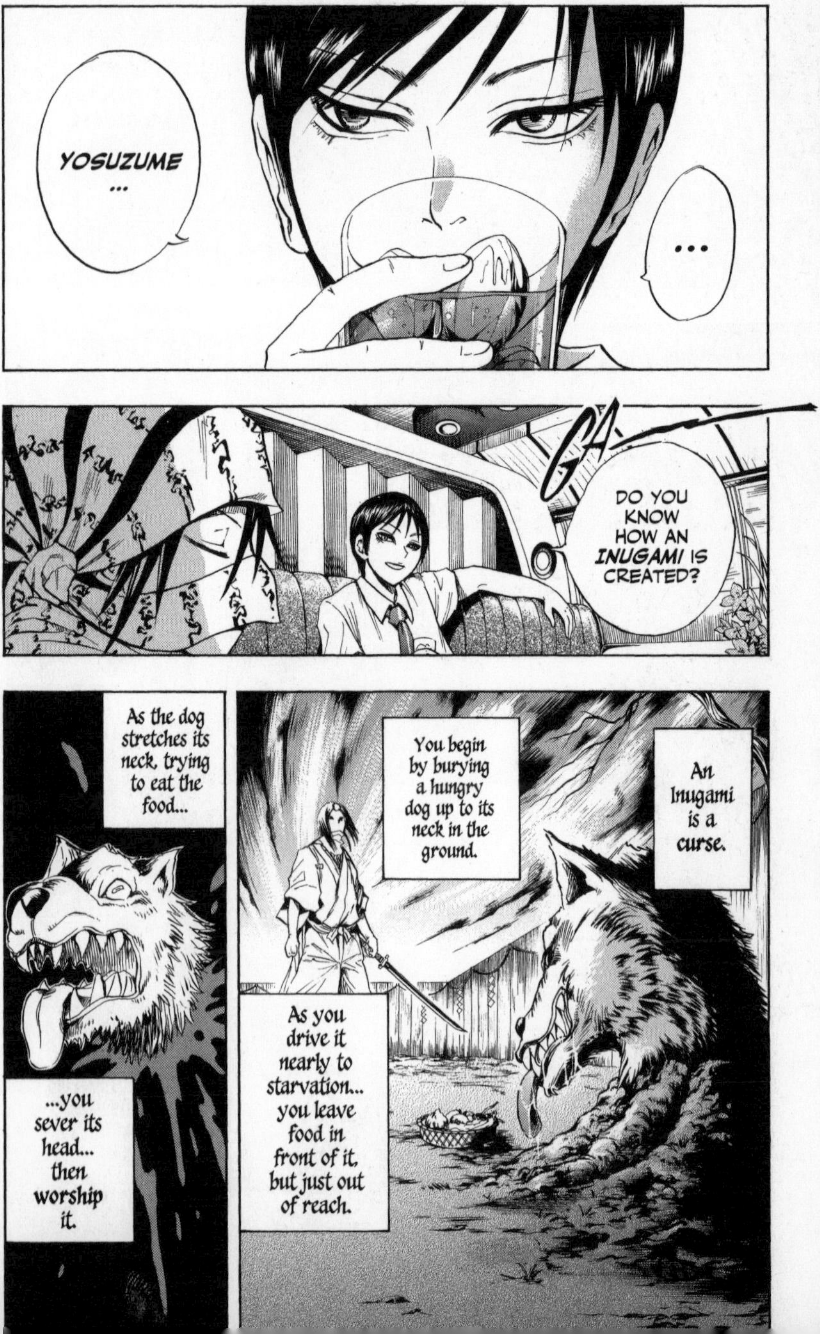
...
YOSUZUME ...
GA
DO YOU KNOW HOW AN *INUGAMI* IS CREATED?
An Inugami is a curse.
You begin by burying a hungry dog up to its neck in the ground.
As you drive it nearly to starvation... you leave food in front of it, but just out of reach.
As the dog stretches its neck, trying to eat the food...
...you sever its head... then worship it.

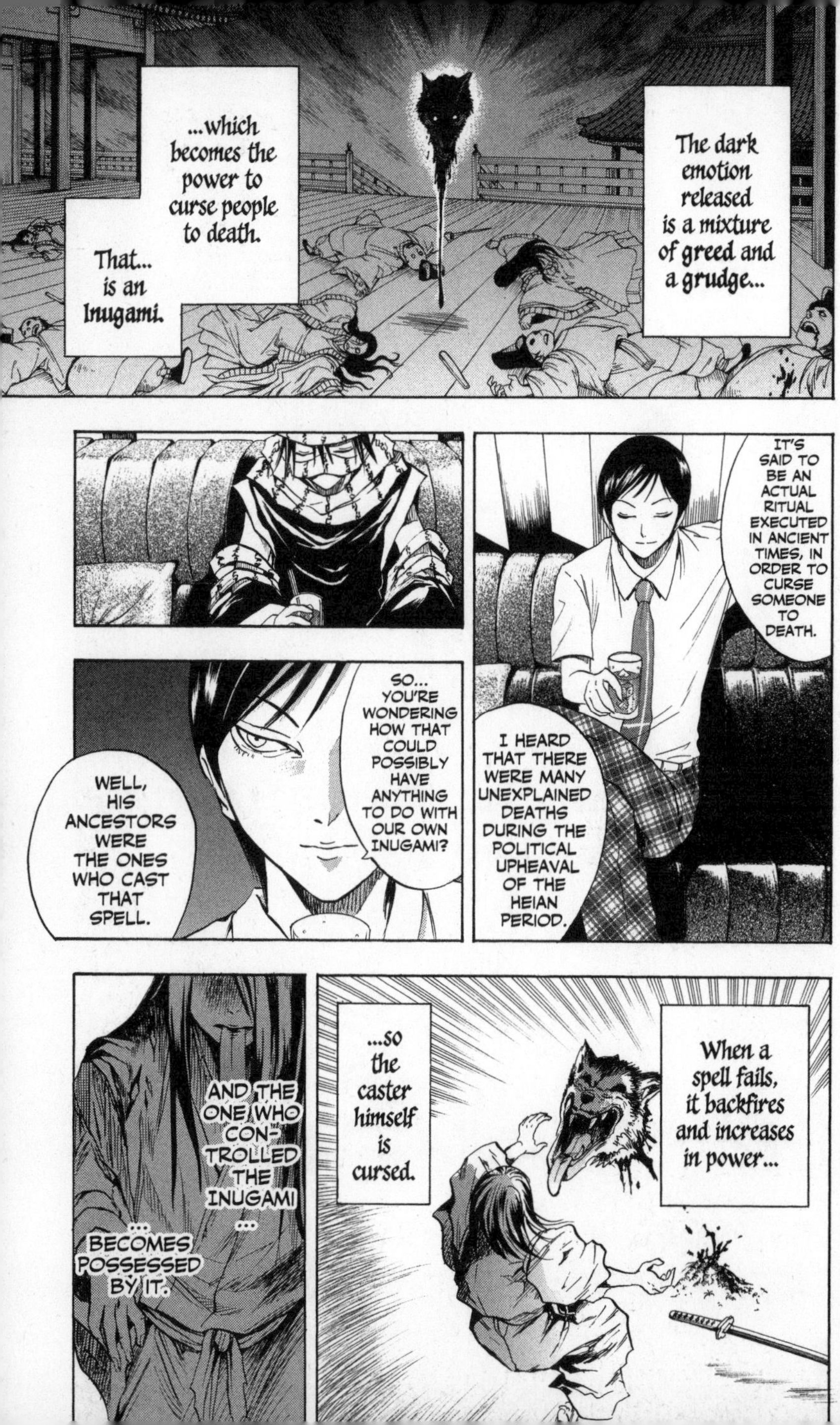
The dark emotion released is a mixture of greed and a grudge...
...which becomes the power to curse people to death.
That... is an Inugami.
IT'S SAID TO BE AN ACTUAL RITUAL EXECUTED IN ANCIENT TIMES, IN ORDER TO CURSE SOMEONE TO DEATH.
I HEARD THAT THERE WERE MANY UNEXPLAINED DEATHS DURING THE POLITICAL UPHEAVAL OF THE HEIAN PERIOD.
SO... YOU'RE WONDERING HOW THAT COULD POSSIBLY HAVE ANYTHING TO DO WITH OUR OWN INUGAMI?
WELL, HIS ANCESTORS WERE THE ONES WHO CAST THAT SPELL.
When a spell fails, it backfires and increases in power...
...so the caster himself is cursed.
AND THE ONE WHO CON-TROLLED THE INUGAMI...
...BECOMES POSSESSED BY IT.

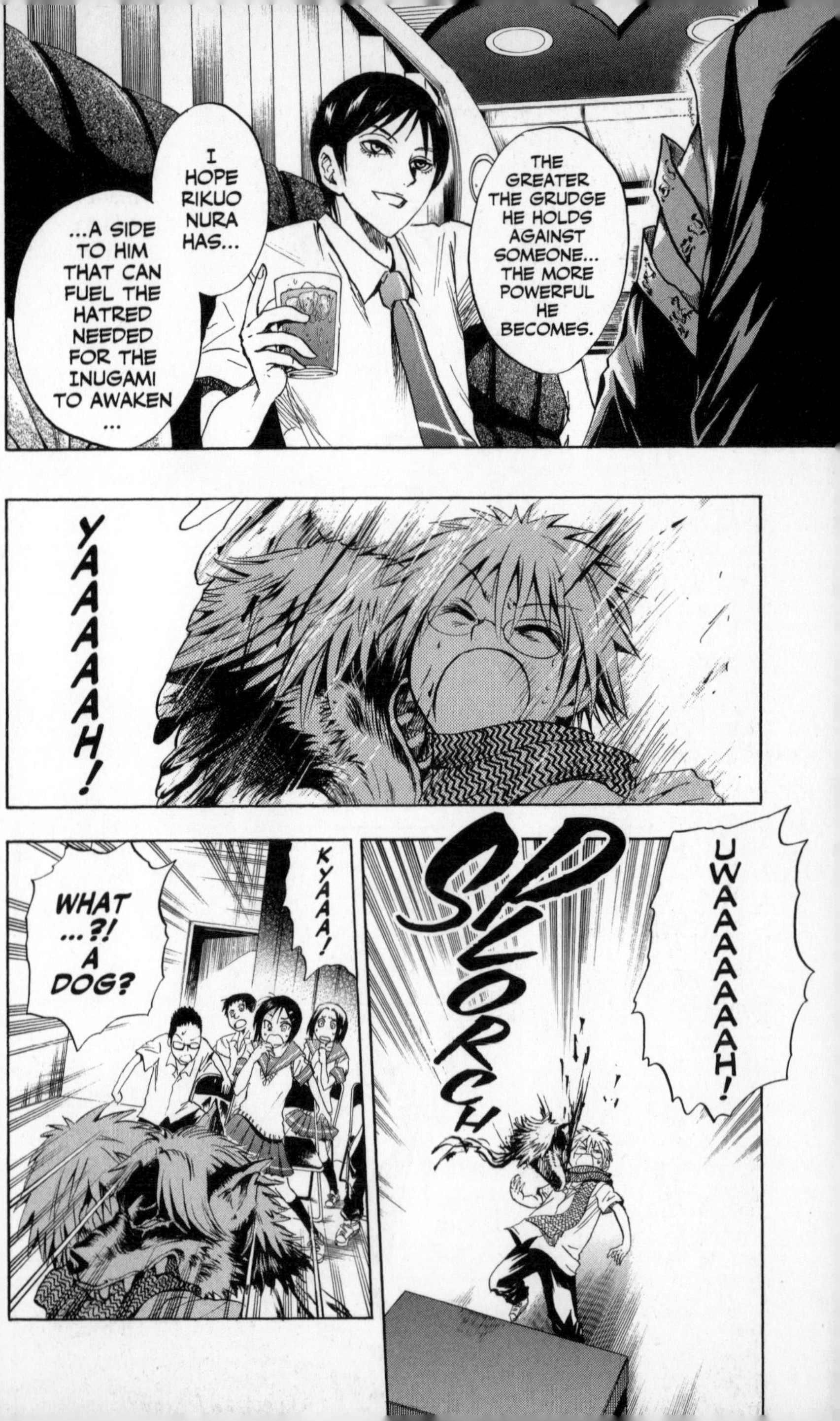
THE GREATER THE GRUDGE HE HOLDS AGAINST SOMEONE... THE MORE POWERFUL HE BECOMES.
I HOPE RIKUO NURA HAS...
...A SIDE TO HIM THAT CAN FUEL THE HATRED NEEDED FOR THE INUGAMI TO AWAKEN...
YAAAAAAAH!
UWAAAAAAAAAH!
SPLORCH
KYAAA!
WHAT...?! A DOG?

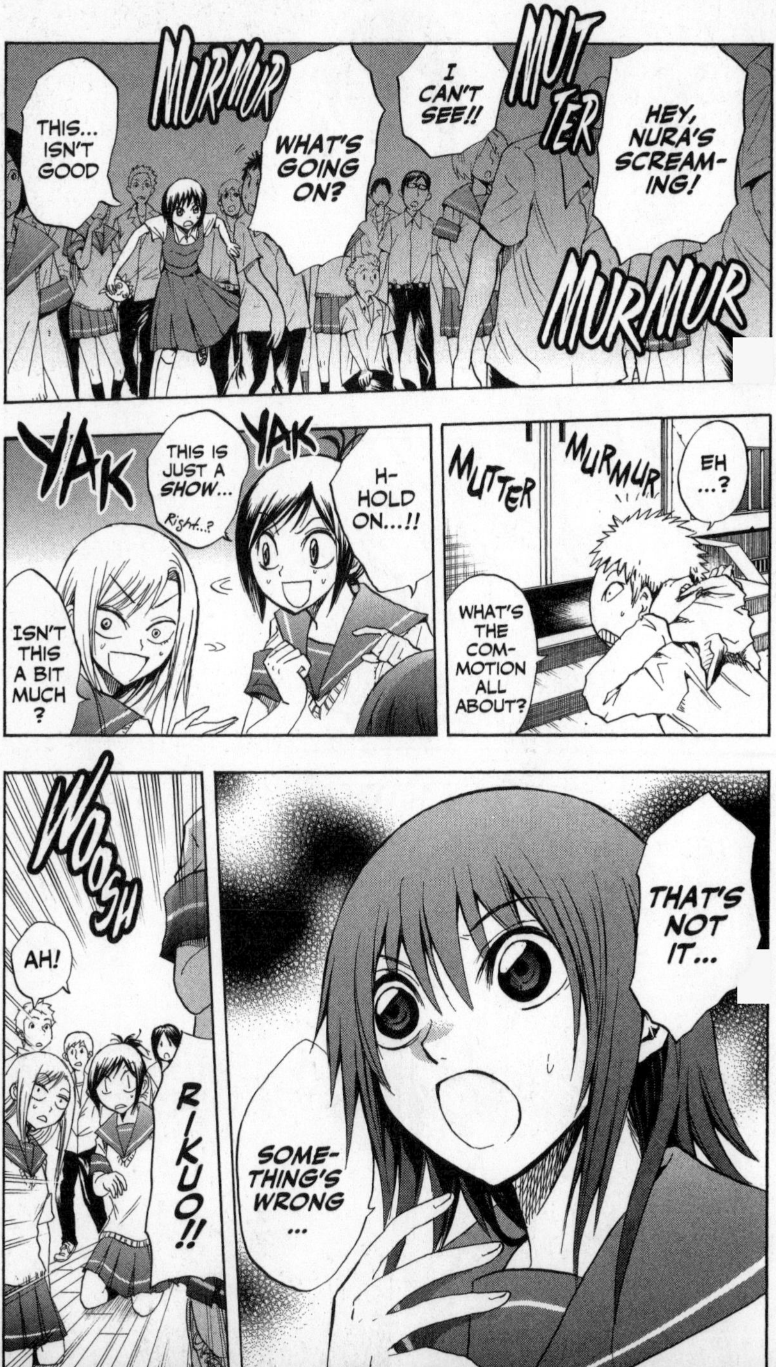
HEY, NURA'S SCREAMING!
MUTTER
MURMUR
I CAN'T SEE!!
WHAT'S GOING ON?
MURMUR
THIS... ISN'T GOOD
EH ...?
MURMUR
MUTTER
WHAT'S THE COMMOTION ALL ABOUT?
YAK
H-HOLD ON...!!
THIS IS JUST A SHOW... Right...?
YAK
ISN'T THIS A BIT MUCH?
THAT'S NOT IT...
SOMETHING'S WRONG ...
WOOSH
AH!
RIKUO!!

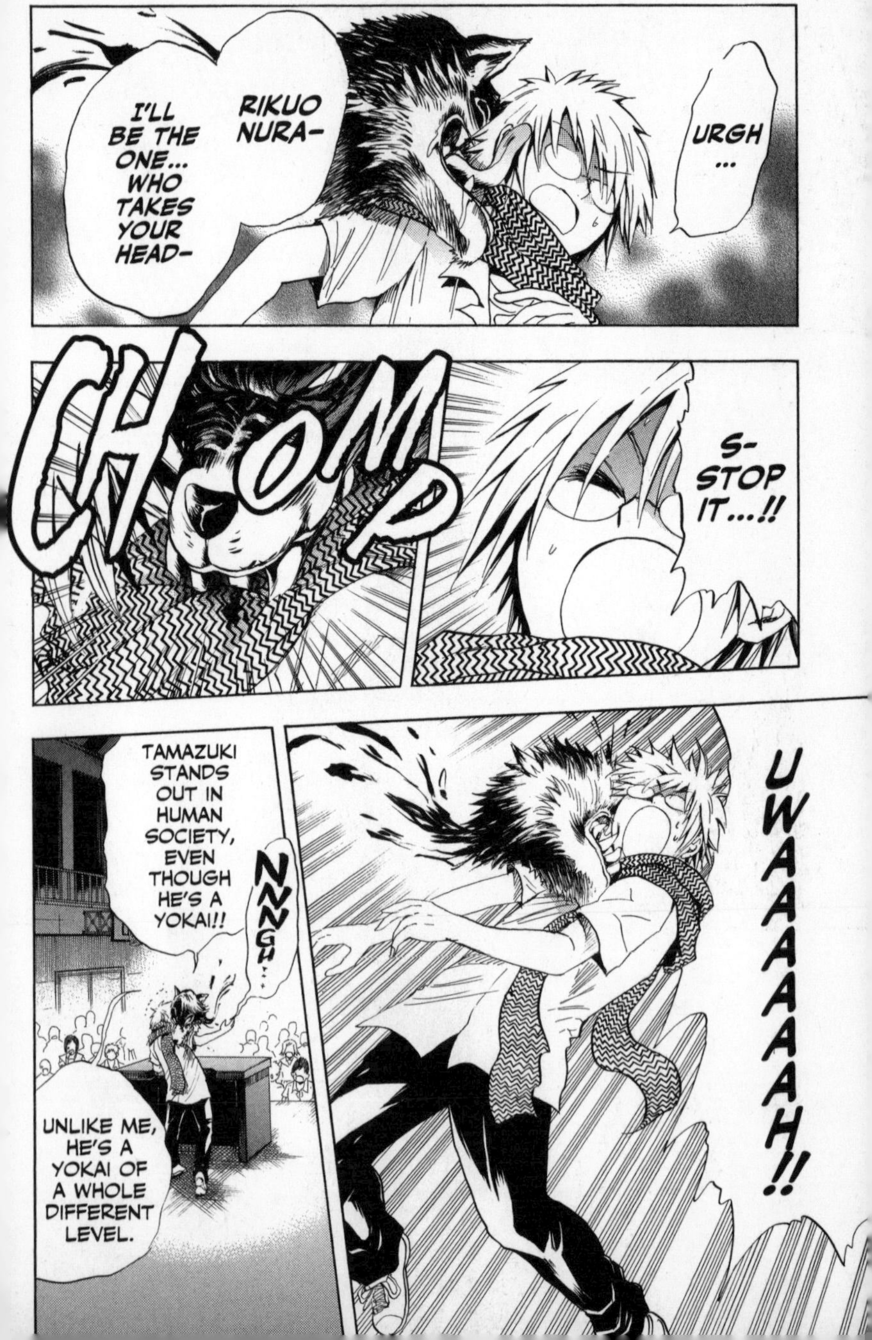
URGH...
RIKUO NURA-
I'LL BE THE ONE... WHO TAKES YOUR HEAD-
S-STOP IT...!!
CHOMP
UWAAAAAAAH!!
NNNGH...
TAMAZUKI STANDS OUT IN HUMAN SOCIETY, EVEN THOUGH HE'S A YOKAI!!
UNLIKE ME, HE'S A YOKAI OF A WHOLE DIFFERENT LEVEL.

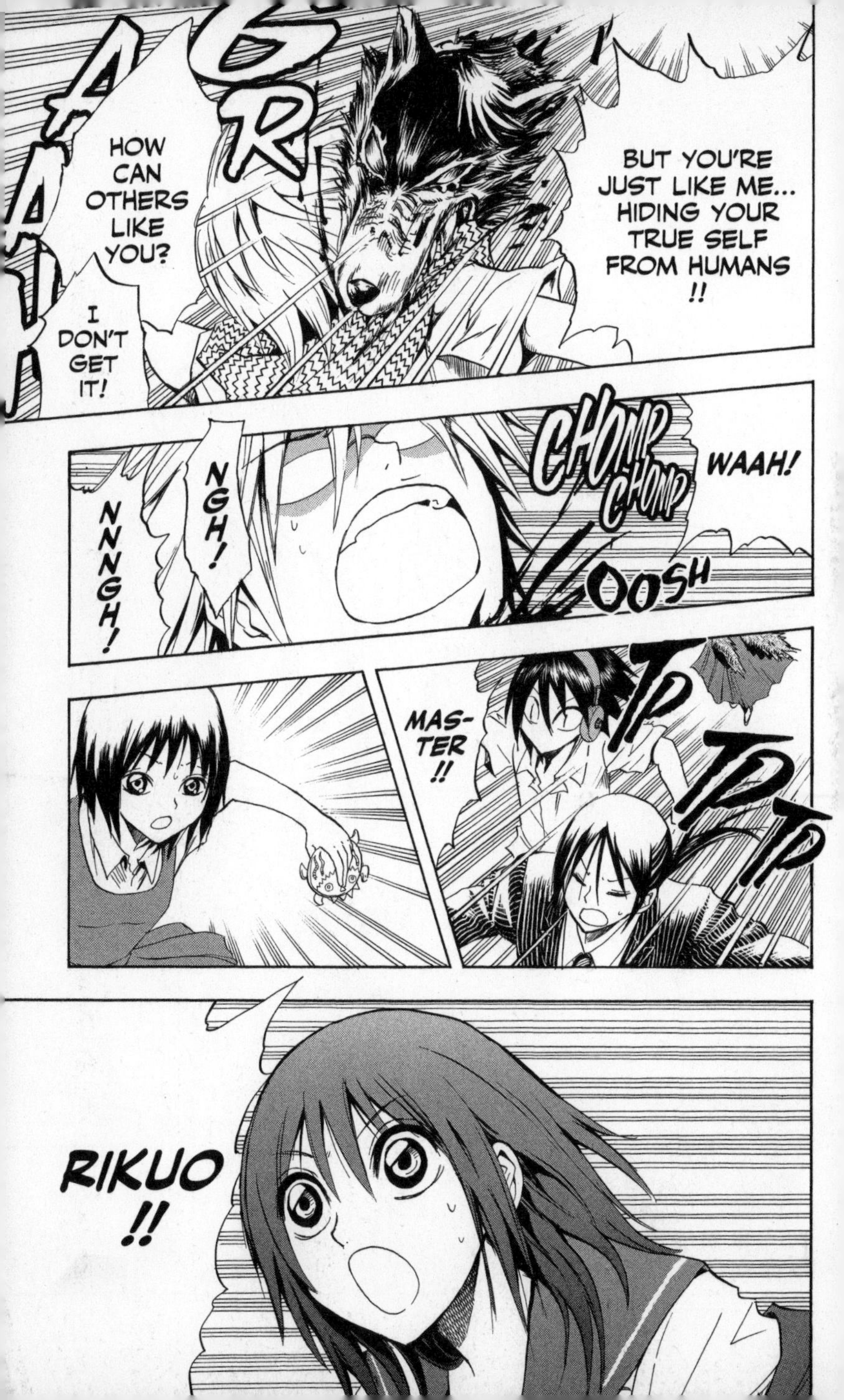
GRAAAAA
BUT YOU'RE JUST LIKE ME... HIDING YOUR TRUE SELF FROM HUMANS !!
HOW CAN OTHERS LIKE YOU?
I DON'T GET IT!
WAAH!
CHOMP CHOMP
WOOSH
NGH!
NNNGH!
TP TP TP
MAS-TER !!
RIKUO !!

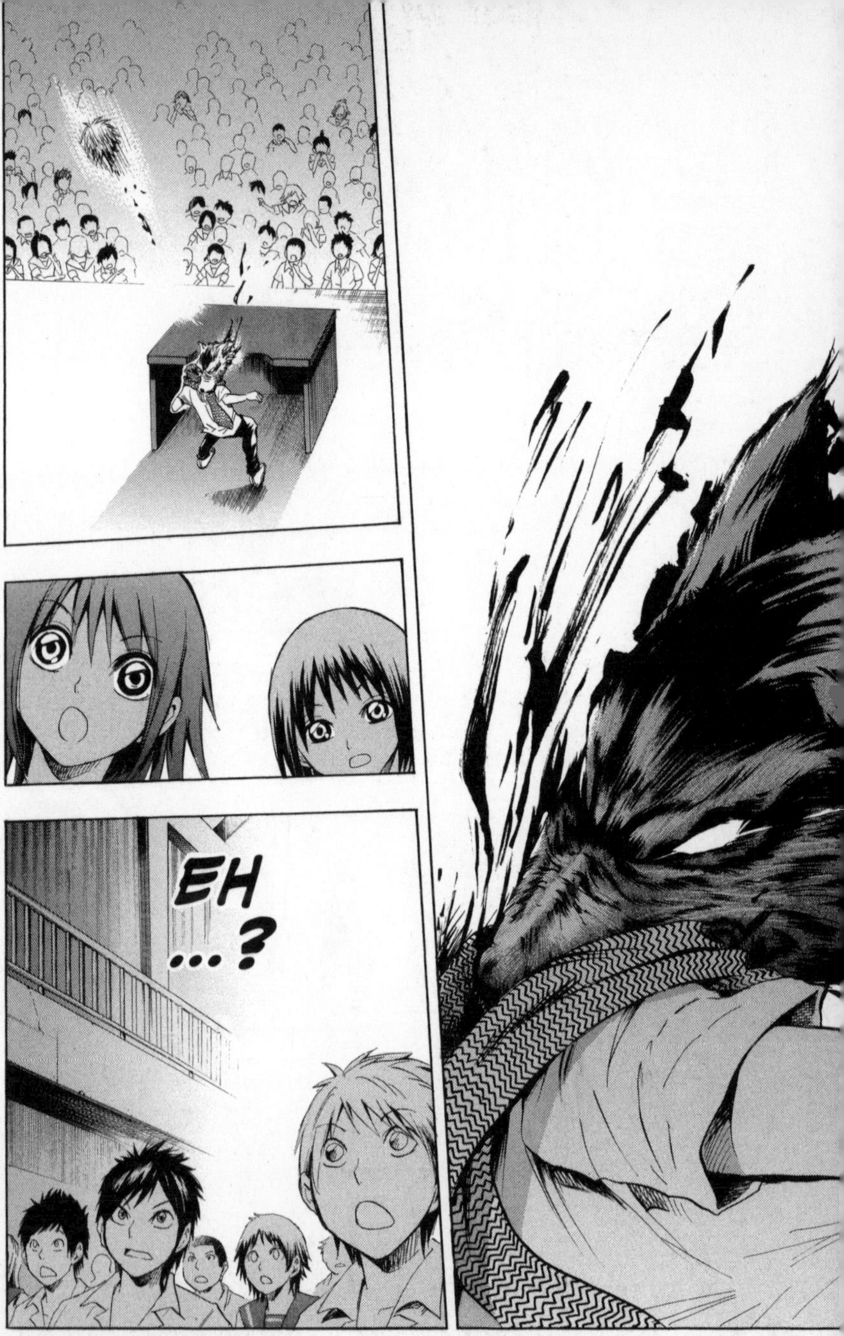
EH ...?

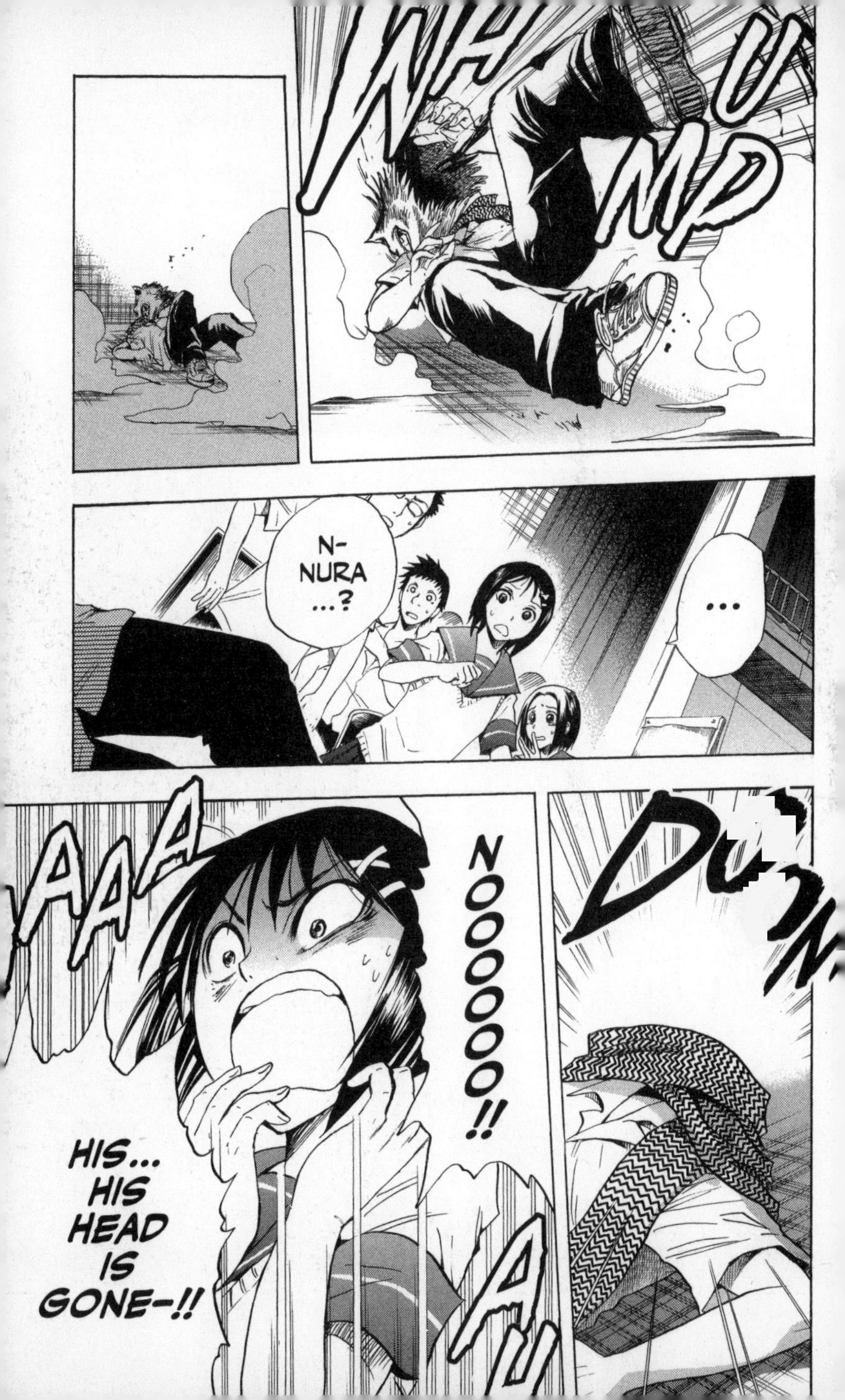
WHUMP
...
N-NURA ...?
NOOOOOOO!!
AAA
A
HIS... HIS HEAD IS GONE-!!

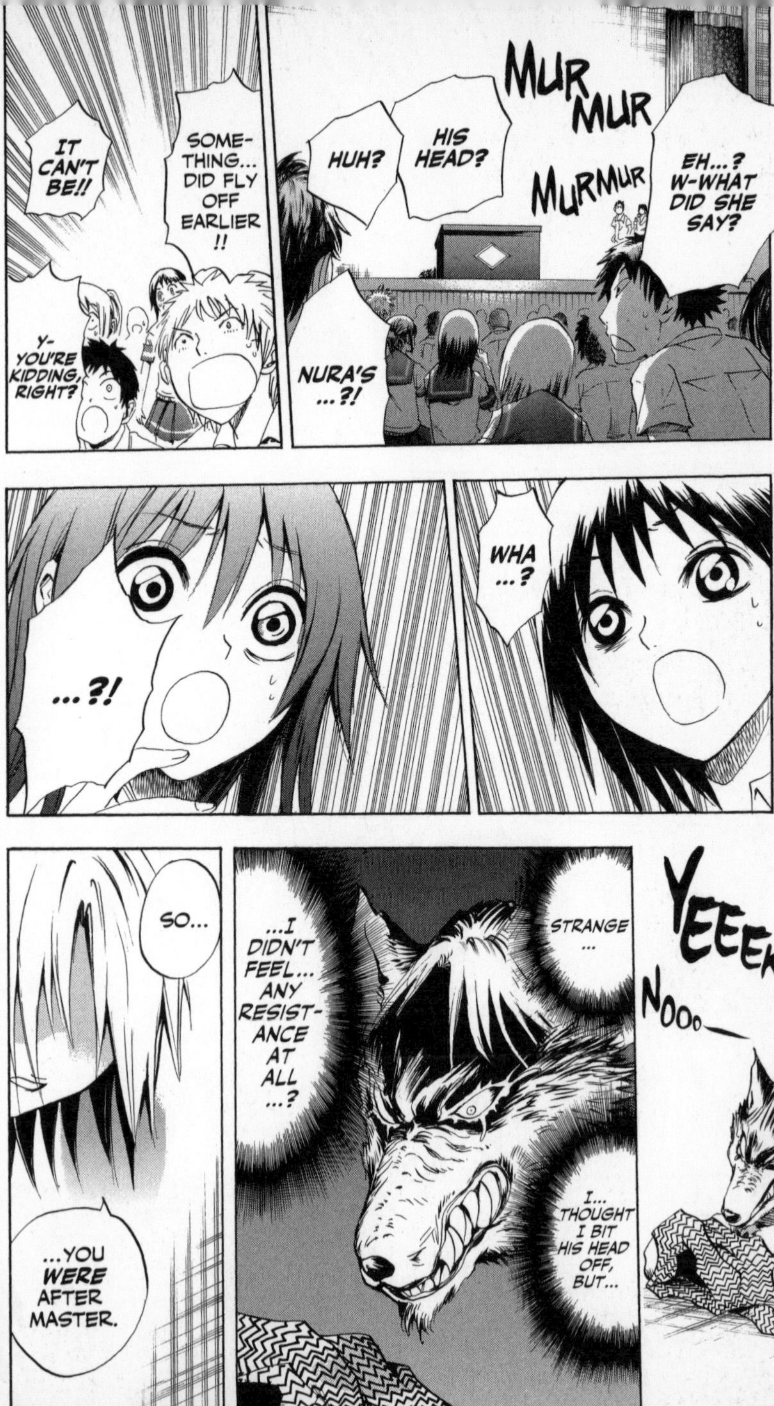
MUR MUR
EH...? W-WHAT DID SHE SAY?
MURMUR
HIS HEAD?
HUH?
NURA'S ...?!
SOME-THING... DID FLY OFF EARLIER!!
IT CAN'T BE!!
Y-YOU'RE KIDDING, RIGHT?
WHA...?
...?!
YEEEK-
NOOO-
STRANGE...
I... THOUGHT I BIT HIS HEAD OFF, BUT...
...I DIDN'T FEEL... ANY RESIST-ANCE AT ALL...?
SO...
...YOU WERE AFTER MASTER.

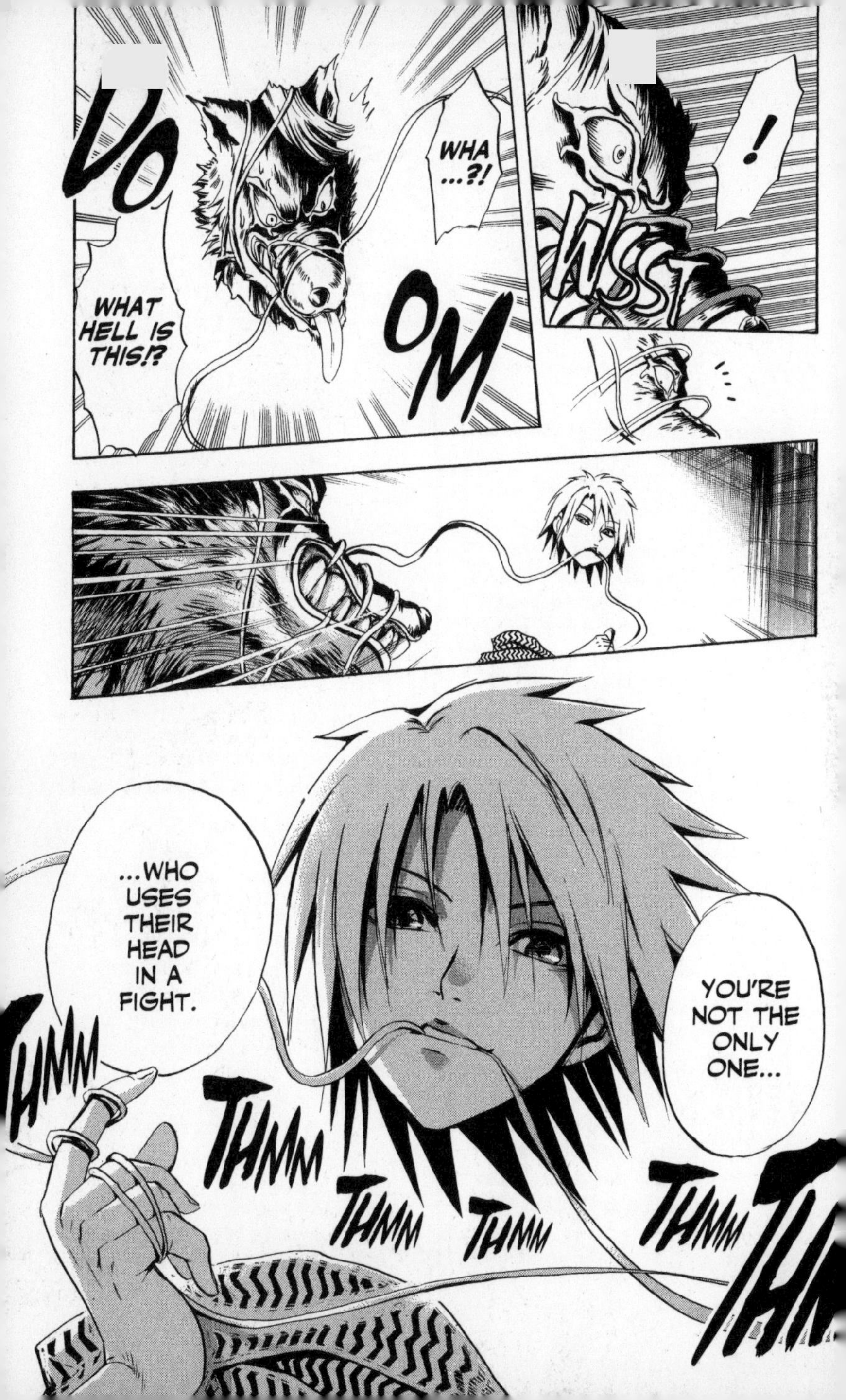
!
WSST
VO
OM
WHA ...?!
WHAT HELL IS THIS!?
YOU'RE NOT THE ONLY ONE...
...WHO USES THEIR HEAD IN A FIGHT.
THMM
THMM
THMM
THMM
THMM
THMM
TH

KIYOTSUGU'S YOKAI BRAIN!

PRINT EDITION #4 by Kiyo

(Continued from page 76)

Question 4: "How much allowance does Kiyotsugu get every month?" —*Nurarihyon's Great-Grandson, Kanagawa Prefecture*

Kiyo: What the heck? This has nothing to do with yokai!! But, I will answer it anyway. At school or at home, I am a super-excellent child who outshines everyone else, so my parents give me an unlimited amount!! Freedom doesn't mean you can just become a delinquent...true freedom comes only to those who choose to live as they desire!! Now, if you understand what I just said, why don't you try hard to join us on the trail of the yokai? All right, next!!

Question 5: "Are 'ayakashi' and 'yokai' the same thing? —*Karasu, Saitama Prefecture*

Kiyo: Hmmm... This is a pretty good question. When Japan entered the Meiji era, it became a nation with a centralized government, and collected all the information from local districts together in Tokyo. It's said that they began to classify "things that aren't quite understandable" as "yokai" at that point. There were dialects and rural folklore, but basically, after the Meiji era they were referred to as "yokai," and before that, everything was "ayakashi." Well, it feels like I've actually answered a question for the first time. All right, I'm on a roll!! Let's move on to the next one!!

Rikuo: Whew... I'm glad. Seems like he cheered up.

Question 6: "Kiyotsugu, what is it about the Lord of the Yokai that attracts you? For me, it's his eyes." —*Ringo-chan, Tokushima Prefecture*

Kiyo: Oooh!! Let's see...yes, you're right... his eyes are certainly attractive!! Definitely!! But that's not the only thing... The Lord of the Yokai is so diminutive, but he stands up against big, scary yokai without fear!! And he wins!! Everything about him is beautiful... Of course, other parts of him are hard to ignore...his distinctive hairstyle is really cool, and the way he wears his kimono is...

Torii & Maki: He's at it again... He's only seen him once, so how can he keep going on like that—?

Kana: But, what really makes that man attractive is...

Tsurara: Tee hee. Rikuo-sama, you're really popular.

Rikuo: Hey!! Tsurara?! Geez... When it comes to this topic, things get out of hand... Oh well... Anyway, for those of you accessing the Yokai Brain, we'll be waiting for more of your questions! Okay, I'll go ahead and post this...

Act 32: The Yokai Inugami, Part 4

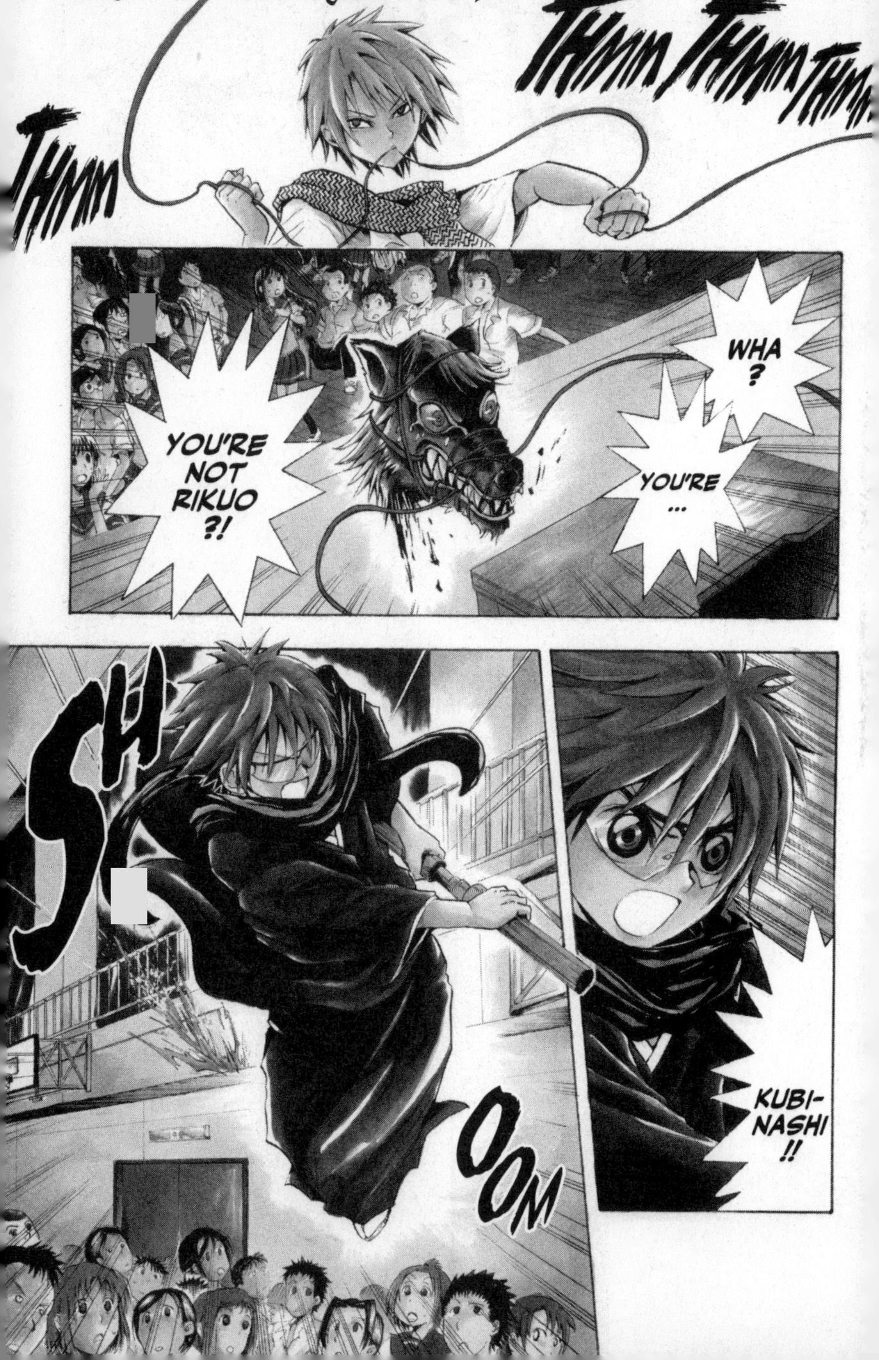
THMM THMM THMM
THMM
WHA ?
YOU'RE ...
YOU'RE NOT RIKUO ?!
KUBI-NASHI !!
SH OOM

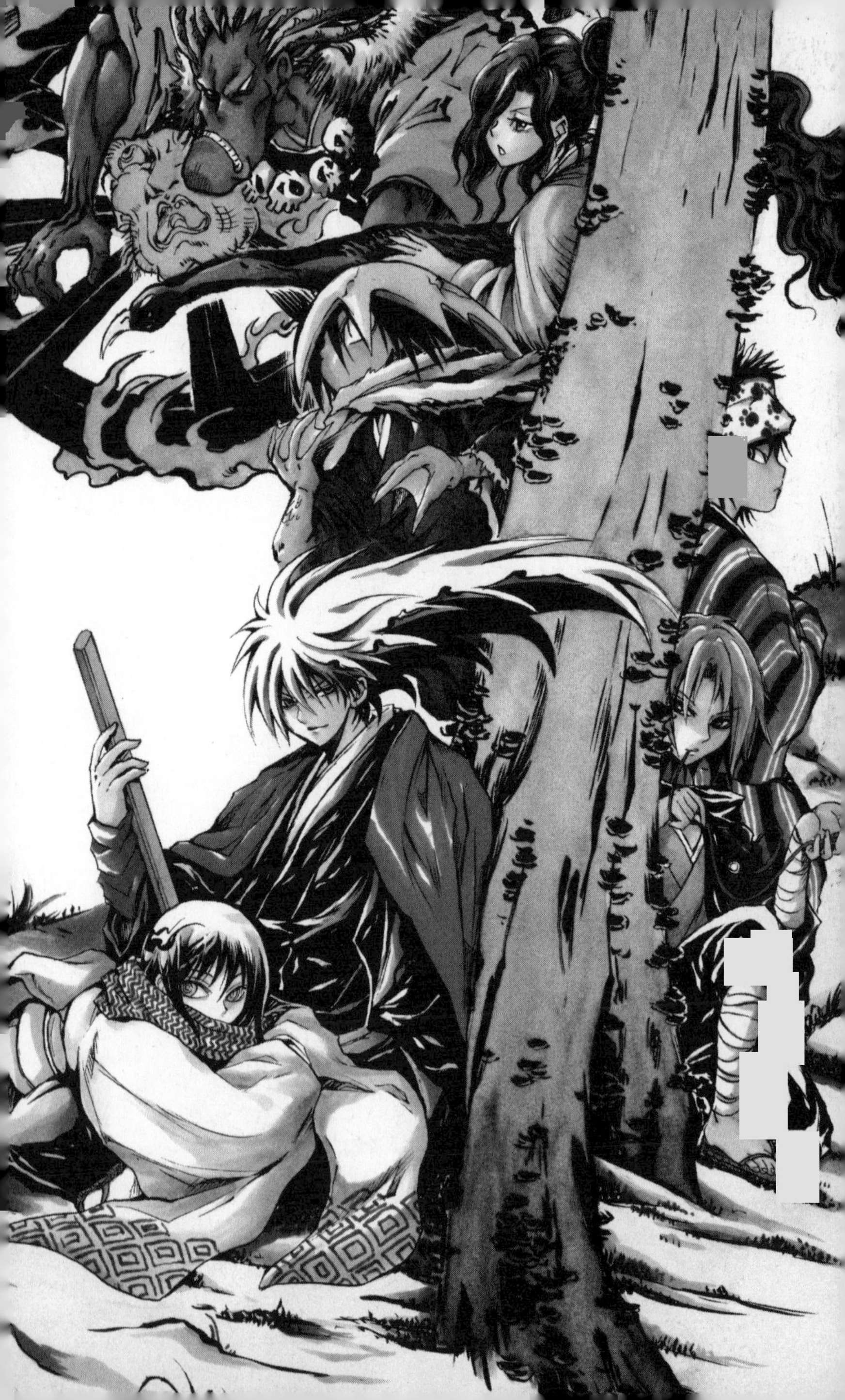

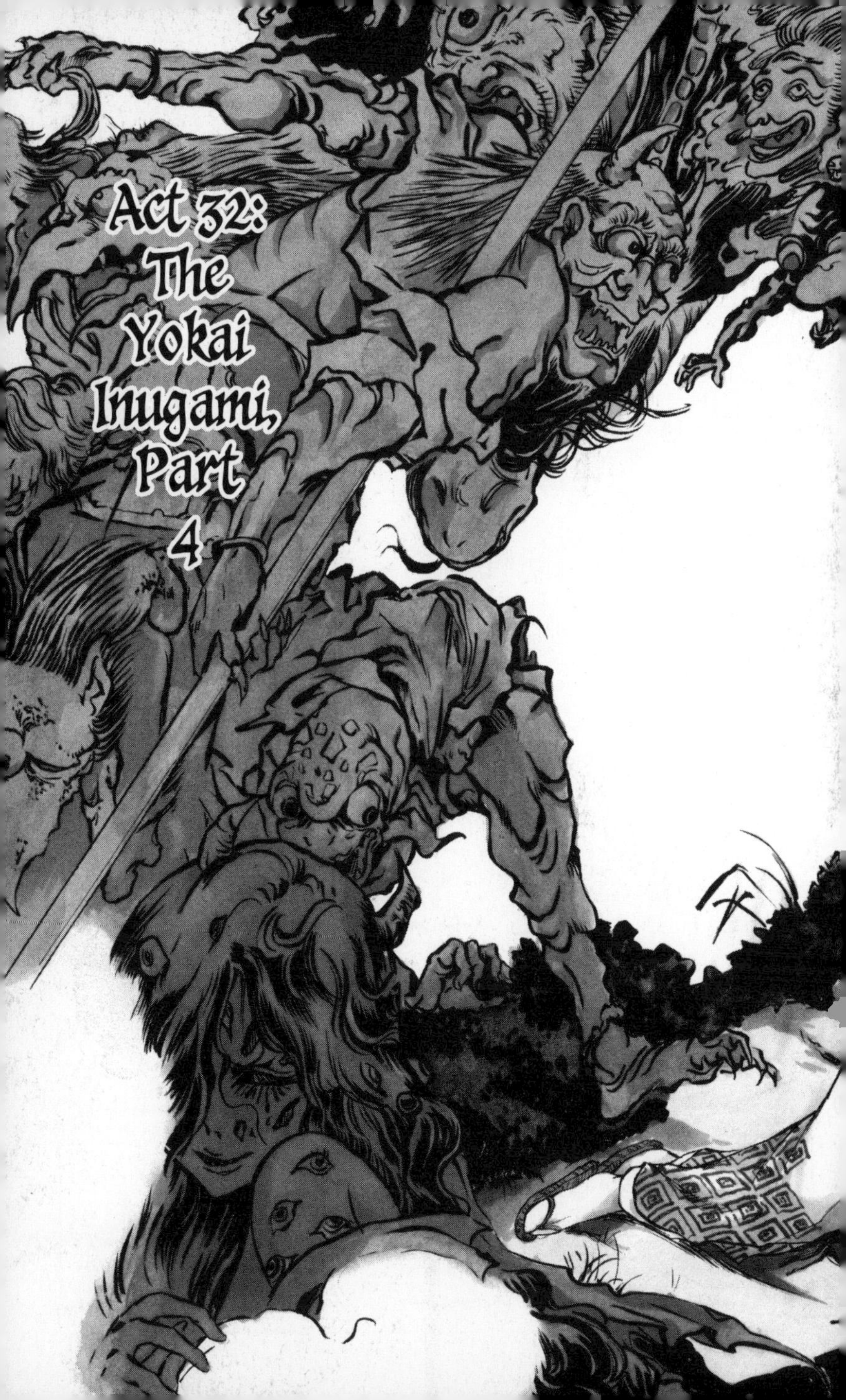
Act 32: The Yokai Inugami, Part 4

YOKAI BRAIN SPECIAL ANNOUNCEMENT

"Yokai Illustration Bulletin Board PixKiyo" Opening!!

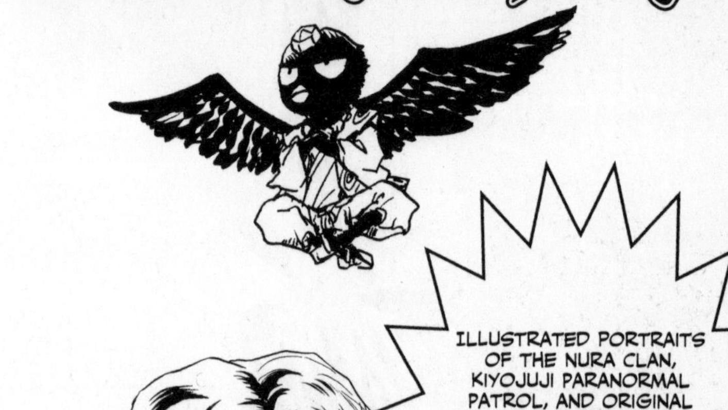
ILLUSTRATED PORTRAITS OF THE NURA CLAN, KIYOJUJI PARANORMAL PATROL, AND ORIGINAL CHARACTERS ARE ALL OKAY! I, KIYOTSUGU (OR SOME OTHER MEMBERS OF THE WEBSITE) WILL COMMENT ON THEM! EVERYONE, PLEASE SEND THEM ALONG TO US! NATURALLY, I'LL BE WAITING FOR EVERYONE'S QUESTIONS AS WELL!

ADDRESS TO

SHUEISHA
SHUKAN SHONEN JUMP EDITOR
NURARIHYON NO MAGO, "KIYOTSUGU-KUN'S YOKAI BRAIN"
2-5-10 HITOTSUBASHI, CHIYODA-KU, TOKYO 101-8050
JAPAN

*PLEASE INCLUDE YOUR NAME, AGE, ADDRESS AND PHONE NUMBER IN THE LETTER. IF YOU DO NOT WANT TO INCLUDE YOUR NAME, PLEASE USE A HANDLE OR NICKNAME. LETTERS AND ILLUSTRATIONS MAILED TO US WILL BE STORED FOR A CERTAIN PERIOD, BUT THEN LATER DISCARDED. IF YOU WISH TO KEEP A COPY, PLEASE MAKE ONE YOURSELF BEFORE MAILING IT IN. IF YOU'D LIKE TO HAVE YOUR NAME AND ADDRESS REMAIN ANONYMOUS, PLEASE INDICATE THAT IN YOUR LETTER. ALL WRITTEN TEXTS MAILED IN WILL BECOME THE COPYRIGHTED PROPERTY OF SHUEISHA.

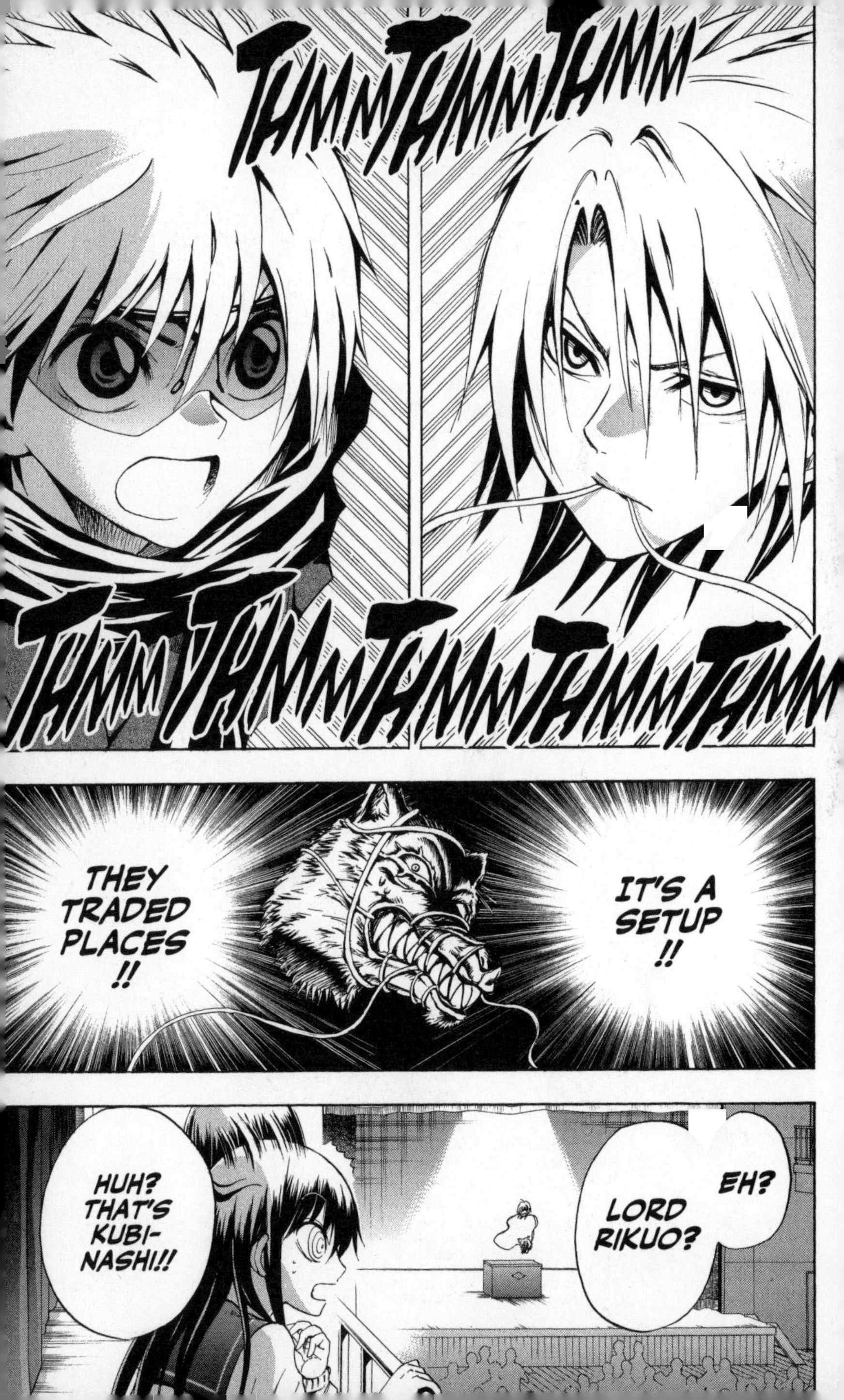
TAMMTAMMTAMM
TAMMTAMMTAMMTAMMTAMM
IT'S A SETUP!!
THEY TRADED PLACES!!
EH? LORD RIKUO?
HUH? THAT'S KUBI-NASHI!!

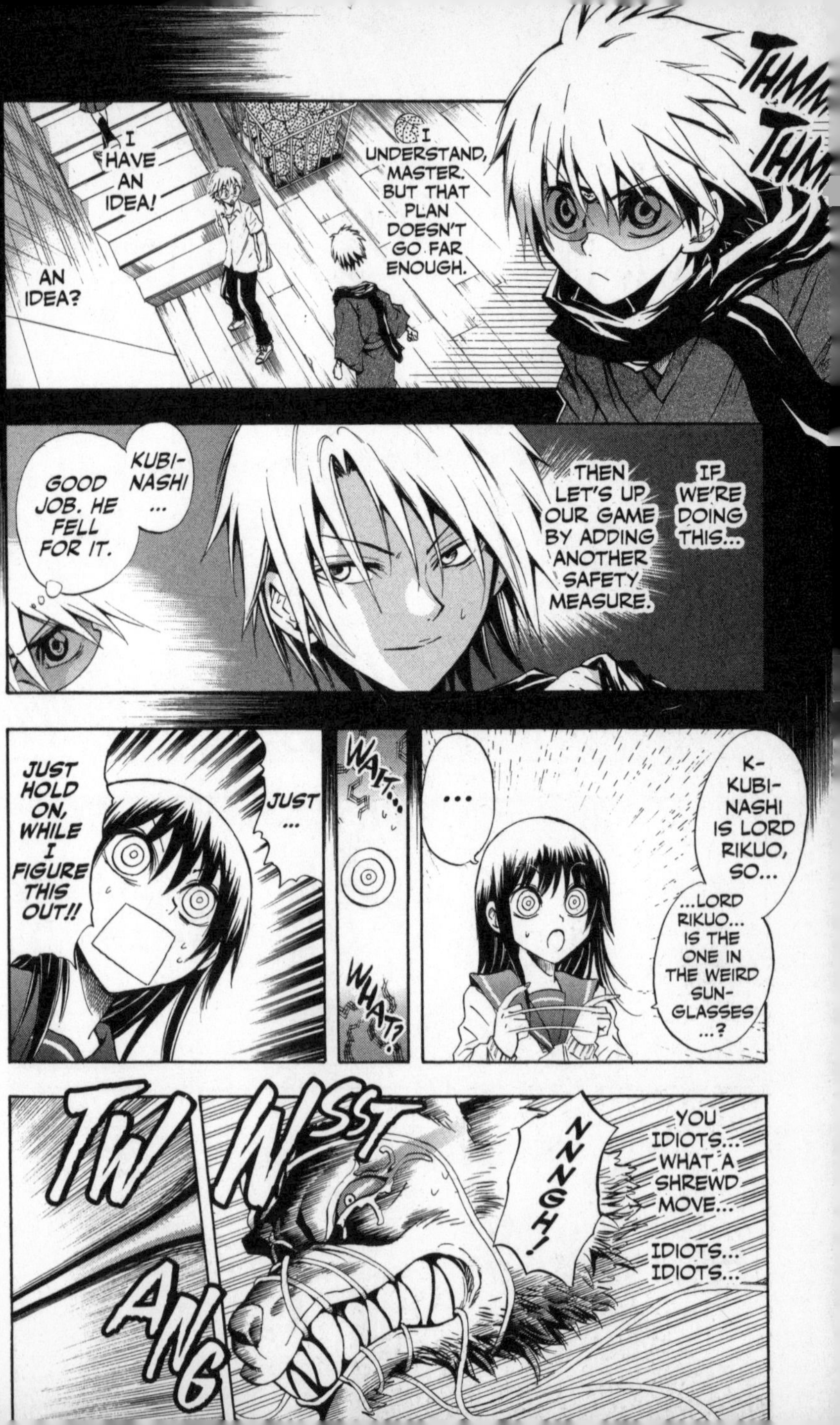
THMM THMM
I UNDERSTAND, MASTER. BUT THAT PLAN DOESN'T GO FAR ENOUGH.
I HAVE AN IDEA!
AN IDEA?
IF WE'RE DOING THIS...
THEN LET'S UP OUR GAME BY ADDING ANOTHER SAFETY MEASURE.
KUBI-NASHI ...
GOOD JOB. HE FELL FOR IT.
K-KUBI-NASHI IS LORD RIKUO, SO...
...LORD RIKUO... IS THE ONE IN THE WEIRD SUN-GLASSES ...?
...
WAIT...
WHAT?
JUST ...
JUST HOLD ON, WHILE I FIGURE THIS OUT!!
YOU IDIOTS... WHAT A SHREWD MOVE...
IDIOTS... IDIOTS...
NNNGH!
TWISST
ANG

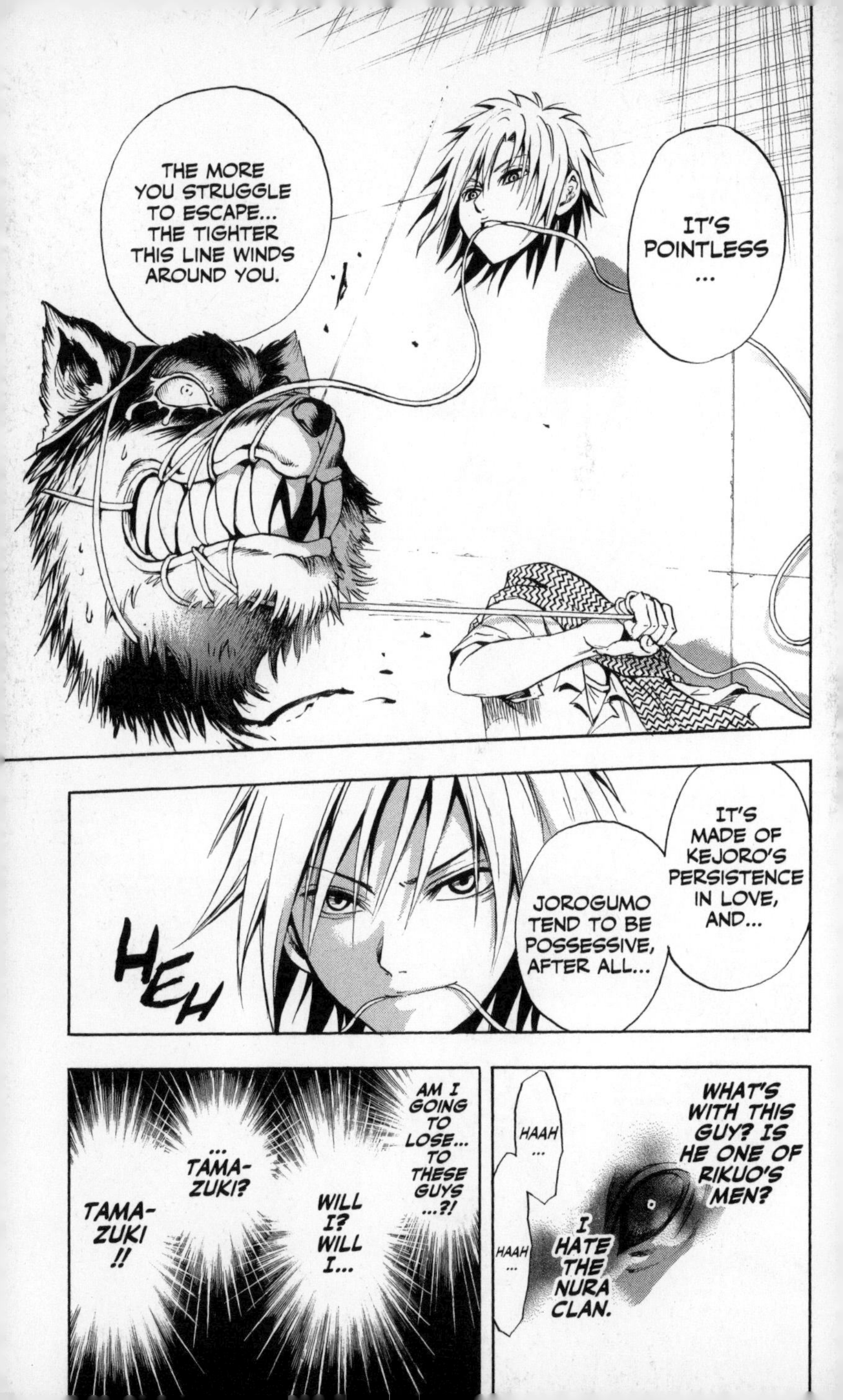
IT'S POINTLESS ...
THE MORE YOU STRUGGLE TO ESCAPE... THE TIGHTER THIS LINE WINDS AROUND YOU.
IT'S MADE OF KEJORO'S PERSISTENCE IN LOVE, AND...
JOROGUMO TEND TO BE POSSESSIVE, AFTER ALL...
HEH
WHAT'S WITH THIS GUY? IS HE ONE OF RIKUO'S MEN?
HAAH ...
HAAH ...
I HATE THE NURA CLAN.
AM I GOING TO LOSE... TO THESE GUYS ...?!
WILL I? WILL I...
... TAMA-ZUKI?
TAMA-ZUKI !!

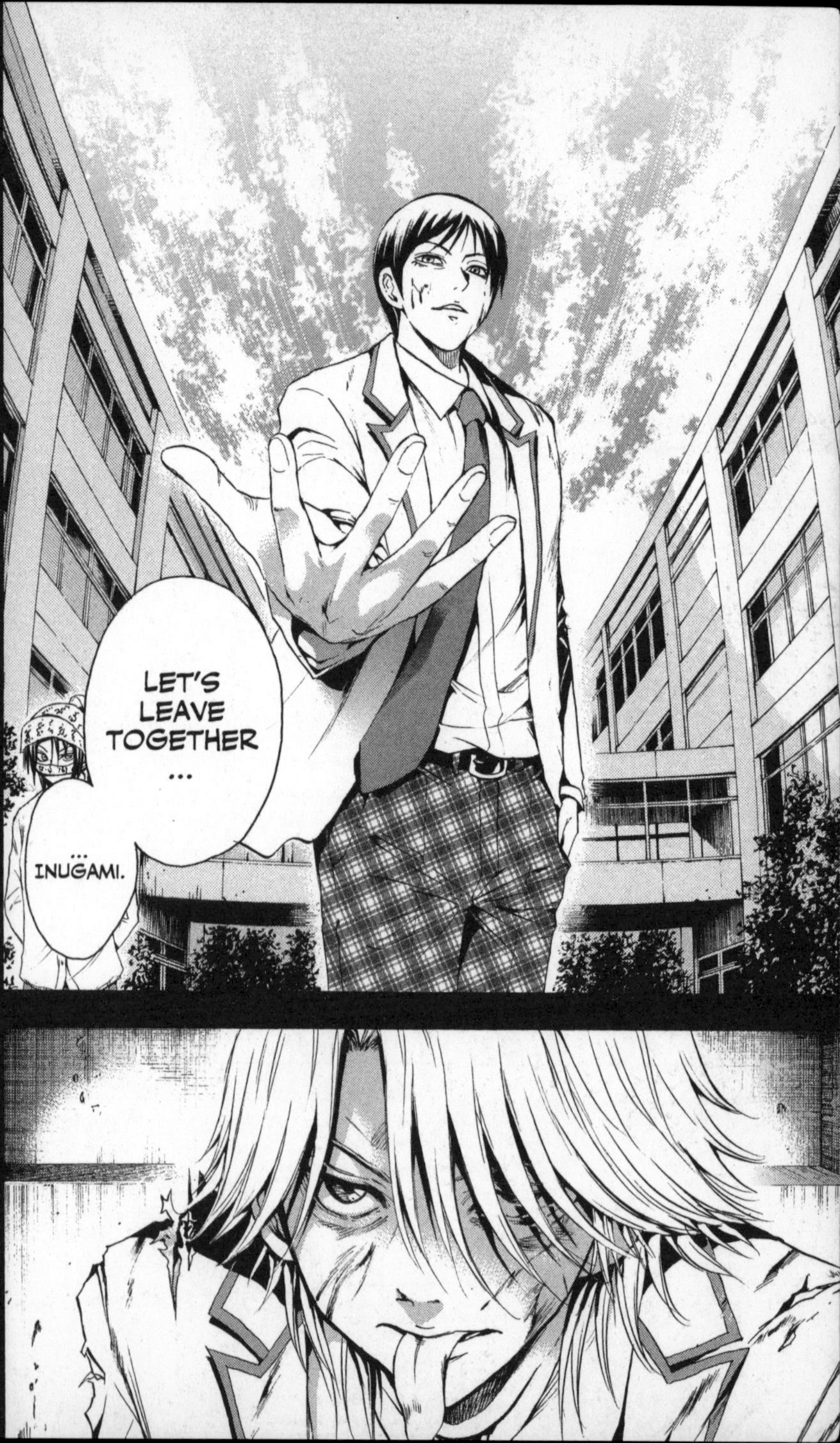
LET'S LEAVE TOGETHER ...
... INUGAMI.

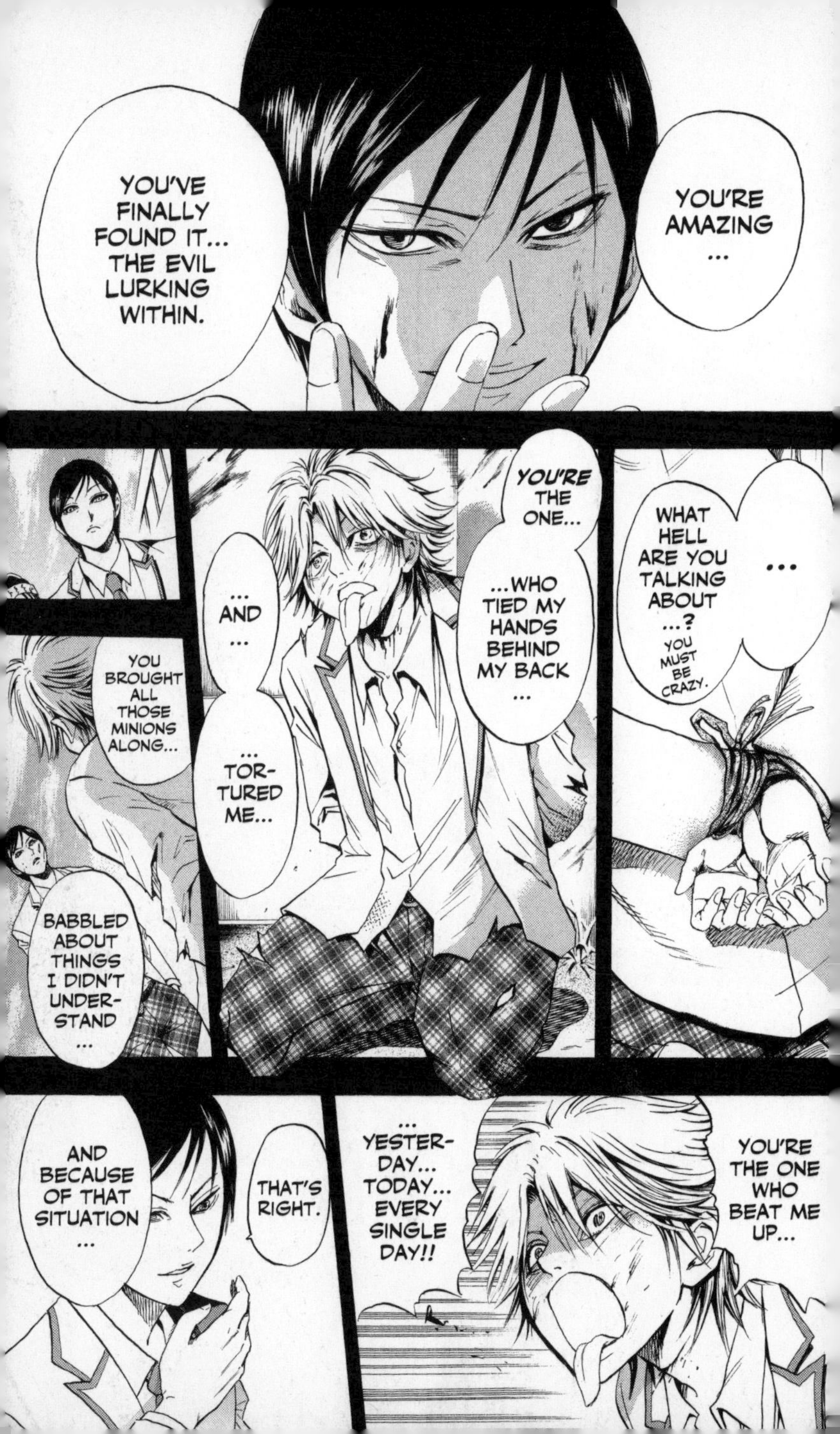
YOU'RE AMAZING ...
YOU'VE FINALLY FOUND IT... THE EVIL LURKING WITHIN.
...
WHAT HELL ARE YOU TALKING ABOUT ...?
YOU MUST BE CRAZY.
YOU'RE THE ONE...
...WHO TIED MY HANDS BEHIND MY BACK ...
... AND ...
... TOR-TURED ME...
YOU BROUGHT ALL THOSE MINIONS ALONG...
BABBLED ABOUT THINGS I DIDN'T UNDER-STAND ...
YOU'RE THE ONE WHO BEAT ME UP...
... YESTER-DAY... TODAY... EVERY SINGLE DAY!!
THAT'S RIGHT.
AND BECAUSE OF THAT SITUATION ...

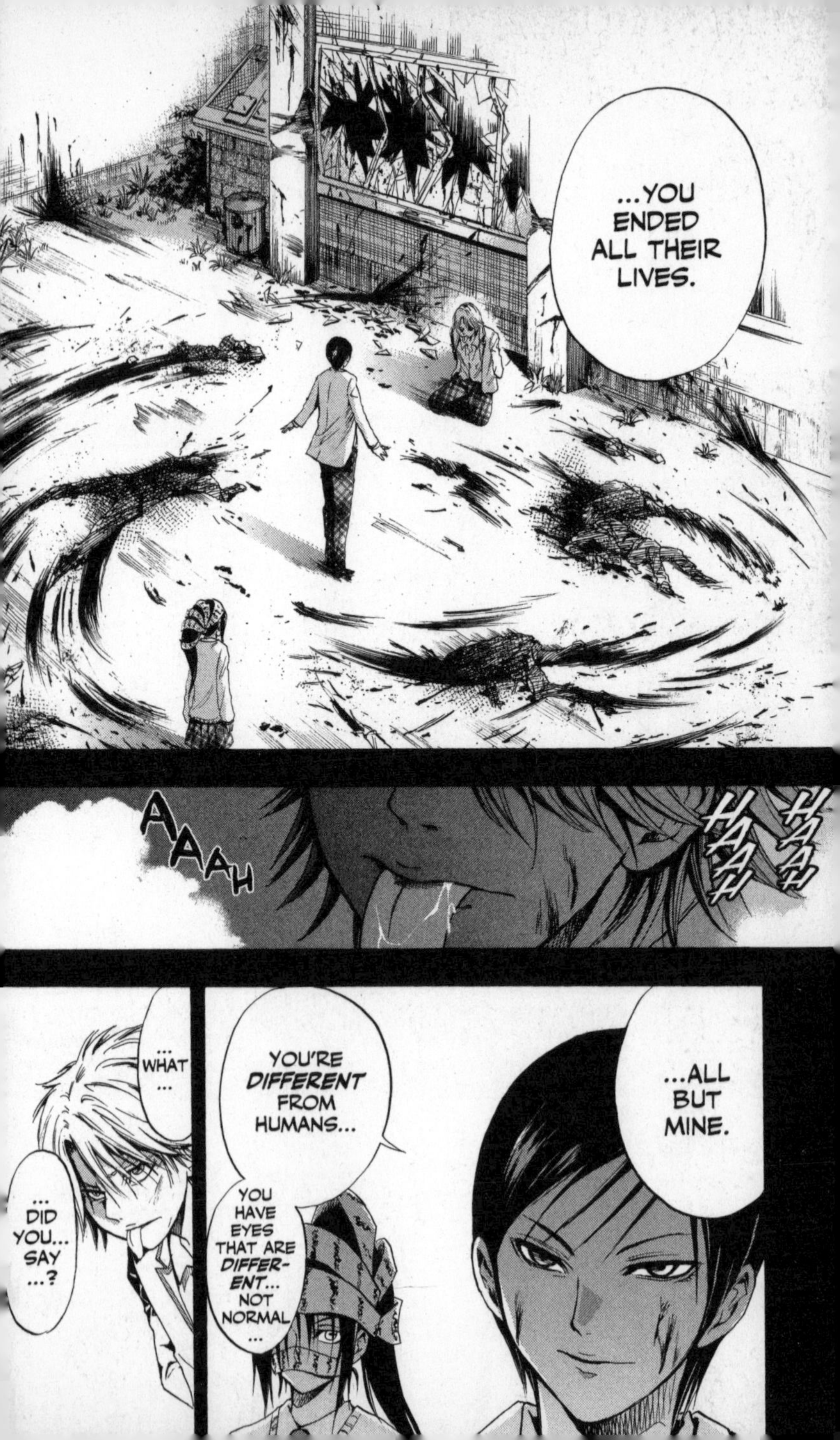
...YOU ENDED ALL THEIR LIVES.
HAAH
HAAH
AAAH
...ALL BUT MINE.
YOU'RE *DIFFERENT* FROM HUMANS...
YOU HAVE EYES THAT ARE *DIFFERENT*... NOT NORMAL...
...WHAT...
...DID YOU... SAY...?

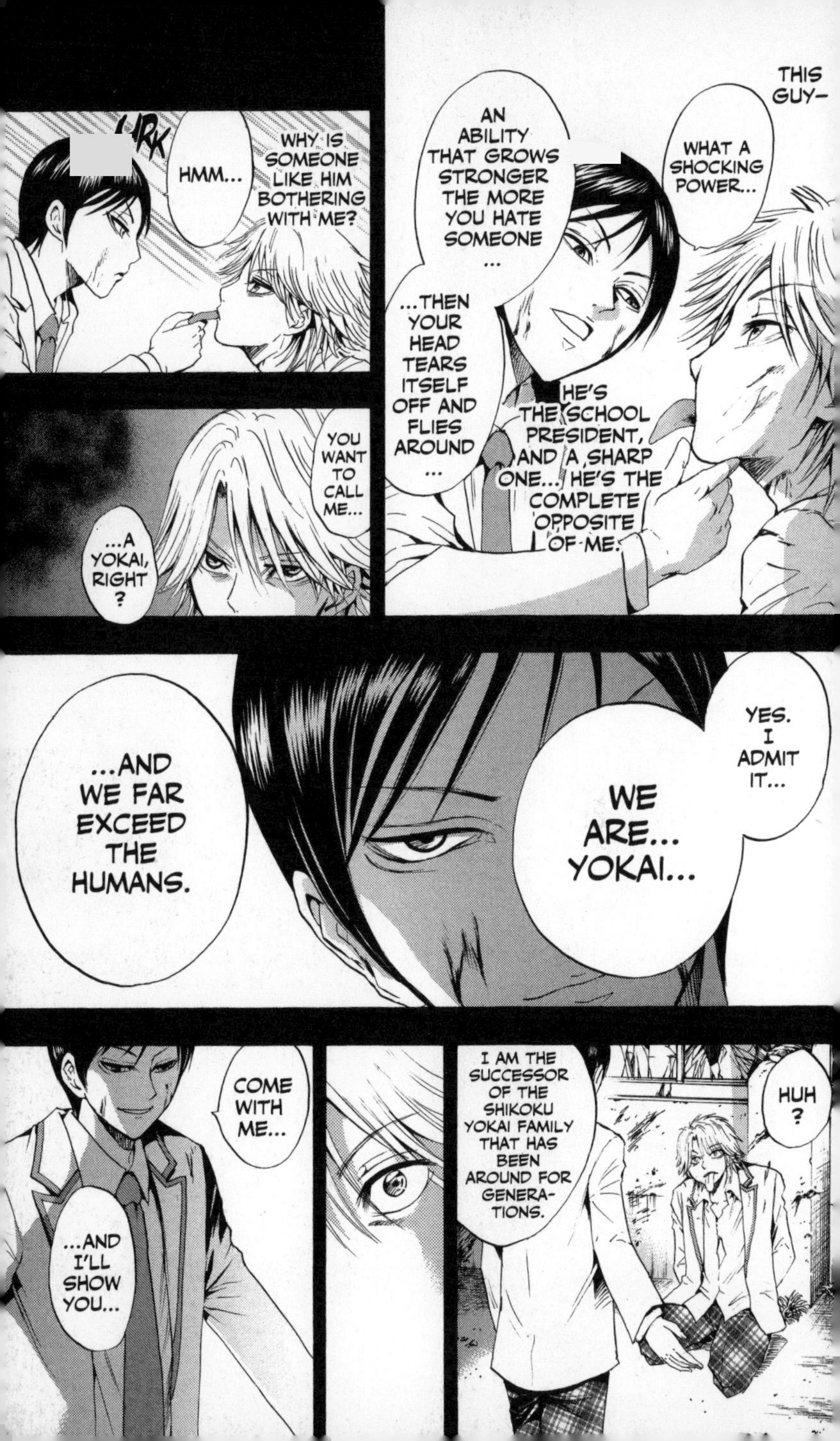
THIS GUY—
WHAT A SHOCKING POWER...
AN ABILITY THAT GROWS STRONGER THE MORE YOU HATE SOMEONE...
...THEN YOUR HEAD TEARS ITSELF OFF AND FLIES AROUND...
HE'S THE SCHOOL PRESIDENT, AND A SHARP ONE... HE'S THE COMPLETE OPPOSITE OF ME.
WHY IS SOMEONE LIKE HIM BOTHERING WITH ME?
HMM...
YOU WANT TO CALL ME...
...A YOKAI, RIGHT?
YES. I ADMIT IT...
WE ARE... YOKAI...
...AND WE FAR EXCEED THE HUMANS.
HUH?
I AM THE SUCCESSOR OF THE SHIKOKU YOKAI FAMILY THAT HAS BEEN AROUND FOR GENERA- TIONS.
COME WITH ME...
...AND I'LL SHOW YOU...

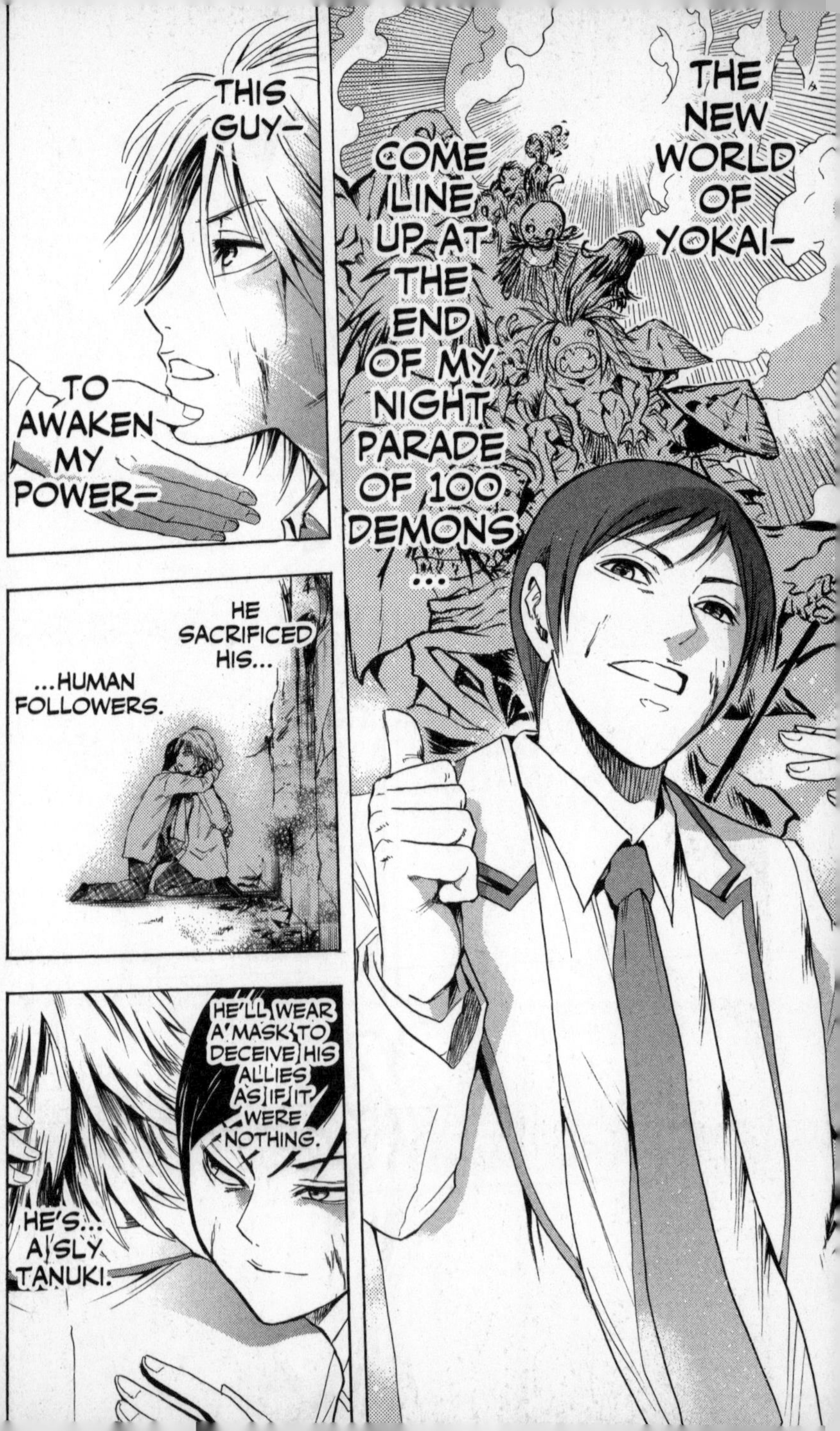
THE NEW WORLD OF YOKAI-
COME LINE UP AT THE END OF MY NIGHT PARADE OF 100 DEMONS...
THIS GUY-
TO AWAKEN MY POWER-
HE SACRIFICED HIS...
...HUMAN FOLLOWERS.
HE'LL WEAR A MASK TO DECEIVE HIS ALLIES AS IF IT WERE NOTHING.
HE'S... A SLY TANUKI.

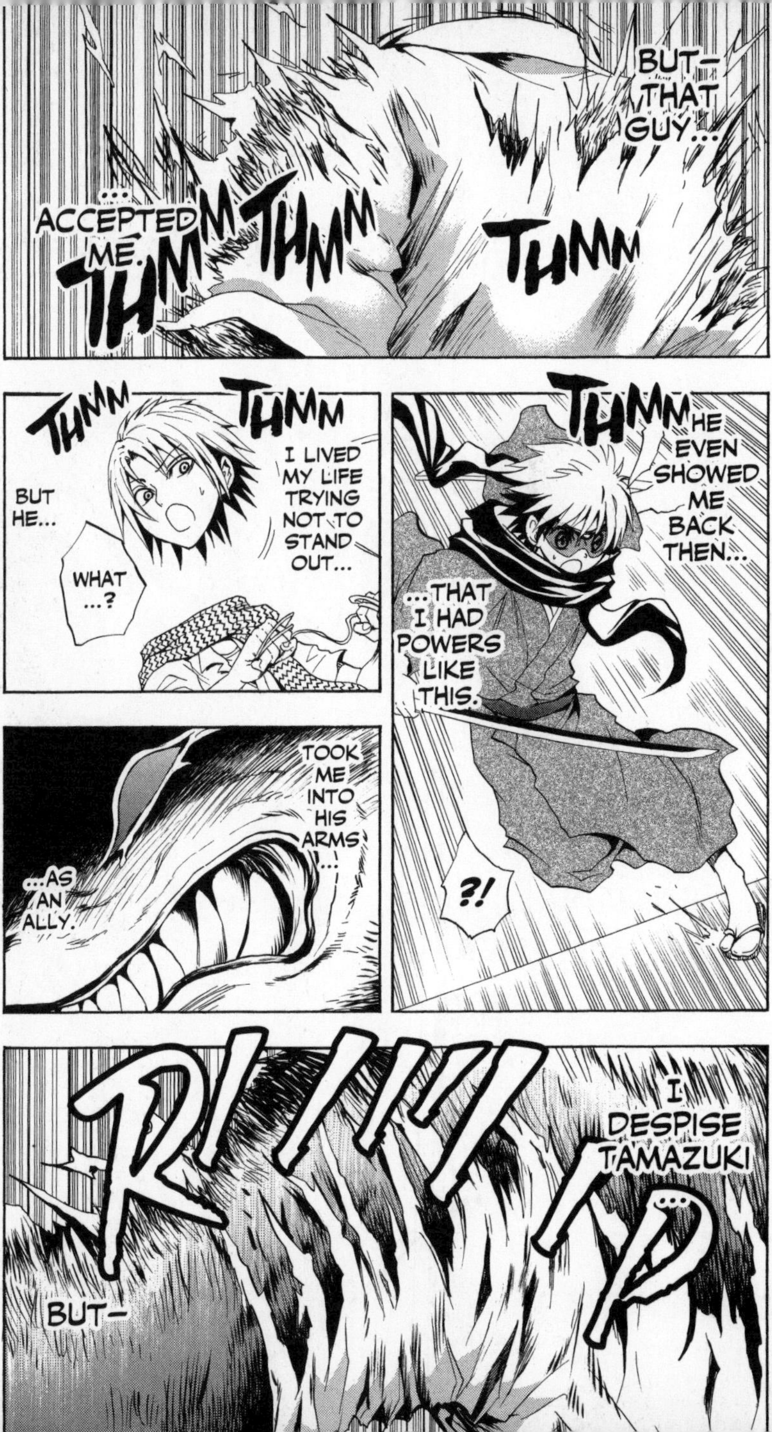
BUT— THAT GUY...
...ACCEPTED ME.
THMM
THMM
THMM
THMM
HE EVEN SHOWED ME BACK THEN...
...THAT I HAD POWERS LIKE THIS.
?!
THMM
THMM
I LIVED MY LIFE TRYING NOT TO STAND OUT...
BUT HE...
WHAT ...?
TOOK ME INTO HIS ARMS...
...AS AN ALLY.
I DESPISE TAMAZUKI...
BUT—
RIIIIP

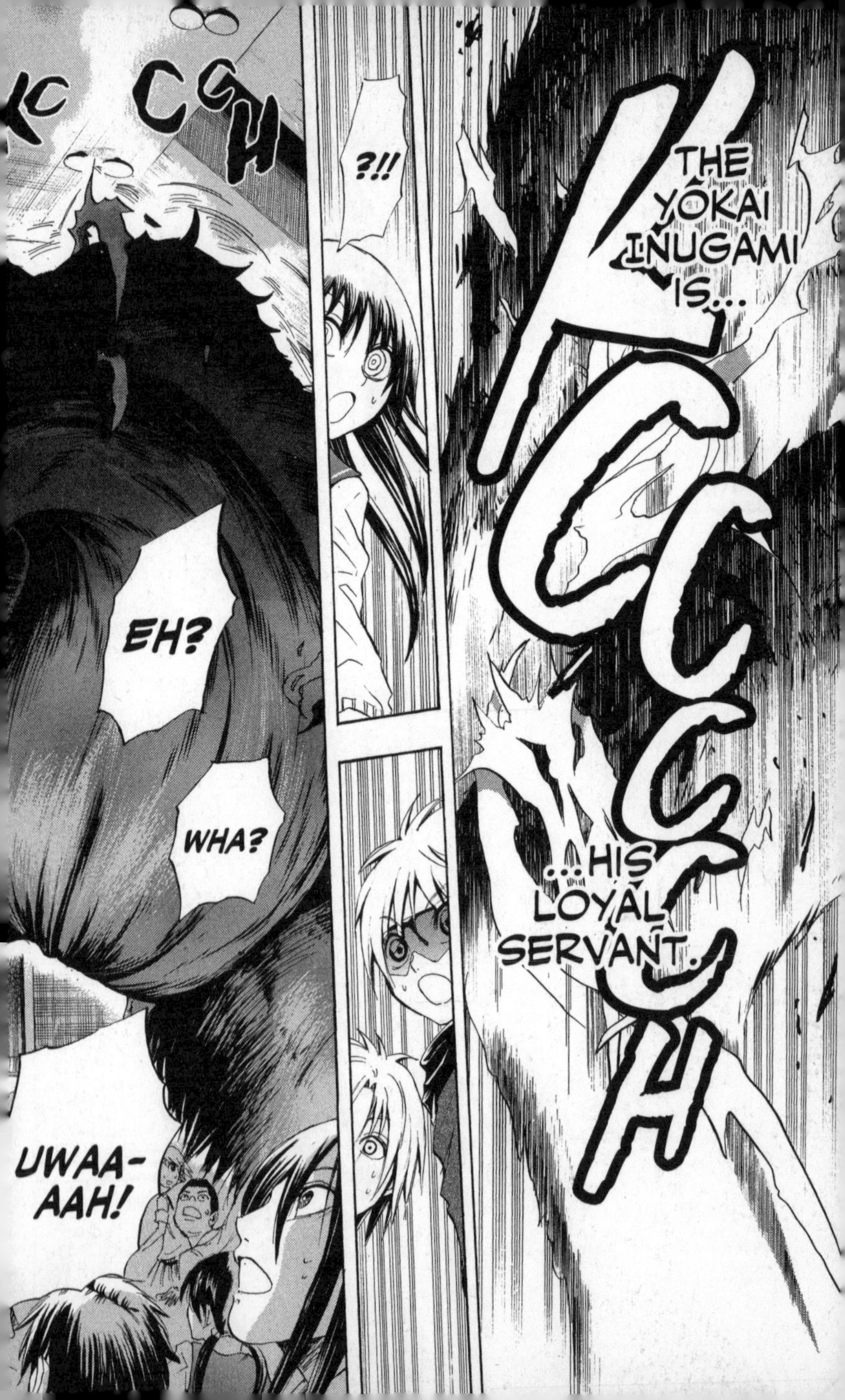
THE YŌKAI INUGAMI IS...
...HIS LOYAL SERVANT.
?!!
KCCH
EH?
WHA?
UWAA-AAH!

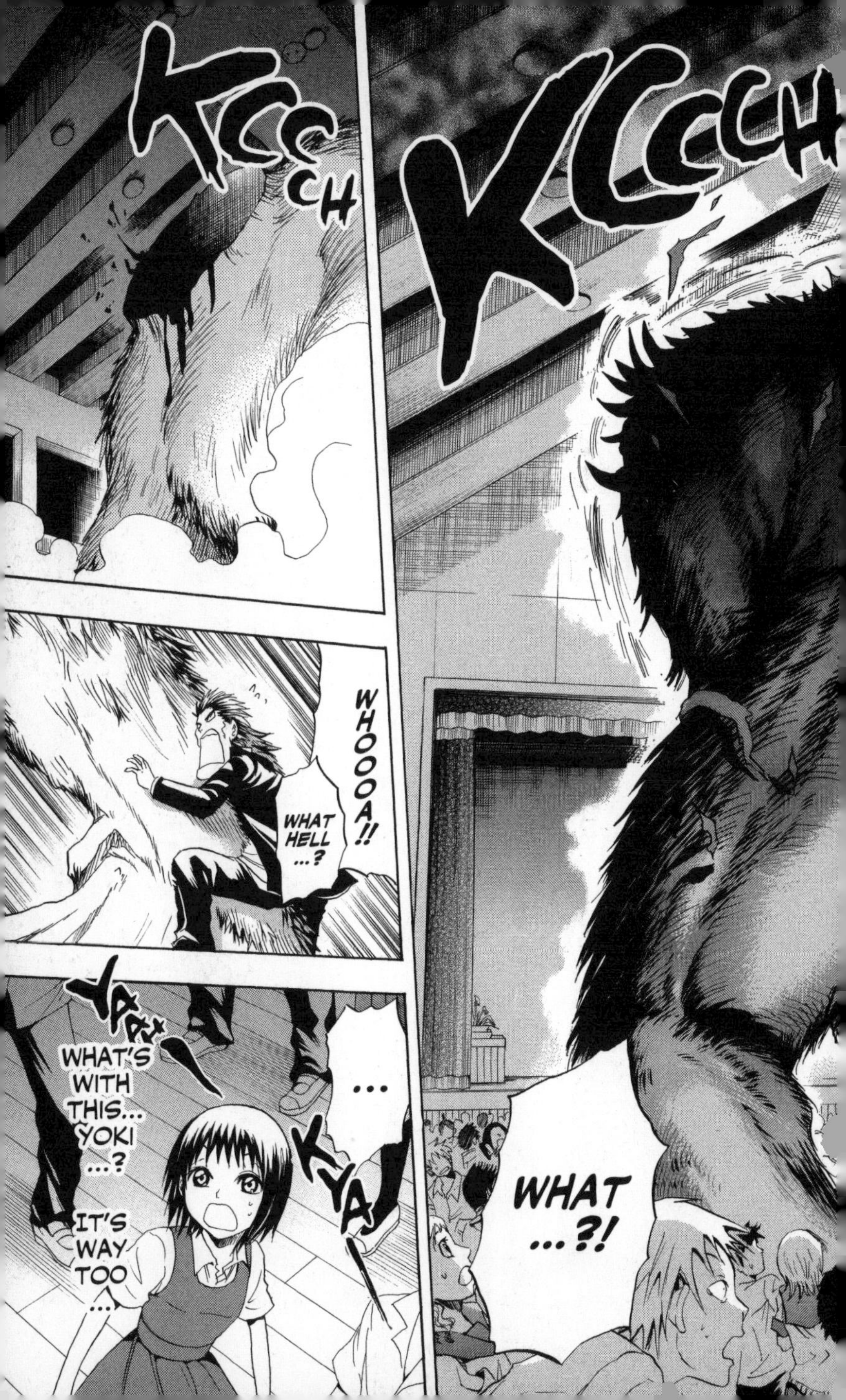
KCCCH
WHAT ...?!
KCCCH
WHOOOOA!!
WHAT HELL ...?
...
KYA
WHAT'S WITH THIS... YOKI ...?
IT'S WAY TOO ...

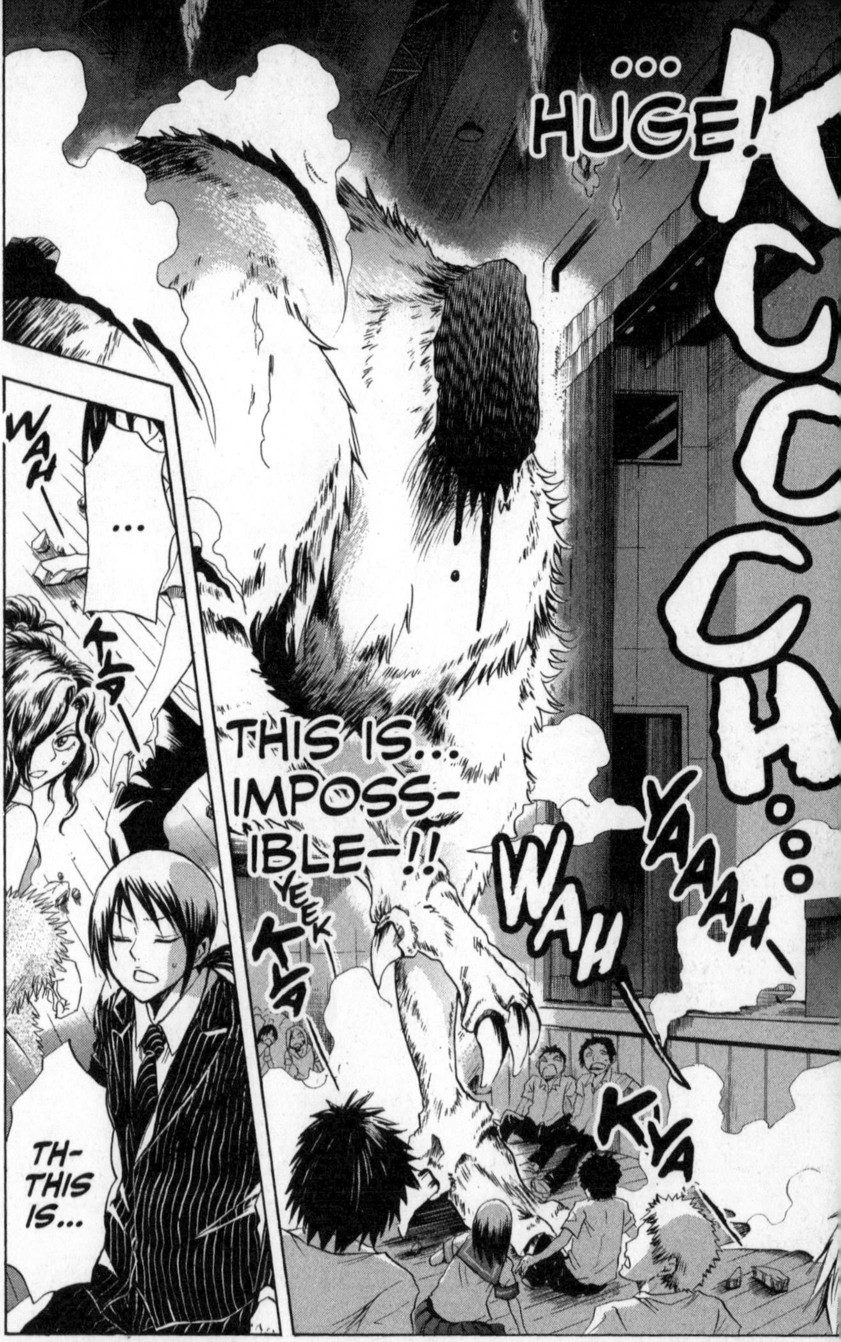
KUCCH...
...HUGE!
YAAAAH
WAH
KYA
THIS IS... IMPOSS-IBLE-!!
YEEK
KYA
WAH
...
KYA
TH-THIS IS...

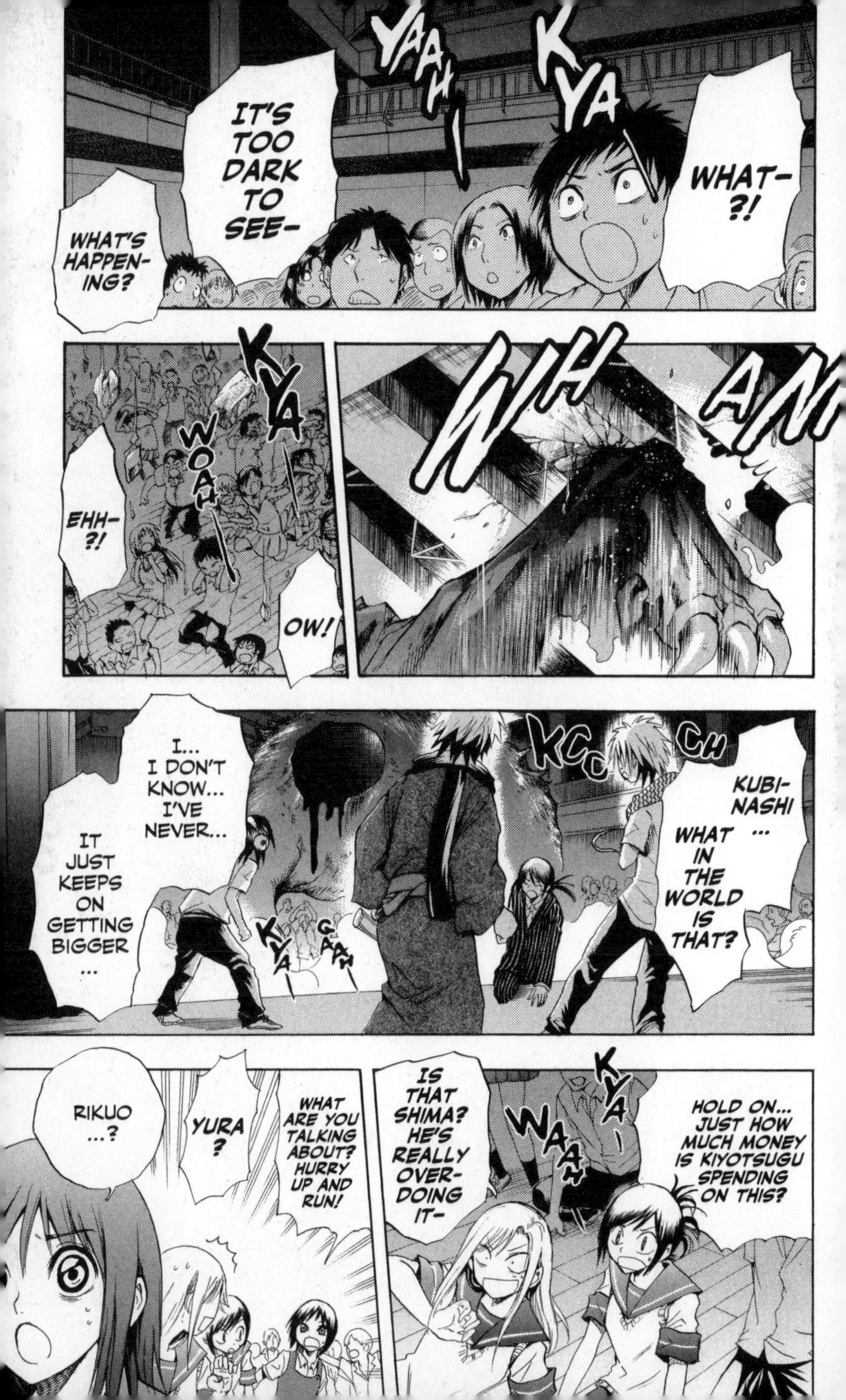
WHAT-?!
KYA
YAAH
IT'S TOO DARK TO SEE-
WHAT'S HAPPEN-ING?
WH AN
KYA
WOAH
EHH-?!
OW!
KUBI-NASHI... WHAT IN THE WORLD IS THAT?
KCO CH
I... I DON'T KNOW... I'VE NEVER...
IT JUST KEEPS ON GETTING BIGGER ...
KYA
GAAH
HOLD ON... JUST HOW MUCH MONEY IS KIYOTSUGU SPENDING ON THIS?
KYA
WAAH
IS THAT SHIMA? HE'S REALLY OVER-DOING IT-
WHAT ARE YOU TALKING ABOUT? HURRY UP AND RUN!
YURA?
RIKUO ...?

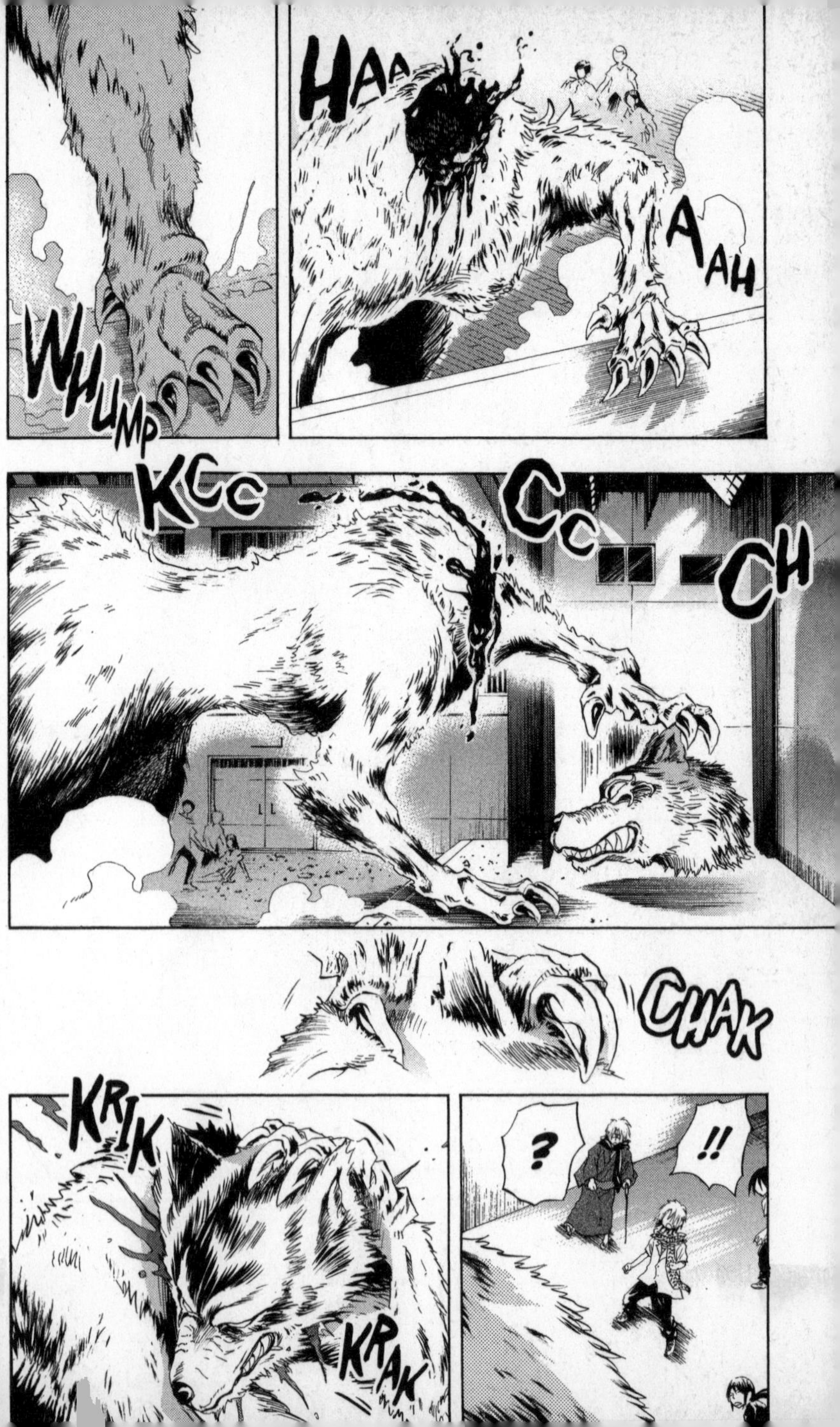
HAA
AAH
WHUMP
KCC
CC
CH
CHAK
?
!!
KRIK
KRAK

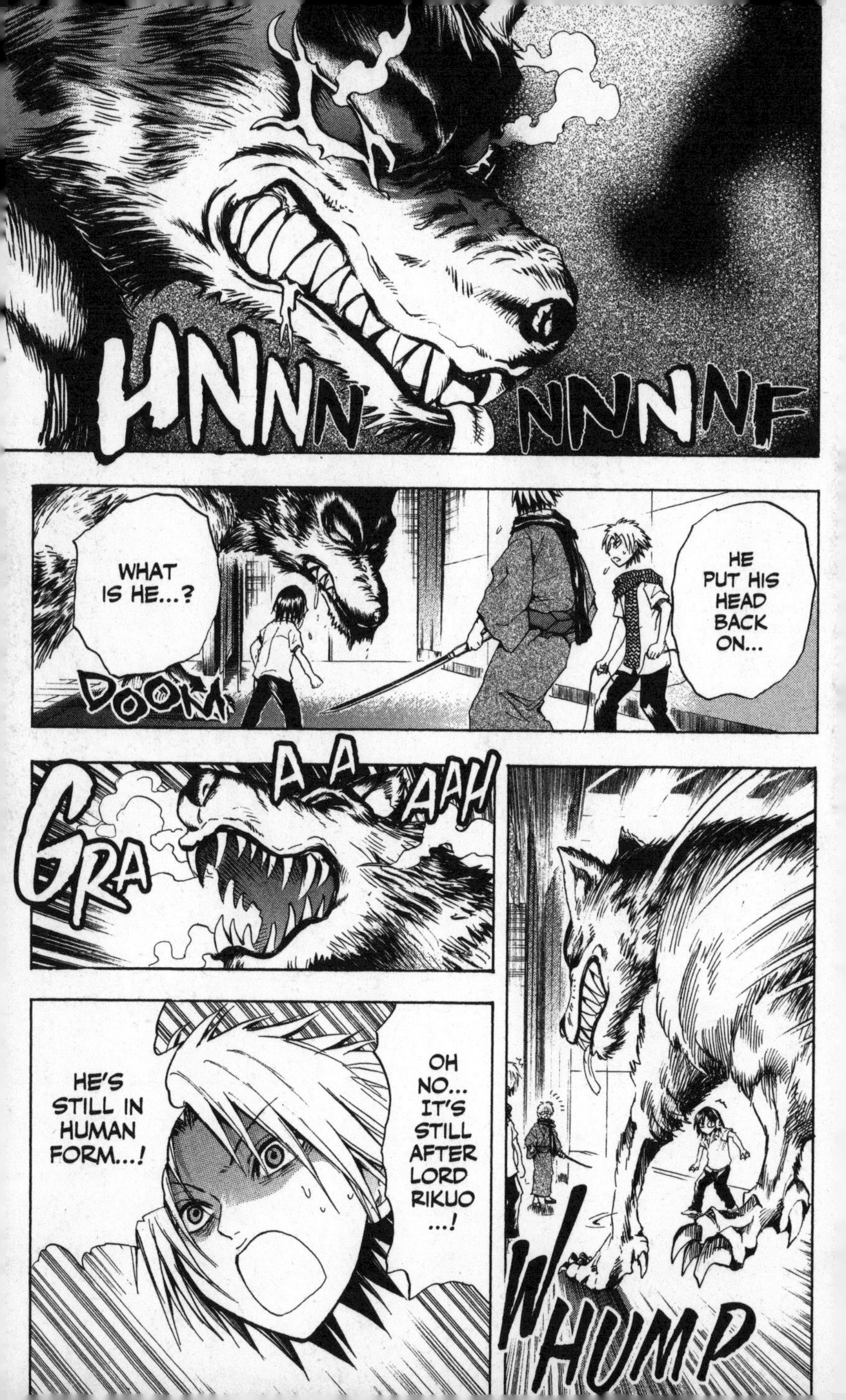
HNNNN NNNNNF
HE PUT HIS HEAD BACK ON...
WHAT IS HE...?
DOOM
WHUMP
GRA A A AAH
OH NO... IT'S STILL AFTER LORD RIKUO ...!
HE'S STILL IN HUMAN FORM...!

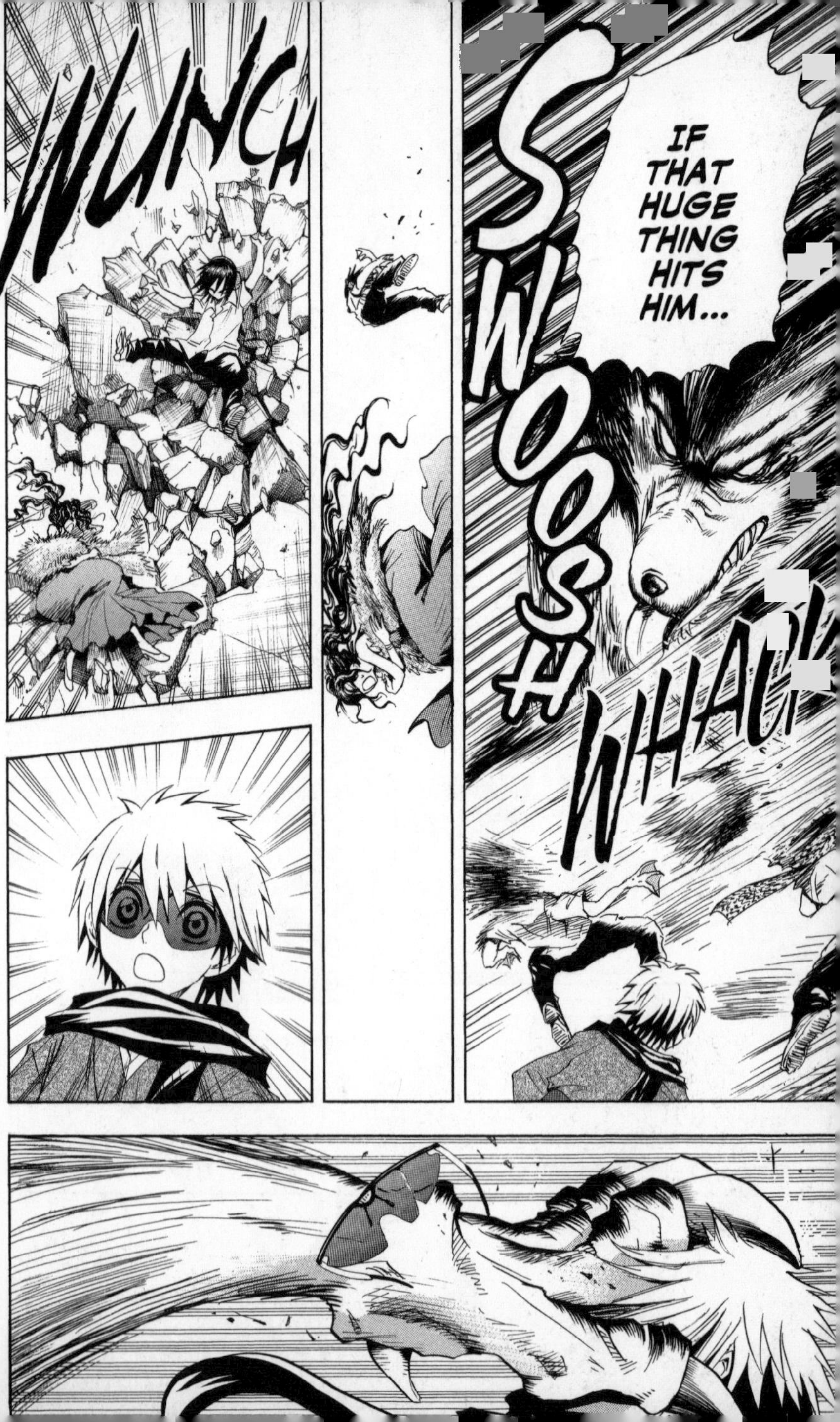
SWOOSH
IF THAT HUGE THING HITS HIM...
WHAC
WUNCH

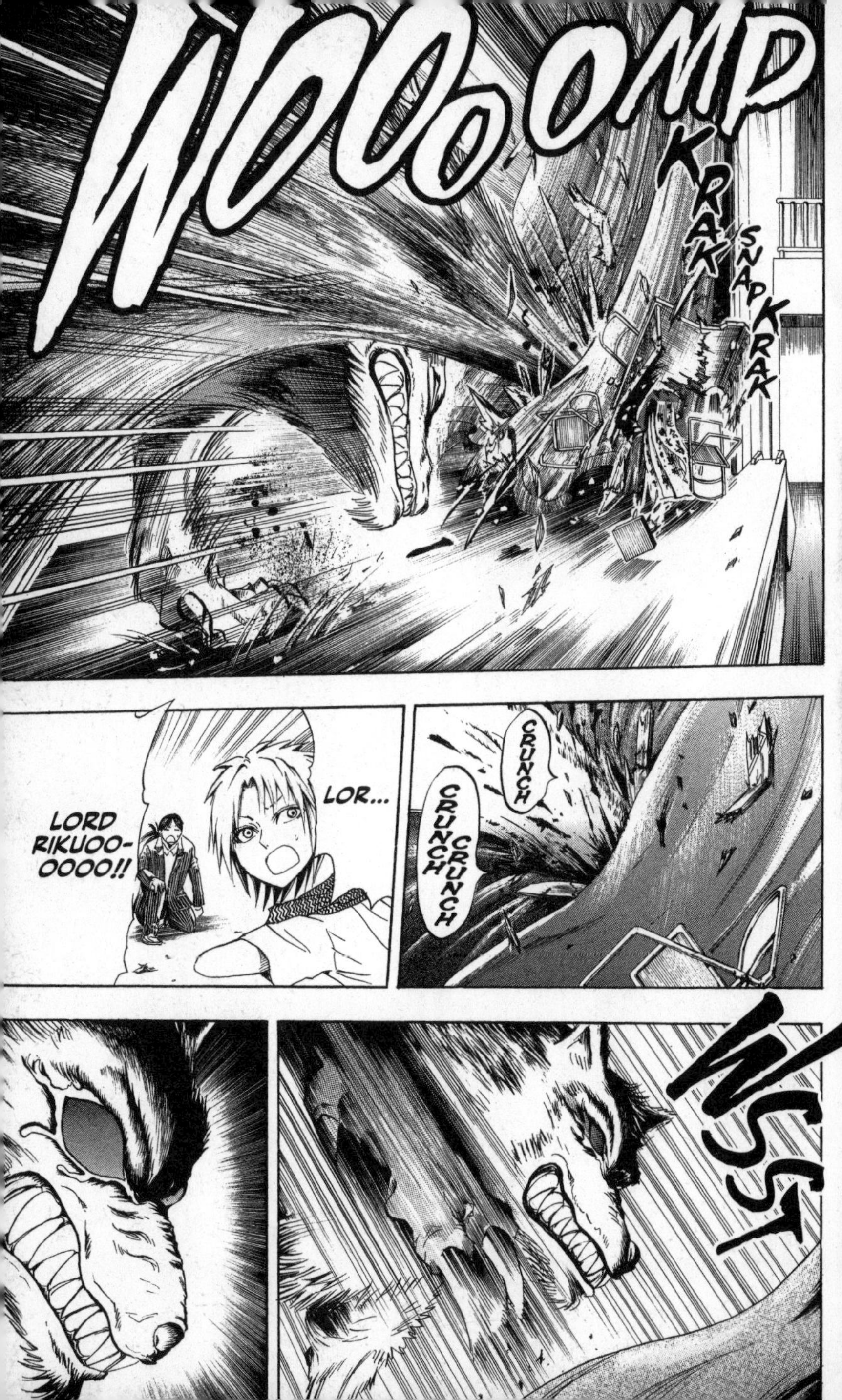
WOOOOMP
KRAK
KRAK
SNAP
KRAK
KRAK
CRUNCH
CRUNCH CRUNCH CRUNCH
LOR...
LORD RIKUOO-OOOO!!
WSST

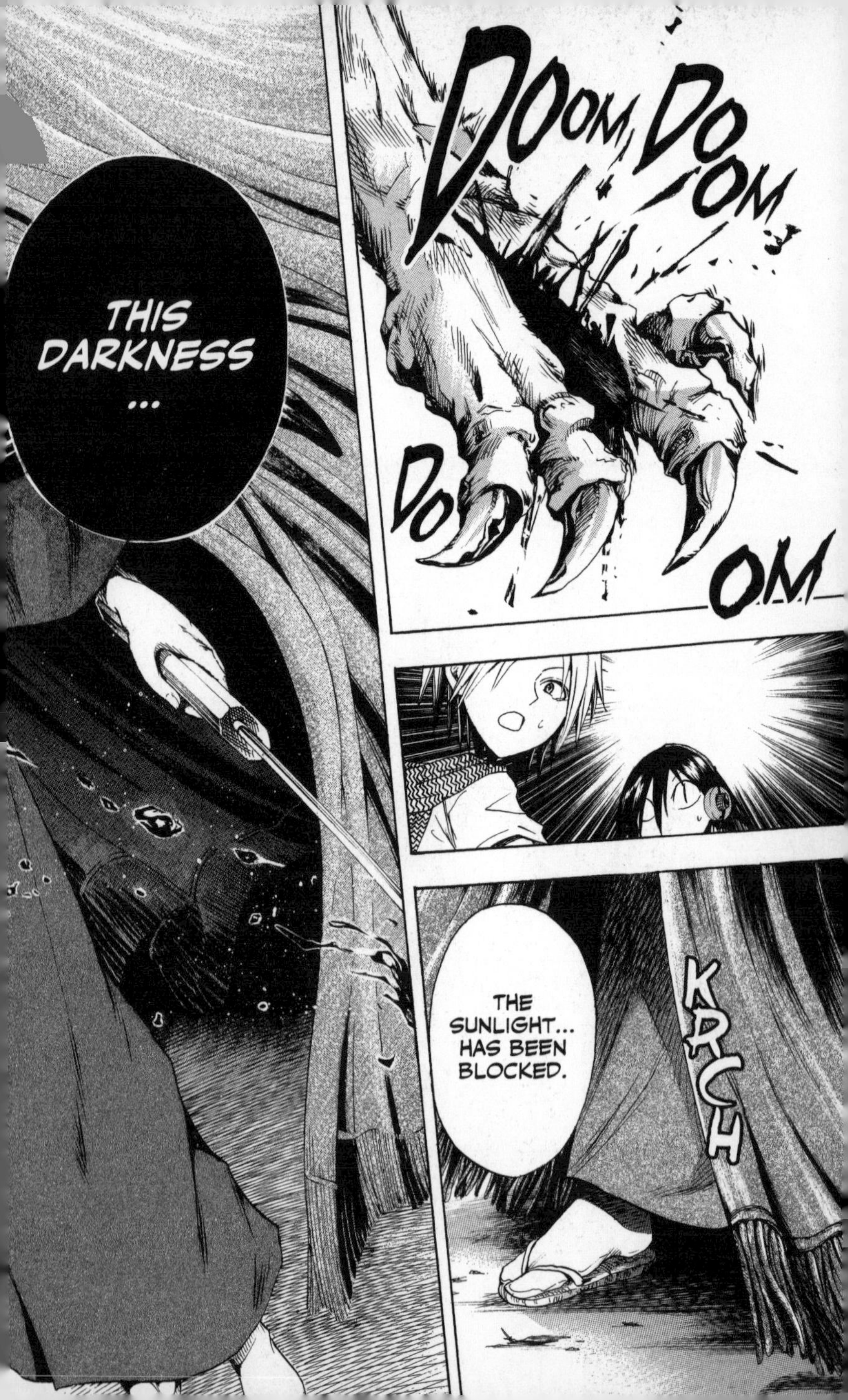
DOOM DOOM
DOOM
THE SUNLIGHT... HAS BEEN BLOCKED.
KRCH
THIS DARKNESS ...

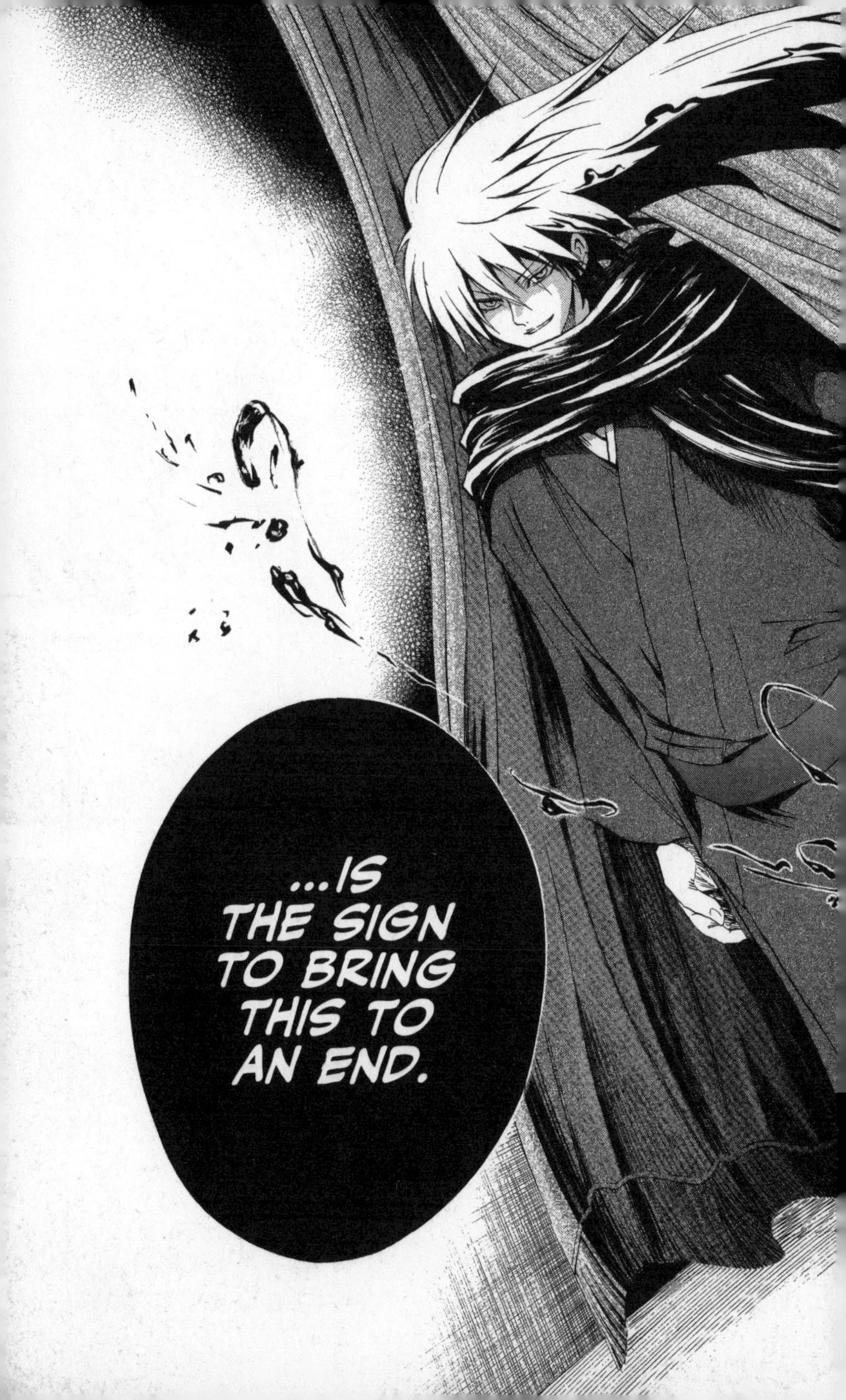
...IS THE SIGN TO BRING THIS TO AN END.

1 Yura 2 Kana 3 Tsurara

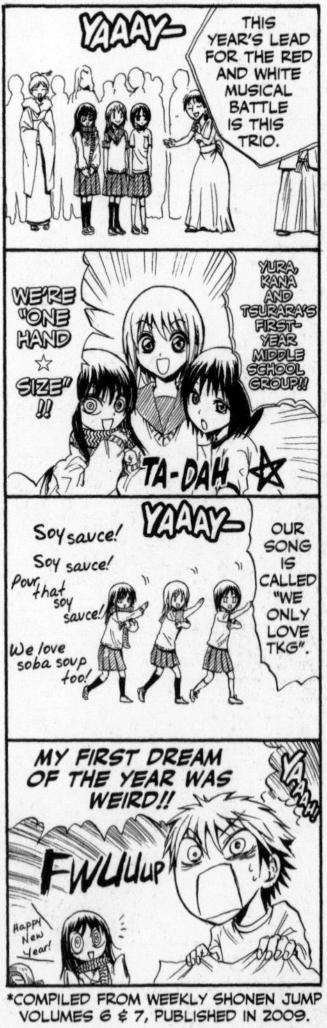
THIS YEAR'S LEAD FOR THE RED AND WHITE MUSICAL BATTLE IS THIS TRIO.
YAAAY-
YURA, KANA AND TSURARA'S FIRST-YEAR MIDDLE SCHOOL GROUP!!
WE'RE "ONE HAND ☆ SIZE" !!
TA-DAH ☆
OUR SONG IS CALLED "WE ONLY LOVE TKG".
YAAAY-
Soy sauce!
Soy sauce!
Pour that soy sauce!
We love soba soup too!
YAAAH!
MY FIRST DREAM OF THE YEAR WAS WEIRD!!
FWUUUP
Happy New Year!

*COMPILED FROM WEEKLY SHONEN JUMP VOLUMES 6 & 7, PUBLISHED IN 2009.

Act 33: The Yokai Inugami, Part 5

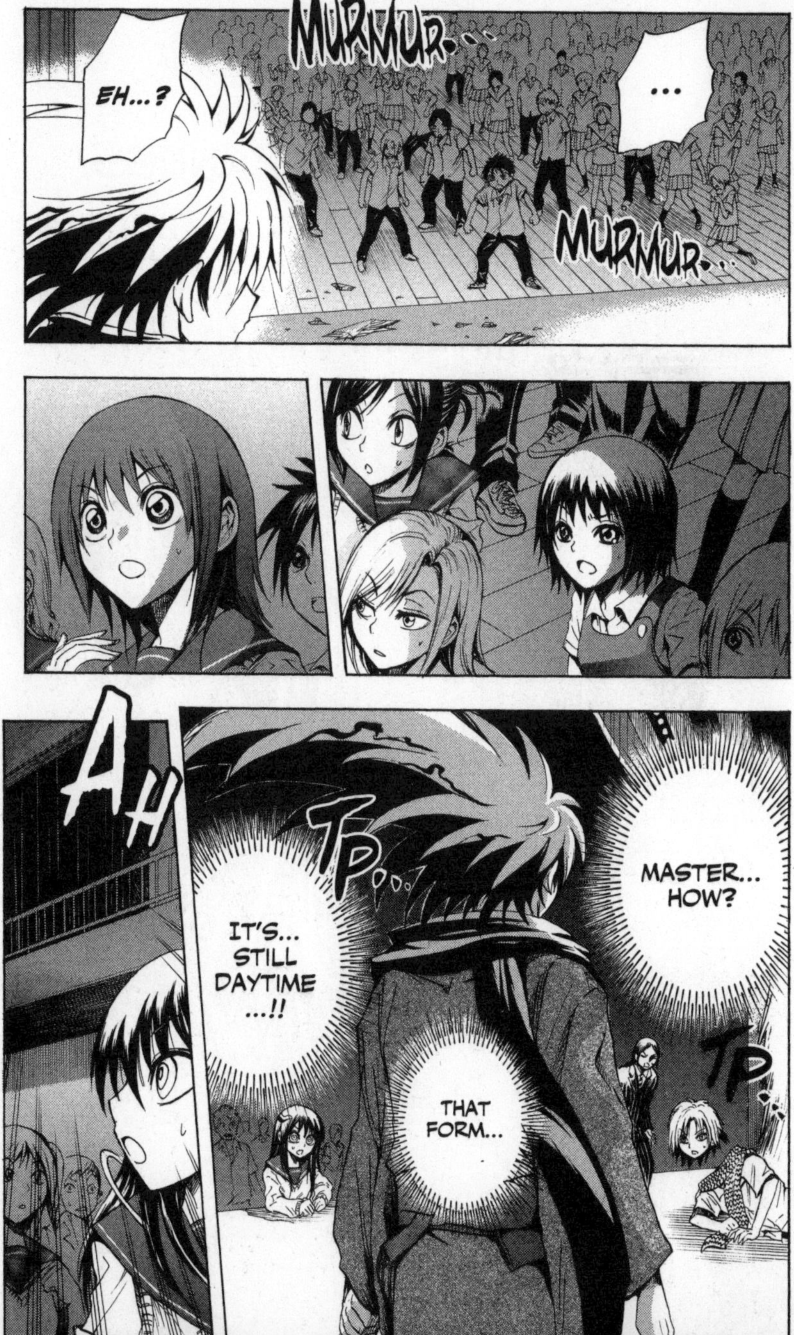
...
MURMUR...
MURMUR...
EH...?
AH
MASTER... HOW?
TP...
TP...
IT'S... STILL DAYTIME ...!!
THAT FORM...

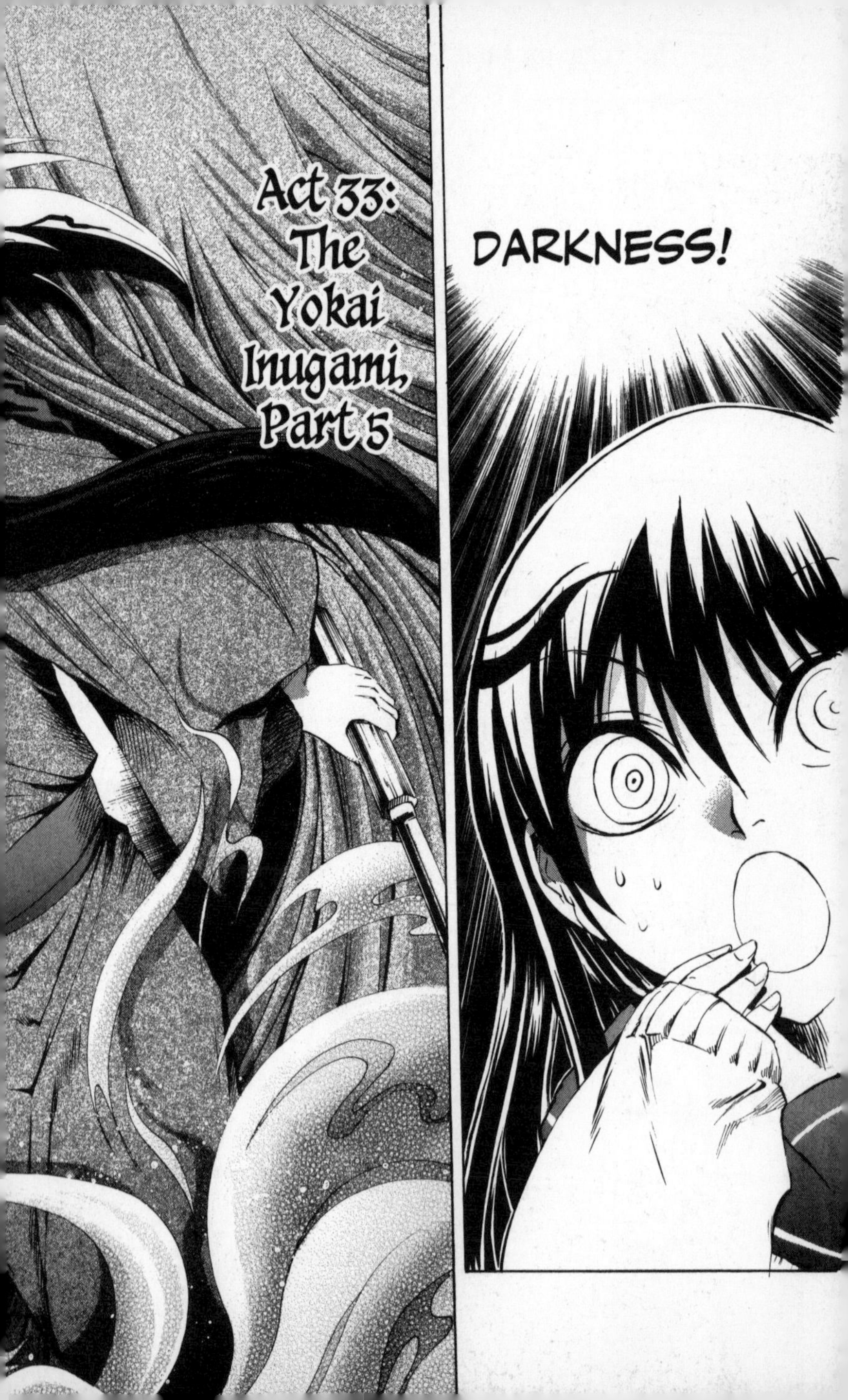
DARKNESS!
Act 33: The Yokai Inugami, Part 5

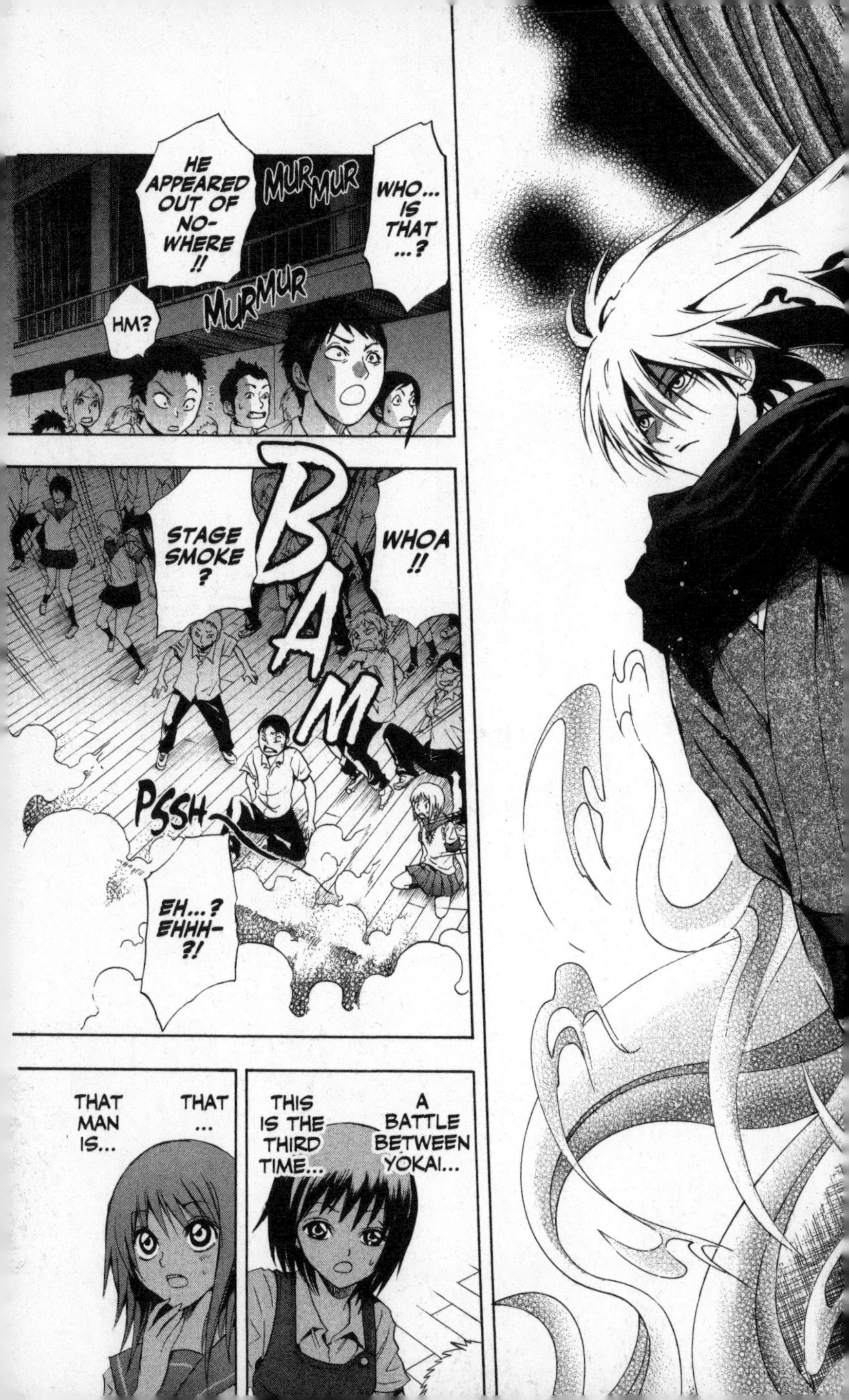
WHO... IS THAT...?
MURMUR
HE APPEARED OUT OF NO-WHERE!!
MURMUR
HM?
WHOA!!
BAM
STAGE SMOKE?
PSSH
EH...? EHHH-?!
A BATTLE BETWEEN YOKAI...
THIS IS THE THIRD TIME...
THAT...
THAT MAN IS...

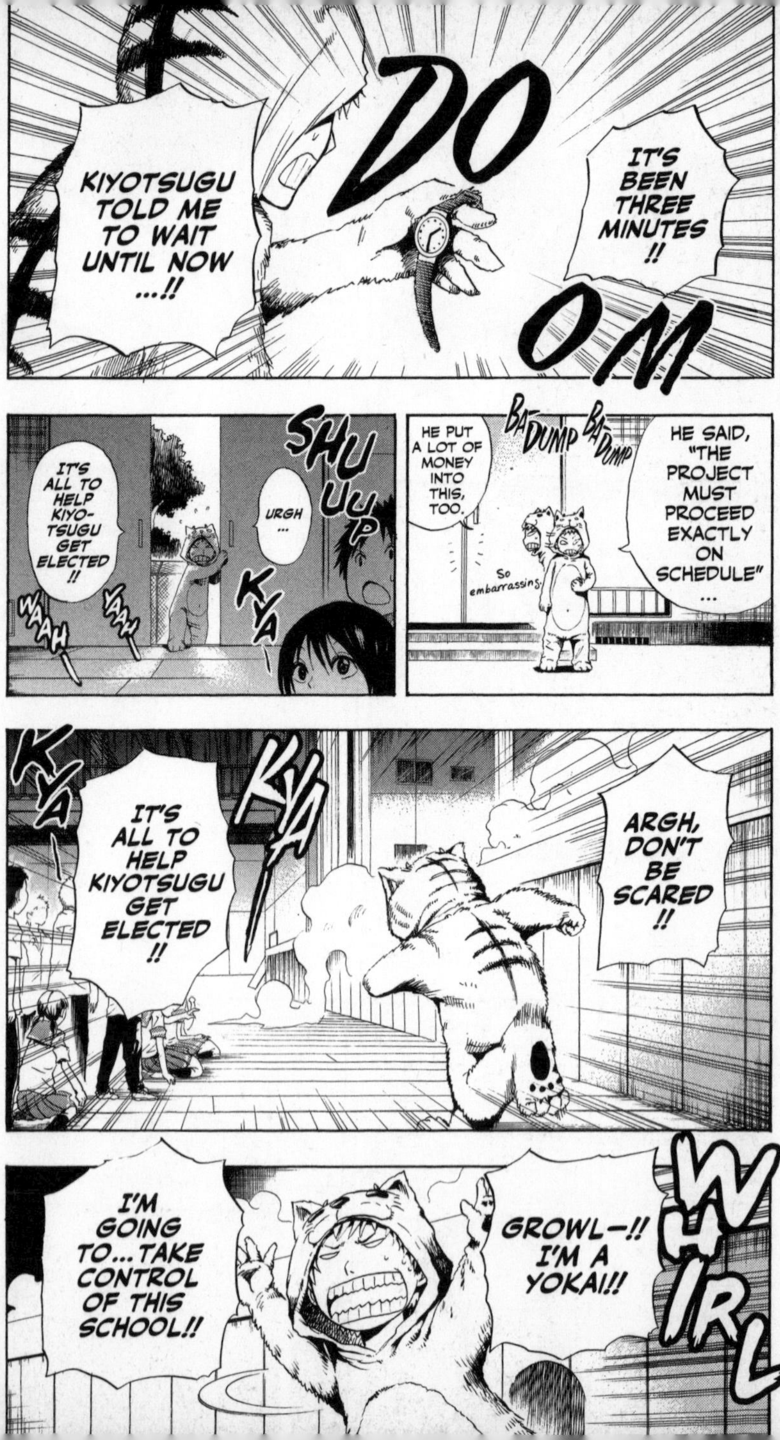
IT'S BEEN THREE MINUTES!!
DO
OM
KIYOTSUGU TOLD ME TO WAIT UNTIL NOW...!!
HE SAID, "THE PROJECT MUST PROCEED EXACTLY ON SCHEDULE"...
BA-DUMP BA-DUMP
HE PUT A LOT OF MONEY INTO THIS, TOO.
So embarrassing.
SHUUUP
URGH...
KYA-
IT'S ALL TO HELP KIYO-TSUGU GET ELECTED!!
YAAH
WAAAH
ARGH, DON'T BE SCARED!!
KYA
IT'S ALL TO HELP KIYOTSUGU GET ELECTED!!
KYA-
WHIRL
GROWL-!! I'M A YOKAI!!
I'M GOING TO...TAKE CONTROL OF THIS SCHOOL!!

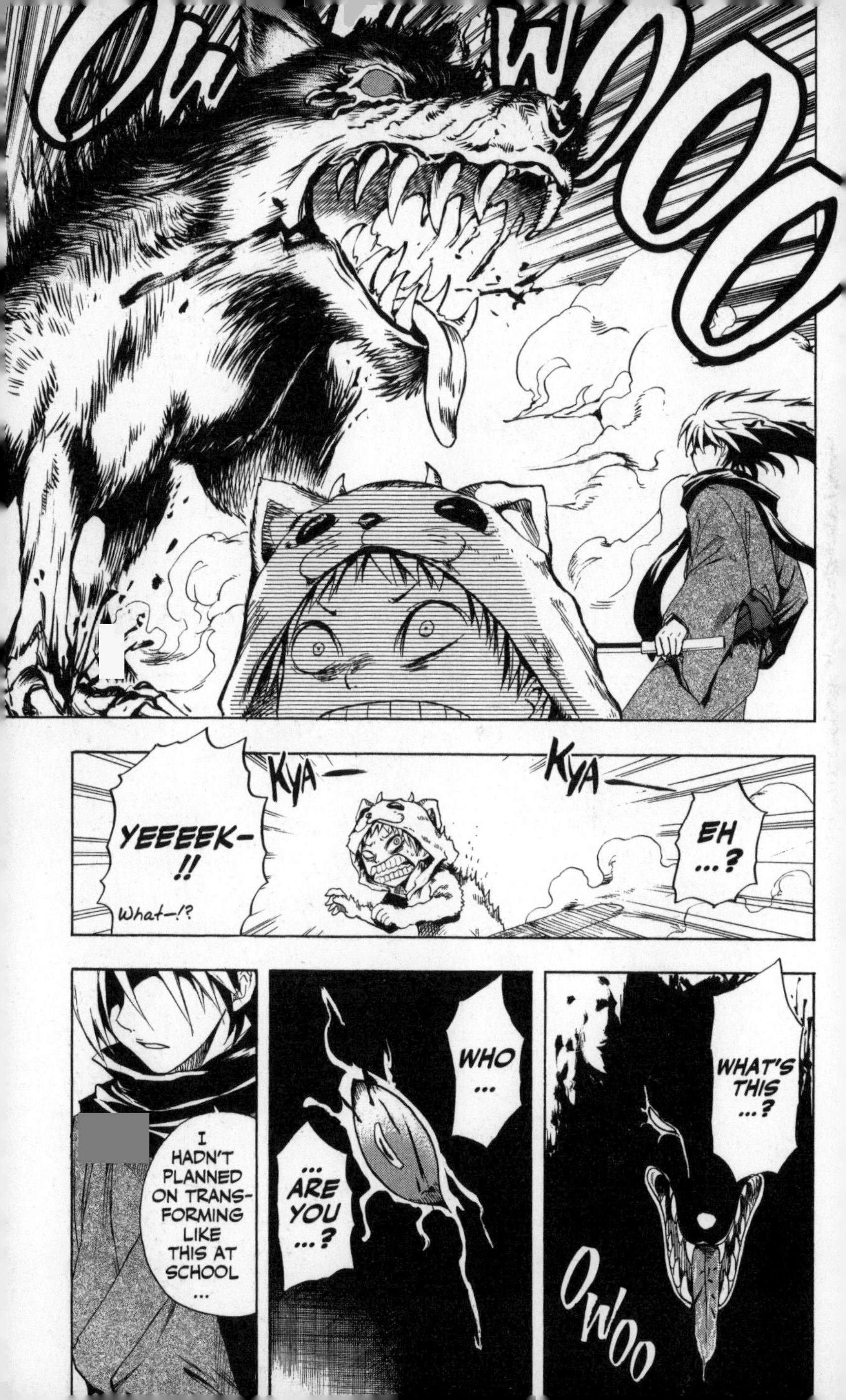
OW WOOOO
EH ...?
Kya—
Kya—
YEEEEK-!!
What-!?
WHAT'S THIS ...?
OWOO
WHO ...
... ARE YOU ...?
I HADN'T PLANNED ON TRANS-FORMING LIKE THIS AT SCHOOL ...

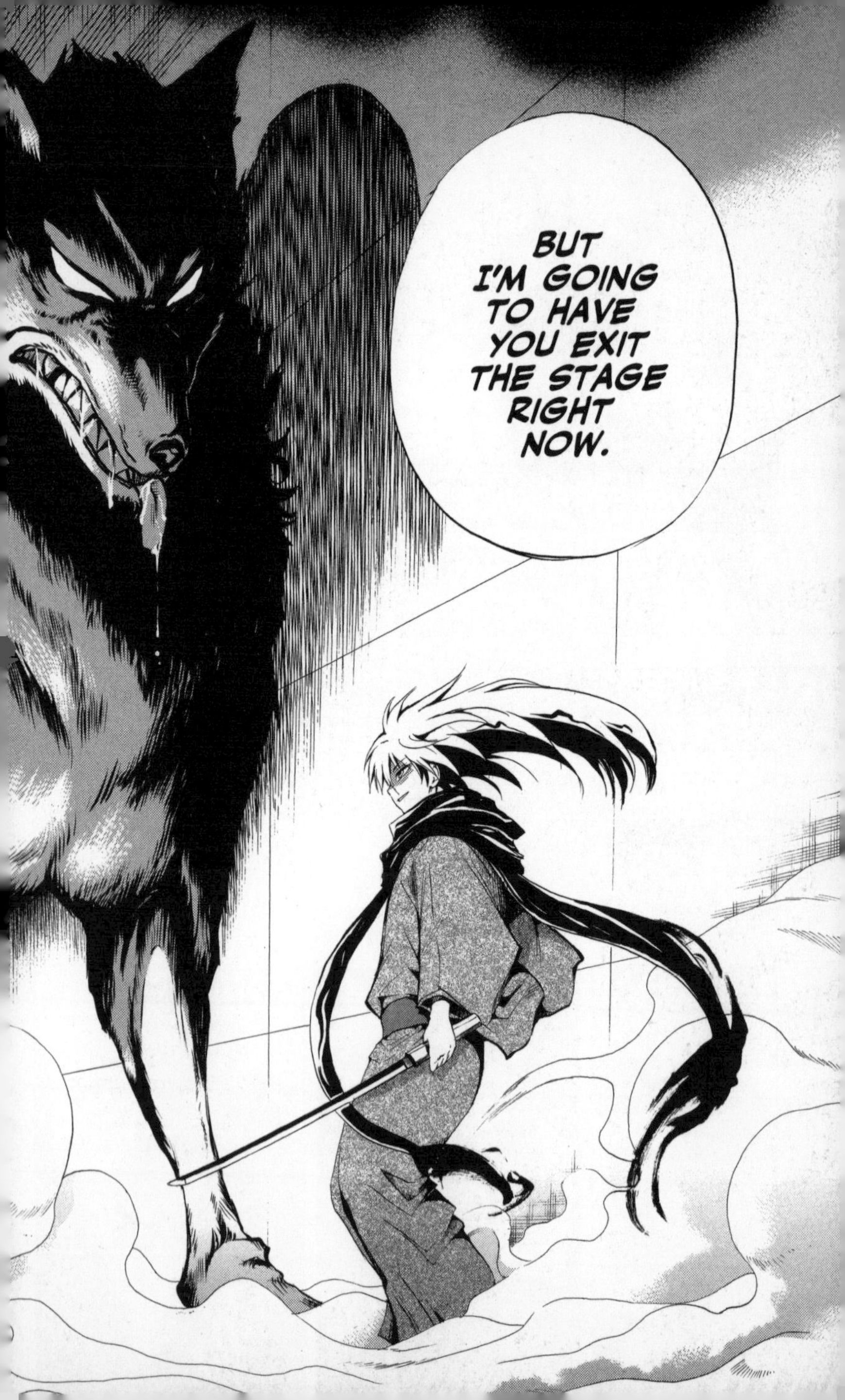
BUT I'M GOING TO HAVE YOU EXIT THE STAGE RIGHT NOW.

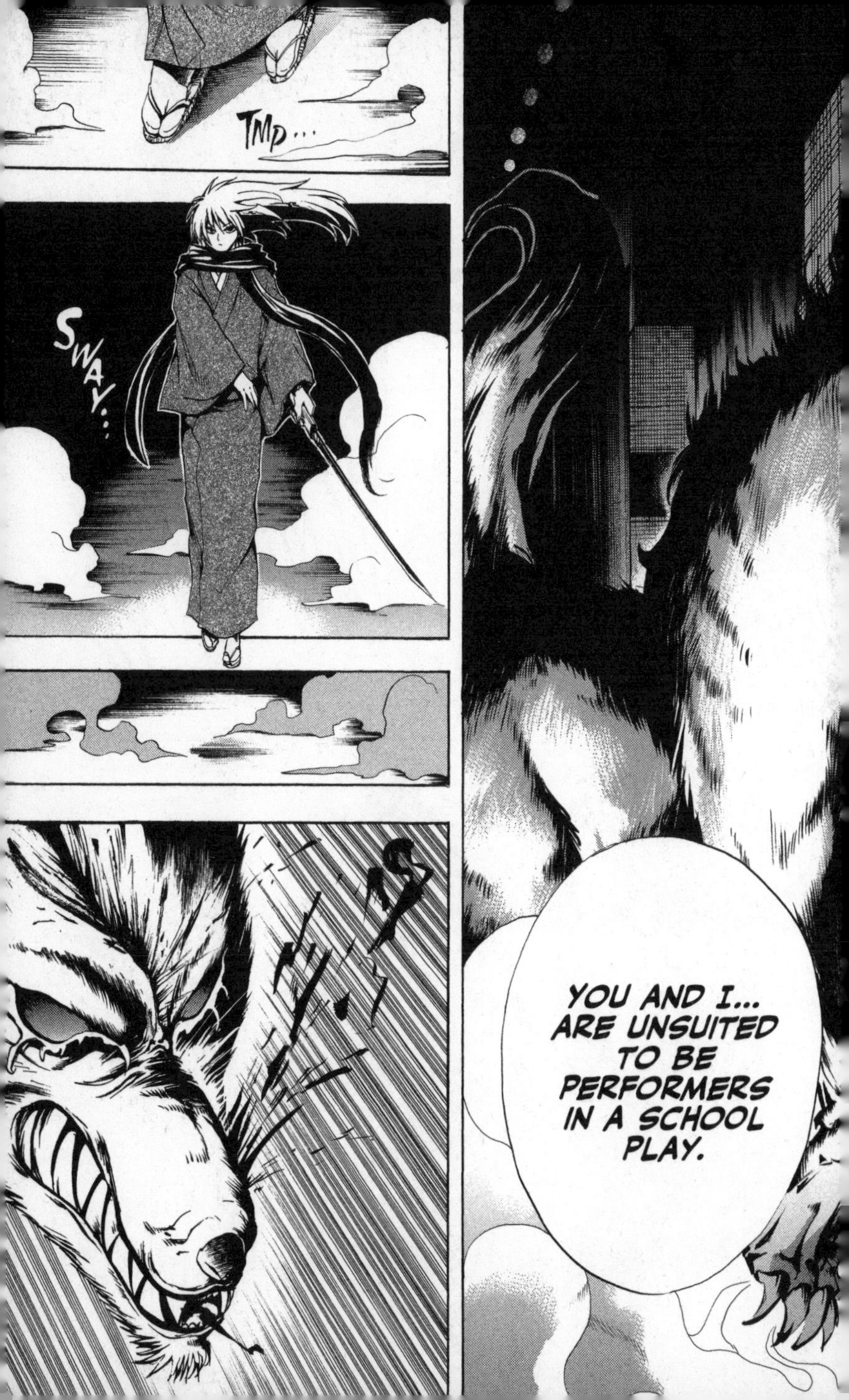
YOU AND I... ARE UNSUITED TO BE PERFORMERS IN A SCHOOL PLAY.
TMP...
SWAY...

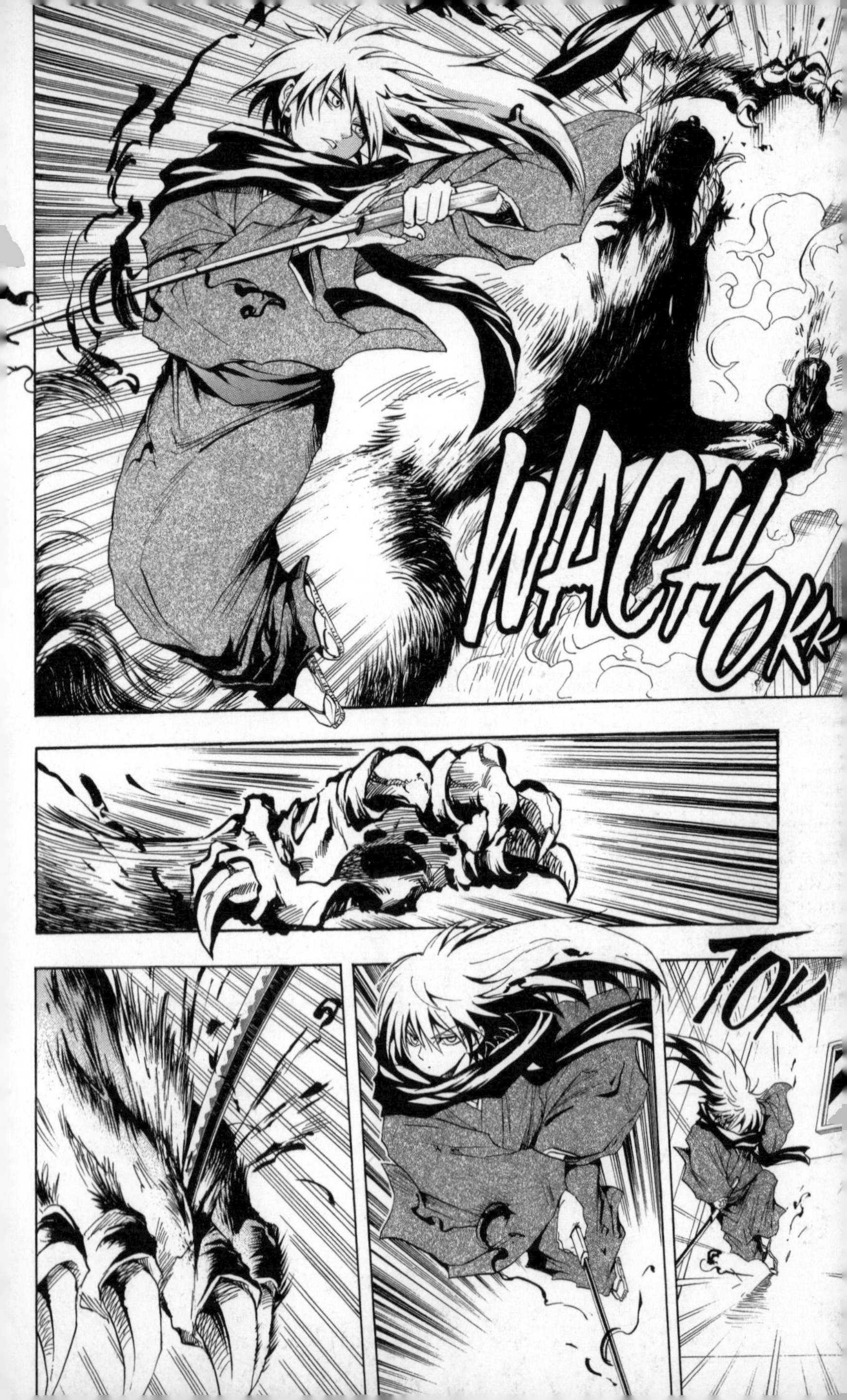
WACHOKK
TOK

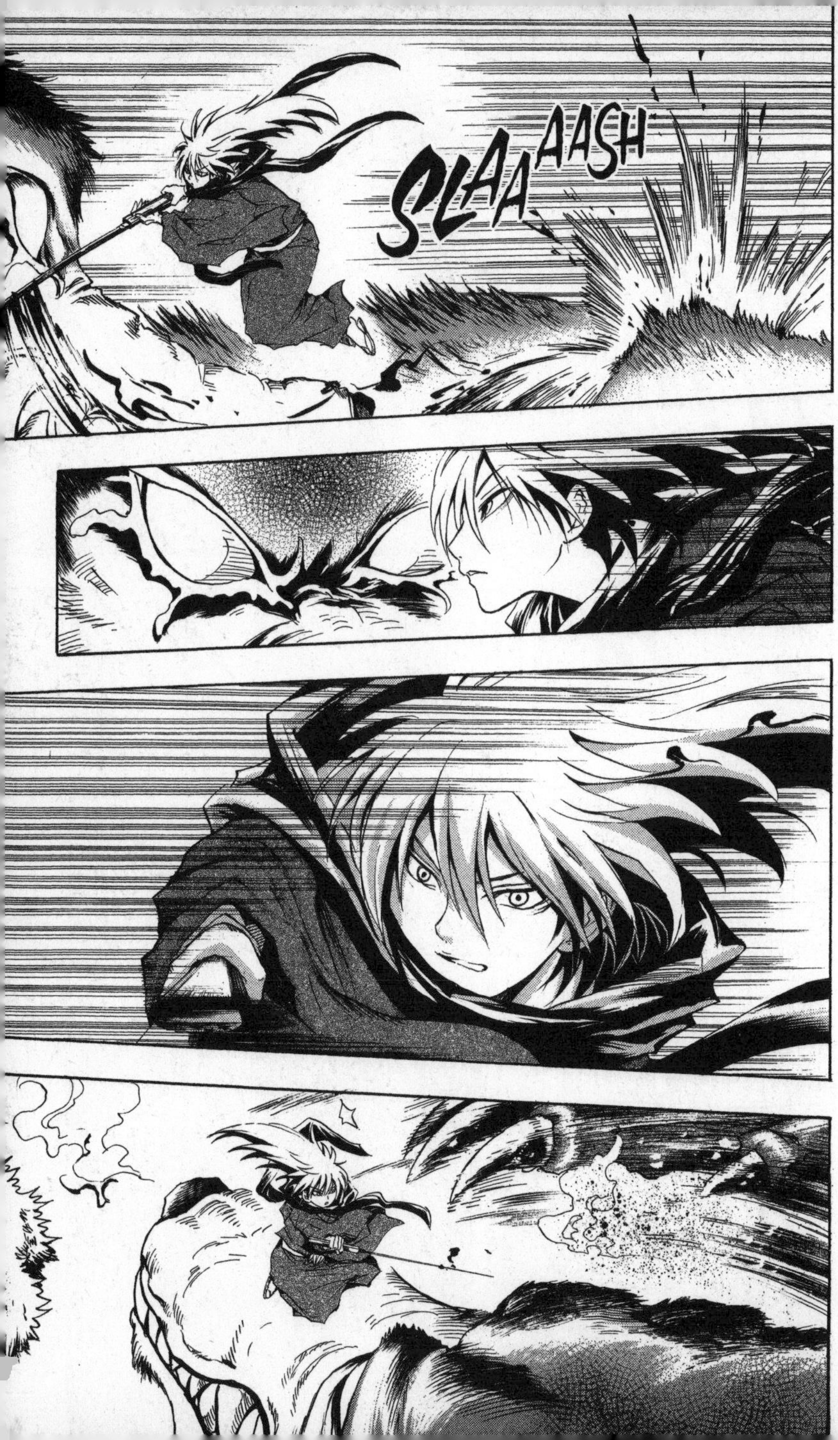
SLAAAASH

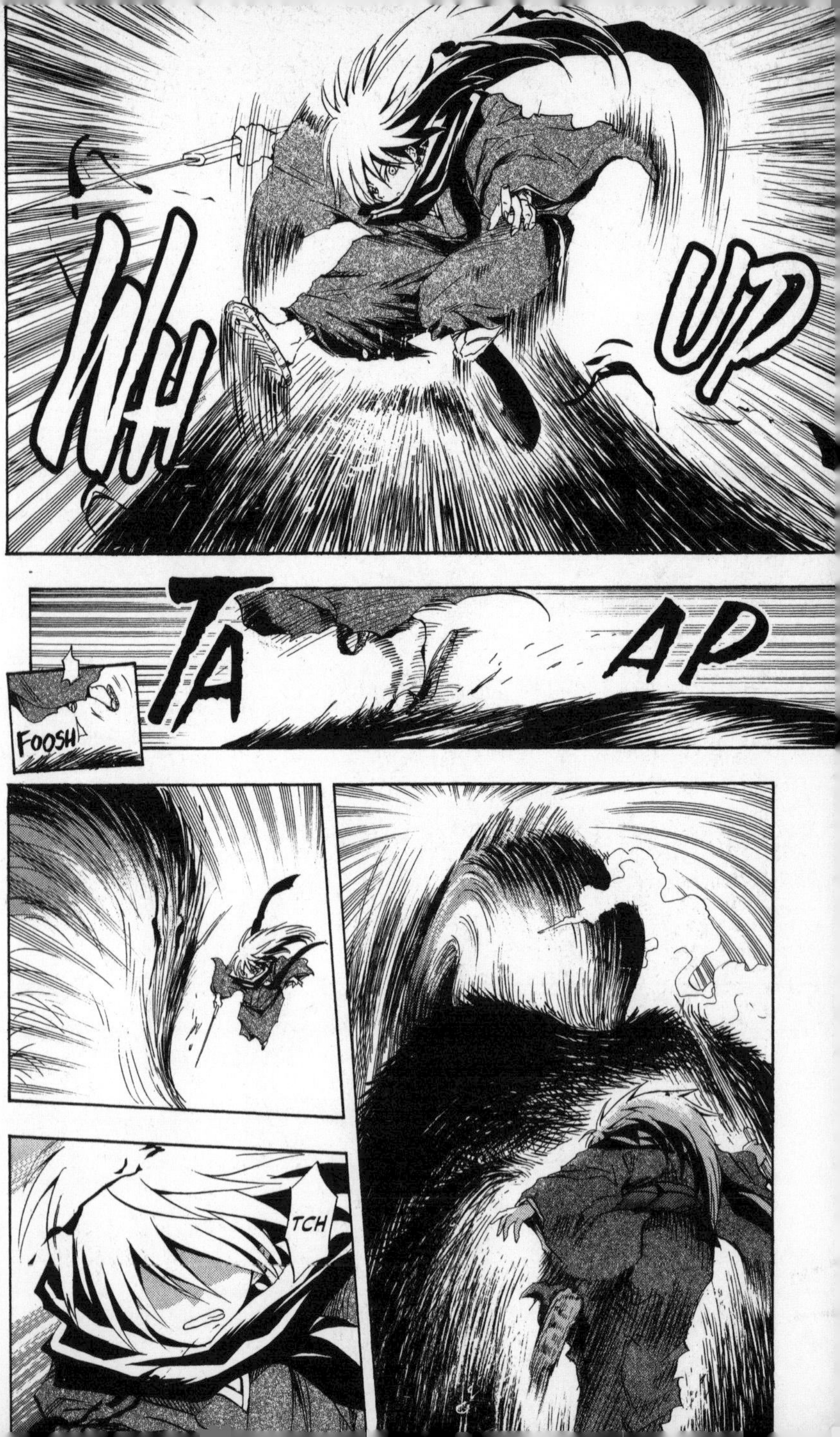
WHUP
TAAP
FOOSH
TCH

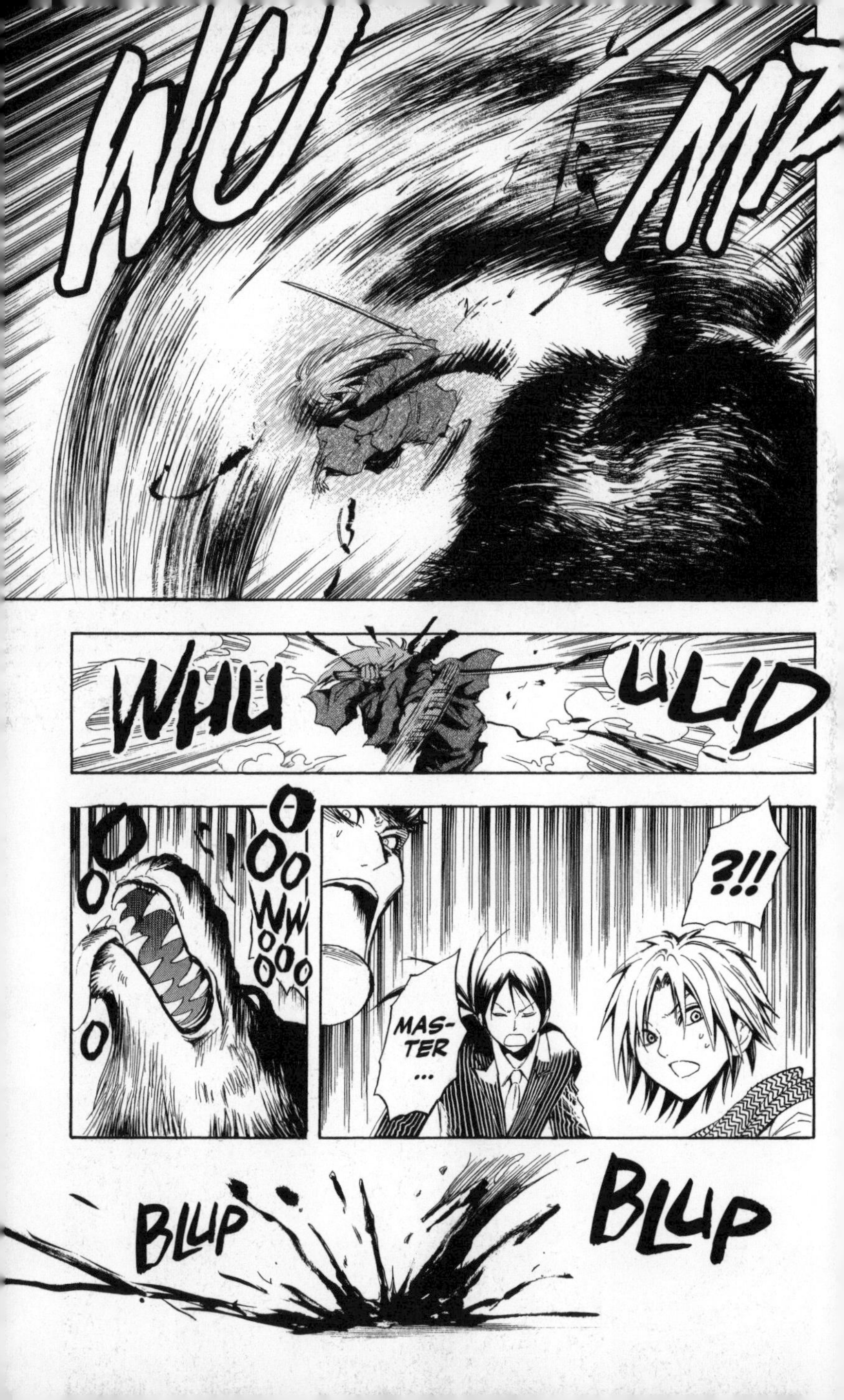
WHU
UUD
?!!
MAS-TER ...
BLUP
BLUP

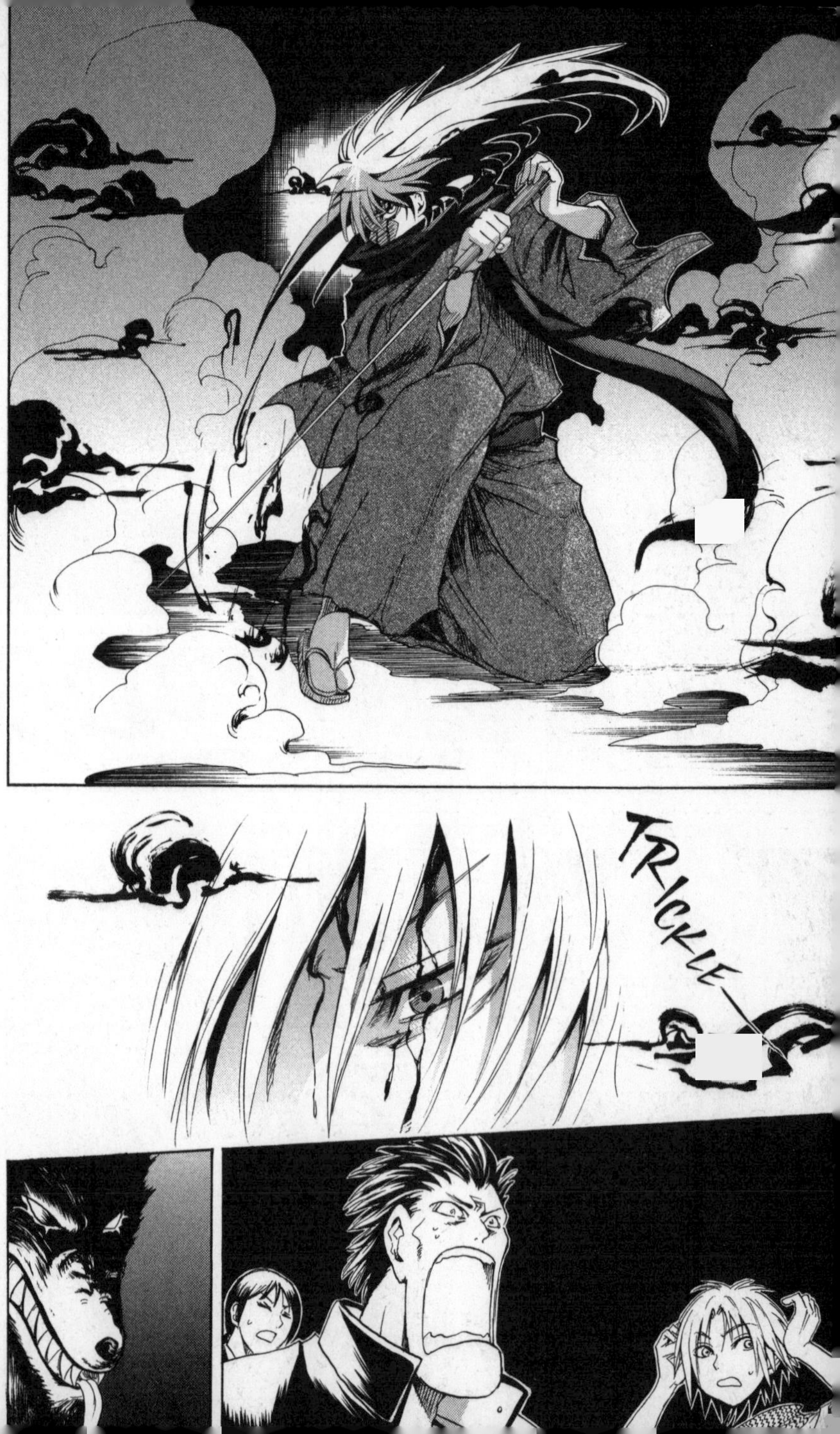
TRICKLE

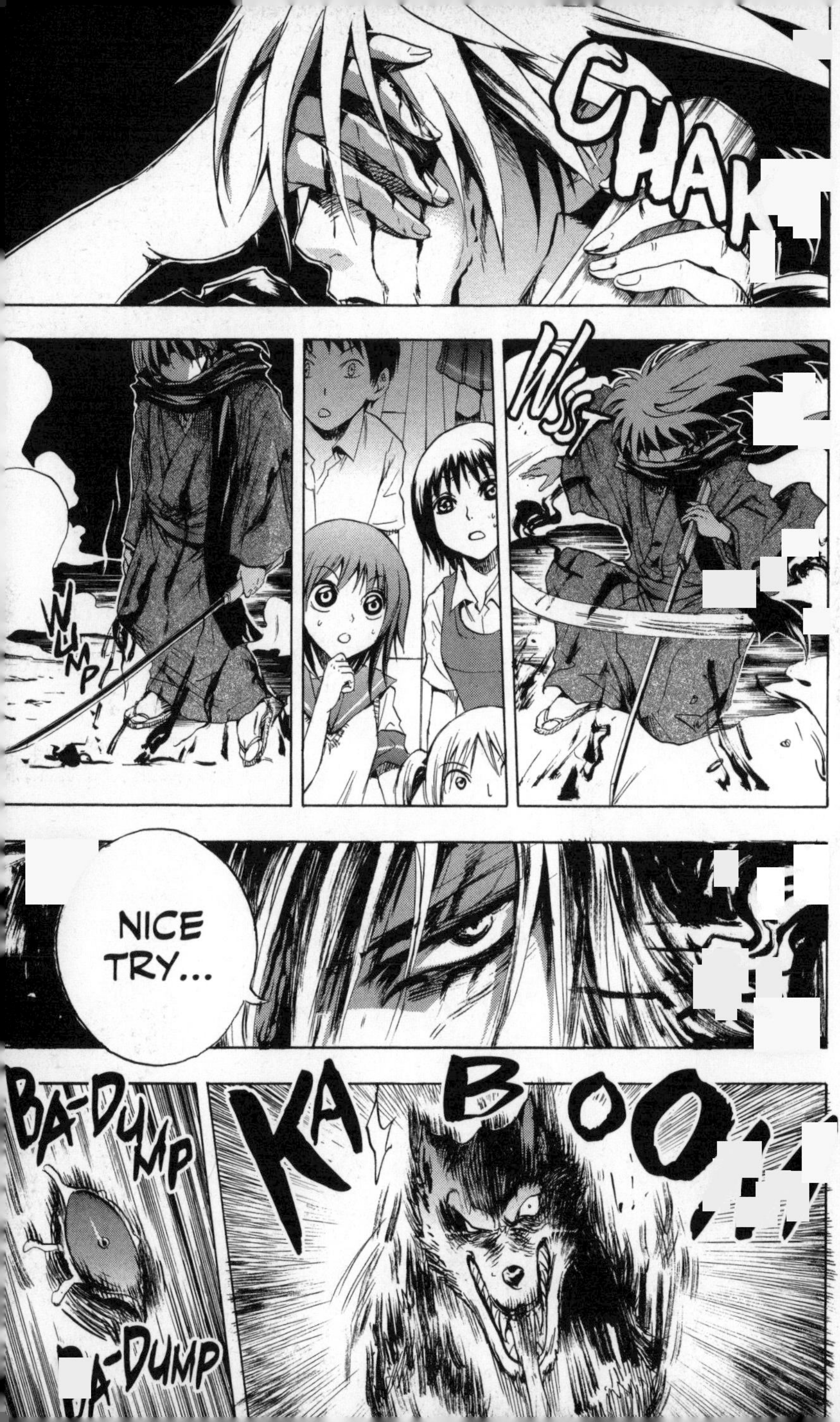
CHAK
WUMP
NICE TRY...
KA BOO
BA-DUMP
A-DUMP

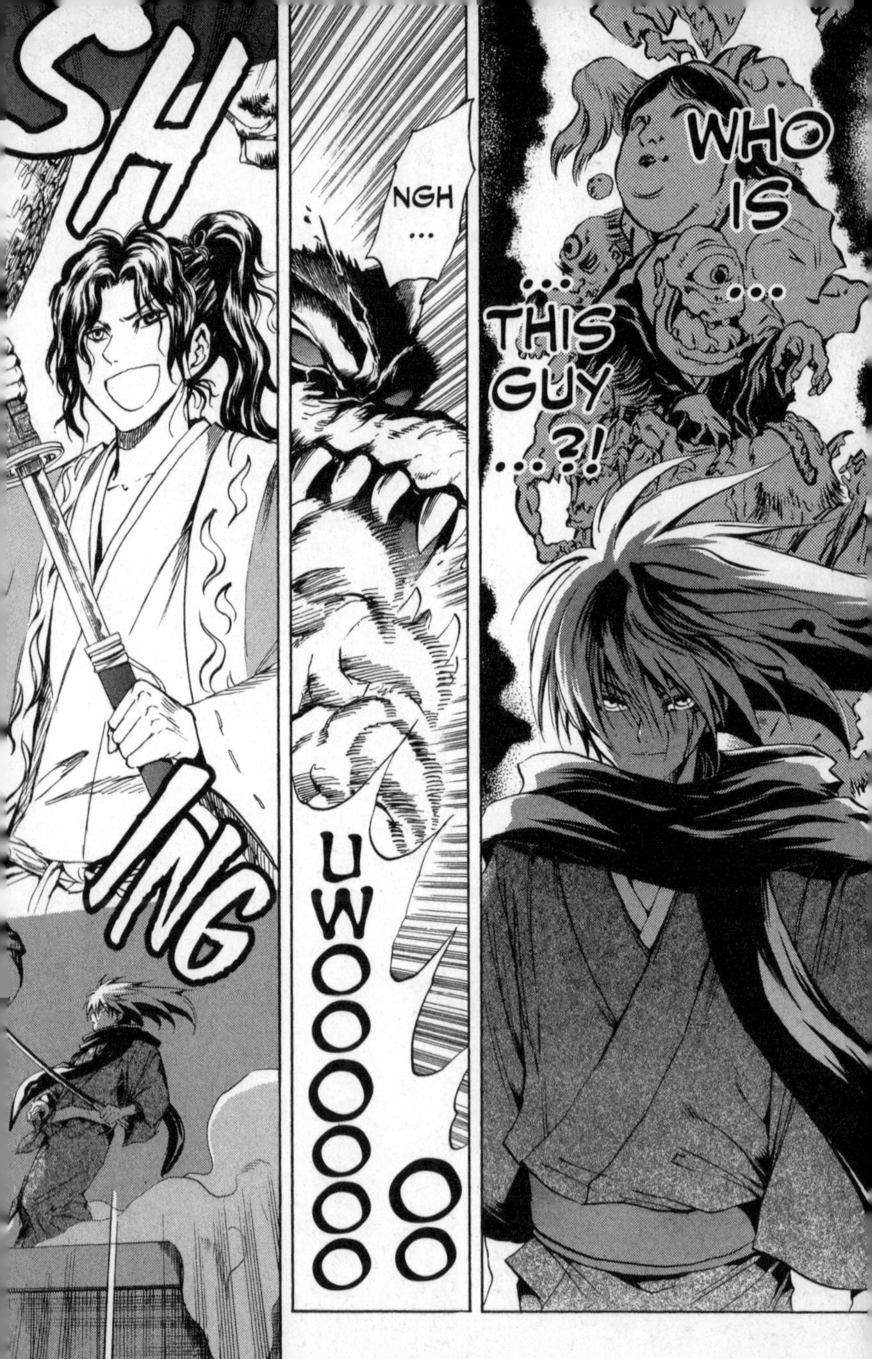
WHO IS ...
... THIS GUY ...?!
NGH ...
UWOOOOOOOOO
SHING

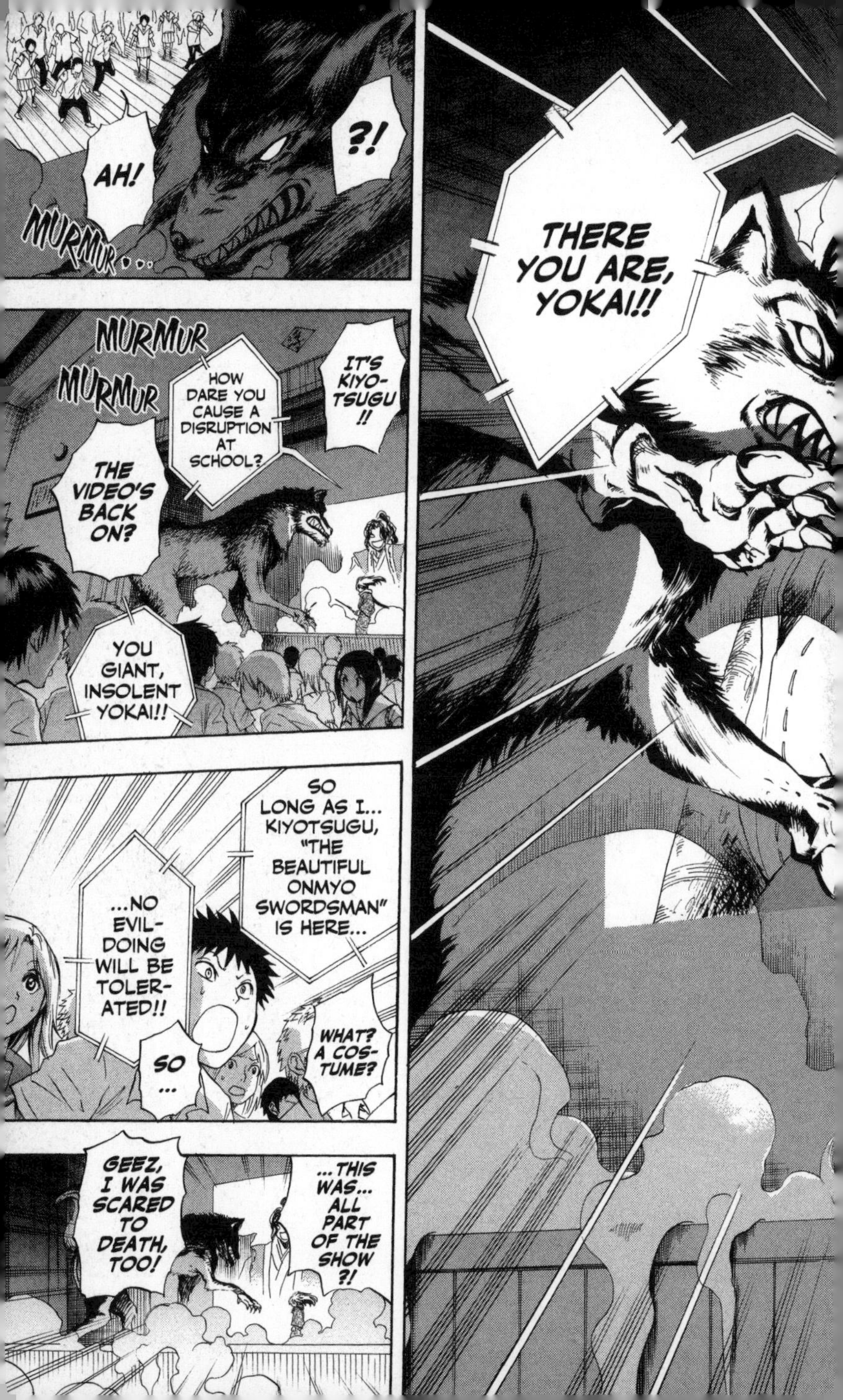
THERE YOU ARE, YOKAI!!
?!
AH!
MURMUR...
IT'S KIYOTSUGU!!
MURMUR
MURMUR
HOW DARE YOU CAUSE A DISRUPTION AT SCHOOL?
THE VIDEO'S BACK ON?
YOU GIANT, INSOLENT YOKAI!!
SO LONG AS I... KIYOTSUGU, "THE BEAUTIFUL ONMYO SWORDSMAN" IS HERE...
...NO EVIL-DOING WILL BE TOLERATED!!
WHAT? A COSTUME?
SO...
...THIS WAS... ALL PART OF THE SHOW?!
GEEZ, I WAS SCARED TO DEATH, TOO!

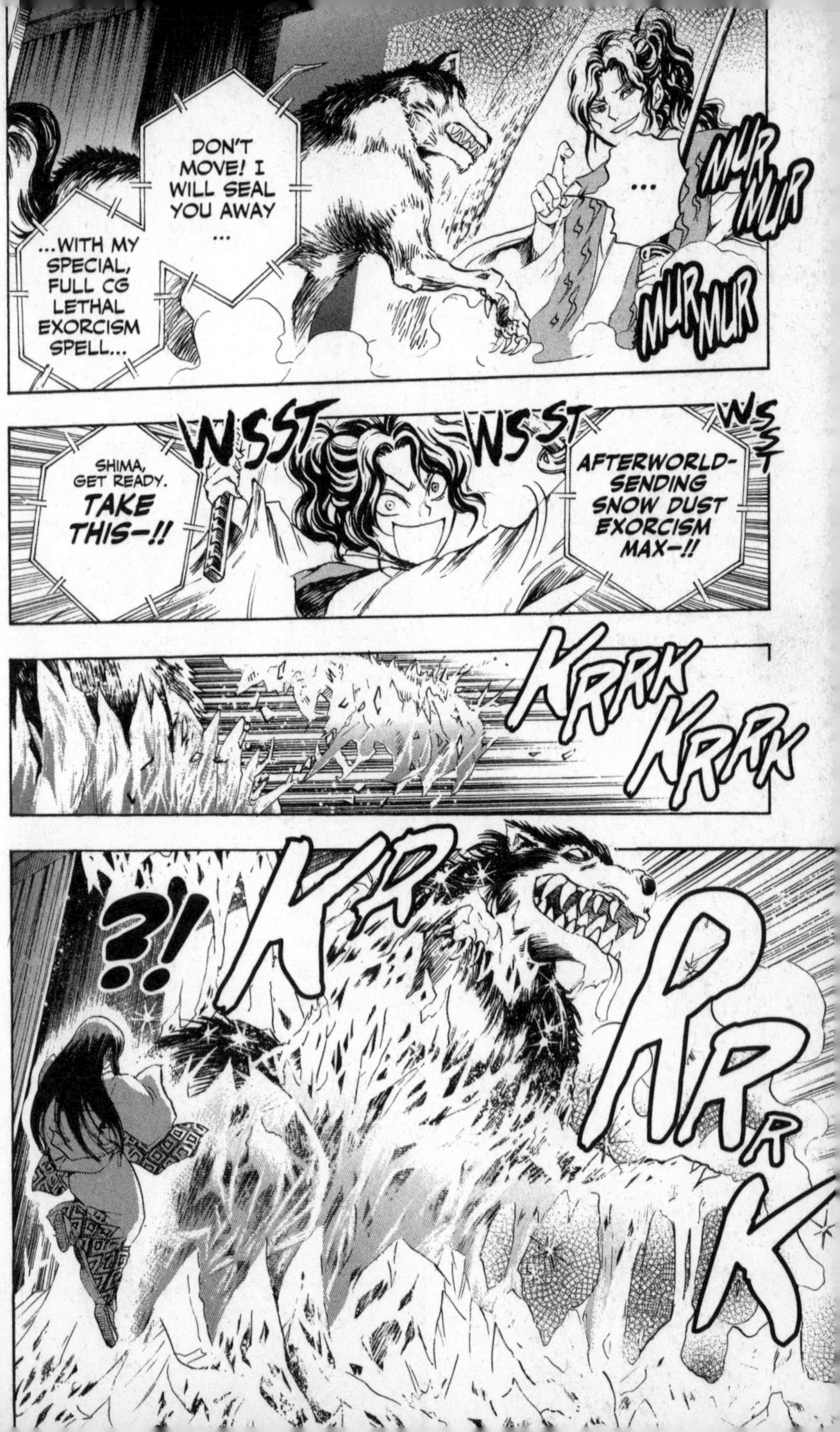
MUR MUR
MUR MUR
...
DON'T MOVE! I WILL SEAL YOU AWAY ...
...WITH MY SPECIAL, FULL CG LETHAL EXORCISM SPELL...
WSST
AFTERWORLD-SENDING SNOW DUST EXORCISM MAX-!!
WSST
WSST
SHIMA, GET READY. TAKE THIS-!!
KRRK KRRK
KR
RRRK
?!!

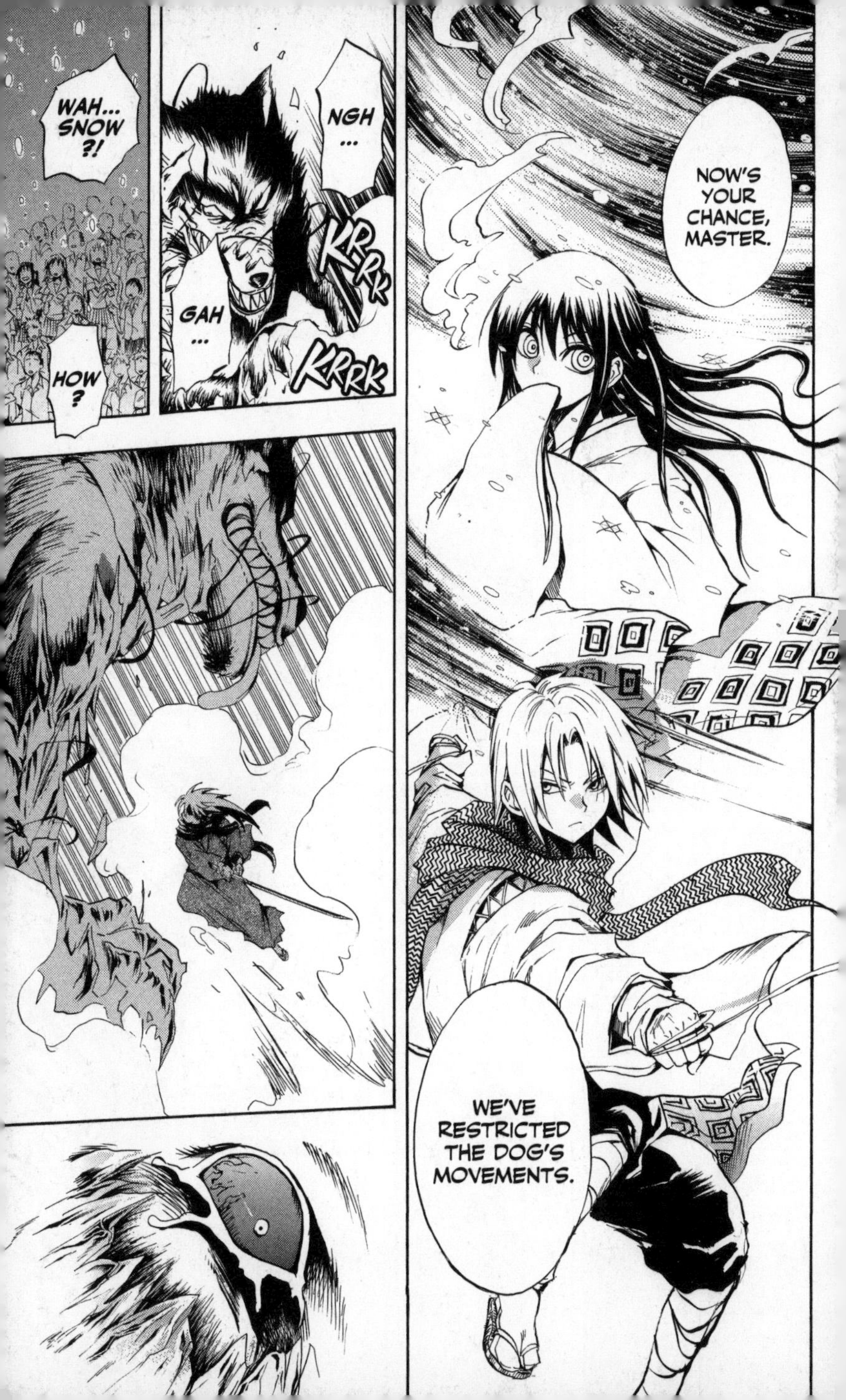
NOW'S YOUR CHANCE, MASTER.
WE'VE RESTRICTED THE DOG'S MOVEMENTS.
NGH...
KRRRK
GAH...
KRRK
WAH... SNOW?!
HOW?

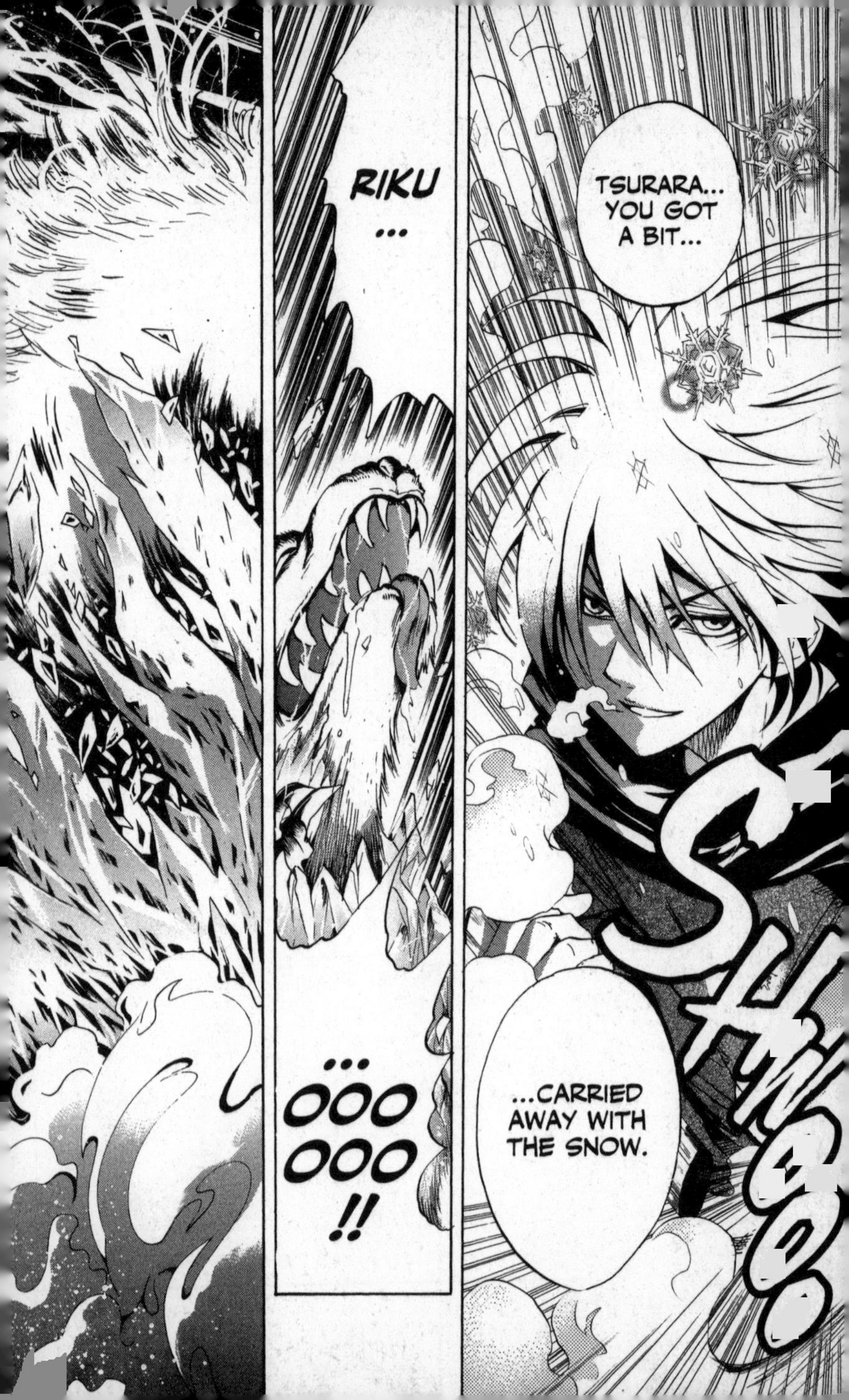
TSURARA... YOU GOT A BIT...
...CARRIED AWAY WITH THE SNOW.
RIKU ...
...OOO OOO !!

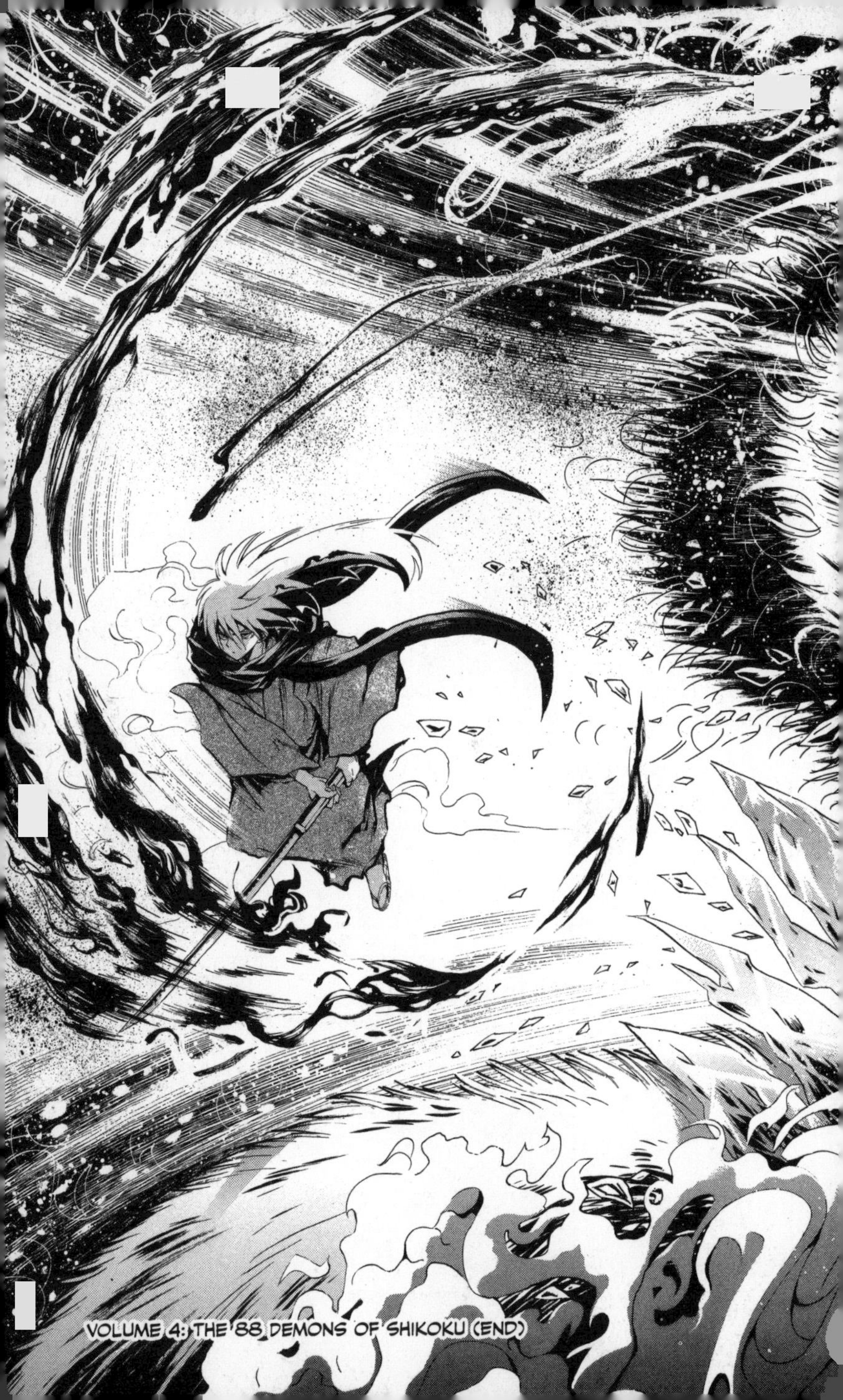
VOLUME 4: THE 88 DEMONS OF SHIKOKU (END)

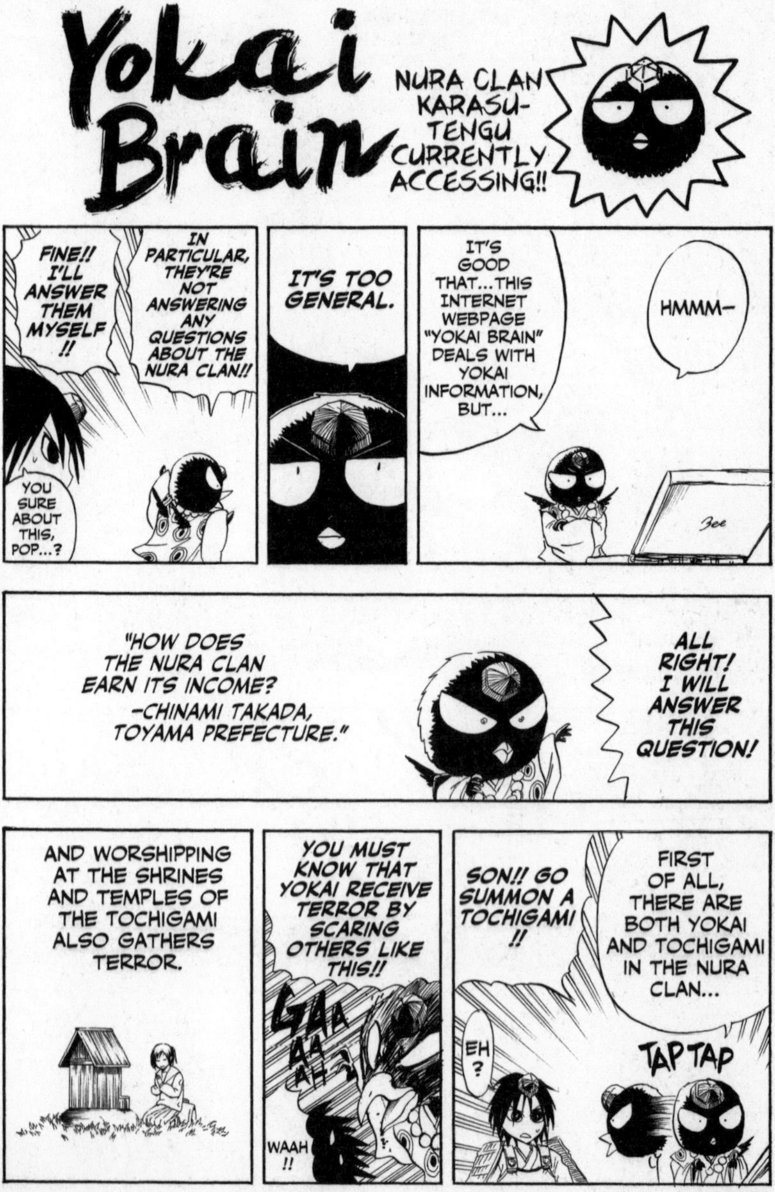
Yokai Brain
NURA CLAN KARASU-TENGU CURRENTLY ACCESSING!!
HMMM–
IT'S GOOD THAT...THIS INTERNET WEBPAGE "YOKAI BRAIN" DEALS WITH YOKAI INFORMATION, BUT...
IT'S TOO GENERAL.
IN PARTICULAR, THEY'RE NOT ANSWERING ANY QUESTIONS ABOUT THE NURA CLAN!!
FINE!! I'LL ANSWER THEM MYSELF!!
YOU SURE ABOUT THIS, POP...?
ALL RIGHT! I WILL ANSWER THIS QUESTION!
"HOW DOES THE NURA CLAN EARN ITS INCOME? –CHINAMI TAKADA, TOYAMA PREFECTURE."
FIRST OF ALL, THERE ARE BOTH YOKAI AND TOCHIGAMI IN THE NURA CLAN...
TAP TAP
SON!! GO SUMMON A TOCHIGAMI!!
EH?
YOU MUST KNOW THAT YOKAI RECEIVE TERROR BY SCARING OTHERS LIKE THIS!!
GAAAAAH
WAAH!!
AND WORSHIPPING AT THE SHRINES AND TEMPLES OF THE TOCHIGAMI ALSO GATHERS TERROR.

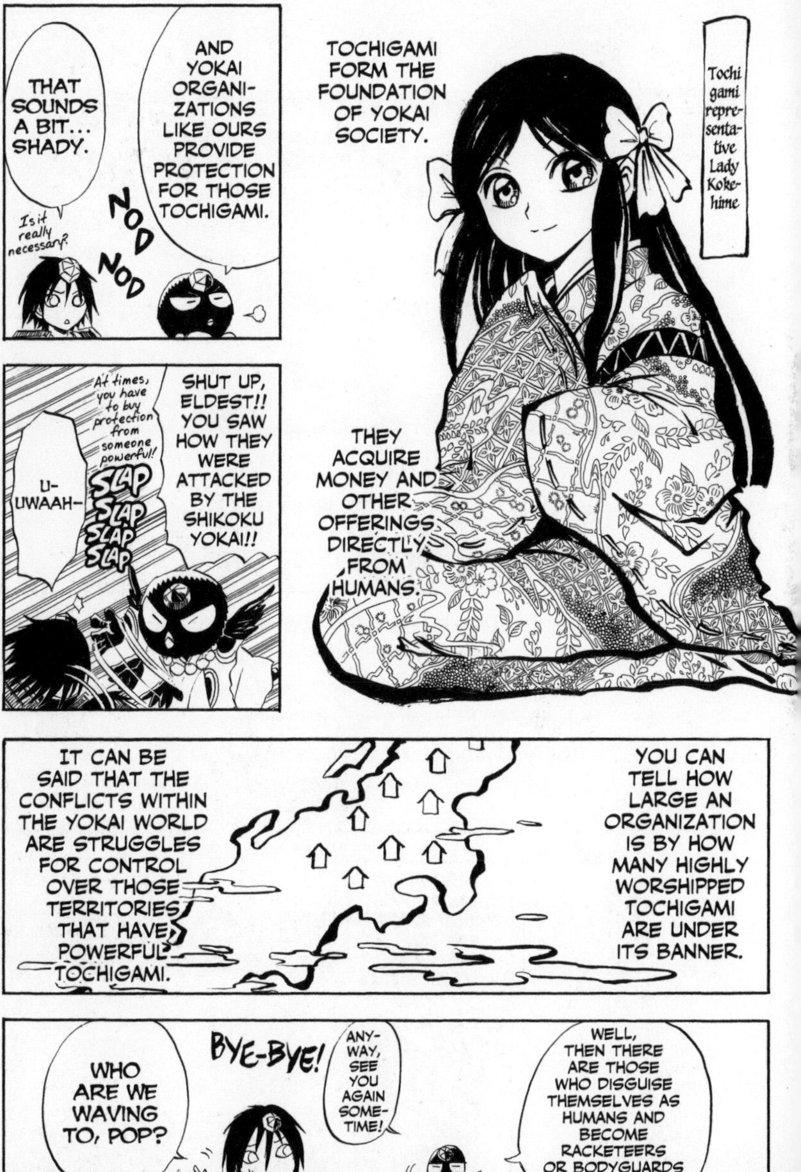
Tochigami representative Lady Kokehime
TOCHIGAMI FORM THE FOUNDATION OF YOKAI SOCIETY.
THEY ACQUIRE MONEY AND OTHER OFFERINGS DIRECTLY FROM HUMANS.
AND YOKAI ORGANIZATIONS LIKE OURS PROVIDE PROTECTION FOR THOSE TOCHIGAMI.
NOD NOD
THAT SOUNDS A BIT... SHADY.
Is it really necessary?
SHUT UP, ELDEST!! YOU SAW HOW THEY WERE ATTACKED BY THE SHIKOKU YOKAI!!
At times, you have to buy protection from someone powerful!
SLAP SLAP SLAP SLAP
U-UWAAH-
YOU CAN TELL HOW LARGE AN ORGANIZATION IS BY HOW MANY HIGHLY WORSHIPPED TOCHIGAMI ARE UNDER ITS BANNER.
IT CAN BE SAID THAT THE CONFLICTS WITHIN THE YOKAI WORLD ARE STRUGGLES FOR CONTROL OVER THOSE TERRITORIES THAT HAVE POWERFUL TOCHIGAMI.
WELL, THEN THERE ARE THOSE WHO DISGUISE THEMSELVES AS HUMANS AND BECOME RACKETEERS OR BODYGUARDS FOR REAL YAKUZA.
ANYWAY, SEE YOU AGAIN SOMETIME!
BYE-BYE!
WHO ARE WE WAVING TO, POP?
TO BE CONTINUED...

IN THE NEXT VOLUME...

A YOKAI WITH WINGS DARKER THAN NIGHT

Rikuo has successfully defended his classmates from the vicious Inugami's mad-dog attack. But that battle is just a hint of what's to come. The sinister Tamazuki has remained in his human form so far, but now he's unleashing his true form: a ferocious yokai leading the 88 Demons of Shikoku, a disciplined demon horde hell-bent on taking the Nura clan out. With Nurarihyon missing, Rikuo must step up as a warrior and a leader.

AVAILABLE OCTOBER 2011!

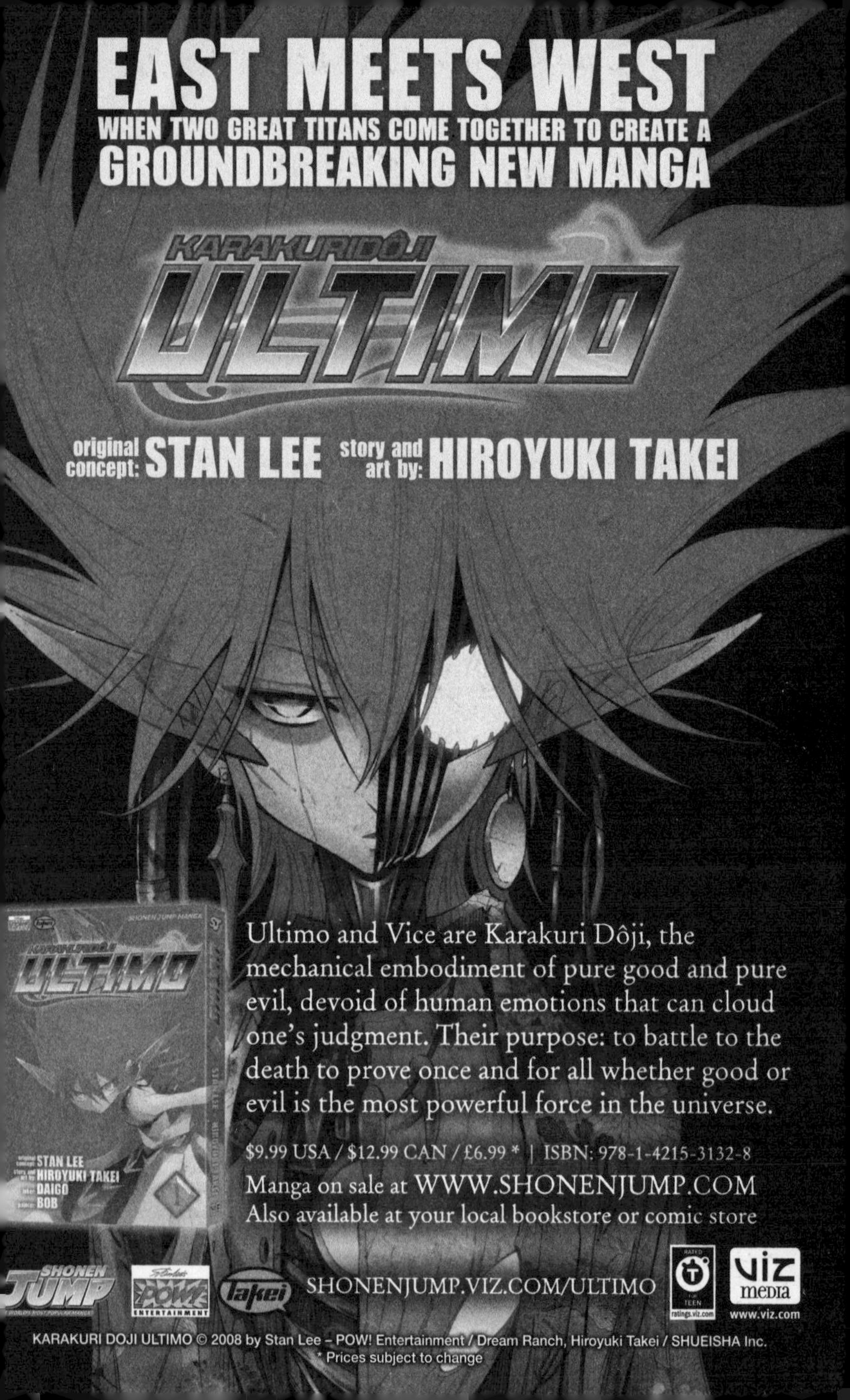
EAST MEETS WEST
WHEN TWO GREAT TITANS COME TOGETHER TO CREATE A
GROUNDBREAKING NEW MANGA
KARAKURIDÔJI
ULTIMO
original concept: STAN LEE story and art by: HIROYUKI TAKEI
Ultimo and Vice are Karakuri Dôji, the mechanical embodiment of pure good and pure evil, devoid of human emotions that can cloud one's judgment. Their purpose: to battle to the death to prove once and for all whether good or evil is the most powerful force in the universe.
$9.99 USA / $12.99 CAN / £6.99 * | ISBN: 978-1-4215-3132-8
Manga on sale at WWW.SHONENJUMP.COM
Also available at your local bookstore or comic store
SHONEN JUMP
POW! ENTERTAINMENT
Takei
SHONENJUMP.VIZ.COM/ULTIMO
RATED T FOR TEEN
ratings.viz.com
VIZ media
www.viz.com
KARAKURI DOJI ULTIMO © 2008 by Stan Lee – POW! Entertainment / Dream Ranch, Hiroyuki Takei / SHUEISHA Inc.
* Prices subject to change

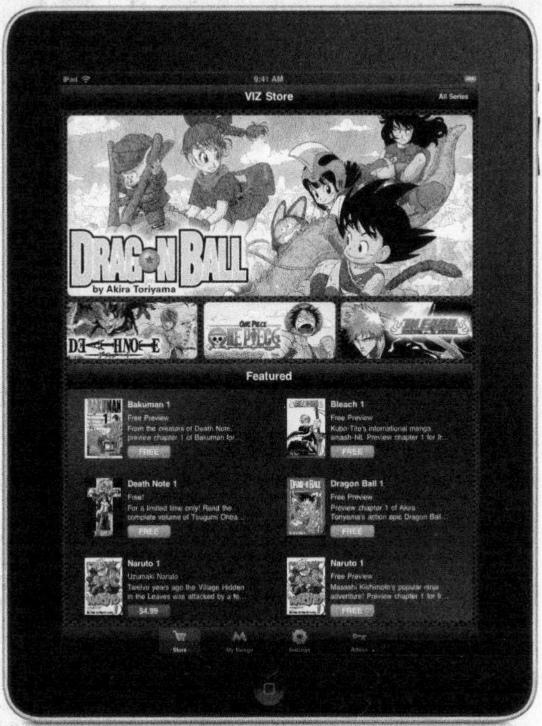

9:41 AM
VIZ Store
All Series
DRAGON BALL
by Akira Toriyama
Featured
Bakuman 1
Free Preview
FREE
Bleach 1
Free Preview
FREE
Death Note 1
Free!
FREE
Dragon Ball 1
Free Preview
FREE
Naruto 1
Uzumaki Naruto
$4.99
Naruto 1
Free Preview
FREE

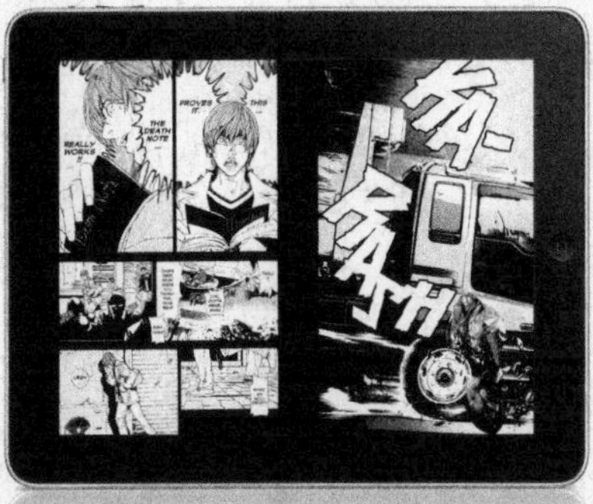